EDUCATION
AND IDENTITY

Arthur W. Chickering
Linda Reisser

EDUCATION AND IDENTITY

SECOND EDITION

Jossey-Bass Publishers · San Francisco

Published by Jossey-Bass
A Wiley Imprint
989 Market Street, San Francisco, CA 94103-1741   www.josseybass.com

Jossey-Bass books and products are available through most bookstores. To contact Jossey-Bass directly call our Customer Care Department within the U.S. at 800-956-7739, outside the U.S. at 317-572-3986 or fax 317-572-4002.

Jossey-Bass also publishes its books in a variety of electronic formats. Some content that appears in print may not be available in electronic books.

Library of Congress Cataloging-in-Publication Data

Chickering, Arthur W., date.
    Education and identity / Arthur W. Chickering, Linda Reisser. — 2nd ed.
      p. cm. — (The Jossey-Bass higher and adult education series)
      Includes bibliographical references and index.
      ISBN 1-55542-591-7
      1. Education, Higher. 2. Educational sociology. I. Reisser,
Linda, date. II. Title. III. Series.
LB2322.2.C45 1993
378'.01—dc20   93-5392
                                                 CIP

Printed in the United States of America
SECOND EDITION
HB Printing   10 9 8 7

The Jossey-Bass
Higher and Adult Education Series

Contents

Preface xi

The Authors xix

1. A Current Theoretical Context for Student
   Development 1

   Part One: The Seven Vectors: An Overview **43**

2. Developing Competence 53

3. Managing Emotions 83

4. Moving Through Autonomy Toward
   Interdependence 115

5. Developing Mature Interpersonal Relationships 145

6. Establishing Identity 173

ix

7. Developing Purpose   209

8. Developing Integrity   235

**Part Two: Key Influences
on Student Development   265**

9. Clear and Consistent Institutional Objectives   283

10. Institutional Size   296

11. Student-Faculty Relationships   316

12. Curriculum   341

13. Teaching   369

14. Friendships and Student Communities   392

15. Student Development Programs and Services   425

16. Creating Educationally Powerful Environments   454

References   487

Name Index   523

Subject Index   531

Preface

This book argues for policies and practices to create higher education environments that will foster broad-based development of human talent and potentials. We believe that this orientation and the resulting changes will restore public confidence and political investments.

Not all those concerned with higher education agree with our orientation. Many did not when the first edition of *Education and Identity* was published in 1969. They doubted that colleges and universities should be concerned about students' personal values, ways of thinking, modes of learning, or interpersonal and intercultural skills. Since educational institutions were not supposed to be churches, parents, or social service agencies, it did not much matter whether the students worked all night, slept all day, fought depression, or abused alcohol. Fostering self-esteem, healthy relationships, and socially responsible behavior was not a priority. Instead, the goal was to give students a limited number of skills, insights, and points of view that would somehow help them find a good job and a satisfying life.

Since that time, society has recognized that higher education's contributions to human learning and development need to reach substantially beyond a limited number of skills, insights, and points of view. Many of those who strongly support development of broad-based talent are concerned about global interdependence and economic competitiveness. They call for a work force that can function at high levels of cognitive complexity, adapt to change, and develop the interpersonal competence and value orientations necessary for effective performance in a multicultural nation and world. They call for persons with motivation and a sense of their own effectiveness who can identify with, and invest themselves in, something larger than their own short-run self-interest.

Certainly we need solid basic skills in oral and written communication, in critical thinking, and in the capacity to process information. We need to be able to distinguish rhetoric from reality and to weigh evidence and diverse logics. Those skills and capacities, however, are necessary but no longer adequate. In addition, we need sufficient interpersonal competence and multicultural understandings to function in a globally interdependent world. We need a strong enough sense of our own identity and of our necessary interdependence that we can appreciate and value similar strength in those who differ from us.

Most people outside higher education recognize these needs. The resistance to this expanded role for our colleges and universities comes mainly from within the academy itself. But the resistance has diminished measurably in the years since *Education and Identity* was first published. In the intervening years, the "student development point of view" has gained substantial currency among professionals in student personnel services. This orientation has been accompanied by appropriate critical examination, with concern for refinement and integration of diverse conceptual perspectives. Concerns about effective implementation also exist. Among academics — administrators and faculty alike — there is growing awareness that higher education needs to contribute more than information transfer and intellectual development, though those remain the central purposes.

During the 1960s and early 1970s, when the senior author

shared the views and implications of *Education and Identity,* the first faculty responses were typically vitriolic attacks, scathing criticism, emotionally loaded defensive reactions, and the like. Working through those reactions always had to precede serious conversations concerning the actual substance and its implications for policies and practices. Since the mid 1980s, that kind of reaction has evaporated. Now there is much more thoughtful, open-minded receptivity. The questions no longer concern legitimacy or validity. Instead, they pose more challenging issues of what is actually required by way of curricula and teaching, faculty behaviors, and institutional norms and expectations.

One reason for moderating earlier views that higher education should restrict itself to information transfer and "cultivating the intellect" lies in the continued accumulation of research into college influences on student learning and development. The research unequivocally demonstrates that college has impact on a wide range of cognitive and affective outcomes. It also demonstrates key aspects of institutional behaviors and characteristics associated with educationally powerful environments. Pascarella and Terenzini (1991) summarize the findings as follows:

> A reasonably consistent set of cognitive, attitudinal, value, and psychosocial changes have occurred among college students over the last four or five decades. Students learn to think in more abstract, critical, complex, and reflective ways; there is a general liberalization of values and attitudes combined with an increase in cultural and artistic interests and activities; progress is made toward the development of personal identities and more positive self-concepts; and there is an expansion and extension of interpersonal horizons, intellectual interests, individual autonomy, and general psychological maturity and well-being [pp. 563–564].

> Perhaps the clearest generalization to be made . . . is that on nearly all of the dimensions on which we find freshman-to-senior change, a statistically signifi-

cant part of that change is attributable to college attendance, not to rival explanations. . . . These effects cannot be explained away by maturation or differences between those who attend and those who do not attend college in intelligence, academic ability, or other precollege characteristics. . . .

These conclusions about the net effects of college on learning and cognitive development are limited by those dimensions that individual scholars have chosen to investigate. It is perhaps useful to think of these dimensions . . . as analogous to geological probes designed to define the nature and extent of mineral or oil deposits. They sample and begin to define the boundaries, but they may not capture the fullness of the phenomenon being measured . . . [p. 567].

Our synthesis of the evidence suggests that college has a rather broad range of enduring or long-term impacts. These include not only the more obvious impacts on occupation and earnings but also influences on cognitive, moral, and psychosocial characteristics, as well as on values and attitudes and various quality of life indexes (for example, family, marriage, consumer behavior). Moreover, it would also appear that the impacts extend beyond the individuals who attend college to the kinds of lives their sons and daughters can expect [p. 573].

Even those of us in academe, who rely so heavily on our long-cultivated, finely honed ability to find a flaw in any argument, in any research method, who can deconstruct the bias underlying any piece of work, cannot sustain self-immunization indefinitely. Ultimately the sheer diversity and volume in samples, types of institutions, research methods, and disciplinary approaches in the larger culture begin to have an impact. It is fortunate that we are becoming more aware, more open, readier to take seriously our capacity for significant contributions to human development. National and global problems cry out for such contributions.

On these grounds, we argue for nothing less than human development, in all its complexity and orneriness, as the unifying purpose for higher education.

Audience

We aim to speak to college and university administrators, faculty, and student educational program professionals. The first edition turned out to be especially useful for top administrators and for professionals responsible for student activities, residential learning, and other student and institutional support programs. That edition has also proved useful as a text for diverse higher education graduate programs. We expect that this update, building on the accumulated research of the last twenty-five years, will be similarly useful to a wide range of people concerned to strengthen higher education's contribution to human development.

Scope and Treatment

We have tried to make our orientation specific, so that it can be translated into concrete policies, practices, leadership activities, and institutional norms. We have done this by suggesting seven "vectors" of human development. We call them vectors because each has direction and magnitude. Although development is expressed more appropriately by a spiral or steps than by a straight line, we retain the term *vectors* in the interests of economy and historical continuity.

All the positions we take are consistent with research and theory up through 1992. We have relied heavily on Pascarella and Terenzini's synthesis (1991) of more than 2,600 research studies on the impact of college on students. Otherwise, we refer to the literature selectively to illustrate our points, but throughout the book, we do not aim to "survey the literature." Therefore, sophisticated readers will know of pertinent studies and conceptual frameworks that we do not cite. We hope they will bring these to bear in interpreting our views and in sharing them with others. Consistent with our orientation toward the "literature," we freely cite earlier work when it has retained its relevance and punch. The references and quotations from past decades remind us that we are all indebted to the work of our predecessors.

Overview of the Contents

The opening chapter summarizes some of the major conceptual frameworks for human development articulated since 1969. These frameworks, in various combinations, integrate two or more dimensions that we leave discrete as our vectors. They all represent significant steps toward a more complex understanding of human development. We decided to keep the original separate vectors because in that form they seem to lend themselves to more convenient application.

Part One elaborates on the seven vectors, with a chapter devoted to each: developing competence, managing emotions, moving through autonomy toward interdependence, developing mature interpersonal relationships, establishing identity, developing purpose, and developing integrity. Each vector is updated to be consistent with the significant contributions made to research since 1969.

Part Two describes how key aspects of our institutions can be addressed to encourage human development in the major areas. In the first two chapters of Part Two (Chapters Nine and Ten), we discuss two fundamentals — institutional objectives and size, respectively. We then turn to the following core academic considerations, devoting a chapter to each (Chapters Eleven, Twelve, and Thirteen): student-faculty relationships, curriculum, and teaching. In the next two chapters (Chapters Fourteen and Fifteen), we turn to friendships and student communities, and then to student development programs and services. The final chapter (Chapter Sixteen), describes the characteristics of educationally powerful environments and suggests how to create and sustain them.

We do not argue for any single model or grand design. On the contrary, the strength of higher education lies in its wide-ranging institutional diversity. We have solid evidence concerning the characteristics of educationally powerful institutions. We know about the necessity for clear purpose and appropriate scale. We know about the critical importance of student-faculty contact, cooperation among students, active learning, engaging curricula, and campus climates and programs that involve students and create a strong sense of community.

Institutions can apply the knowledge to their own mission, in relation to their own constituencies, using existing faculty, administrators, student service professionals, and support staff. Doing so does not require huge infusions of new dollars or human resources. Change can begin at the level of a course, a curriculum, a residence hall, a department, a school. It can begin with reward systems and institutional architecture, with campus climate or cultural norms. We need only the will, and the ability to persevere, to sustain effort and commitment through time.

We want to emphasize that by proposing human development as a unifying purpose, we do not suggest that every student major in human development. Nor do we propose that the developmental needs of a particular student be the sole basis for laying out an educational program. Individual interests and needs must be addressed in light of requirements for knowledge, competence, and human capacities that have been determined by particular plans and aspirations, particular disciplines or professions, and particular social problems. We do not espouse a self-centered, narcissistic glorification of individual needs and desires over the hard, realistic requirements for effective careers, social contributions, and satisfying lives. But we believe that by taking developmental needs as an organizing framework, we will better prepare all our students, and ourselves, for the kinds of lives as workers and citizens required by the social changes rushing toward us.

Acknowledgments

In creating the revised edition, we owe most to the committed practitioners and researchers who have so significantly augmented our sophistication about human development and educationallv powerful environments during the past twenty years. Many of these are by now long-standing friends and colleagues, too numerous to mention here. Without their outstanding work, there would have been no need for a revision.

We also owe much to the diverse students with whom we have worked in various roles and relationships. Firsthand encounters formed the bedrock that supports our feeble attempts to capture the complexities of college impacts on human development. We are especially grateful to students and former students who shared their written observations of their own developmental turning points. We also acknowledge invaluable assistance from the staff at Jossey-Bass, the reviewers who made excellent suggestions, and professional colleagues and personal friends who supported our efforts.

This revision has been a true collaboration. The differences in our age, gender, and professional experiences have enriched the perspectives we brought to this work. We have learned together. We have provided each other with a steady diet of tough-minded critiques, thoughtful suggestions, and warm support. The result, for whatever it is worth, is far superior to what either of us could have achieved alone.

September 1993

Arthur W. Chickering
Fairfax, Virginia

Linda Reisser
Suffern, New York

The Authors

Arthur W. Chickering is a University Professor of educational leadership and human development at George Mason University. He received his B.A. degree (1950) in modern comparative literature from Wesleyan University, his M.A. degree (1951) in teaching English from the Graduate School of Education, Harvard University, and his Ph.D. degree (1959) in school psychology from Teachers College, Columbia University.

Chickering began his career in higher education as psychology teacher and coordinator of evaluation at Goddard College from 1959 to 1965. From 1965 to 1969, he directed the Project on Student Development in Small Colleges, a four-year action research project on interactions between educational practices, college environments, and student development. In 1969–70, he was a visiting scholar in the Office of Research at the American Council on Education, then directed by Alexander Astin. From 1970 to 1977, as founding vice president for academic affairs, Chickering played a major role in creating Empire State College. From 1977 to 1988, he was distinguished professor and director of the Center for the Study of Higher Education at Memphis State University.

Chickering is the author of many publications, including *Commuting Versus Resident Students: Overcoming Educational Inequities of Living Off Campus (1974), The Modern American College: Responding to the New Realities of Diverse Students and a Changing Society* (1981), and *Improving Higher Education Environments for Adults: Responsive Programs and Services from Entry to Departure* (1989, with N. K. Schlossberg and A. Q. Lynch). He has received the E. F. Lindquist Award from the American Educational Research Association for his studies of college impacts on student development, the Outstanding Service Award from the National Association of Student Personnel Administrators, and the Distinguished Contribution to Knowledge Award from the American College Personnel Association. He has been a board member and chaired the boards of the American Association for Higher Education, the Association for the Study of Higher Education, and the Council for Adult and Experiential Learning. He has received an honorary degree in humane letters from the University of New Hampshire and the E. F. Newman Award from Lourdes College. He has served on the editorial boards of the *Journal of Higher Education* and the *Journal of Higher Education Administration.*

Linda Reisser is dean of student services at Rockland Community College. She received her B.A. degree (1968) in English and her M.Ed. degree (1970) in counseling from the University of California, Santa Barbara. She received her Ed.D. degree (1973) in higher education from the University of Massachusetts, Amherst.

As a graduate student at the University of California, Santa Barbara, Reisser designed admissions procedures for the newly formed University Without Walls and advised undergraduates designing individualized learning contracts at the University of Massachusetts. From 1973 to 1978, she served as associate dean of student services and director of student activities at South Dakota State University, initiating the Nontraditional Student Program for returning adults and teaching graduate courses in counseling and personality development. From 1978 to 1985, she was dean for students at Whatcom Community College in Bellingham, Washington. From 1986 to 1991, Reisser taught graduate and undergraduate courses in student development theory, higher education, and human services at Western Washington University's Woodring College of Education.

In addition to serving as a consultant and workshop presenter, Reisser coordinated a regional conference on "New Educational Strategies for Adult Learners" in 1981 and a national conference on "Student-Centered Learning" in 1988. She has been a participant in the National Institute for Leadership Development "Leaders of the '80's" program and a fellow of the National Center on Adult Learning. She is the author of several articles, including "Approaches to Recruiting the Adult Learner" in New Directions for Community Colleges no. 29, *Serving Lifelong Learners,* and "On the Evolution of Student Personnel Workers" in the *Journal of the National Association of Women Deans, Administrators, and Counselors.*

EDUCATION
AND IDENTITY

ONE

A Current Theoretical Context for Student Development

Prior to Nevitt Sanford's work, no developmental theory other than Erik Erikson's was available to describe the changing patterns of thinking, feeling, and behaving in college-age students. Sanford (1962, 1966) set the stage for a new level of thinking about student development, proposing that colleges should foster development by providing an empowering balance of challenge and support. Too much challenge could be overwhelming, but too much support created a static comfort zone. Like other theorists, Sanford knew that disequilibrium was an essential catalyst for learning new skills and knowledge, for differentiation and integration. New cognitive and psychosocial theories were introduced during the 1970s and 1980s, generating much research and experimentation. This chapter briefly summarizes some of the most relevant student development theories as context for our "vectors."

In their monumental study *How College Affects Students: Findings and Insights from Twenty Years of Research* (1991), Pascarella and Terenzini reviewed every major research report since 1967 on the impact of higher education on student development. We have relied heavily on their synthesis of research in reviewing

1

the validity of Chickering's earlier theory. Like other authors (Knefelkamp, Widick, and Parker, 1978; Moore, 1990; Rodgers, 1990; Strange and King, 1990), Pascarella and Terenzini suggested broad categories for organizing the diverse array of theories:

1. *Psychosocial theories* view development as a series of developmental tasks or stages, including qualitative changes in thinking, feeling, behaving, valuing, and relating to others and to oneself. Examples:

> Erikson's (1959) eight developmental crises
> Chickering's (1969) seven vectors of development
> Marcia's (1965, 1966) model of ego identity status
> W. Cross's (1971) model of black identity formation
> Heath's (1968, 1978) maturity model
> Life-span theories of adult development (Chickering and Havinghurst, 1981; Gould, 1972; Levinson, 1978; Neugarten, 1964, 1968, 1975; Sheehy, 1974; Vaillant, 1977; Knox, 1977)
> Josselson's (1987) pathways to identity development in women

2. *Cognitive theories* describe changes in thinking and the evolving frames of reference that structure values, beliefs, and assumptions. Examples:

> Perry's (1970) scheme of intellectual and ethical development
> Belenky, Clinchy, Goldberger, and Tarule's (1986) women's ways of knowing
> Baxter Magolda's (1992) epistemological reflection model
> Kohlberg's (1969) theory of moral development
> Gilligan's (1982) different voice model
> Loevinger's (1976) theory of ego development
> Kegan's (1982) evolving self
> Fowler's stages of spiritual development (1981)
> Kitchener and King's (1981, 1990a, 1990b) reflective judgment model

3. *Typology theories* describe distinctive but stable differences in learning style, personality type, temperament, or socioeconomic background as contexts for development. Examples:

Kolb's (1976) learning styles
The Myers-Briggs typology (Myers, 1980a, 1980b)
Keirsey and Bate's (1978) temperaments
K. P. Cross's (1971, 1981) work on sociodemographic
  characteristics

4. *Person-environment interaction theories* focus on how the environment influences behavior through its interactions with characteristics of the individual. Examples:

Campus ecology theories (Banning and Kaiser, 1974;
  Barker, 1968)
Holland's (1966, 1985) theory of vocational personalities
  and work environments
Perceptual models (Moos, 1976, 1979; Stern, 1970; Pervin, 1967, 1968a, 1968b)

The last two types of theories—typology theories and person-environment interaction theories—are not technically developmental theories, since they do not describe the hallmarks of development, the means of measuring it, or the ways to foster it. Thus, we will discuss them only briefly.

Typology theorists shed light on how personal characteristics or preferences affect students' experiences and can assist students in matching preferences to career plans or academic majors. For example, Kolb's (1981) theory of learning styles, proposes that we have preferred ways of learning. Kolb's Learning Style Inventory measures two dimensions: (1) concrete experiencing (CE) of events versus abstract conceptualization (AC), and (2) active experimentation (AE) versus reflective observation (RO).

Kolb, like other typology theorists, warns against labeling or stereotyping people based on where they score on these instruments. The specific situation and the larger cultural context influence which cognitive processes are used. For example, if African tribespeople are more skillful at measuring grain than at measuring distance, it may not signify a lack of abstract thinking abilities. It may instead mean that they have not lived in a setting that valued or fostered abstract thinking. A person with strengths or preferences at one end of the continuum might feel extremely out of place in a context or an academic major that values the other polarity, and the result may be a lowering of self-esteem. For example, Kolb (1981, pp. 246–248) found more alienation and isolation and more frequent perceptions that the workload was heavy among students whose learning styles were incongruent with their disciplines' norms than in cases where they were congruent.

The Myers-Briggs Type Indicator measures the perceptual preferences, sensing (S) or intuition (N), and the judgment preferences, thinking (T) or feeling (F). It also measures two attitudes or orientations: (1) extraversion (E) or introversion (I), which describe the person's focus of attention and source of energy in the world (outward toward people, objects, and actions or inward toward ideas and inner reflection), and (2) judgment (J) or perception (P), which reflects ways of interacting with the world. A judgment orientation is toward organization, planning, and control, while a perception orientation is toward openness, flexibility, and spontaneous reactions to events. The test generates scores on each of these four dimensions:

E = extroversion	I = introversion
N = intuition	S = sensing
T = thinking	F = feeling
P = perceiving	J = judging

When students are given an opportunity to compare their learning styles or Myers-Briggs patterns with others, they can gain both self-awareness and tolerance of styles other than their own. They might also experiment by consciously using styles or patterns that are less familiar. The extravert may learn to savor solitude, and the thinking type may tune into feelings.

To summarize, typology models provide valuable frameworks for thinking about how institutional challenges, environmental factors, and occupational settings influence different types of students and "how different individuals may manage, delay, progress through, or retreat from developmental tasks" based on their cognitive style or ethnic background (Knefelkamp, Widick, and Parker, 1978, p. xiii).

Person-environment interaction theories begin with the premise that individual students can experience the same environment differently, based on their own level of development. For example, a student who prefers independent learning and discussion of different points of view may give high ratings to an instructor who facilitates this, but a student who is trying to learn the right answers in order to succeed on a multiple-choice test may feel that the instructor is not effective.

Holland's self-directed search technique (1990) helps students categorize interests and preferences into six vocational types: realistic, investigative, artistic, social, enterprising, or conventional. While this approach resembles the typology theories, Holland (1985) also proposes six model environments that correspond to the types; he believes that people gravitate toward work environments that suit them. Satisfaction and stability result when personality and environment interact smoothly. Discrepancies lead to dissatisfaction and change.

Other person-environment interaction theories focus on the environments provided by colleges. Banning (1989) offers an ecological perspective, whereby students are viewed not as a collection of individuals but as part of an ecosystem. The college environment consists of physical spaces and buildings, services, programs, events, and policies. Banning recommends designing environments that offer opportunities, support systems, and rewards for movement toward value-based educational goals. Thus, the environment should foster development, while helping students feel at home.

Environmental managers should assess students' perceptions of the environment and changes in their behavior as a way of creating more educationally powerful environments. However, most of the published research on campus ecology has focused on students' perceived satisfaction with the environment, without assessing changes in development or performance (Rodgers, 1990). While an environment that is satisfying to students may help retention, it does not necessarily foster student development.

Person-environment interaction theories remind us that individual differences must be taken into consideration when we structure programs, activities, and offices. They invite us to become more attuned to students' needs and to select from an array of theoretical lenses rather than using one preferred model and assuming it works for everyone.

In this chapter, we focus on the cognitive theories (Perry; Belenky, Clinchy, Goldberger, and Tarule; Baxter Magolda; Kohlberg; and Gilligan) and the psychosocial theories (Erikson, the earlier Chickering model; Kegan and Loevinger are also included, even though they are frequently treated as cognitive theorists). These cognitive and psychosocial theories bear most directly on our seven vectors, and they raise basic questions for all student development theorists. Are there predictable "stages" or "positions" that mark developmental shifts? Are they sequential, invariant, and irreversible? Are some developmental tasks prerequisites for others? Are there basic differences between males and females, either in the process of development or in the content of their thoughts, feelings, and values? Are there differences based on ethnic background, sexual orientation, or age?

Cognitive Theories

Cognitive theories describe changes in how students think. For example, Piaget (1932) conceptualized cognitive development along two dimensions—from a concrete view of the world to an ability to form abstract ideas, and from an egocentric, active model to a reflective, internalized way of knowing (Kolb, 1981, p. 236). He presented three fundamental principles of the cognitive approach:

1. *Cognitive structures.* Individuals form "cognitive structures" to make sense of what they experience. The structures consist of an interrelated set of assumptions, which have their own internal logic. They provide the frames of reference for in-

terpreting the meaning of events, for choosing behavior, and for solving problems. Like programs in a computer, they become relatively fixed patterns for processing information and can therefore be called stages.

2. *Developmental sequence.* The cognitive structures evolve, becoming more complex, differentiated, and integrated. One stage of thinking provides the foundation for the next, which is more "adequate" than the prior one. Development proceeds through a predictable sequence, but at an uneven pace. Each stage is qualitatively different from earlier structures, which, at some point, were found to be inadequate for interpreting reality. Development proceeds through a process of preparing for the shift to the next, more complex stage, and once attained, expanding and integrating gradually within the stage (*horizontal décalage*).

3. *Interaction with the environment.* Both maturity or readiness within the person and stimulation from the environment are essential for growth to occur. When life presents challenges or new information that existing cognitive structures cannot handle, the resulting dissonance or disequilibrium forces a new accommodation or alteration of the cognitive structure.

Perry

While Piaget and Bruner studied children's intellectual processes, William Perry was curious about how intellectual and ethical development continued in young adults. Apparently there was some question that it *did* continue, as Robert W. White wrote in his forward to Perry's book (1970, p. v): "Research with intelligence tests suggested that the maturing of intellectual power was finished by the time a student entered college; never again would capacity be higher." Perry and his associates used open-ended questions to interview students at Harvard in each of their college years, beginning in 1955. As they listened to the tape-recorded interviews, they detected "behind the individuality of the reports a common sequence of challenges to which each student addressed himself in his own particular way" (p. 8). They heard changes in the *forms* of seeing, knowing, and caring that transcended the mastery of the content; they conceptualized these evolving frames of reference as changing cognitive structures, each of which incorporated the forms of the preceding stages in a coherent way.

Perry and his colleagues envisioned a continuum with nine positions, each representing a more differentiated and integrated way of thinking. The positions can be combined into four broad levels (see Figure 1.1). Perry's influential book includes in-depth descriptions of each position, illustrated with detailed transcript excerpts. His model has given us a valuable tool for conceptualizing intellectual development — not in terms of retaining content but as changing frames of reference for interpreting reality.

Perry describes developmental turning points that can affect relationships, integrity, and identity. The shift out of dualistic, black-and-white thinking leads naturally to an increase in tolerance, which in our model is addressed as the process of developing mature interpersonal relationships. Growing acceptance of others' interpretations and values is essential in forming truly intimate relationships and for living in a pluralistic society. When students discover that absolute truths and simple solutions no longer suffice, a liberalizing or humanizing process follows. Empathizing with people from different backgrounds who hold differing interpretations of reality fosters this process. Eventually, students can critically examine values and beliefs in light of evidence and experience and personalize them — transform them and claim them as abiding principles for daily living. A new level of integration occurs when students make conscious choices to take positions, to live out their values, and to continue searching for meaning and congruence.

Perry's description of the shifts through multiplistic and relativistic patterns to commitment within relativism parallels components of our seventh vector, developing integrity. His descriptions of the highest levels of cognitive development (positions 6 to 9) also relate to our fifth vector, establishing identity. He describes these students as "moving off the fence" and making commitments to ideas, values, religious beliefs, careers, and relationships. These are all vital components of identity. Perry's theory laid the groundwork for further inquiry. Other researchers used the open-ended interview process to gather qualitative data on broader samples of students. For example, Perry's book did not include any excerpts from women's reports, only two of which were in the sample, but Belenky, Clinchy, Goldberger, and Tarule (1986) organized ways to more clearly hear the voices of women students.

Belenky, Clinchy, Goldberger, and Tarule

In the late 1970s, Mary Belenky, Blythe Clinchy, Nancy Goldberger, and Jill Tarule observed that women students often doubted their intellectual competence and spoke frequently of problems and gaps in their learning. As psychologists interested in human development, they had studied the intellectual, ethical, and psychological development of adolescents and adults in educational and clinical settings. They noticed that women often felt alienated in the academic environment, setting much greater store in the lessons learned in relationships with friends and teachers, life crises, and community involvements.

Belenky and her colleagues decided to interview women about their experiences as learners and their changing concepts of self and relationships. They analyzed 135 transcripts — 90 from students in six diverse academic institutions (including a high school) and 45 from clients referred by family agencies providing assistance or information on parenting. The subjects differed in age, class, ethnic background, and academic interests and performance. Each interview began with the question, "Looking back, what stands out for you over the past few years?" and proceeded gradually to questions about self-image, relationships, education and learning, moral dilemmas, personal development, catalysts for change, impediments to growth, and views of the future.

In 1986, they published *Women's Ways of Knowing*, which describes five epistemological *perspectives* that they found in their subjects. They did not attempt to delineate why and when the shifts occurred, nor whether they had stagelike qualities. The five perspectives parallel Perry's scheme, with some important differences. For example, the first position is *silence*, a perspective

Figure 1.1. Perry's Model of Intellectual and Ethical Development.

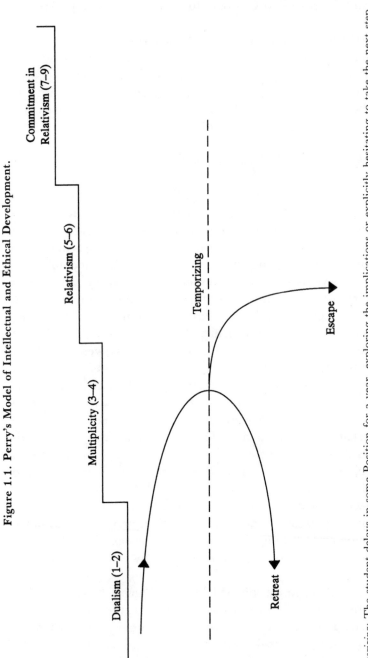

Temporizing: The student delays in some Position for a year, exploring the implications or explicitly hesitating to take the next step.
Escape: The student exploits the opportunity for detachment offered by the structures of Positions 4 and 5 to deny responsibility through passive or opportunistic alienation.
Retreat: The student entrenches in the dualistic, absolutistic structures of Positions 2 or 3 (quotation from Perry, 1970, p. 10).

Dualism (Positions 1 and 2)	Multiplicity (Positions 3 and 4)	Relativism (Positions 5 and 6)	Commitment in Relativism (Positions 7, 8, and 9)
• Knowledge exists absolutely.	• Students accept diversity and uncertainty as legitimate but still temporary in areas where Authority "hasn't found The Answer yet."	• All knowledge (including authority's) now is viewed as contextual and relativistic.	• Students have a growing realization that they need to find their own choices, based on multiple "truths."
• "Right answers" are known by authorities.	• Questions now can legitimately have multiple answers.	• Dualistic right-wrong thinking exists only within certain contexts.	• They move "off the fence" and begin to align choices with personal themes.
• Tasks that require thinking about options or many points of view are confusing.	• Students assume that Authorities grade on "good expression" but remain puzzled as to standards.	• Students differentiate between an unconsidered belief and a considered judgment.	• Active affirmation of themselves and their responsibilities in a pluralistic world clarifies identity.
• Legitimacy of alternate perspectives is not yet acknowledged.	• Those who hold different beliefs are no longer seen as simply "wrong."	• Authorities are no longer resisted, but can be valued for their expertise.	• Personal commitments in such areas as marriage, religion, and career are made from relativistic frame of reference.
• Judgments are stated as though they are self-evident.	• All opinions are equally valid outside of the Authority's realm where right-wrong still prevails.	• Their judgments, too, can be evaluated.	
• Diversity of opinion or uncertainty among Authorities is viewed as inadequacy on their part, or an exercise "so we can learn to find The Answer for ourselves."	• Students are unable to adequately evaluate points of view, and question the legitimacy of doing so.	• Differing perspectives are now not merely acknowledged, but seen as pieces of a larger whole.	
		• Personal Commitments are seen as ways to orient oneself in a relativistic world (vs. unconsidered commitment to simple belief in certainty).	

apparently unfamiliar to Perry's subjects. In fact, none of the subjects in this category were doing college-level work. They were among the youngest and most socially, economically, and educationally deprived. Women in this position felt "deaf and dumb." Authorities were all-powerful. Words were weapons, not tools. Representational thinking was not well developed, in part because the women rarely engaged in dialogue and therefore missed vital opportunities to speak and listen, reflect and share. They saw life in terms of polarities (good or bad, win or lose) and stereotyped roles (women are incompetent, passive, and dependent on men).

Perspective 2 is *received knowledge* and is similar to Perry's dualistic positions. Women at this stage believed that learning is done through listening carefully to authorities and receiving the right answers from them. They valued structure, clarity, and predictability. Whereas the women were awed by authorities, Perry's males appeared to identify with them, to look to them as mentors, and to speak in their presence as a demonstration of their learning. Even though the men argued and debated more, they tended to view discussion as a waste of time, since only authorities had the truth and peers did not. In contrast, the females at this level built almost symbiotic relationships, valued conversation, and were surprised and relieved to hear others saying "the very same things that they would say" (p. 37).

At perspective 3, *subjective knowledge,* the interviewees had moved from silence and passivity to a "protesting inner voice and infallible gut" (p. 54). They no longer viewed knowledge as absolute or authorities as infallible. They differed in their view of themselves as learners, however. Perry's men saw themselves as defenders of everyone's right to have their own opinion and publicly offered their own, insisting it was just as good as the teacher's. For them, the next step was to learn the analytical methods and objective procedures for joining the ranks of academic authorities. The women interviewed by the authors were less confident about their opinions, often did not express themselves, wanted others to affirm their views, and frequently felt that truth was personally intuited and perhaps uncommunicable.

Of the 135 interviewed, almost half were predominantly subjectivist in their thinking. Many told stories about loss of trust in male authority, and the authors found that "sexual abuse appears to be a shockingly common experience for women. In our sample of seventy-five women, 38 percent of the women in schools and colleges and 65 percent of women contacted through the social agencies told us that they had been subject to either incest, rape, or sexual seduction by a male in authority over them — fathers, uncles, teachers, doctors, clerics, bosses" (pp. 58–59).

The subjectivists expressed the strongest levels of anger about their naive trust, their silent submission to abuse, and the unresolved issues that they had not yet worked through. In addition, they had difficulty describing themselves clearly. The authors felt that a secure, integrated, and enduring self-concept was not yet in place for these women. "Whereas in the position of received knowledge, women derive a sense of 'who I am' from the definitions others supply and the roles they fill, subjectivist women shift away from this perspective and experience a wrenching away of the familiar contexts and relationships within which the old identity has been embedded. Their place in life is no longer a matter of adopting the values of the community and fulfilling the expectations of those they care about" (p. 81).

This statement makes an important link between intellectual development and identity. It brings to mind Josselson's (1987) finding that women who "foreclosed" on their identities — that is, who stayed with or returned to identities rooted in unquestioned values provided by their family or religion — tended to be less anxious than those who constructed identities through crisis and commitment. The latter women tended to be more flexible and autonomous, but they also knew that risk and uncertainty might recur at any moment, bringing on another round of struggle. The pull of the familiar is strong, and the anxiety that comes with letting go of the known to move into the unknown can be terrifying, especially if supportive people and resources are not visible.

In addition to leaving familiar contexts, a move toward autonomy is often, for women, a break with past relationships.

Painful partnerships and negative self-images from the past need to be replaced by nurturing relationships and empowering self-definitions in order for identity and purpose to take a positive form. Thus, the ability to hear a trustworthy inner voice can lead to a rebirth of the self, and the authors saw this occurring in thirty-, forty-, and fifty-year-old subjects—further testimony to the fact that development continues throughout life.

Perspective 4 is *procedural knowledge*. When earlier ways of knowing were challenged, absolutism and subjectivism gave way to reasoned reflection. Instructors asked students to justify opinions, to analyze and evaluate according to objective criteria, and to think critically. As a result, students found that some conclusions had more credibility than others, based on evidence or logic. Intuitive knowing no longer sufficed. One could no longer "just know." Real knowing required careful observation and the right form or methodology. Learning how to do it required formal instruction.

The authors found two styles of procedural knowing. The more familiar academic approach is *separate knowing,* because truth is established through impersonal procedures, doubt and debate, public defense, and the exclusion of personal feelings or beliefs. It is easier to recognize than the second type because "Piaget, Kohlberg, and Perry have tuned our ears to it, and it rang out loud and clear in our interviews, especially with women from highly selective, rigorous, and traditional colleges like the one from which Perry drew his sample" (p. 102). The other style, *connected knowing,* was harder to hear. From this angle, truth emerges from firsthand experience, from understanding another's ideas, from conversation rather than debate, from clarifying rather than judging, and from collaborating and nurturing emerging ideas rather than critiquing them. For subjectivists, learning to use systematic procedures, whether separate or connected, is a step forward, since they "learn to get out from behind their own eyes and use a different lens, in one case the lens of a discipline, in the other the lens of another person" (p. 115).

The two voices come together in perspective 5, *constructed knowledge.* The student learns to integrate knowledge felt to be personally important with knowledge learned from others. In this way, the knower becomes part of the known, weaving together rational and emotive thought, objective and subjective information. This engenders a reverence for different ways of knowing and different parts of the self. Rather than compartmentalizing thought and feeling, conscious and unconscious perceptions, work and home, self and other, learners look for ways to transcend boundaries, resist oversimplification, and see that the answers to all questions vary depending on the context in which they are asked and on the frame of reference of the person doing the asking (p. 138). Authorities are now seen as experts based on their competence, not their status. Constructivists can collaborate with them in seeking new awareness, using intellectual competence to make a contribution in a larger sphere, and using the self as an instrument of understanding and expanding knowledge.

Belenky, Clinchy, Goldberger, and Tarule augmented our understanding of intellectual development, adding depth and contrast to Perry's earlier work and the educational practices that can foster it. They also highlighted the importance of the family of origin and the "politics of talk" in influencing development during college.

Baxter Magolda

Marcia Baxter Magolda (1992) investigated students' perceptions of the nature of knowledge and the role of gender in their changing patterns of reasoning. She found parallels to both Perry and Belenky, Clinchy, Goldberger, and Tarule after interviewing 101 students in their beginning year of college and then each year until the first year after graduation. Seventy students participated for the full five years. Her sample was less diverse than that of Belenky and her colleagues in that all were students at Miami University in Oxford, Ohio, 80 percent were eighteen years old, and only 3 percent were from nondominant populations. However, the research did include both males (44 percent) and females (56 percent).

Baxter Magolda's epistemological reflection model describes

four ways of knowing and their development throughout college. The first three categories feature two patterns, and they appear to be gender related, although not "gender dictated" (Baxter Magolda, 1992, pp. 37–72):

1. *Absolute knowers* viewed knowledge as certain and authorities as having access to the absolute truths in all areas of knowledge. The two patterns of reasoning were (a) *receiving* knowledge (used more frequently by women in the study) and (b) *mastering* knowledge (used more frequently by men in the study).

2. *Transitional knowers* viewed knowledge as absolute only in some areas but not in others. They expected authorities to go further than simply imparting knowledge, to help students understand and apply knowledge. The two patterns of reasoning were (a) *interpersonal* (used more frequently by women in the study) and (b) *impersonal* (used more frequently by men in the study).

3. *Independent knowers* viewed knowledge as mostly uncertain. They wanted authorities to promote independent thinking, an exchange of opinions in class, and support for more intellectual autonomy. The two patterns of reasoning were (a) *interindividual* (used more frequently by women in the study) and (b) *individual* (used more frequently by men in the study).

4. *Contextual knowers* saw some knowledge claims as better than others in a particular context. Judgments about what to believe are possible although not absolute, they are based on evidence, and learning changes from thinking independently to thinking through problems and integrating and applying knowledge in context. This mode of knowing was rarely found during college and was seen in only 12 percent of the interviews done one year after graduation. There were too few data to identify gender differences.

Reflecting on these students' stories, Baxter Magolda saw that the boundaries between patterns were fluid and that more similarities than differences existed in these women's and men's ways of knowing: "I discovered that some consistently used similar patterns over time, whereas others moved back and forth between patterns. Some who used one pattern fairly consistently would still occasionally exhibit reasoning from the other patterns. I began to understand the patterns as a continuum bounded by a pattern on each end, with numerous variations and combinations in between" (p. 13).

These cognitive theorists give us new tools for understanding the development of intellectual competence, a component of our first vector. While others have researched the acquisition of knowledge and aesthetic appreciation, and the growth of academic skills such as critical thinking, changes in *how* students think are probably more enduring than the accrual of facts and figures. Belenky, Clinchy, Goldberger, and Tarule, Perry, Baxter Magolda, and other theorists such as Kitchener and King (1981, 1990a, 1990b) have charted parallel shifts from simple to complex, from passive to active, from narrow to broad. We propose that developing intellectual competence involves learning to use different modes of thinking and knowing based on chosen purposes; gaining skill in reflecting on one's own thinking processes; and generating questions, content, and conclusions that have both objective and subjective validity.

More and more work is being done on intellectual development. Now that some basic constructs are widely known, researchers are probing for differences based on gender, class, ethnicity, and age. Nancy Goldberger (forthcoming) is studying the effects of acculturation on ways of knowing as students from different ethnic communities, races, and immigrant groups move into the American educational system, with its explicit norms about the "right way to know." She cites Collins's (1990) exploration of a black feminist epistemology that values concrete experience, dialogue and narrative, wisdom (versus knowledge), and "mother wit," and Luttrell's (1989) interviews with black and white working-class women, who rely on personal experience, common sense, and intuition as central to knowing.

Kohlberg

Another family of cognitive theories deals with moral development. Here, too, debate continues about the role of gender in the development of ethical thinking. Lawrence Kohlberg's theory is widely known. After analyzing how respondents justified their opinions about hypothetical moral quandaries, such as the now famous "Heinz dilemma" (should penniless Heinz steal the experimental drug for his dying wife?), he delineated six stages of moral development and refined a method for assessing them. When first proposed, the model described a conceptual hierarchy for making decisions based on (1) fear of punishment and gratification of one's own needs, (2) opportunities to meet one's needs or to instrumentally bargain with others for mutual benefit, (3) the need to conform to a peer group's wishes or society's rules and to be a "nice boy/nice girl" in earning approval from others, (4) respect for "law and order," duty, and authority, (5) adherence to legal rights or social contracts or to personal values, and (6) adherence to personally chosen ethical principles or universal moral principles. In his later work, Kohlberg had difficulty finding enough empirical evidence for the separate existence of stage 6 (Kohlberg, Levine, and Hewer, 1983).

Each stage in the theory represents a qualitatively different and more comprehensive system of mental organization and a different conception of right and wrong. Progress occurs in an invariant sequence, with thinking becoming less concrete and more abstract, less based on self-interest and more based on principles such as justice, equality, and the Golden Rule. Kohlberg's scoring manual was modified to give greater importance to caring and empathy as indicators of postconventional reasoning (Kohlberg, 1984). After all, he said, a universal principle such as the Golden Rule has two elements, one that emphasizes fairness (Do unto others as you would have them do unto you) and another that emphasizes compassion (Love thy neighbor as thyself).

Gilligan

The change in emphasis may be related to questions raised by Carol Gilligan, whose research on women's concepts of self and morality revealed discrepancies between their experience and the prevailing theories of Piaget, Erikson, and particularly Kohlberg, whose sample of subjects were all boys, age ten to sixteen. Gilligan (1977) noticed that women consistently scored at lower stages of development than men when instruments operationalizing Kohlberg's model were used. She hypothesized that there were flaws in the theory, not in the women. After interviewing women about their approach to a real-life moral dilemma (whether or not to terminate a pregnancy), she proposed that Kohlberg's overemphasis on the rights of individuals as separate and autonomous tended to discount women's valuing of relationships. If moral development involves impartial analysis of conflicting arguments, decisions based on caring, supporting, healing, and preserving relationships might look like "nice girl" attempts to make everyone feel better.

If the "objective" application of rules, contracts, and principles of fairness represents the apex of moral reasoning, posing questions about the concrete details and situational contexts looks like ambivalence or unwillingness to take a firm position. For example, Gilligan listened to eleven-year-old Jake reason that Heinz should steal the drug, after deciding that the value of life was greater than the value of property rights, even if a flawed system of justice punished him. Young Amy, however, considered neither law nor property but how stealing the drug would affect the relationship between Heinz and his wife and the wife's future. After all, what if he had to go to jail? What if his wife got sicker again and the money-grubbing pharmacist remained implacable? She thinks "they should really just talk it out and find some other way to make the money" (1982, p. 28). Heinz should not have to decide between stealing and letting her die. The conflict should be worked out through communication, and if that is done, relationships remain intact between wife, husband, and druggist.

The so-called "Kohlberg-Gilligan debate" has continued since Gilligan identified "a different voice," the *care and responsibility voice,* and criticized Kohlberg's theory as biased in favor of the *justice voice.* Researchers have reported conflicting findings. Some continue to find two different, gender-related voices (Gilligan, 1982, 1986a, 1986b; Lyons, 1983; Johnston, 1985) and lower scores for women on Kohlberg's scale (Langdale, 1983; Baumrind, 1986; Haan, 1985). Others have found one structure of moral reasoning — the justice structure — but two different styles of expressing it (fairness and compassion), similar to Baxter Magolda's (1992) work exploring each mode of reasoning with two patterns of expression. Several have disputed the lower scores for females (Kohlberg, 1984; Walker, 1984; Brabeck, 1982; Denny, 1988; Gibbs, Arnold, and Burkhart, 1984; Rest, 1986). The debates continue, with new camps forming around "cultural feminist essentialists" and "poststructuralist" genderless theorists (Alcoff, 1988).

Focusing too much energy on who is right can sidetrack us from responding to the students who sit before us. The idea that polarities may exist within each stage or mode of reasoning adds an intriguing element to the study and practice of student development. Perhaps our theoretical lenses have now become bifocals, the better to see these splits within the stages or vectors. The voices of care and justice express complementary processes for development, just as the Myers-Briggs preferences are complementary patterns of perceiving and deciding. For us, debating whether the differences stem from gender or personality or conditioning seems less important than recognizing that there *are* differences and creating learning environments responsive to them. For our purposes, it seems important to acknowledge the work of Gilligan and other researchers as valuable moves toward inclusiveness and as sobering reminders that any theory based on a limited sample cannot be automatically applied to the entire human race.

The debate about moral development theory adds to our understanding of the seventh vector, developing integrity. In our model, movement along this vector involves consciously affirming core values that are socially responsible, bringing beliefs and behavior into greater alignment, and gaining skill and consistency in the use of principled thinking. Both the ethic of care and the ethic of justice are socially responsible principles; both are needed to live in the world and help it flourish. Students moving along this vector are learning to make moral decisions and personal commitments based on these universal values and others as well.

Both Kohlberg's and Gilligan's theories also describe movement away from self-serving impulsiveness and unthinking conformity toward inner directedness—movement guided by awareness and the will to make difficult choices. Their principles shed light on aspects of the second vector—managing emotions—which involves impulse control as well as learning appropriate expression of feelings. In Kohlberg's image of the postconventional thinker, willing to risk ostracism in protesting unjust laws or invoking higher principles than convention dictates, we see movement toward autonomy. In Gilligan's image of the caring choice maker, who balances self-interest with the interests of important others, we see a process of moving through autonomy toward interdependence (our third vector).

Psychosocial Theories

Many of our theories of student development have emerged from a rich psychological tradition that began with Freud. Adler, Jung, and Erikson kept some of his ideas, disputed and modified others, and added new perspectives. Others set off in divergent directions—Rogers and the client-centered counselors, Skinner and the behaviorists, Berne and the transactional analysts, Perls and the Gestalt therapists, Ellis and the rational-emotive therapists, and Satir and the family therapists. Personality theorists like Harry Stack Sullivan and Jean Baker Miller added insight based on clinical experiences. Like different facets of a diamond, each theory clarified a different perspective on human development, and in doing so, provided theoretical tools for college counselors and current theorists. All were interested not only in how people thought about themselves and the world but also in how they felt, behaved, and interpreted the meaning of experience.

Erikson

Erik Erikson, the progenitor of the psychosocial models, belonged to Freud's circle of psychoanalysts. Freud was the first stage theorist, linking the age of children to predictable "fixations." Erikson (1959) saw stages of development beyond childhood and put more emphasis on social context and strengths built throughout life than on internal energy dynamics or the struggling ego's defense mechanisms. He believed that certain challenges are systematically presented when physical growth and cognitive maturation converge with environmental demands. He outlined eight stages or periods in psychosocial development, each with a life challenge that can lead to progress, regression, standstill, or recurring bouts with the same issue in a new context.

The first challenge for infants is to decide whether the world is safe. If their needs are met and their environment is nurturing, they learn basic *trust*. Similar strengths develop when children experience the *autonomy* that comes with muscle control and coordination (versus the *shame* that comes with self-consciousness about lack of coordination), the *initiative* to move around and make things (versus the *guilt* that comes from being punished), and the *industry* to succeed in school (versus the *inferiority* that comes from inadequate performance). Each resolution of the eight crises bestows an ego strength or "virtue." Adolescents face *identity* versus *identity diffusion* and learn the virtue of fidelity. Young adults face *intimacy* versus *isolation* and learn the virtue of love. Adults face *generativity* versus *stagnation* and learn the virtue of caring. Old age brings *integrity* versus *despair,* with the chance to gain wisdom and acceptance.

Erikson believed that each part of the ego has a time of special ascendency, just as each part of the embryo arises according to a master plan. He called this the *epigenetic principle.* Each part exists in some form before the time when it becomes "phase-specific" — that is, when the individual's readiness and society's pressure precipitate its psychosocial coming of age. Identity became phase-specific at the end of adolescence and has to "find a certain integration as a relatively conflict-free psychosocial arrangement — or remain defective or conflict-laden" (1959, p. 130).

Since the stabilization of identity was the primary task for adolescents and young adults, it was a logical anchor point for Chickering's attempt to synthesize data about college student development into a general framework that could be used to guide educational practice. College students, in his earlier work, meant young adults. In his review of research and in students' written self-assessments, he saw growing differentiation and integration, greater coherence and stability, and more effectiveness in adapting to the world. As noted earlier, *Education and Identity* (1969) proposed seven vectors of development, each of which could be seen as more specific aspects of the central concept of "identity." Chickering's original seven vectors were (1) developing competence, (2) managing emotions, (3) developing autonomy, (4) establishing identity, (5) freeing interpersonal relationships, (6) developing purpose, and (7) developing integrity.

The Earlier Chickering Model

Chickering followed in Erikson's footsteps by proposing that establishing identity depended in part on movement along the first three vectors, since one had to clarify who one was, apart from others, before interpersonal relationships could be freed from symbiosis. When Erikson saw adolescent females defining their identity *through* relationships with others, he concluded that they deviated from the normal pattern because they confused identity with intimacy. From this perspective, a woman at midlife may appear to be regressing to the unfinished business of adolescence when she struggles to find her own voice.

A review of more recent research has led us to reorder and rename some of the vectors. For example, researchers have challenged the assumption that autonomy must precede intimacy. New findings suggest that it may be the other way around. For example, Straub and Rodgers (1986) administered the Student Development Task Inventory (SDTI) to 241 female students at a large Midwestern university. All classes scored significantly higher on the Mature Interpersonal Relationships task than on the Autonomy task, suggesting that "regardless of when work is begun on the Autonomy task or when it is resolved (whether on time or delayed), the Mature Interpersonal Relationships task preceded the Autonomy task for the women in this study" (p. 222).

Furthermore, Straub (1987) theorized that women may need to become autonomous in their relationships before becoming autonomous in their own right. She interviewed students who scored significantly higher than the mean on the Autonomy scale of the SDTI in order to find out which kinds of experiences had significant impact on development of autonomy. Her subjects reported relational events most frequently (38.5 percent), with educational events a close second (37 percent).

Other findings caution us about oversimplification of gender differences. For example, Greeley and Tinsley (1988) used the Developing Mature Interpersonal Relationships and Developing Autonomy scales with 441 traditional-age students at a large Midwestern university. They found that scores for intimacy were significantly higher for women than for men, but they also found that the women scored slightly but not significantly higher on autonomy than the men did. Furthermore, men scored significantly higher on intimacy than autonomy at all class levels.

The interplay between autonomy, interdependence, and intimacy is complex. Recognizing that relationships provide powerful learning experiences about physical expression of feelings, others' evaluations, levels of self-esteem, and other aspects of identity, we moved that vector to an earlier place in the sequence and renamed it "developing mature interpersonal relationships," since we were broadening the scope of the vector to include increasing tolerance and capacity for intimacy.

We also wished to put greater emphasis on interdependence as the capstone of autonomy. Robert Kegan, whose theory recognizes the interaction between intimacy and autonomy, warns us about the futility of insisting on a lockstep sequence. While Kegan is regarded as a cognitive theorist, his model of development relates to our vectors on developing mature interpersonal relationships and to the renamed vector, moving through autonomy toward interdependence.

Kegan

In *The Evolving Self* (1982), Kegan proposed a helix of "evolutionary truces" to portray the dynamic between "the yearning to be included, to be a part of, close to, joined with, to be held, admitted, accompanied [and] the yearning to be independent or autonomous, to experience one's distinctness, the self-chosenness of one's directions, one's individual integrity" (p. 107). (See Figure 1.2.)

Development involves becoming temporarily embedded in one pattern until its inherent imbalance impels us to break away from it and move toward the other polarity. Each shift involves a change in how we construct meaning. To develop a new way to interpret our experience, we must first be able to observe the old one with greater detachment and to see a new boundary between what is "me" (subject) and what is "not me" (object).

People move from stage 1 — the *impulsive balance* — by learning to control their impulses (to *have* them, not to *be* them). This fundamental shift occurs between the ages of five and seven. Stage 2 is the *imperial balance* because others are judged according to whether or not they "meet my needs, fulfill my wishes, pursue my interests" (p. 91). A sense of shared reality with others does not yet exist, and therefore others have to be controlled, manipulated, or at least "predicted" in terms of their behavior.

To move to stage 3, the *interpersonal balance,* one must somehow detach and observe that "'I' no longer *am* my needs (no longer the imperial I); rather, I *have* them. In having them I can now coordinate, or integrate, one need system with another, and in so doing, I bring into being that need-mediating reality which we refer to when we speak of mutuality" (p. 95). This kind of shift away from self-centeredness was portrayed in *The Doctor,* a film based on the real-life experiences of E. E. Rosenbaum (1988), in which a successful surgeon (subject) is forced into the position of patient (object). After a crisis of forced dependency on an impersonal health care system and a confrontation with a fellow patient incensed at the staff's self-protective lies, he realizes that he has distanced himself not only from his patients but also from his own vulnerability. He sees the pattern of holding people at arm's length and admits that he does not know how to "lower his arm" enough to connect. Having hatched out of his embeddedness in separation, he becomes a more caring physician.

In Kegan's model, stage 3 is "interpersonal" but it is not

Figure 1.2. Kegan's Helix of Evolutionary Truces.

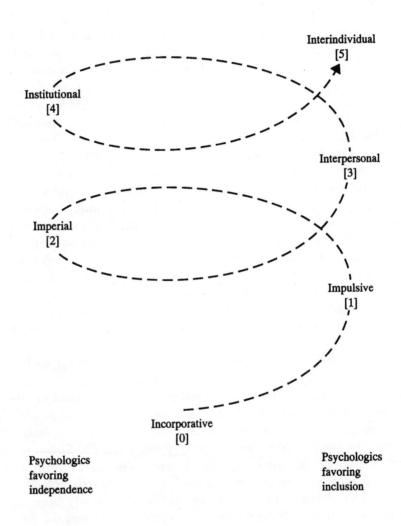

"intimate." Mature intimacy requires a self that exists independently, whereas at this stage, a significant other is needed in order to feel complete, to define oneself, and to make life meaningful. "There is no self to share with another; instead the other is required to bring the self into being. Fusion is not intimacy. If one can feel manipulated by the imperial balance, one can feel devoured by the interpersonal one" (pp. 96–97). To get to stage 4, the *institutional balance,* a person must realize that "I *am not* my relationships." Instead, "I *have* relationships." Before this can occur, there must be a relatively autonomous self who can accomplish this having, who can take control of the personality, administering it like a sort of psychic institution, which it then identifies with.

When the institutional balance is achieved, emotional life becomes more internally controlled. The threat of rejection is not as powerful as attacks on the interior polity. "The question is not, as it was earlier, 'Do you still like me?' but, 'Does my government still stand?'" (p. 102). The will to stand alone, without the group's approval or fusion with another person, signals a major developmental step, as this student reports:

> I became less dependent on a relationship to feel good about myself or loved. The old way of thinking: I felt empty, lonely, and lost if I wasn't with a man. The new way of thinking: I don't need a man to be happy. I can set my own goals, feel motivated, and be a total person all by myself. I moved out of an unhealthy relationship with a crisis that got me into counseling. I gradually began to piece myself together and understood how destructive my behavior and the relationship had been for me. I knew I had really changed because I began to follow through with all my decisions. I was happy by myself.
>
> I began to control my self-talk, I began to nurture and talk to the scared, lonely child within me. I no longer depended on external situations or people for my sense of well-being. [What helped?]

My counselor really helped by listening to me while
I tried to get in touch with the feelings I had been
avoiding all my life. A split-up with my ex, his
remarrying almost immediately, and my going back
to school in order to support myself. I felt that I
was finally doing the right thing. I was feeling the
pain, the loneliness, and dealing with the feelings
of fear that had held me back.

This story illustrates the interrelationship between managing emotions, developing autonomy, recognizing an unhealthy
relationship and moving out of it, and "piecing together" a new,
more satisfying identity. It remains to be seen whether this student will reach Kegan's stage 5, the *interindividual balance*. To
do so involves separating the self from the psychological institution it was identified with. What was subject becomes object
again; the individual is now a self who can reflect on, as though
observing from a distance, the regulations and purposes of a
psychic administration. There is now a self who *directs* the organization, rather than a self who *was* the organization. Stage
5 is called interindividual because here people can truly experience interdependence as the capstone of autonomy and the foundation of community.

Kegan disputes the idea that development is a linear, sequential series of accomplishments, with independence as the
desired result: "The model also recognizes the equal dignity of
each yearning, and in this respect offers a corrective to all present
developmental frameworks which unequivocally define growth
in terms of differentiation, separation, increasing autonomy, and
lose sight of the fact that adaptation is equally about integration, attachment, inclusion. The net effect of this myopia, as
feminist psychologists are now pointing out . . . has been that
differentiation (the stereotypically male overemphasis in this
most human ambivalence) is favored with the language of growth
and development, while integration (the stereotypically female
overemphasis) gets spoken of in terms of dependency and immaturity" (pp. 108–109).

Nancy Chodorow (1974) proposed that female identity

formation takes place in a context of ongoing relationship, since girls experience themselves as like their mothers. The experience of attachment, with its inherent foundation for empathy, is fused with the process of identity formation. In contrast, boys must separate from their mothers in order to define themselves as masculine. Kegan picks up this theme, observing that men have more difficulty moving from stages that favor autonomy (the imperial and the institutional stages), and women have more difficulty moving from stages that favor inclusion (the interpersonal and the interindividual stages). According to Kegan, if Chodorow is right that there is some intrinsic bias toward separation in males and inclusion in females, then men may move through all of the levels in a more differentiated way and women may move through them all in a more integrated way (p. 210).

But regardless of gender, human beings need to find the balance between too much dependence and too much independence. Women and men must learn to blend care of the self with concern for others and to speak and act authentically, without confusing genuine caring with placating. Gilligan (1982, p. 171) says that this redefinition of care marks the shift from childhood to adulthood: "When the distinction between helping and pleasing frees the activity of care from the wish for approval by others, the ethic of responsibility can become a self-chosen anchor of personal integrity and strength."

When college students move through autonomy toward interdependence, doors are opened within the self and new levels of emotional and ethical integration are possible. A growing capacity for healthy detachment decreases defensiveness. Since "I" exist (at Kegan's interindividual level) apart from my role or my performance, I can become less defensive about how others evaluate me. I can not only receive but also seek out information that helps me function more smoothly, even if it takes the form of criticism. "The self seems available to 'hear' negative reports about its activities; before, it *was* those activities and therefore literally 'irritable' in the face of those reports. . . . Every new balance represents a capacity to listen to what before one could only hear irritably, and the capacity to hear irritably what before one could not hear at all" (p. 105).

This capacity to take in feedback from others must also parallel increased access to feelings and impulses that were formerly held hostage by an internal censor guarding a somewhat fragile ego from threatening emotions. One can begin to observe conflicts within the self and not be so quick to suppress them. As Kegan says, "At ego stage 4, one's feelings seem often to be regarded as a kind of recurring administrative problem which the successful ego-administrator resolves without damage to the smooth functioning of the organization. When the self is located not in the institutional but in the coordinating of the institutional, one's own and others, the interior life gets "freed up" (or "broken open") within oneself, and with others; this new dynamism, flow, or play results from the capacity of the new self to move back and forth between psychic systems within itself" (p. 105). Perhaps the ability to tolerate an internal plurality of inner voices enables increasing tolerance of external conflict. Rather than dismissing others, one can begin to take them in.

In fact, the interest in diversity has been noted as a mark of ego development in Jane Loevinger's theory, which also emphasizes the development of autonomy and the growth of an internal set of standards to guide behavior.

Loevinger

While primarily a cognitive stage theorist, Loevinger's model (1976) is more holistic than theories concerned primarily with thinking processes. Its nine stages encompass impulse control, character development, interpersonal style, conscious preoccupations, and cognitive style. She contends that these are all facets of a single coherent process, since like Adler, she stresses the unity of personality: "What one perceives and understands bears the imprint of the ego" (p. 9), which she believes is a process, not a thing. Its essence is "the striving to master, to integrate, to make sense of experience" (p. 59). "It is close to what the person thinks of as his self" (p. 67).

Loevinger (1976) proposed a linear, sequential model, basing her research initially on sentence completion tests with girls and women. (See Table 1.1.) Her first three stages (*symbi-*

otic, impulsive, and *self-protective*) are generally not manifested by college students. At the *conformist* stage, individuals want to belong. They tend to adopt the language, appearance, and opinions of whatever group becomes significant. They are more likely to judge differences negatively and to think in stereotypes. To develop, they must discover who they are, apart from the group. The transition from the conformist stage to the conscientious stage is called the *self-aware* level. It is characterized by greater self-consciousness, a willingness to move away from external controls, and a discovery of multiple perspectives and alternatives. Her model fits well with our perspective on developing autonomy in college settings, where students can literally move away from the family, reflect on the values taught at home, and consider different points of view, both inside and outside of the classroom.

At the *conscientious* stage, behavior is aligned with values and standards chosen by a self less affected by others' opinions. Awareness of emotions, beliefs, and priorities increases. Relationships become more reciprocal. New levels of detachment, empathy, and complex reasoning are possible. The transition to the next stage — described as the *individualistic* level — involves an even greater sense of one's uniqueness and value. Tolerance of self and others increases, as does an openness to paradox and contradiction. Issues related to dependence and independence begin to surface, and at the next stage, they become more problematic as conflicts between personal needs and others' interests becomes more pronounced. In our model, capacity for intimacy and growing tolerance of differences in others are dimensions of developing mature interpersonal relationships (the fourth vector).

The highlight of Loevinger's *autonomous* stage is conceptual complexity — an ability to integrate apparently contradictory ideas and a high tolerance for ambiguity. As values become clearer, choices become more difficult. Should I do my duty or follow my dream? Should I settle for security or stretch myself? Should I buck the system or fit into it? A stronger sense of autonomy and selectivity about partners and friends enhances a capacity for more satisfying interdependence. Purposes and

Table 1.1. Some Milestones of Ego Development.

Stage	Code	Impulse control, character development	Interpersonal style	Conscious preoccupations	Cognitive style
Presocial			Autistic		
Symbiotic	I-1		Symbiotic	Self versus nonself	
Impulsive	I-2	Impulsive, fear of retaliation	Receiving, dependent, exploitative	Bodily feelings, especially sexual and aggressive	Stereotyping, conceptual confusion
Self-protective	△	Fear of being caught, externalizing blame, opportunistic	Wary, manipulative, exploitative	Self-protection, trouble, wishes, things, advantage, control	
Conformist	I-3	Conformity to external rules, shame, guilt for breaking rules	Belonging, superficial niceness	Appearance, social acceptability, banal feelings, behavior	Conceptual simplicity, stereotypes, clichés
Conscientious-conformist	I-3/4	Differentiation of norms, goals	Aware of self in relation to group, helping	Adjustment, problems, reasons, opportunities (vague)	Multiplicity
Conscientious	I-4	Self-evaluated standards, self-criticism, guilt for consequences, long-term goals and ideals	Intensive, responsible, mutual, concern for communication	Differentiated feelings, motives for behavior, self-respect, achievements, traits, expression	Conceptual complexity, idea of patterning

Individualistic	I-4/5	*Add:* Respect for individuality	*Add:* Dependence as an emotional problem	*Add:* Development, social problems, differentiation of inner life from outer	*Add:* Distinction of process and outcome
Autonomous	I-5	*Add:* Coping with conflicting inner needs, toleration	*Add:* Respect for autonomy, interdependence	*Add:* Vividly conveyed feelings, integration of physiological and psychological causation of behavior, role conception, self-fulfillment, self in social context	Increased conceptual complexity, complex patterns, toleration for ambiguity, broad scope, objectivity
Integrated	I-6	*Add:* Reconciling inner conflicts, renunciation of unattainable	*Add:* Cherishing of individuality	*Add:* Identity	

Note: Add means in addition to the description applying to the previous level.
Source: Loevinger, 1976, pp. 24–25. Reprinted by permission.

values grow more important. In contrast to the recognition of individual differences at the self-aware level and the acceptance of them as truly legitimate at the conscientious stage, the new pattern is to cherish, celebrate, and actively seek them out at the autonomous stage.

The *integrated* stage may only be reached by Maslow's self-actualized persons. They are the paragons who have achieved a high level of integration, autonomy, identity, objectivity, and self-transcendence. They have let go of intensive striving and can balance task-orientedness with spontaneity and relaxation. They balance vivid perception of the outer world and inner life. They can be concrete or abstract. Their democratic character structure keeps them respectful and open to learning from anyone, and on top of all that, they are fun to be with. They have an unhostile sense of humor and exhibit "gaiety, particularly in sexual and other love relations" (Loevinger, 1976, p. 140).

Principles from Loevinger's model reappear in several of our vectors, including moving through autonomy toward interdependence (vector 3), developing purpose (vector 6) — which involves choosing future directions for career, family, life-style, and community — and developing integrity (vector 7).

The Seven Vectors

Our model does not portray development as one predominant challenge or crisis resolution after another, each invariably linked to specific ages. Development for college students, which today includes persons of virtually all ages, is a process of infinite complexity. Just as students are notorious for not proceeding through the institution according to schedule, they rarely fit into oversimplified paths or pigeonholes. We propose the seven vectors as maps to help us determine where students are and which way they are heading. Movement along any one can occur at different rates and can interact with movement along the others. Each step from "lower" to "higher" brings more awareness, skill, confidence, complexity, stability, and integration but does not rule out an accidental or intentional return to ground already traversed. We assume that "higher" is better than "lower," because in adding the skills and strengths encompassed by these vectors, individuals grow in versatility, strength, and ability to adapt when unexpected barriers or pitfalls appear.

We also recognize that developmental patterns described by psychosocial theorists may have been skewed by the exclusivity of their samples, as was the case for cognitive theorists. Women were less prominent in Erikson's thinking, and males were initially excluded from Loevinger's sample. Nontraditional students and members of minority groups often were left out altogether. These deficiencies are now being corrected. For example, there have been studies on identity formation for women (Josselson, 1987), on nonwhite students (Cross, 1971; Helms, 1990, Sue and Sue, 1971; Martinez, 1988; Johnson and Lashley, 1988; Atkinson, Morten, and Sue, 1983; Ho, 1987; Branch-Simpson, 1984), and on homosexual students (Cass, 1979; Coleman, 1981–1982; Dank, 1971; Minton and McDonald, 1983–1984; Plummer, 1975; Troiden, 1979). Many of these studies seem to be turning up variations in style and sequence, but the fundamental themes reappear and continue to serve as foundations for the seven vectors.

The vectors describe major highways for journeying toward individuation — the discovery and refinement of one's unique way of being — and also toward communion with other individuals and groups, including the larger national and global society. We propose that while each person will drive differently, with varying vehicles and self-chosen detours, eventually all will move down these major routes. They may have different ways of thinking, learning, and deciding, and those differences will affect the way the journey unfolds, but for all the different stories about turning points and valuable lessons, college students live out recurring themes: gaining competence and self-awareness, learning control and flexibility, balancing intimacy with freedom, finding one's voice or vocation, refining beliefs, and making commitments.

Since we refrained from describing development in terms of Erikson's age-specific crises, we are hesitant to portray it as movement from one stage or position to the next. Rest (1979) differentiated between "simple-stage models" and "complex-stage models." Using simple-stage models, a typical assessment question was, "What stage is a person in?" Assuming one stage at a time with no overlapping, no skipping of stages, and no steps backward, it should be easy to pinpoint where a student is and design challenges to foster the next step. Loevinger, Perry, and Kohlberg, following Piaget's lead, envisioned cognitive structures that evolved in an orderly fashion. Like windows built into a house, they became relatively fixed lenses for interpreting reality and screening input. Major remodeling was needed to change the windows. Once the new model was installed, it was as hard to go back to the old structure as to replace stained glass with a plain windowpane. Furthermore, the brain would not move from windowpane to stained glass in one leap. A sliding glass door had to come next, and then beveled, leaded designs, perhaps with inset mirrors and magnifying glasses. Perry differed from his colleagues in allowing for escape, retreat, and delay in his theory of intellectual development. For others, it was onward and upward, and while it was easy for a student to look back with disdain on an earlier way of thinking, it was hard to see beyond the next level of complexity, let alone understand an instructor who was teaching two or more stages ahead.

King (1990, pp. 83–84) warns against an overly simplified description of cognitive processes, which are inconsistent with many research findings. "For example, people don't seem to change from the exclusive use of one set of assumptions to the exclusive use of those of the next adjacent stage; rather, the use of assumptions characteristic of several stages at once often has been found. Stage usage seems to be influenced by a variety of individual factors (e.g., consolidation of existing structures, fatigue, readiness for change) and environmental factors (e.g., whether one is asked to create one's own solution to a problem or to critique someone else's solution, explaining one's beliefs verbally or in writing)." Different test characteristics and demands call forth different cognitive structures. Rest (1979, p. 63) proposes that instead of trying to assess what stage the person is in, we should ask, "To what extent and under what conditions does a person manifest the various types of organizations of thinking?"

A linear perspective may also frustrate those who want to help students achieve the upper reaches of stage theories. Pascarella and Terenzini (1991, p. 35) found no evidence of college students functioning at any of the final three stages of Loevinger's model. Kohlberg (1972) found that stage 4 (law and order) was the predominant stage in most societies. Perry (1970) was more optimistic, saying that perhaps 75 percent of the seniors in his study had reached positions 7 and 8. Subsequent research found Perry position scores ranging from 2 to 5, with no students scoring at the committed positions (Kurfiss, 1975; Pascarella and Terenzini, 1991, p. 30). This does not mean that higher levels are not present or possible. In fact, as our student populations diversify, the likelihood that all the stages will be represented increases. It may mean that the strategies for assessing developmental levels still need refining, or it may mean that the journey is a more logical priority than the destination.

Given the limitations of sequential models, we have proposed a sequence in order to suggest that certain building blocks make a good foundation (see Table 1.2). Some tasks are more likely to be encountered early in the journey. College students, regardless of age, will be challenged to develop intellectual competence. If the college does nothing else, it will try to move students along this vector. If it requires physical education or encourages athletics and if it supports participation in music, art, drama, or dance, it will foster physical and manual competence. Unless the new student makes a serious effort to remain isolated, the experience of meeting new people inside and outside of class will stimulate interpersonal competence. Whether leaving home for the first time or returning to college late in life, students will face loneliness, anxiety, frustration, and conflict. They will be required to make decisions, set goals, and develop greater autonomy. While younger students may be more obsessed with sex and romance, older students may be forming new relationships and perhaps reexamining earlier ones in light of what they are reading and whom they are meeting. Therefore, it is likely that a college will move students along these first four vectors, and growth in each area helps construct identity. Most students also experience greater clarity about purposes, values, and ways

Table 1.2. The Seven Vectors: General Developmental Directions.

From	To
Developing Competence	
Low level of competence (intellectual, physical, interpersonal)	High level of competence in each area
Lack of confidence in one's abilities	Strong sense of competence
Managing Emotions	
Little control over disruptive emotions (fear and anxiety, anger leading to aggression, depression, guilt, and shame, and dysfunctional sexual or romantic attraction)	Flexible control and appropriate expression
Little awareness of feelings	Increasing awareness and acceptance of emotions
Inability to integrate feelings with actions	Ability to integrate feelings with responsible action
Moving Through Autonomy Toward Interdependence	
Emotional dependence	Freedom from continual and pressing needs for reassurance
Poor self-direction or ability to solve problems; little freedom or confidence to be mobile	Instrumental independence (inner direction, persistence, and mobility)
Independence	Recognition and acceptance of the importance of interdependence
Developing Mature Interpersonal Relationships	
Lack of awareness of differences; intolerance of differences	Tolerance and appreciation of differences
Nonexistent, short-term, or unhealthy intimate relationships	Capacity for intimacy which is enduring and nurturing
Establishing Identity	
Discomfort with body and appearance	Comfort with body and appearance
Discomfort with gender and sexual orientation	Comfort with gender and sexual orientation
Lack of clarity about heritage and social/cultural roots of identity	Sense of self in a social, historical, and cultural context
Confusion about "who I am" and experimentation with roles and lifestyles	Clarification of self-concept through roles and lifestyle
Lack of clarity about others' evaluation	Sense of self in response to feedback from valued others
Dissatisfaction with self	Self-acceptance and self-esteem
Unstable, fragmented personality	Personal stability and integration

Table 1.2. The Seven Vectors: General Developmental Directions, Cont'd.

From	To
Developing Purpose	
Unclear vocational goals	Clear vocational goals
Shallow, scattered personal interests	More sustained, focused, rewarding activities
Few meaningful interpersonal commitments	Strong interpersonal and family commitments
Developing Integrity	
Dualistic thinking and rigid beliefs	Humanizing values
Unclear or untested personal values and beliefs	Personalizing (clarifying and affirming) values while respecting others' beliefs
Self-interest	Social responsibility
Discrepancies between values and actions	Congruence and authenticity

of thinking. If they are lucky, they will discover interests and people they care deeply about and will make lasting commitments. And they will expand their awareness of who they are and of how valuable they are.

Few developmental theories have paid much attention to emotions and relationships. More work has been done on thoughts and values. Our theory assumes that emotional, interpersonal, and ethical development deserve equal billing with intellectual development.

How does this revision differ from the earlier version of *Education and Identity?*

1. The fifth vector, *freeing interpersonal relationships,* had been retitled *developing mature interpersonal relationships* and moved back in sequence, prior to *establishing identity.* We did this primarily to recognize the importance of students' experiences with relationships in the formation of their core sense of self.
2. The chapter on the *managing emotions* vector has been broadened beyond the earlier focus on aggression and sexual desire to address anxiety, depression, anger, shame, and guilt, as well as more positive emotions.

3. We have placed more emphasis on the importance of interdependence, while not denying the significance of learning independence and self-sufficiency. Instead of retaining the term *developing autonomy*, we have renamed this vector *moving through autonomy toward interdependence*.
4. More emphasis has been placed on the intercultural aspects of tolerance as a component of developing mature interpersonal relationships, which also entails a growing capacity for intimacy.
5. We have added more complexity to the *developing identity* vector. We have noted issues raised by recent researchers concerning differences in identity development based on gender, ethnic background, and sexual orientation.
6. More current research findings have been cited as they relate to the vectors (although this book is not meant to contain a thorough review of the literature).
7. We have added illustrative statements from students to reflect greater diversity. Where earlier statements reinforce the text, they have been left in.

Like many humanistic models, this one is founded on an optimistic view of human development, assuming that a nurturing, challenging college environment will help students grow in stature and substance. Erikson believed in an epigenetic principle. Rogers saw a benign pattern at work in human beings, similar to the process that turns acorns into oak trees. The ancient Greeks had a concept alien to our modern-day emphasis on specialization and fragmentation between body and mind, between the physical and the spiritual. It is called *aretê*. According to the Greek scholar H.D.F. Kitto (1963, pp. 171–172), it was their ideal:

> When we meet it in Plato we translate it "Virtue" and consequently miss all the flavour of it. "Virtue," at least in modern English, is almost entirely a moral word; *aretê* on the other hand is used indifferently in all the categories and means simply "excellence." It may be limited of course by its con-

text; the *aretê* of a race-horse is speed, of a cart-horse strength. If it is used, in a general context, of a man it will connote excellence in the ways in which a man can be excellent — morally, intellectually, physically, practically. Thus the hero of the *Odyssey* is a great fighter, a wily schemer, a ready speaker, a man of stout heart and broad wisdom who knows that he must endure without too much complaining what the gods send; and he can both build and sail a boat, drive a furrow as straight as anyone, beat a young braggart at throwing the discus, challenge the Phraecian youth at boxing, wrestling, or running; flay, skin, cut up, and cook an ox, and be moved to tears by a song. He is in fact an excellent all-rounder; he has surpassing *aretê*.

Kitto says that "this instinct for seeing things whole is the source of the essential sanity in Greek life" (p. 176). Institutions that emphasize intellectual development to the exclusion of other strengths and skills reinforce society's tendency to see some aspects of its citizens and not others. Just as individuals are not just consumers, competitors, and taxpayers, so students are not just degree seekers and test takers. To develop all the gifts of human potential, we need to be able to see them whole and to believe in their essential worth. In revising the seven vectors, we hope to offer useful tools to a new generation of practitioners who want to help students become "excellent all-rounders." We also hope to inspire experienced faculty, administrators, and student services and support staff to recommit to the mission of nurturing mind, body, heart, and spirit.

PART ONE

The Seven Vectors: An Overview

Lasting personality changes may not occur in a blinding flash. As Dylan Thomas (1939, pp. 29–30) said, "Light breaks where no sun shines . . . Dawn breaks behind the eyes . . . Light breaks on secret lots . . . On tips of thought. . . . " While some epiphanies are dramatic and sudden, most occur gradually and incrementally. We may not know for years that a single lecture or conversation or experience started a chain reaction that transformed some aspect of ourselves. We cannot easily discern what subtle mix of people, books, settings, or events promotes growth. Nor can we easily name changes in ways of thinking, feeling, or interpreting the world. But we can observe behavior and record words, both of which can reveal shifts from hunch to analysis, from simple to complex perceptions, from divisive bias to compassionate understanding. Theory can give us the lenses to see these changes and help them along.

The challenges students, faculty, and administrators face today can be overwhelming. While the 1960s brought protest marches, drug busts, demands for curricular relevance, and students insisting on shared power, it was also an era of expanding budgets, new construction, and innovative programs. The boom lasted through the 1970s, and longer in some states. The resources were there to support adequate staffing, burgeoning specialization, and bold experiments. Perhaps we should have foreseen the pendulum swinging backward. Now administrators spend a great deal of time stretching dollars, consolidating services, and managing crises. Faculty are teaching larger classes or worrying about too few enrollees, fretting about retirement, relying on adjunct instructors, scrutinizing contracts, and going to union meetings. Students are facing higher tuition, longer lines, and fewer seats in the classroom. With higher costs, bleaker job prospects, and more evident crime statistics, students may focus more on security than on self-improvement.

Student development theory must apply to this generation of students as well as to future ones. It must be useful to institutional leaders as they cope with retrenchment as well as expansion. Without a developmental philosophy at the core of the college, it can become a dispensary of services, a training ground for jobs that may not exist, or a holding tank for those not sure what to do next. Institutions that impart transferable skills and relevant knowledge, bolster confidence and creativity, and engender social responsibility and self-directed learning are needed more than ever. To be effective in educating the whole student, colleges must hire and reinforce staff members who understand what student development looks like and how to foster it.

The seven vectors provide such a model. Though they were originally proposed as major constellations of development during adolescence and early adulthood, we have attempted to apply the vectors to adults as well. We have tried to use language that is gender free and appropriate for persons of diverse backgrounds. The vectors have stood the test of time as conceptual lenses. They have enabled higher education practitioners to view their students, their courses, and their programs more clearly and to use them as beacons for change. Those who have kept up to date on research, or who want more specificity and complexity, may be frustrated by our level of generality. Yet we believe that the original version of the model has been useful precisely because of its broad conceptual nature, leaving practitioners the options of putting their own understanding and interpretation into it and applying it within their own contexts.

We have also attempted to tie this model to student perceptions of their experience. We have drawn excerpts from student self-assessments, short reflection exercises, and papers on
developmental theories where autobiographical examples were
included. Over a period of three years, I (Reisser) invited students in my classes and professionals attending my presentations to complete a "developmental worksheet" by writing anonymous responses to the following:

1. Briefly describe a change in yourself that had
    a major impact on how you lived your life.
    What was the "old" way of thinking or being,
    vs. the "new" way? What did you move *from*
    and what did you move *to?* How did you know
    that a significant change had occurred?
2. What were the important things (or persons)
    that *helped* the process? What did the person
    do? What was the experience that catalyzed the
    shift? Were there any *feelings* that helped or ac-
    companied the process?

In all, 120 worksheets were collected, and though they
were not based on carefully designed sampling procedures, the
statements excerpted from them bring to life the potentially dry
formality of theory. When students' research or reflection papers
included relevant examples; I (Reisser) asked to keep copies for
future writing projects on student development. Students' statements from the 1969 edition were also used here to illustrate
developmental stages.

The seven vectors are summarized below.

1. *Developing competence.* Three kinds of competence develop in college — intellectual competence, physical and manual
skills, and interpersonal competence. Intellectual competence
is skill in using one's mind. It involves mastering content, gaining
intellectual and aesthetic sophistication, and, most important,
building a repertoire of skills to comprehend, analyze, and synthesize. It also entails developing new frames of reference that
integrate more points of view and serve as "more adequate" structures for making sense out of our observations and experiences.

Physical and manual competence can involve athletic and artistic achievement, designing and making tangible products, and gaining strength, fitness, and self-discipline. Competition and creation bring emotions to the surface since our performance and our projects are on display for others' approval or criticism. Leisure activities can become lifelong pursuits and therefore part of identity.

Interpersonal competence entails not only the skills of listening, cooperating, and communicating effectively, but also the more complex abilities to tune in to another person and respond appropriately, to align personal agendas with the goals of the group, and to choose from a variety of strategies to help a relationship flourish or a group function.

Students' overall sense of competence increases as they learn to trust their abilities, receive accurate feedback from others, and integrate their skills into a stable self-assurance.

2. *Managing emotions.* Whether new to college or returning after time away, few students escape anger, fear, hurt, longing, boredom, and tension. Anxiety, anger, depression, desire, guilt, and shame have the power to derail the educational process when they become excessive or overwhelming. Like unruly employees, these emotions need good management. The first task along this vector is not to eliminate them but to allow them into awareness and acknowledge them as signals, much like the oil light on the dashboard.

Development proceeds when students learn appropriate channels for releasing irritations before they explode, dealing with fears before they immobilize, and healing emotional wounds before they infect other relationships. It may be hard to accept that some amount of boredom and tension is normal, that some anxiety helps performance, and that impulse gratification must sometimes be squelched.

Some students come with the faucets of emotional expression wide open, and their task is to develop flexible controls. Others have yet to open the tap. Their challenge is to get in touch with the full range and variety of feelings and to learn to exercise self-regulation rather than repression. As self-control and self-expression come into balance, awareness and integration ideally support each other.

More positive kinds of emotions have received less attention from researchers. They include feelings like rapture, relief, sympathy, yearning, worship, wonder, and awe. These may not need to be "managed" so much as brought into awareness and allowed to exist. Students must learn to balance self-assertive tendencies, which involve some form of aggressiveness or defensiveness, with participatory tendencies, which involve transcending the boundaries of the individual self, identifying or bonding with another, or feeling part of a larger whole.

3. *Moving through autonomy toward interdependence.* A key developmental step for students is learning to function with relative self-sufficiency, to take responsibility for pursuing self-chosen goals, and to be less bound by others' opinions. Movement requires both emotional and instrumental independence, and later recognition and acceptance of interdependence.

Emotional independence means freedom from continual and pressing needs for reassurance, affection, or approval. It begins with separation from parents and proceeds through reliance on peers, nonparental adults, and occupational or institutional reference groups. It culminates in diminishing need for such supports and increased willingness to risk loss of friends or status in order to pursue strong interests or stand on convictions.

Instrumental independence has two major components: the ability to organize activities and to solve problems in a self-directed way, and the ability to be mobile. It means developing that volitional part of the self that can think critically and independently and that can then translate ideas into focused action. It also involves learning to get from one place to another, without having to be taken by the hand or given detailed directions, and to find the information or resources required to fulfill personal needs and desires.

Developing autonomy culminates in the recognition that one cannot operate in a vacuum and that greater autonomy enables healthier forms of interdependence. Relationships with parents are revised. New relationships based on equality and reciprocity replace the older, less consciously chosen peer bonds. Interpersonal context broadens to include the community, the society, the world. The need to be independent and the longing for inclusion become better balanced. Interdependence means respecting the autonomy of others and looking for ways to give and take with an ever-expanding circle of friends.

4. *Developing mature interpersonal relationships.* Developing mature relationships involves (1) tolerance and appreciation of differences (2) capacity for intimacy. Tolerance can be seen in both an intercultural and an interpersonal context. At its heart is the ability to respond to people in their own right rather than as stereotypes or transference objects calling for particular conventions. Respecting differences in close friends can generalize to acquaintances from other continents and cultures. Awareness, breadth of experience, openness, curiosity, and objectivity help students refine first impressions, reduce bias and ethnocentrism, increase empathy and altruism, and enjoy diversity.

In addition to greater tolerance, the capacity for healthy intimacy increases. For most adolescent couples, each is the pool and each the Narcissus. Satisfying relationships depend on spatial proximity, so that each can nod to the other and in the reflection observe himself or herself. Developing mature relationships means not only freedom from narcissism, but also the ability to choose healthy relationships and make lasting commitments based on honesty, responsiveness, and unconditional regard. Increased capacity for intimacy involves a shift in the quality of relationships with intimates and close friends. The shift is away from too much dependence or too much dominance and toward an interdependence between equals. Development means more in-depth sharing and less clinging, more acceptance of flaws and appreciation of assets, more selectivity in choosing nurturing relationships, and more long-lasting relationships that endure through crises, distance, and separation.

5. *Establishing identity.* Identity formation depends in part on the other vectors already mentioned: competence, emotional maturity, autonomy, and positive relationships. Developing identity is like assembling a jigsaw puzzle, remodeling a house, or seeking one's "human rhythms," a term that Murphy (1958) illustrated by photic driving. A person watching an instrument that emits flashes at precise intervals eventually hits a breaking point—the point at which the rhythm induces a convulsion. If, for example, the number is sixteen, the observer may rapidly

lose consciousness as this number is presented in the standard time interval. Seventeen and fifteen, however, are safe numbers. It is not until thirty-two or some other multiple of sixteen is reached that a breakdown recurs. Like the piano wire that hums or like the glass that shatters, we all have our critical frequencies in a variety of areas. Development of identity is the process of discovering with what kinds of experience, at what levels of intensity and frequency, we resonate in satisfying, in safe, or in self-destructive fashion.

Development of identity involves: (1) comfort with body and appearance, (2) comfort with gender and sexual orientation, (3) sense of self in a social, historical, and cultural context, (4) clarification of self-concept through roles and life-style, (5) sense of self in response to feedback from valued others, (6) self-acceptance and self-esteem, and (7) personal stability and integration. A solid sense of self emerges, and it becomes more apparent that there is an *I* who coordinates the facets of personality, who "owns" the house of self and is comfortable in all of its rooms.

College student concern with appearance is obvious. Though gowns no longer prevail except at Oxford and Cambridge, town residents recognize students, especially younger ones who don emblems of student culture. Whatever the limitations or prescriptions, experimentation occurs. With clarification of identity, however, it diminishes. By graduation, most of the early creative — or bizarre — variations are given up. Experimentation with dress and appearance herald pathways to sexual identity. Looking at old high school yearbooks confirms the evolution of hairstyles. Macho, androgynous, or femme fatale "looks" come and go, but identity hinges on finding out what it means to be a man or a woman and coming to terms with one's sexuality.

Establishing identity also includes reflecting on one's family of origin and ethnic heritage, defining self as a part of a religious or cultural tradition, and seeing self within a social and historical context. It involves finding roles and styles at work, at play, and at home that are genuine expressions of self and that further sharpen self-definition. It involves gaining a sense of how one is seen and evaluated by others. It leads to clarity and stability and a feeling of warmth for this core self as capable, familiar, worthwhile.

6. *Developing purpose.* Many college students are all dressed up and do not know where they want to go. They have energy but no destination. While they may have clarified who they are and where they came from, they have only the vaguest notion of who they want to be. For large numbers of college students, the purpose of college is to qualify them for a good job, not to help them build skills applicable in the widest variety of life experiences; it is to ensure a comfortable life-style, not to broaden their knowledge base, find a philosophy of life, or become a lifelong learner.

Developing purpose entails an increasing ability to be intentional, to assess interests and options, to clarify goals, to make plans, and to persist despite obstacles. It requires formulating plans for action and a set of priorities that integrate three major elements: (1) vocational plans and aspirations, (2) personal interests, and (3) interpersonal and family commitments. It also involves a growing ability to unify one's many different goals within the scope of a larger, more meaningful purpose, and to exercise intentionality on a daily basis.

We use the term *vocation* in its broadest sense — as specific career or as broad calling. Vocations can include paid work, unpaid work, or both. We discover our vocation by discovering what we love to do, what energizes and fulfills us, what uses our talents and challenges us to develop new ones, and what actualizes all our potentials for excellence. Ideally, these vocational plans flow from deepening interests, and in turn, lend momentum to further aspirations that have meaning and value. Considerations of life-style and family also enter the equation. As intimate relationships increasingly involve the question of long-term partnership and as formal education and vocational exploration draw to a close, next steps must be identified. It is difficult to construct a plan that balances life-style considerations, vocational aspirations, and avocational interests. Many compromises must be made, and clearer values help the decision-making process.

7. *Developing integrity.* Developing integrity is closely related to establishing identity and clarifying purposes. Our core values and beliefs provide the foundation for interpreting experience, guiding behavior, and maintaining self-respect. Developing integrity involves three sequential but overlapping stages: (1) humanizing values — shifting away from automatic application of uncompromising beliefs and using principled thinking in balancing one's own self-interest with the interests of one's fellow human beings, (2) personalizing values — consciously affirming core values and beliefs while respecting other points of view, and (3) developing congruence — matching personal values with socially responsible behavior.

Humanizing values involves a shift from a literal belief in the absoluteness of rules to a more relative view, where connections are made between rules and the purposes they are meant to serve. Thus, the rules for a ball game can change to accommodate limited numbers of players or other unusual conditions; rules concerning honesty, sex, or aggressiveness can vary with circumstances and situations, while overriding principles (such as the Golden Rule) become more important. This change has also been called "liberalization of the superego" or "enlightenment of conscience"— the process by which the rigid rules received unquestioned from parents are reformulated in the light of wider experience and made relevant to new conditions (Sanford, 1962, p. 278).

Students bring to college an array of assumptions about what is right and wrong, true and false, good and bad, important and unimportant. Younger students may have acquired these assumptions from parents, church, school, media, or other sources. When others' values are internalized, most behavior conforms even when the judge is absent. Disobedience produces either diffuse anxiety or specific fear of discovery and punishment. Most of the values are implicit and unconsciously held; therefore, they are hard to identify or explain. With humanizing of values, much of this baggage comes to light. The contents are examined. Many items are discarded on brief inspection, sometimes with later regret. Some items are tried and found unsuitable. A few are set aside because they still fit and can be incorporated into a new wardrobe.

Personalizing of values occurs as the new wardrobe is assembled. Ultimately, the items selected are those required by the characteristics of the wearer, by the work expected to be done, by the situations to be encountered, and by the persons who are seen as important. In short, individuals select guidelines to suit themselves and to suit the conditions of their lives. In time, the components of this wardrobe are actively embraced as part of the self and become standards by which to flexibly assess personal actions.

Personalizing of values leads to the development of congruence — the achievement of behavior consistent with the personalized values held. With this final stage, internal debate is minimized. Once the implications of a situation are understood and the consequences of alternatives seem clear, the response is highly determined; it is made with conviction, without debate or equivocation.

These, then, are the seven major developmental vectors for college students. Each has additional components, and more detailed study reveals further ramifications. This overview, however, suggests the major configurations. The following chapters consider research and theory relevant to each vector in more detail.

TWO

Developing
Competence

Competence is a three-tined pitchfork. Intellectual competence, physical and manual skills, and interpersonal competence are the tines. But the handle is most important. Without it, no work can be done, no matter how sharp and sturdy the tines. A sense of competence stems from the confidence that one can cope with what comes and achieve goals successfully. The pitchfork metaphor is appropriate not only because of its connection with productivity and achievement, but also because its parts are interrelated. Long before technological developments increased our muscle and mobility, extended our vision, and sharpened our hearing, our human gifts for thinking, learning, acting, and interacting were essential tools for staying alive.

This chapter focuses on three interrelated forms of competence — intellectual competence, physical and manual competence, and interpersonal competence — as well as on the overarching sense of competence that reflects people's assessment of their capabilities. Intellectual competence involves using the mind's skills to comprehend, reflect, analyze, synthesize, and interpret. It entails mastering content, acquiring aesthetic appreciation and cultural interests, and, perhaps most important, developing the ability to reason, solve problems, weigh evidence, think originally, and engage in active learning. Physical and manual competence involve using the body as a healthy vehicle for high performance, self-expression, and creativity. Interpersonal competence is skill in communicating and collaborating with others. These aspects of competence are worth considering separately, despite their interrelatedness, because each is fostered or inhibited by different conditions and experiences. Actions that serve one may overlap, augment, or conflict with the others. Each of the components, as part of a larger whole, needs to be understood in order for systematic educational efforts to be successful.

Intellectual Competence

Fostering intellectual competence in students is the top priority of most postsecondary institutions. The Higher Education Research Institute at the University of California at Los Angeles surveyed 35,478 professors at 392 institutions on a broad range of issues. When asked to describe their institutions' highest priorities, more than three-fourths (76.1 percent) of all professors cited students' intellectual development (Mooney, 1991).

It is difficult, however, to find agreement about what intellectual competence looks like. The National Institute of Education's *Involvement in Learning* (1984) calls for specific standards for awarding degrees. In addition to student outcomes such as self-confidence, persistence, leadership, empathy, social responsibility, and understanding of cultural and intellectual differences, the report recommends measuring academic outcomes such as knowledge and intellectual skills, emphasizing that while grades and credits reflect time spent in class and performance on tests, they do not necessarily reflect how much students learned and retained. It also expressed concern that few institutions have undertaken in-depth efforts to identify learning outcomes or student development goals.

The Association of American Colleges (1985) is one of many organizations that have attempted to define essential intellectual goals for undergraduate education. These include: (1)

the ability to engage in inquiry, abstract thinking, and critical analysis, (2) literacy (for purposes of writing, thinking, and critical analysis), (3) the ability to handle quantitative information, (4) historical consciousness, (5) exposure to science, art, and international and multicultural experiences, (6) the study of value formation, and (7) an in-depth study integrating this intellectual development.

Despite disagreement over what it is, intellectual development has been studied more than any other aspect of development in college. Three broad areas have been researched: (1) acquisition of subject matter knowledge and academic (usually verbal and quantitative) skills tied directly to specific academic programs, and (2) gains in cultural, aesthetic, and intellectual sophistication, and expanding interests and activities in humanities and performing arts, philosophy, and history, and (3) the development of general intellectual or cognitive skills, which can be applied regardless of content areas. These include critical thinking, reflective judgment, the ability to process and use new information and to communicate it well, the ability to reason objectively and to draw objective conclusions from data, the ability to evaluate new ideas, arguments and claims critically, and the ability to become more objective about beliefs, attitudes, and values (Michael, 1975).

Students do show gains in the first area of intellectual development — subject matter knowledge. Studies conducted by the Educational Testing Service and others conclusively demonstrate progressive yearly increases in both general and specific knowledge as students move from entrance to graduation (Lannholm and Pitcher, 1956a, 1956b, 1959; Spaeth and Greeley, 1970; Pace, 1974; Hyman, Wright, and Reed, 1975; Bisconti and Solomon, 1976; Dumont and Troelstrup, 1981). Pascarella and Terenzini (1991) note that findings from studies of gains in subject matter knowledge and academic skills, as measured by standardized tests, are consistent across nearly five decades of research. The research documents the reassuring conclusion that the more students study in a particular major, the more they acquire knowledge and skill specific to that major.

As for the second category of intellectual development,

research has consistently found cultural, aesthetic, or intellectual attitudes and values are enhanced during the college years (Pascarella and Terenzini, 1991, p. 271). For example, Hyman, Wright, and Reed (1975) drew on fifty-four nationally representative surveys conducted between 1949 and 1971, which included some 80,000 people. They found educational level to be strongly related not only to knowledge level but also to intellectual outlook, receptivity to further knowledge, and interest in reading and continuing education. The literature also shows that college graduates seem to develop a taste for lifelong learning. They read more newspapers, books, and magazines, remain more informed about public affairs, and engage in more formal and informal continuing education than high school graduates.

The third category of intellectual development involves ways of knowing and reasoning. As we saw in Chaper One, cognitive theorists have created some interesting models for conceptualizing shifts in thinking and learning. These skills are vitally important, because much of the factual material presented in college is soon forgotten and because factual knowledge quickly becomes obsolete (Blunt and Blizard, 1975; Brethower, 1977; Gustav, 1969; Macleish, 1968; Rosen, 1975).

Researchers have studied communication skills, reasoning ability, critical thinking, and conceptual complexity, finding that students make statistically significant gains in their abilities to communicate orally and in writing, to use reason and evidence in analyzing problems, to distinguish between strong and weak arguments, to weigh evidence, to determine the validity of data-based generalizations, and to use concepts skillfully and flexibly (Pascarella and Terenzini, 1991, pp. 115–160). They "have greater intellectual flexibility in that they are better able to understand more than one side of a complex issue, and can develop more sophisticated abstract frameworks to deal with complexity" (p. 155).

These findings seem consistent with the work of Perry (1970), Belenky, Clinchy, Goldberger, and Tarule (1986), and Baxter Magolda (1992). The overall trend is away from passive, receptive, concrete, superficial, and absolutistic ways of thinking and learning to more active, creative, abstract, in-depth, objective, and complex ways of engaging with subject matter. Students moving along this vector become less interested in memorizing and more interested in understanding, less fixated on completing the teacher's assignment than engaging with the material from their own frame of reference, less worshipful of authors and more able to see them as human and fallible. Like Perry's students, they can see more than one side of an issue, formulate their own questions and opinions, and even observe their own thinking processes. Like Belenky, Clinchy, Gold-berger, and Tarule's subjects, they can blend objective and sub-jective, concrete and abstract, intuitive and empirical ways of knowing. They are finding their voices and using their talents, rather than feeling inadequate and unaware of what they can do intellectually.

Intellectual development is also marked by the process of reframing, or *frame-changing,* as Haswell (forthcoming) calls it. "Developmental episodes, if induced by teachers, will involve more than just an elaboration or filling in of frames the students already have, more than just a learning of new content. They will involve such a restructuring of frames that students will have to re-interpret both new and old content, at deeply embedded levels". This process unfolds as follows: "Old frames meet the unassimilable ('the most startling event'), old frames prove in-adequate ('I felt something was missing'), frame conflict creates unpleasant vacillation ('I had most trouble with'), frame reor-ganization sets in unannounced ('it seemed to click'), new frames take on the guise of solvers ('at first I was puzzled'), or the guise of saviors ('at last I have found')."

Mezirow (1990, p. 1) says that the essence of learning is making a new or revised interpretation of the meaning of an experience, which guides subsequent understanding, appreci-ation, and action. He highlights the skill of reflection: "Perhaps even more central to adult learning than elaborating established meaning schemes is the process of reflecting back on prior learn-ing to determine whether what we have learned is justified un-der present circumstances. This is a crucial learning process egre-giously ignored by learning theorists" (p. 5).

Kitchener and King (1990b, p. 160) identify reflective

thinking as a goal of education: "A reflective thinker understands that there is real uncertainty about how a problem may best be solved, yet is still able to offer a judgment about the problem that brings some kind of closure to it. This judgment, which Dewey refers to as a 'grounded' or 'warranted' assertion, is based on criteria such as evaluation or evidence, consideration of expert opinion, adequacy of argument, and implications of the proposed solution."

Kitchener and King's (1981, 1990b) model of growth in reflective judgment parallels Perry and Loevinger's approaches. It involves a seven-stage sequence of increasingly complex stages relating to what people "know" or believe and how they justify their knowledge claims and beliefs. The process of forming judgments becomes more and more complex, sophisticated, and comprehensive from lower to higher stages (Kitchener and King, 1990b, pp. 162–165):

> Stage 1 — Knowing is characterized by a concrete, single-category belief systems: what a person observes to be true is true.
>
> Stage 2 — Since truth is not available to everyone, some people hold "right" beliefs while others hold "wrong ones" (Perry's dualism).
>
> Stage 3 — In some areas, truth is temporarily inaccessible, even for those in authority, but concrete information will some day clarify things. Where evidence is incomplete, no one can claim any authority beyond his or her own personal impressions or feelings.
>
> Stage 4 — Uncertainty is clearly accepted as an intrinsic characteristic of knowing, although some "well-structured" problems can be described completely and solved with certainty (like math problems). "Ill-structured" problems, like what career path to follow or how to reduce pollution, are acknowledged as important but difficult since it is hard to decide when and whether an adequate solution has been found. Such reasoning is most typical of college seniors.

Stage 5 — Here individuals move beyond the idiosyncratic justifications of stage 4 to argue that knowledge must be placed in a context and understood based on interpreting evidence within a particular perspective.

Stage 6 — In addition to knowing that knowledge is uncertain and contextual, there is the awareness that some perspectives, arguments, or points of view are better than others.

Stage 7 — Knowledge can be constructed via critical inquiry and through the synthesis of existing evidence and opinion.

Kitchener and King (1990a) found that average reflective judgment scores for both traditional-age and older-age freshmen were almost the same and that they were substantially lower than those of seniors. While age and verbal ability have been found to affect reflective judgment, college attendance seems to have a greater effect than does maturation. However, research by Kitchener, King, Wood, and Davison (1989) found that among a college-educated sample, the majority did not typically use reasoning higher than stage 4 prior to the age of twenty-four, that individuals were consistent in their reasoning across different tasks, that subjects' scores tend to move up in sequence one step at a time every six years, with regression occurring only rarely.

Waluconis (1992) draws from student self-evaluations in a variety of Washington Community Colleges to convey some of the excitement and frustration that comes when students are asked to reflect on their own intellectual development.

I've had to work very hard at critical thinking in this class. In real-life situations, I feel that I do more analyzing to come to decisions, but the situations that were presented in class were more confusing to me because I wasn't familiar with laws. In class I noticed that I was quick to come to a conclusion, but as you brought up more issues, I found myself switching sides. It's uncomfortable to find out that

you don't know which side to take in a situation.
It shows that people need to examine all sides of
an issue, ask more questions, and research rules
and regulations when it comes to legal issues concerning contracts (or anything).

Writing skills seemed so much different here
than in an English Composition class. In English,
my pen flowed much more freely. In this class, I
found I would stumble over words, write things
down, and then scratch them out as I thought of
new ideas and new solutions. Law can be very confusing.

This student notices the need to master more information about
a new subject area (law) in order to analyze more smoothly,
voices the universal feeling of discomfort when one's position
is not immediately clear, and appears self-conscious about the
new mode of expression, like a young bicycler who has just removed the training wheels and is wobbling down the street.

Another student illustrates the links between growing intellectual competence and the development of autonomy and
purpose:

Learning how to learn is the single most important
attribute one can ever achieve. I've learned to recognize my learning barriers. . . . This class has
helped me to plan out the direction I want to go
in school. . . . If I had to describe this quarter in
boxing terms, I guess this analogy would sum it
up: this quarter was a comeback fight. I picked a
soft opponent (schedule) that I should have handled easily. I was overconfident based on past performances and didn't train as hard as I should have.
Consequently, the opponent turned out to be more
formidable than I anticipated. I suffered a few
knockdowns, but after a rally in the later rounds
hopefully I squeaked out a decision to continue my
comeback.

Still another student becomes more aware of her feelings through the writing process and clearly shifts from the position of pleasing the teacher to having a voice and making a point:

> When I wrote my second essay, which was about the personal and cultural experiences I had in Ethiopia, I began to feel angry. . . . I wanted to shout while I was writing. I wanted the words I was writing to have a voice, to shout as loud as I would if I was speaking. . . . I wanted to say something through the essay. I wanted to make sense instead of counting the words and wondering if it met the amount of words our teacher told us to write. I was conscious of what I was doing; it was like I was speaking.

Assignments that invite students to engage emotionally as well as intellectually can assist them with the management of emotions, which must first be brought into awareness before they can be given powerful expression.

Writing assignments not only help students to clarify thoughts and assumptions, hone analytical skills, and touch inner feelings; they can also provide vehicles for learning representational thinking — for seeing and naming with symbols. E. M. Bower (1966, pp. 109, 112) attempted to make such connections between intellectual development and other aspects of change:

> The adjustment of an individual in the school (and later in society) can be conceptualized as a function of his competence to use referents or representations of objects and events. Such referents or representations are systematized in words, language, mathematics, and other symbol systems. Symbols are learned by individuals as a function of "experiencing" objects, events, and relationships. To convert an event or a happening into an experience (something learned) its essence must be ingested,

processed, and assimilated via symbolic vehicles such as words or mathematical formula. . . . The sparking between an event or object and its eventual incorporation within self through ego processes is a function of the symbolic posts to which the event or object can be tied. An event which cannot be tied securely to a symbol has limited educational utility. An object which has no representational correlate cannot be conceptualized or held in the mind. Our basic tool for this sparking between objects and symbol has been the written and spoken word. Indeed, language is our royal road to defining not only what surrounds us in the environment but what we are as an organism.

Thus all facets of development may depend partially on the ability to symbolize abstractly the events and objects of our experience, and in so doing to detach from our embeddedness in an experience and view it as object. This is a key developmental principle for Kegan and others interested in object relations. Conversely, for the person whose learning experiences are primarily verbal or otherwise symbolic, firsthand encounters with concrete materials and objects are also required if symbols are to be recognized as merely inexact representatives of objects and events, rather than as the objects or events themselves.

A student affairs staff member described a developmental turning point in a way that illustrates the power of symbolizing, or naming: "I remember lying in bed and discovering that a good friend was a 'significant other' to me. I learned the term in an Education class. In a sense, it suddenly didn't matter to me what others thought about me because this person liked and cared about me and valued me. I could be 'who I was' and not lose her. It was a great feeling and I got out of bed and went to her room and told her."

More research is needed on other aspects of intellectual competence, such as the following:

- The ability to identify problems and define them in clear, workable terms
- The ability to synthesize and integrate information from diverse sources for a particular purpose
- The ability to invent answers or hypotheses rather than simply to search for and find them
- The ability to operate creatively within existing conditions and to establish and maintain conditions that enable continued creativity

Colleges must guard against defining intellectual competence as skill at passing tests or mastery of some "essential" knowledge. Beyond the ability to memorize facts lies the ability to seek them out with well-formed questions. Beyond the ability to score well on tests lies the ability to construct meaning, using words, images, and theories. Beyond skill at finding the right answer lies the ability to generate many answers and choose between them based on reasoned argument, credible evidence, or other appropriate criteria. Skills in listening, questioning, reflecting, and communicating can be built in any course that engages students in actively searching for valuable knowledge rather than passively receiving prepackaged material.

Physical and Manual Competence

Many college students invest substantial time in athletic and artistic activities to develop a variety of physical and manual skills. For a few, such skills and their augmentation become a vocation; for more, they become an avocation around which much of life is organized; for many, they become a source of occasional satisfaction or status. Yet despite their importance, and even though athletic programs are a major expense in many college budgets, little research exists on the development of physical or manual skills or on the developmental consequences of participation in such activities. Perhaps the development is so obvious when one learns to shoot baskets, jump hurdles, play rhapsodies, dance, sail, somersault, design, sculpt, or photograph that systematic observation seems superfluous.

Winter, McClelland, and Stewart (1981) found that gains in critical thinking (as measured by the Test of Thematic Analysis) were positively correlated with intercollegiate athletic participation, especially for men. They noted that the same two qualities needed for success in athletics—disciplined, thorough practice and adaptability to complex and rapidly changing circumstances—could enhance one's intellectual abilities. Good players got help from the game in formulating and expressing concepts and organizing complex experience. "Thus coaches in many sports, for example, speak of a player's ability to diagnose or 'read' the other team's intentions or the course of the game" (p. 134).

Pascarella and Smart (1990) analyzed a national sample of college students over a nine-year period to determine whether participation in intercollegiate athletics influenced completion of the bachelor's degree. They found a small but significant advantage for male athletes but could not break out the impact of different kinds of participation (for example, revenue-producing sports such as football and basketball versus regional or intramural play). Other studies found that college graduates saw athletics as helping them with career development, particularly in the areas of competitiveness and teamwork (Bisconti and Kessler, 1980; Alumni Office, Princeton University, 1967). Ryan (1989) found that athletic participation has a positive net impact on the development of interpersonal and leadership skills during college.

Earlier research by Ryan (1958a, 1958b) sought to understand the differences among successful and unsuccessful competitors. Ryan sent questionnaires to track coaches throughout the nation. The poor competitors turned out to be unhappier, more constricted, and more poorly adjusted. They had difficulty expressing their aggression. Their inability to compete in athletics seemed to be a specific example of that difficulty. In contrast, the good competitors were more conflict free, less constricted, and better adjusted; they expressed aggression more appropriately (pp. 119, 120).

These findings suggest that experiences encountered in athletics provoke reactions sharply relevant not only to developing competence and sense of competence, but also to increased awareness of emotions and ability to manage them. Athletics offers a context in which concrete, unequivocal, and public performance provides clear evidence of achievement and of developmental progress. In this arena, students' attitudes toward personal abilities and potentials are starkly revealed, and competence or the lack of it must be faced squarely. If the competence is there, it is publicly acclaimed and the sense of competence is likely to soar. Disappointed or indifferent observers may have the opposite effect.

For adolescents, athletic prowess almost always leads to rising self-esteem. Though dated, Bower's (1940) study of adolescent boys produced findings that may still hold true today. He found that popularity was unrelated to intelligence, height, home ratings, or school achievement but significantly related to strength and to physical ability. These adolescents not only placed a high premium on athletic proficiency, but also associated strength and other aspects of physical ability with traits they regarded as favorable, such as activity, aggressiveness, and leadership (p. 117).

> My junior year in high school was a turning point. At that time, schools did not play external sports for girls. This event took place midyear. The junior girls played the senior girls in a basketball game in front of the entire student body. I was the starting guard. I was quick and good. I loved the attention and cheers for my talent and ability. My teachers took notice of me and singled me out in the classroom during the next few days. I felt noticed and important. Before, I was shy and silent in class — invisible. Now I became involved and felt seen by the school. I later became involved in college varsity teams and Olympic development programs. My confidence as a whole person was increased due to the entire experience and process [student affairs staff member].

This statement illustrates the power of athletic success in changing a student's overall sense of competence as well as her intellectual competence, leading her to participate more actively in class. Similar shifts can occur in college.

Participation in intercollegiate and intramural athletics also can foster increased awareness of emotions and increased ability to manage them. Pleasures purely sensual and aesthetic derive from smooth, forceful, well-coordinated muscular activity. Those who have carved a turn on skis or hit a long straight drive with a bat or golf club know the feelings well. In athletics, the open and direct expression of feelings that elsewhere must be properly muted or denied is legitimate. Rage and delight are expected reactions; their expression in voice, gesture, and action are part of the game. Anger and frustration from other encounters can also be vented. I (Chickering) know a tennis-playing dean. When he bashes his cannonball serve, he often shouts the name of a teacher. Those serves usually do not go in, but they have plenty of zip. And the teacher probably gets better treatment.

Learning to manage aggression and anxiety are developmental tasks required for movement from immaturity to self-regulation. The full experience and expression of emotions that athletics provokes and legitimizes may relax restraint enough to permit productive carryover to other arenas. Hair let down in one situation may be loosened more readily in another. This can be an advantage when students get in touch with deeper levels of feeling or relieve pent-up tensions. It can also be a problem if students engage in high-risk behavior. A study of student athletes representing a variety of sports and including a nearly equal number of males and females by the medical school at the University of California, Los Angeles, found that student athletes were more likely than other students to say they drank too much, drove under the influence of alcohol or drugs, or did not use seat belts. They were also more likely to engage in sex without contraceptives, to have a higher number of sex partners, or to have a sexually transmitted disease ("Risky Business," 1992).

Our culture glorifies winning. Pearson (1986) contends

that we live in a "Warrior culture," informed by endless variations of the hero/villain/victim myth. Like many other aspects of our culture, sports involve a contest between winners and losers. Losing is still considered shameful, whether it is in athletics, politics, law, or business. Winning can be an empty ritual or a deeply satisfying event, depending on the frame of reference used. If athletes play the role of the gladiator vanquishing an enemy, they are acting out the Warrior archetype on a less developed plane. Like the other archetypes in Pearson's *The Hero Within,* Warriors must learn that the goal is not necessarily to slay the dragon, or to convert it or rescue it, but to engage with it, to play with it, to appreciate its strengths. They must also learn courage, mastery, agency.

> In each modality explored so far, our hero has learned to deal with a difficult experience: the Orphan has dealt with powerlessness; the Martyr, pain; the Wanderer, loneliness; and now the Warrior confronts fear. The levels Warriors experience . . . also are related to how well they have learned to confront fear. At the early stages — the stages in which the only answer seems to be a literal slaying of the enemy — fear is rampant. . . . The symbolic contest in politics/business/sports/school is mild in comparison, but its fears are real as well: the fear of losing, of not being the best, of being inadequate, inferior, a loser [pp. 82–83].

When fear, revenge, or anger dominate the field, attacking and defending take precedence over enjoying the matching of wits and the exercise of skills. By learning to trust their abilities, to do their best, to strive for the goal, to play by the rules, and to respect their opponents, students can transform any contest into a measure of internal development. "The stronger and more confident Warriors become, the less they must use violence, the more gentle they can be — with themselves and others. Finally, they need not define the other as villain, opponent, or potential convert, but as another hero like themselves" (Pearson, 1986, pp. 84–85).

Developmental challenges are inherent in competing but losing; playing the game but suffering injury; feeling too uncoordinated, overweight, or otherwise disabled to participate but learning to enjoy participation for its own sake. There are many ways to work with the physical body to learn courage, flexibility, self-discipline, and self-care. To feel physically competent, one must be relatively healthy or at least able to cope well with physical limitations. For one woman, changing her appearance was an Olympian effort:

> For the first time in my life, I have gained control of a difficult aspect of my life — my weight. For me, my physical appearance has had an impact on my self-concept. Since this quarter started, I have learned more than ever before about myself and why I lose control of my eating habits. I feel that control is now in my hands, toward all aspects of my life. This class concentration on learning more about myself has given me the power to look at aspects of my life that need work. I recognize the things that need work and I verbalize them to other people around me, and as I do so, I gain more power and control [junior].

Again we see a change in one area carrying over to others. Other major changes can occur when students acknowledge problems with addiction. Freeing the body from drug or alcohol abuse can clear the way for healthy relationships, purpose, and integrity, as this student reports:

> The change in my life was a realization that "life only has as much meaning (fulfillment, joy, and so on) as I *allow* it to have. This realization came to me after months of treatment for heroin addiction. My old way of behaving was generated out of fear, and I thought I could get what I wanted or needed by taking it. Today, I get what I want and need through being honest, empathetic, and having an emotional connection with the world around me.

[What helped this process?] *Treatment* was the most important thing that helped in the process. The people that helped were my counselor (I forget his name but he had enough guts and care to fight things out with me). Then there was a judge that showed me he cared when I did not. He put me in jail, and when I broke probation, he put me in treatment (two and a half years inpatient and out). Then he married my wife and me. Fear turned to realization, relief, contentment, and happiness [junior].

This middle-aged man, making a daily commitment to his own health and welfare, lays the foundation for ongoing success as a student and as a person.

Another student athlete learned a new way to channel the drive toward competence when he became disabled:

Having my leg broken in the summer had a major impact on my development. My old way of thinking was that I could be "successful" and support myself through sports — football or basketball — which I was good at. I developed a new way of thinking after breaking my leg and finding that I was left with limited mobility. I quickly became interested in the arts (painting and music) and college academics. [What helped this process?] After having my leg broken and spending a great deal of my time in the hospital (half of the summer and part of the fall), I was assigned a tutor, Mr. C., who was also a counselor in psychology. Mr. C. took a personal interest in me and began to help prepare me for college. He kept me interested in the arts and helped to motivate me toward the academic arena. I had always had a desire to grow and learn about other ways of thinking, and I took advantage of what Mr. C. was presenting to me [graduate student].

Encounters with wood, stone, clay, or paint, and the development of skills needed for artistry, offer potentials similar to those of athletics. Like the unequivocal triumphs on the field and the measurable achievement of weight loss or recovery, tangible creations and visible performances offer clear evidence of progress and accomplishment. The creative process requires similar confrontation of emotions and enables similar legitimized expression of feelings. Watch the child of an angry parent try to draw a friendly adult. Warm smiles become toothy grimaces or fanged snarls; soft hands become crooked claws; casual posture becomes a fixed stance. Observe the campus art of creative students and see the same process working, perhaps more subtly.

Experiences to develop skills in arts and crafts also interact with intellectual competence and the development of identity. Many students bring to college a high level of verbal facility. They handle abstractions well and can pursue discussion of concepts close to the edge of infinity. Yet these same students have limited experience with solid materials. They cannot look at a piece of machinery and grasp its logic, cannot use tools or convert raw materials into some kind of product, cannot handle their own bodies with ease, cannot manage tasks requiring large-muscle coordination or small-muscle dexterity. Consequently, the abstractions handled with such facility are little grounded in tangible realities; their meanings are hazy and limited. Experiences of designing, modeling, and building, of learning the requirements, limitations, and possibilities inherent in different materials, may not only enrich understanding of abstractions but also be transferred productively to more nebulous ideas. A student, for example, applies principles from a treatise on creativity:

> Being creative is knowing how one operates oneself, and how to set up conditions which enable one to be creative. It is also knowing how to fit into existing conditions in order to operate creatively with them. And I have seen that in ceramics quite a bit. When you have had enough experience with clay and have tried a variety of ways, you kind of know how you work with it. You also know what your present position is and what the alternatives are

which are possible. The more you work the more
alternatives you see and the more you find out about
your own position.

The abstractions concerning creativity were enriched and "brought
home" by the student's experience with clay. Similar learning
can occur through experiences in music ensembles, drama
groups, poetry readings, and dance concerts. Once meaningful concepts are attached to integrated systems of concrete experience, they will be retained as working knowledge.

Thus, development of physical and manual skills can foster
development in other areas by permitting objects and events
to be tied to symbols through action. When ideas are implemented in specific acts, when abstractions are translated into
tangible and visible products, and when goals are realized
through concrete behaviors, an integrated system results. Conceptualization, perception, and implementation join to constitute a larger whole. As Bower (1966, pp. 121, 131–132) observes:

> It is . . . important for schools to provide real events,
> objects, and relationships to which symbols can be
> tied. "Democracy" or "freedom," as words, are
> meaningless and their use dangerous unless a child
> learns them in a context of doing and thinking. Such
> symbols, unless tied down by first-hand experi-
> ences, are like boats in a storm, to be tossed this
> way or that, depending on the wind or current. . . .
>
> If objects are not bound into symbols by ac-
> tion, they tend to remain unintegrated and frag-
> mented. Bergson suggested that, in some men, per-
> ceiving and acting are separate entities. When such
> persons look at a thing "they see it for itself not for
> themselves." These are people who are born with
> or have developed a detachment from life. This is
> a reminder of the Swiss gentlemen who, when given
> a choice between going to paradise or going to a
> lecture about paradise, chose the latter.

In most colleges, intellectual activities are restricted to manipulation of abstractions. Awareness of feelings and expression of them in thought or action are to be tempered in the service of propriety or simple self-protectiveness. In most colleges, learning is more passive than active. Thus, most colleges need a counterbalancing commitment to encouraging athletic and artistic participation, promoting wellness and healthy living, and balancing mental overload with hands-on learning. Pounding nails on a Habitat for Humanity project can boost interdependence and integrity and foster personal integration.

Interpersonal Competence

Interpersonal competence includes an array of discrete skills, like listening, asking questions, self-disclosing, giving feedback, and participating in dialogues that bring insight and enjoyment. It also involves broader abilities to work smoothly with a group, to facilitate others' communication, to add to the overall direction of a conversation rather than go off on tangents and to be sensitive and empathic with others. White (1963, p. 73) says that

> every interaction with another person can be said to have an aspect of competence. Acts directed toward another are intended consciously, or unconsciously, to have an effect of some kind, and the extent to which they produce this effect can be taken as the measure of competence. When interactions are casual, when we are merely "passing the time of day," the element of competence may be minimal, although even in such cases we are surprised if we produce no effect at all, not even an acknowledging grunt. When matters of importance are at stake, the aspect of competence is bound to be larger. If we are . . . seeking help or offering it, trying to evoke love or giving it, warding off aggression or expressing it, resisting influence by others or trying to exert influence, the effectiveness of our behavior is a point of vital concern.

A student's comments illustrate White's point. At the end of her first semester, she said: "I started out with the tendency to monopolize the discussion, to be dogmatic about my ideas, and to mainly be interested in what I was contributing. I became aware of this—through seeing it myself and having it pointed out to me—and tried to fit myself in as a part of the whole."

At the end of her fourth semester, she said:

In the beginning of this semester my whole life seemed to center around the public affairs council, of which I am chair. I spent almost all my time trying to run the committee and arrange the affairs. I got into what I can term a "twitch"—being constantly upset. After talking my problems out and getting more experience in administering, I was able to calm down and things proceeded more smoothly. Toward the end of the semester, when all my undone work piled up, I didn't carry out all my PAC duties. The committee didn't fall apart, but I didn't do all I could. I learned a lot about organizing and working with people and feel confident things will go better next semester. . . .

When it became apparent to me that the majority of the group was not really working and seemed to be relatively uninterested in the class (Literature and Social Relations), I became discouraged and tried to figure out how to change this. At the same time, I realized that for me to do so much of the leading and initiating didn't help the group develop its own leadership responsibilities. Thinking it would be more help to the class and good practice for me, I attempted to play a following and resource role, rather than a leadership one. Thus, I dropped my attempts to reform the working habits of the group. I became aware, as I stopped fighting the class, that there was some kind of group feeling and purpose that didn't coincide with

mine. I then accepted what the group seemed to
be moving toward and acted accordingly. It was
hard not to play leader, and often I became too ex-
cited to restrain myself, but during the times I was
a follower, I also became aware of the different ways
that people do operate.

And at the end of the fifth semester, she said: "I carried out my
duties as public affairs committee chair in a much easier manner than last semester. I learned how to work with people more
successfully and was able to be a successful administrator."

These excerpts reveal some of the requirements for the
development of interpersonal competence. The student recognized that as part of a cooperative effort she must listen as well
as talk, follow as well as lead, understand the concerns and motives of others, vary her role in response to the requirements
of varying conditions, and avoid excessive imposition of her own
viewpoint. She recognized that the job of chair required decisions concerning use of time and the development of some system of organization; it required also sensitivity to group processes and to individuals. Those comments support White's
(1963, p. 91) proposition that a sense of interpersonal competence develops through effort and its efficacy in human interactions. As a committee chair and in class, the student could clearly
see the effects of modifying her own behavior. Consequently,
her competence and sense of competence could increase.

Another student leader illustrates a slightly different direction. Her experience with less motivated cohorts led her to become more cynical and perhaps more realistic.

I used to be very trusting of others and always believed that people would do what they said and keep
promises that were made. It wasn't until I moved
away from home that I found that some people were
not true to their word. I now take promises and
commitments with a grain of salt, unless I know
the person very well. [What helped the process?]
I worked on a committee and became the chair.

> Of the four other members, I was the only one who
> contributed to the organization, although subcom-
> mittees had been established. . . . I was very frus-
> trated and spent countless hours trying to pull
> everything together within the allotted budget. . . .
> I now try to prepare contingency plans when I'm
> faced with similar situations [junior].

This student has not really progressed with interpersonal competence. Unlike the student quoted earlier, she did not learn new skills for interacting, but instead looked for ways to protect herself from overcommitment. Perhaps with more experience or training, she would add to her repertoire some interpersonal skills like the ability to invite others to participate and to offer them feedback about their level of commitment, the ability to make better discriminations about which people to appoint to subcommittees, the ability to make explicit contracts or plans with others, and the ability to make more accurate assessments about who can be counted on and who cannot.

These skills carry over into friendships and love relationships as well. Learning to communicate directly and diplomatically involves much observation and trial and error. With positive experiences, students begin to feel an overall sense of effectiveness in their interactions. They learn to be adaptable in taking the initiative or easing up, in self-disclosing or holding back, in expressing opinions or testing the waters.

Interpersonal competence is a complex of subskills. Breen, Donlon, and Whitaker (1977, p. 15) refer to "interpersonal literacy"—knowing *when* and *how* to communicate *what* to *whom* in order to achieve specified goals. A person with interpersonal competence knows how to make appropriate choices about (1) timing—when to make comments or suggestions, and when to listen; (2) the medium of communication—verbal, nonverbal, or in writing; (3) the content—information, questions, feelings, values; (4) the target of communication—which individual or group to select and how to structure the message(s); and (5) how to be intentional in using communication skills to "maximize the attainment of goals that are congruent with their own and others' feelings, actions, and interpretations and to be able to recognize when they are not congruent" (p. 16). These authors provide a detailed inventory of interpersonal competencies, under several categories: mentoring, managing, leading, negotiating, instructing, supervising, consulting, persuading, communicating, and entertaining.

Students also find that these skills are transferable — they can be used in a variety of private, public, and professional settings. Breen and Whitaker (1983) include human relations and interpersonal skills among seventy-six transferable skills and propose that these are inherent in liberal arts learning. Their list includes thirteen human relations and interpersonal skills (p. 16):

- Guide a group toward achievement of a common goal
- Maintain group cooperation and support
- Delegate tasks and responsibilities
- Interact effectively with peers, superiors, and subordinates
- Express your feelings appropriately
- Understand the feelings of others
- Use argumentation techniques to persuade others
- Make commitments to others
- Be willing to take risks
- Teach a skill, concept, or principle to others
- Analyze behavior of self and others in group situations
- Demonstrate effective social behavior in a variety of settings and under different circumstances
- Work under time and environmental pressures

Some colleges are now giving greater emphasis to the importance of interpersonal skills. For example, Alverno College's competence-based curriculum requires students to demonstrate up to six levels of skill within eight categories (Alverno College Faculty, 1992). Competence 1 is "develop communications ability (effectively send and respond to communications for varied audiences and purposes)". Competence 5 is "develop facility for

social interaction" and ranges from level 1 (identify own interaction behaviors utilized in a group problem-solving situation)
to level 6 (facilitate effective interpersonal and intergroup relationships in one's professional situation).

Interpersonal competence is also important for job success. Klemp (1977) added to a large body of research that identifies the skills, abilities, and other characteristics required for
effective work. He and his associates identified successful individuals in a variety of work roles and examined what they were
doing that made them successful. One of the major factors involved interpersonal skills: (1) communications skills, including fluency and precision in speaking and writing, and the nonverbal component both in sending and receiving information,
and (2) accurate empathy, defined as both the diagnosis of a
human concern (based on what a person says or how he or she
behaves) and as an appropriate response to the needs of the person (pp. 102–109).

The development of these skills is a prerequisite for building successful friendships and intimate relationships. They are
essential for career and family and for playing one's role as a
citizen. When colleges provide opportunities to practice these
skills and offer explicit instruction and feedback, the third component of competence can come into balance with the other two.

Sense of Competence

While it is possible to observe and assess intellectual, physical,
and interpersonal competence by breaking them into specific
behaviors, the overall sense of competence is subjective. It comes
from how students feel about the worth of their accomplishments,
how well they believe they have solved problems or at least coped
with them, and how steadfastly they have maintained their
equilibrium in the ebb and flow of their college experience. Have
they learned to trust their abilities, or are they constantly plagued
by worries? Is their orientation toward themselves and their
world characterized by openness and strength, or by defensiveness and self-blame?

White (1963, p. 74) describes a sense of competence:

The competence of a living organism means its fitness or ability to carry on those transactions with the environment which result in its maintaining itself, growing, and flourishing. . . . To describe it neurologically, competence is an achieved state of affairs in the nervous system which makes effective action possible; . . . The subjective side of this can be called sense of competence. . . . In clinical work, sense of competence has been widely recognized in negative forms: feelings of helplessness, inhibition of initiative, the inferiority complex. The positive side has perhaps been poisoned for many of us by that hastily conceived dream-figure of perfect mental health who has attained invulnerable self-confidence and serene self-esteem — obviously a conceited fool. . . . Our best insight comes from the ordinary phenomenon of confidence, which is an aspect of virtually every act.

Students' sense of competence is directly related to the reality of their competencies. A genuine and sound sense of security depends on the ability to solve, or otherwise cope with, life's problems and to maintain equilibrium. Thus, development of intellectual, social, and physical skills is important. Yet the productivity and effectiveness achieved with a given level of intellectual, interpersonal, or physical ability vary greatly with the feelings about, and orientations toward, the levels of competence attained. Some students take their high levels of competence for granted; others feel that no matter how well they do, it is never enough. Some students do not know how to gauge their competence accurately, since they rarely receive specific feedback on their strengths and weaknesses. Students who have been disadvantaged or discriminated against may have high levels of competence but too little support or acknowledgment.

Yet college students are constantly identifying and testing their competencies. Those who are given guidelines for evaluating their own development in specific ways are more likely to have a strong sense of competence. For example, this Univer-

sity of Washington student analyzes progress in clear, sophisticated terminology (Waluconis, 1992, p. 15):

> Analysis of these pieces has opened my eyes to the
> fact that I have become much more adept at inter-
> twining critical thinking, the use of previous and
> newly required knowledge, and an incorporation
> of a geographic mind set to effectively present my
> research and ideas on paper. My writing process
> as presented in these pieces has shown a direct link
> between thinking, writing, and reading. At each
> stage I have thought out how I could present some-
> thing more effectively, what relevance or place my
> own critical analysis and/or research had with the
> problem and solutions I was trying to present, and
> what I could learn from a critique of other people's
> writing. I also was constantly reading, whether it
> was going through an article for the fifth time try-
> ing to find that critical piece of evidence or skim-
> ming through one of my drafts again to look for
> places it did not flow very well.

This increased trust in one's abilities may be less dramatic
when older students make strides in college. While returning
adults have more life experiences to draw on in confirming their
skills, many come into college with distorted fears about performance. Some feel that their academic skills have become too
rusty during years of working or raising families. When they
discover that they can do well on papers and exams and that
younger students and instructors value their experience, the
sense of competence can break through the self-protective shell
of fear and bring life to the whole endeavor.

Regardless of age, increased sense of competence makes
for more open and energetic action in the service of learning
and development. There is greater readiness to take risks and
greater willingness to persist at difficult tasks because success
seems more likely. A female sophomore reports, for example:
"I have changed a great deal. I can connect ideas more easily

now and I have just realized that I have a fine mind and can have good ideas of my own. I am much more able to stick with a problem for a longer period of time now and thereby develop ideas. I am progressively finding it easier to communicate, both orally and in writing. I also have a lot more to say these days." And an exchange with a male sophomore went as follows: "I feel that from now on I won't be nearly as hesitant to talk in class just from my change in feelings. In fact, I will probably be a pest in some classes because the way I feel now, if I've got something to say, I guess I'll just say it. If it takes two hours out of three hours, they will just have to put up with me if they can." The instructor commented, "It sounds like you are trying to get a little revenge." The student answered, "Not that, but it makes me feel good that I feel I'll be able to. I really do. It means so much to have more self-confidence. I don't think I have too much, just a lot compared with what I had."

Pascarella and Terenzini (1991) differentiate between self-concept and self-esteem in reviewing a substantial amount of research on these aspects of psychosocial development. They propose that *self-concept* is the student's judgment about personal competence (whether academic or social) *relative to other students.* It is also hierarchical, in that a pyramid of individual experiences is capped with an overall belief about where one stands. In contrast, *self-esteem* is based on an internal standard of how one "should" be, versus where one "is," and is not specific to any particular dimension of self. Self-esteem is a personal judgment of one's own worthiness, capability, success or significance, and the feeling of approval or disapproval that goes with it (pp. 171–172). Since the latter implies that internal ideals for the self have emerged and been solidified, the self-esteem literature relates more directly to the development of identity, while the self-concept research may shed light on sense of competence.

While the direction is not always linear, the evidence points to overall growth in students' academic self-concept over the four years of college. When students were asked to rate themselves "compared to other students you know" on various intellectual skills, several researchers found a pattern of declining sense of competence during the first year. This would not be surprising, given the culture shock of entering a new institution, with an academically competitive environment. Others found little change in students' academic self-concepts over the first year. Students' academic self-images become progressively more positive, however, during the ensuing years, according to research reviewed by Pascarella and Terenzini (pp. 172–174).

Research on changes in students' social self-concepts revealed similar patterns. "The transition from high school to college appears to be as hard on students' social self-concepts (popularity, popularity with the opposite sex, leadership ability, social self-confidence, understanding others, and the like) as it is on their academic self-images" (p. 174). This may indicate that students are discovering that they cannot rely on past history or their position in a social subgroup to gain companionship. Interpersonal skills must be developed in order to connect with a broader range of cohorts and to find common ground based on inner character versus outward appearance. Pascarella and Terenzini (1991) see a change by the end of the sophomore year. They cite evidence from large national studies that as seniors, students become much more confident in their ability to interact socially and use leadership abilities (pp. 190–194, 203). An anecdote from a female student illustrates this shift:

> When I was in high school I was pretty popular and had lots of friends. I was prom princess and homecoming queen. I tried to be nice to people who weren't in my group, but I never really got to know them. I think I was judgmental in many ways. When I went to college, all of the limelight was gone. I was just the same as everyone else. I didn't have lots of friends, and I felt I didn't fit into a group. . . . Now I don't have to hang around friends that only shop at Nordstrom's and are attractive and popular. I think I am a better human being since I eventually got to accept people not for their outward appearances but for their inward feelings and personality. I can be friends with people from different age groups and also learn from them [senior].

Another interesting theme emerges from nationally representative data gathered by UCLA and the American Council on Education's Cooperative Institutional Research Program (Astin, 1977), as well as by other studies of institutional effects on students. Apparently the size, selectivity, prestige, predominant race of a school, and type of control had little direct influence on students' academic and social self-concepts. These institutional characteristics did, however, have indirect effects on self-concepts through their influence on the kinds of academic and social experiences students had, which were in turn related to students' self-concepts (Pascarella and Terenzini, 1991, p. 184). In other words, "what happens to students after they arrive on campus has a greater influence on academic and social self-concepts than does the kind of institution students attend" (p. 184). One notable exception was the positive but indirect effect of attending a predominantly black institution on both the academic and social self-concepts of African-American women.

Increasing competence leads to increasing readiness to take risks, to try new things, and to take one's place among peers as someone not perfect, but respectable as a work in progress. Colleges that help students take concrete steps based on their abilities and readiness level are laying the cornerstone for long-range progress, even if the steps involve "precollege" reading and writing skills, "elective" courses in art or music, or "extracurricular" interpersonal encounters. It is through these increments of growing mastery and assuredness, not through the numbers of credits acquired toward graduation, that the development of competence occurs.

THREE

Managing Emotions

Students come to colleges loaded with emotional baggage. In varying degrees, they come with repressed anger, unhealed wounds, distorted ideas about sex, festering self-doubts, old resentments, unmet needs. With each new semester or quarter, they must face the anxieties of new instructors, new subjects, new challenges. For some, excessive anger, anxiety, or depression becomes overwhelming. Many struggle with frustration, fear, boredom, or desire, without ever exploring the sources of these feelings or learning how to shift out of them. Others suppress their feelings and divert attention to what others want, not what *they* feel.

The calm of the campus is increasingly threatened by date rape and other forms of violence, bias-related incidents, suicide, theft, vandalism, and alcohol and drug abuse. As staff devote more time to managing crises, conducting disciplinary procedures, investigating complaints, and confronting disruptive behavior, they have less energy to direct toward building a positive environment. The growing diversity of our campuses requires us to become more astute about the feelings that drive students' behavior and more skilled at helping them manage those unruly emotions that can so easily block progress.

All members of the college community are affected by the emotions of the students as they live out their dramas inside and outside of the classroom. Some feelings are disruptive and self-defeating. Others, like caring and optimism, are valued. These need cultivation. Learning to master fear or anger is a different proposition from mastering math or sociology. Becoming more adept at identifying feelings and giving them appropriate expression may have some elements in common with learning to write papers or conduct experiments, but there is a difference. Mastery implies using will and discipline to practice new skills. Emotions have a way of confounding will and discipline.

It is easier to conceptualize the development of competence, whether intellectual, physical, or interpersonal. We build competence by learning behaviors and linking them together. The process, whether it involves memorizing a computer keyboard, playing a chess game or a piano, or writing an essay or giving a speech, requires a certain amount of practice or repetition. Gradually, learning becomes integrated, until a single pattern can be activated as a unit. When the letter habits of a keyboard have been stamped in, whole words and phrases can be run off automatically. The pianist can take in a whole musical phrase at a glance, rather than focusing on each note. The skilled basketball player can maneuver and shoot, while at the same time watching the other players, calling up a strategy diagram, and observing the timeclock. Developing competence involves building a hierarchy of integrated perceptual-motor skills into larger and more complex structures. Learning to think, write, and communicate also involves practice, concentration, learning the rules, discovering what works, and using conscious choice to guide the overall performance. More practice and feedback lead to higher levels of integration.

The problem with some emotions is that they seem to crop up unexpectedly and confound all of our hard work and planning. Players going to the field and students going to an exam both feel tension. They may have drilled long and hard. They may have studied the material. But when anxiety hits like a tidal wave, it can block energy and paralyze action. This student reports an example:

I never did get nervous or have problems with confidence while playing any sport but football. It wasn't my small size or my lack of experience that got me nervous. I'm not sure exactly what it was, but the problem began to perpetuate itself until I began to freeze out on the field. I played like a superstar in practice but was so nervous during games that I would see double. One situation that exemplified my problem was when I was sent in to play linebacker during a game. I had a chance to intercept a pass but instead let it slip through my arms into my opponent's. I was instantly crushed as my teammates began to criticize me. They were very upset and felt afterwards that that play had lost the game. I felt myself saying I was a bum and a lousy player. I felt like I was making a mistake by even playing [graduate student].

Fear can debilitate. Anger and fright can trigger emergency responses, even when there is no real emergency. When stresses are great, the adrenal glands go to work. Heart rate accelerates. Blood sugar pours into the hungry muscles. Digestion slows down. Pupils dilate. Muscles tense. We sweat, to cool off heat generated by the impending struggle with the examiner or the rival team. The crowd roars. We get goosebumps, even though our skin no longer has long hair to bristle at an attacker. The body prepares for self-protective action, flooded by nervous impulses. Involuntary responses also occur when we see something we desire. Delicious food stimulates salivation; attractive strangers stimulate sexual yearnings; impending intimacy fires the blood.

Koestler (1967) calls these reactions "overstatements of the body." They are innate, autonomous responses to stimuli "which carry an echo, however faint, of situations that held a threat or promise in the remote past of the species; which once were biologically relevant, though they no longer are" (p. 58). The result is a tendency toward violent movement, to "work off" or at least "shake off" the physiological effects of emotion.

The chief mediators of this general mobilization are the sympathetic division of the autonomous nervous system and the hormones secreted by the adrenal medulla, stimulated by rage, fear, pain, desire, and other types of stress. Koestler says:

> These involve incomparably heavier machinery, acting on the whole body, than the process of thinking, which, physiologically speaking, is confined to the roof of the brain. The chemical and visceral states induced by the action of the sympathico-adrenal system tend to persist; once this massive apparatus is set in motion it cannot be called off or "change its direction" at a moment's notice. Common observation provides daily, painful confirmation of this. We are literally "poisoned" by our adrenal humours; reason has little power over irritability or anxiety; it takes time to talk a person out of a mood, however valid the argument; passion is blind to better judgment; anger and fear show physical after-effects long after their causes have been removed. . . . These changes are governed by phylogenetically much older parts of the brain than the roof-structures which enable us to think in verbal symbols [p. 58].

Pain, fear, and anger stimulate impulses toward muscular action, usually to fight or to flee, in much the same ways that hunger and arousal produce urges to approach and control (Lange and James, 1967). These "overheated drives" can build up enormous pressure when they have no outlet, or when the mechanisms for release are insufficient. The result is tension, resentment, and suffering. If some sort of consummatory option is in sight, frustration can change to incipient relief. A little pressure can be pleasurable. We feel arousal, attraction, or appetite as we imagine the reward coming. Afterward, if the pressure is too low, we get bored and go looking for stimulation. We usually register anger, fear, hurt, or longing whether we want to or not.

These are the emotions that need good management. Development involves finding appropriate channels for releasing irritations before they explode, dealing with fears before they immobilize, counteracting pain and guilt, and controlling impulses to exploit others or give in to unwanted pressures. It involves learning that some amount of boredom and tension is normal and that immediate gratification or instant diversion can block optimum performance and quiet reflection.

There are other kinds of emotions that psychologists have left largely to the poets. These feelings are harder to measure, because they do not drive toward aggressive or defensive behavior. They are not related to the survival of the fittest, and so perhaps were not as interesting to researchers concerned about the acquisitive and competitive aspects of social behavior. Nevertheless, these emotions are as real as rage and fear: feelings of inspiration, wonder, love, happiness, grief, surrender to the inevitable. They are usually expressed not through observable, muscular action but through internalized, visceral and glandular changes. Sometimes laughter or tears are the only external indicators. Rather than needing to be controlled, these emotions should simply be brought into conscious awareness and permitted to exist. Emotional development also involves learning to seek out, create, and savor the positive emotions of love, joy, and hope.

To conceptualize development in this arena, it is helpful to borrow an analogy from Koestler (1967). He says we must first differentiate between the various emotions according to the nature of the drive, originating in various physiological, social, or psychological needs and urges, such as hunger, sex, protection of offspring, curiosity (the "exploratory drive"), conviviality, and so on. He imagines each of these represented by a different tap in a bar, each beverage providing a different flavor (p. 276). A second dimension can be represented by the pressure in the tap. How strong is the drive, and is it pleasurable or not? Does it flow smoothly out of the tap, or does it foam and spurt because too much pressure is built up in the pipes? A third dimension can be represented by the alcohol content in the tap. Is it stimulating or soothing, toxic or beneficial? Koestler proposes that for every emotion, the polarity of self-assertive versus self-transcending (or participatory) can enter in. Self-assertive tendencies involve some form of aggressiveness or defensiveness, whereas participatory tendencies involve transcending the boundaries of the individual self, identifying or bonding with another, or feeling part of a larger whole. Thus, one can see a loved one and feel entranced, devoted, and happy (self-transcending), or one can feel jealous of rivals and driven to possessive rage (self-asserting).

We can conceptualize development along this vector as first becoming more aware of feelings and then as learning flexible control and appropriate means of expression or integration. Development also entails findings ways to balance negative or painful feelings with positive, uplifting emotions, and integrating feeling with thought and action. Using Koestler's metaphor, awareness of emotions includes (1) becoming more aware of the full range of feelings and gaining skill at differentiating between the various emotions; (2) becoming more adept at gauging the intensity of the feeling, the "pressure in the tap"; and (3) understanding whether the feelings are toxic or nurturing, self-protective or self-transcending. We can also add awareness of the causes or sources of feelings, acceptance of feelings as valuable sources of information, and learning the consequences of acting on impulse. Developing balance, control, and appropriate expression involves practicing new skills, learning coping techniques, directing feelings toward constructive action, becoming more flexible and spontaneous, and seeking out rewarding and meaningful experiences.

There is relatively little research on changes in students' emotional adjustment. Hood and Jackson (1986, p. 1) describe one of the Iowa Student Development Inventories, which attempts to measure awareness of emotions and integration of emotions. Five categories of emotions were selected for inclusion in the inventory: happiness, attraction, anger, depression, and frustration. Studies using this inventory and other similar scale scores over varying periods of time generally report increases in students' self-understanding and control of emotions, as well as gains in personal integration over varying periods of time (Hood and Jackson, 1986; Bennett and Hunter, 1985; King, 1970, 1973; Brawer, 1973; Newcomb and others, 1971; Heath, 1968). Earlier studies found change in the direction of increased awareness of emotions and increased freedom of expression in words or behavior. Webster, Freedman, and Heist (1962, p. 830) reported that at both Bennington and Vassar, "the older students are more developed, more mature, more free to express impulses than the younger students." Feldman and Newcomb (1969, p. 34), reporting their comprehensive review of research on change and stability during the college years, say that "college students tend to become somewhat more impulsive and somewhat less self-controlled, orderly, and conscientious."

Pascarella and Terenzini (1991, p. 225) report that only two large-scale projects measured changes in students' emotional adjustment: Clark and his colleagues' (1972) study of students at eight diverse institutions, and Chickering and his associates' study of thirteen small colleges (Chickering, 1969, 1971, 1974b; Chickering and Kuper, 1971; Chickering and McCormick, 1973). Chickering and his associates (1969, pp. 48–49) found increases on the Personal Integration scale of the Omnibus Personality Inventory (OPI). The higher the score, the less students reported intentionally avoiding others, feeling lonely, rejected, and isolated, or expressing hostility and aggression. Anxiety level was also measured, and sixteen cases changed in the hypothesized direction, meaning that fewer admitted to being worried or nervous.

Both Clark's and Chickering's research found increases of 14 to 16 percentile points on the Impulse Expression scale of the OPI, which assesses "a general readiness to express impulses and to seek gratification either in conscious thought or in overt action. The high scorers value sensations, have an active imagination, and their thinking is often dominated by feelings and fantasies" (Center for the Study of Higher Education, 1964, p. 5). Very high scores indicate a tendency toward aggression (Heist and Yonge, 1968, p. 5). Chickering, McDowell, and Campagna's study (1969) indicates that half or more of any shift in impulse expression may occur in the first two years of college, stabilizing in the latter two years.

Changes in impulse expression, at the general level at which they have been assessed, can reflect two quite different patterns. For some people, increasing scores may reflect better achievement of flexible control and increased ability to manage emotions symbolically, perceive underlying complexities and realities, gratify impulses vicariously, or intelligently moderate behavior. Others may simply have traded a punitive conscience for rampant impulsiveness. They may still be driven. A different drive is in control but self-control has not increased. Furthermore, the responses that students give to questionnaires and personality inventories may not reflect actual behavior. Students may give the "approved" answer or may exaggerate descriptions of behavior that is much more pallid in real life.

For some students, the challenge is to become aware of the different flavors of feelings and to understand their legitimacy. Some come with the faucets of impulse expression wide open, and their task is to develop flexible controls. Others have yet to open the tap. Their challenge is to loosen repressions from earlier years and to let off pressure stored in the system. Then they can experience the full range and variety of feelings and experiment with safe, and hopefully creative, ways to use emotional energy. They can explore how feelings convey vital information, some urging us to pay attention or protect ourselves, others cementing an experience in our memory or adding intensity and meaning to a new idea. Or they can channel feelings into artistic, political, religious, or athletic activities. Each must learn to exercise self-regulation — not the controls inherited unwittingly from parents, not the controls called for by peers or by the dominant culture, but controls reconstructed as one's own, linked to personal purpose. As self-control and self-expression must come into balance, awareness and integration ideally support each other.

Toxic Feelings

What kinds of feelings are likely to give students the most trouble? The most toxic are those which can interfere with daily life and academic success: (1) fear and anxiety, (2) anger leading to aggression, (3) depression, guilt, and shame, and (4) dysfunctional sexual or romantic attraction.

Fear and Anxiety

A certain amount of anxiety can help students get "psyched up" for a test or a speech or a game. Too much leads to a freeze-up. Gaudry and Spielberger (1971, p. 14) describe the Facilitating Anxiety Scale (FAS), which includes such items as: "Nervousness while taking a test helps me to do better"; "I look forward to exams"; "The more important the exam or test, the better I seem to do." They found that anxiety appears to facilitate performance on simple straightforward tasks and to interfere with performance on more complex tasks. In conditions where ego involvement is low, a number of studies have found anxiety to be unrelated to performance. In conditions of high ego involvement, anxiety has typically been found to interfere with performance (p. 96). In other words, when students really care about what they are doing and have a certain amount of their self-concept wrapped up in how well they perform, the threatening power of self-consciousness and anxiety is amplified.

Test anxiety can afflict even the most stable and accomplished students. It escalates when students anticipate failure and blame themselves for it. Preoccupation with the dire consequences of failure and the critical evaluations of others multiply worry and emotionality (Crouse, Deffenbacher, and Frost, 1985, p. 315). Negative self-talk perpetuates and worsens the tightness.

Students are anxious about all kinds of things. Archer and Lamnin (1985) identified academic stressors reported by undergraduates at the University of Florida. The list included concerns about tests, grade competition, time demands, professors and classroom environment, and career choice and future success. Less stressful concerns included procrastination, studying, papers, and speaking in class. Students worried about intimate relationships, parental conflicts, finances, and interpersonal conflicts with friends. Some gender and racial differences were found. For example, older students and African-American students were more likely to feel financial concerns than younger, Caucasian students. Female students listed roommate conflicts and personal appearance items more frequently, and male students listed concerns about approaching and meeting other students, judgment and acceptance by peers, and peer pressure more often (p. 212). This community college counselor's observation is typical: "The students I am seeing tend to have not one frustration, but seven or eight at a time. During this past week, one returning adult student was faced with a car that was stolen, a baby-sitter who didn't show up, no money to buy her textbooks or a bus pass, a boyfriend who became abusive, and an instructor who made disparaging remarks about single parents on welfare. Since she is struggling to get off public assistance, the instructor's remark was the last straw. No wonder she wants to drop out."

Anger Leading to Aggression

When anxiety and frustration build up, they create walking powder kegs. Students, and sometimes their parents, lose their tempers when they feel victimized by what they perceive as arbitrary authorities, bureaucratic procedures, inflexible rules, and closed courses. Competition for precious seats in prerequisite courses, for good grades, even for the best parking spaces adds to the tensions on campus. Students encounter people with different backgrounds, tastes, habits, and values. Whether they are attracted or repelled, new behaviors are needed. Younger students, on their own for the first time, may struggle with setting up a new home for themselves and venturing into new relationships, freed from parental constraints. Experimentation may lead to rejection, disappointment, resentment, acting on impulse. Older students are not exempt from unconscious expression of feelings. They may be biased or oversensitive, needy or overbearing, manipulative or naive.

Many students are unaware of their aggressive impulses. If they received early messages that anger is unacceptable, it may get rerouted through more socially acceptable patterns, such as anxiety, depression, guilt, overeating, self-imposed starvation, insomnia, constant sleeping, obsessions, compulsions, denial, self-sabotage, being accident prone, overworking, over-sexing, overexercising, and problems with drugs and alcohol (Rubin, 1969). Males may be taught that aggressiveness is fine, especially in competition. Females are rewarded for yielding and taunted about being "overemotional."

Aggressive behaviors learned in childhood tend to persist (Eron, 1987; Eron and Huesmann, 1984; Huesmann and Eron, 1984). Early aggression also predicts reduced intellectual achievement in adulthood. Feshback and Price (1984) found that motivational factors in children linked to poor academic performance also correlated with aggressive and delinquent behaviors. They speculated that the same factors that lead to a lack of interest in school — poor self-evaluation, internal conflict, suppressed anger — also produce a pattern of aggression. Students who come to college with long-standing problems with anger may wreak havoc on the learning environment. Development involves learning specific cognitive skills and social competencies that can decrease aggressive behavior and increase constructive interaction (Feshback and Feshback, 1984; Spivak and Shure, 1974). These skills include social problem solving, perspective taking, role playing, and discriminating and responding to one's own and others' feelings.

Sexual coercion and violence have long been hidden problems on college campuses. They were documented some years ago by Makepeace (1981, 1983) in studies of premarital dating. More than one student in five has had direct personal experience with courtship violence (forceful attempt at intercourse that led to the woman's fighting, crying, or screaming) on a date. Many students have absorbed subtle messages that forced sex is justifiable if the woman hitchhikes, goes braless, initiates a date, goes to a man's apartment or hotel room, or gets drunk and then has sexual intercourse with someone she just met at a party. Sandberg, Jackson, and Petretic-Jackson (1987) studied dating patterns and attitudes of 408 college men and women. They found that "the dating atmosphere is prone to misinterpretation, miscommunication, and misunderstandings" that may result in coercive behavior by both men and women. Problems with relationships are major contributors to depression, guilt, and shame.

Depression, Guilt, and Shame

Lopez (1986) estimates that 25 percent of college students suffer from depression and that 33 percent of all college dropouts suffer serious depression just before leaving school. The majority of the sufferers are women. Moreover, the incidence rates for depression and suicide are 50 percent higher for college students than for their noncollege peers. Suicide is twice as frequent and is the second or third highest cause of death in this population (Nagelberg, Pillsbury, and Balzer, 1983, p. 525).

Depression can be an appropriate reaction to loss. While it is a drain on energy and motivation, it does not normally get in the way of working, eating, sleeping, thinking, or social interaction. When it does, students may need help in recognizing that they are in a danger zone. If they are uninformed about the symptoms of clinical depression or if they blame themselves for feeling down, they may never seek help. Even if they do, physicians may prescribe tranquilizers without checking for other underlying physical problems. Up to 40 percent of all diagnoses of depression are misdiagnoses of common and uncommon physical illnesses, such as thyroid disease, heart disease, alcoholism, Alzheimer's disease, diabetes, mononucleosis, nutritional deficiencies, or cancer. At least seventy-five diseases first appear with emotional symptoms, and depression can be a side effect of virtually any prescription or illegal drug (Gold, 1987, p. xv).

Depression is not a single emotion, but a collection of behaviors and feelings that often — but not always — go together. These include: (1) *negative emotions*, such as sadness, guilt, pessimism, feelings of worthlessness and inadequacy, sense of failure, dissatisfaction, expectation of punishment, and self-dislike; (2) *behavioral patterns*, such as irritability, passivity, social withdrawal, indecisiveness, and problems interacting or concentrating; (3) *physical problems*, such as lethargy, sleep disturbances, loss of appetite, weight loss or weight gain, increased headaches, stomachaches or intestinal difficulties, and reduced interest in sexual activity (Beck, 1967; Lewinsohn, Muñoz, Youngren, and Zeiss, 1986). Since going to work or class takes effort, depression may lead to passivity and solitary activities like watching television, eating, or napping. These are not the kind of acting-out problems that attract staff members' attention.

Like those with an alcohol or drug problem, student sufferers may not want to admit that these feelings are overwhelming, that life is becoming meaningless, or that suicide is a serious possibility. If they have an internal rule that they should not feel bad, the result can be shame — "the affective-cognitive state of low self-esteem" (Lewis, 1987, p. 39). Students who violate rules or fail to meet standards, either naively or maliciously, may remember guilty feelings forever. One student reports an example:

> My freshman and sophomore English teacher, Dr. H., took an interest in me, in who I really was. She exposed me to J. D. Salinger, T. S. Eliot, Lawrence Ferlinghetti, and Shakespeare. She had us talk about ourselves and our thoughts. We read out loud several full plays and poems. She had little soirées at her apartment for some of us. Except for this teacher, few of our instructors challenged us. My friends and I were bored and thought ourselves "above the law." We began to cheat during exams. We were so bold about it that we thought all the teachers knew. One day at the end of sophomore year, Dr. H. saw me cheating. She told me she saw me and was so disappointed in me. Of course I couldn't say, "We were all cheating. Haven't you been noticing?" I carried the burden of being the *big disappointment*. I still carry it. I felt such shame to let down this person who was so important to me [graduate student].

Rather than exploring the problem with the student or privately holding her accountable for unacceptable behavior, the faculty member passed judgment on her as a person. Without a way to reflect on her mistake, learn from it, and resolve it, it poisons an otherwise valuable relationship. Peterson, Schwartz, and Seligman (1981) found that "blame of character" (who I am) is related to symptoms of depression in college

students. "Blame of behavior" (what I do), however, is equated
with lack of depressive symptoms.

Dysfunctional Sexual or Romantic Attraction

Emotions arising from sexual impulses offer the most pressing
challenge to flexible self-control, the greatest provocation for
either repression and asceticism or preoccupation with pursuit
and gratification. Successful integration — where sexual behavior
becomes a vehicle for expressing complex feelings of affection,
nurturance, and respect and for satisfying a similarly complex
network of needs in ourselves — requires a great deal of awareness and trial-and-error learning. This returning adult student
reports a painful story of disappointment:

> When I was a freshman, I started going out with
> a senior. I was very innocent and uninformed about
> sex. He was a good looking, experienced, aggres-
> sive, exciting football player and I was way out of
> my league with him. I was a prime candidate for
> date rape, and before long, it happened. I was a
> bewildered, forced participant who didn't know how
> to stop his advances. This left me feeling victimized,
> angry, used, ashamed, ruined, and terribly guilty.
> Now I was a "bad girl." While I still looked the part
> (and was) a nice person, inside I felt deceptive and
> dirty. I thought if people knew what I had done,
> they would think I was cheap. I tried to rationalize
> my nonvirgin status by saying that we were going
> to get married anyway so it didn't make any differ-
> ence. I stayed in this unhealthy relationship because
> I thought I loved him and because I had had sex
> with him; that meant I should marry him. Later
> when he began to drink heavily and go out on me,
> I would break up with him. But he would come cry-
> ing for forgiveness, promising he wouldn't do it
> again, and even though I didn't want to, I'd go back
> with him [graduate student].

This student's report contains some components of awareness. She names the feelings ("victimized, angry, used, ashamed, ruined, and terribly guilty"). She identifies the myths and assumptions that exacerbated the already-disturbing emotions (she was now "bad" and "cheap," and since she had had sex with him, she had to stay with him). She acknowledges that she didn't have the information she needed (about sex or about assertiveness) or the will to insist on what she wanted ("even though I didn't want to, I'd go back with him"). Development involved becoming informed about sexuality, rape, and domestic violence, replacing outmoded beliefs with more mature frames of reference, and learning that she had the right to set firm boundaries.

Increasing Awareness of Emotions

Awareness of emotions increases when students learn to identify and accept feelings as normal reactions to life experience, when they can understand and amend outdated assumptions that amplify negative feelings, and when they become well informed about sexuality, interpersonal communication, and personal rights. Opportunities to share their stories in supportive groups or through reflective writing assignments can help this process.

Reflecting on one's family history can also aid awareness of emotions. We learn our primary lessons about managing emotions as we are growing up. Parents can model spontaneity, rigidity, or denial. Some families yell at each other regularly, while in others, polite decorum prevails. One clan easily hugs and kisses; another keeps its distance. For some, only positive feelings are acceptable; others revel in complaining and criticizing. Many students receive explicit or implicit messages rooted in a Puritan heritage: "Be good." "Work hard." "Save for a rainy day." "Don't rock the boat." More unrealistic messages might have been: "Nothing's wrong." "Never lose control." "Be perfect." "Look good." Adolescents who observe aggression or loss of control at home but are pressured to maintain a cool facade can bring to college a distorted view of what is "normal." Worriers and perfectionists are more vulnerable to depression. Overly dependent individuals as well as introverts are also at risk. One student learned through family dynamics how to depress herself:

> I would tell myself I was as good as other people, that I wasn't inferior or dumb, but the underdog usually prevailed. . . . No matter what I did that was good, I would find something negative about myself to concentrate on. For example, although I was an attractive person, I didn't think I really was. Instead I'd focus on the fact that I had small breasts, big feet, that I was too tall, and so on. I was also adept at people-pleasing, just trying to be liked and fitting in. I was brought up as an understudy to my martyr mother, who always encouraged me to "just be nice" (and not pay attention to my own needs). Consequently, I was an easy target and a pushover for anyone loud, aggressive, and intimidating. I would simply shrink away from a fight with a red face and try to avoid a scene. It was "Christian" to turn the other cheek, my censor would tell me. It is interesting to realize that for three generations of two sisters in our family, the younger, martyr, peacemaker sister has allowed the older aggressive and insensitive sister to get away with unreasonable behavior. We (the wimps) have experienced pain and humiliation from their unchecked, oppressive acts. It seems we have been so concerned with being "nice" that we haven't been able to bring ourselves to do battle with them. Instead, we have been careful and oversensitive to their moods, trying to keep peace and avoid confrontations [graduate student].

Historians studying the evolution of the family and therapists working with dysfunctional families have begun to uncover the extent of sexual abuse and domestic violence. Students in social sciences classes or wellness programs may recognize themselves in presentations about victimization. For example,

Middleton-Moz (1990, pp. xiii–xiv) reported similarities in adults who were shamed or abused during childhood: they are afraid of being vulnerable, intimate, or committed; they suffer extreme shyness, embarrassment, and feelings of inferiority; they appear either grandiose and self-centered or selfless; they feel worthless and unlovable no matter what they do; they become defensive when any negative feedback is given; they feel angry and judgmental about qualities in others that they are ashamed of in themselves; they feel they must do things perfectly or not at all. These patterns can lead to performance anxiety, procrastination, compulsive behaviors, dependency, and feeling constantly violated by others.

Many students are relieved to discover that they are not the only ones struggling with these patterns and that understanding family dynamics can allow them to find more positive alternatives to the old self-defeating habits. Similarly, students taking biology classes may learn that depression may have roots in neurochemical deficiencies and genetic, environmental, socioeconomic, and nutritional factors (Gold, 1987, pp. 201–202). Wellness workshops and chemical dependency training may shed light on how the brain chemistry and metabolism of alcoholics differ from those of nonalcoholics. In both cases, shame and guilt can be lifted as new information comes in.

Psychology students may see themselves reflected in discussions of the "affective domain" or in textbook content on neurotic behavior. Likewise, English majors may learn about jealousy and despair by reading Hardy's *Far from the Madding Crowd,* about lust and shame by reading Hawthorne's *The Scarlet Letter,* about hope and courage by reading Alice Walker's *The Color Purple.* Whereas many instructors would prefer that feelings be parked outside the door of their classrooms, others look for ways to elicit feelings as well as thoughts, to stir passions, to inspire enthusiasm and enjoyment as natural elements of any learning experience. Belenky, Clinchy, Goldberger, and Tarule (1986, p. 227) describe "connected teachers" as intensely interested in students' feelings, able to retain objectivity while presenting themselves as real persons, and interested in connecting with students by entering into their perspective.

Residence hall advisers can help students discover feelings simply by being attentive listeners.

> I remember one night during my first semester in
> the residence hall. I went to the lounge to get some
> coffee, and a resident assistant invited me to come
> down to her room for my coffee break. She asked
> me all kinds of questions about how I was getting
> along with my roommate and how my classes were
> going. I felt myself putting into words for the first
> time those nebulous but powerful feelings of excite-
> ment, uneasiness, homesickness, and confusion.
> She listened for a long time and responded with
> genuine interest and sensitivity. I'd never experi-
> enced that kind of probing attentiveness before. It
> was the first of many long, intense dialogues, and
> soon I was asking other people around me about
> their experiences, listening intently, and asking
> questions, as she had done. From that time on, peo-
> ple's feelings and relationships — including my own —
> became an endless source of fascination [student
> affairs staff member].

Awareness involves not only noticing but also identifying the feeling, or at least the family to which it belongs, and
its intensity level. Students not familiar with the language of
emotions may only say they are "upset." It may take skilled questioning to determine whether they are slightly irritated or ready
to explode, completely devastated or a little disappointed. This
second-year student expresses the hesitant first steps toward acting on his own feelings, rather than functioning unconsciously
or trying to stiffly reason out the correct thing to do:

> I guess I began to realize that I wasn't really un-
> derstanding how I felt about a lot of things. I real-
> ized that I had been ignoring this for a long time.
> But realizing that you don't know what you are feel-
> ing and changing it are two different things. You

can't change when you are threatened by anything
substantial. You can't relax enough to stop thinking objectively and sort of interpret and feel, sort
of pay attention to yourself and interpret. Looking
back, there has been a gradual process of knowing
what was going on and feeling things around more.
It feels sort of strange to me. . . . When I was little,
I was constantly getting told I should do that and
shouldn't do this, more than other kids I think. . . .
I think I got so I tried to behave on an objective
level. I tried to decide objectively what correct behavior was, because I couldn't really feel the reasons or feel the demands after awhile. And that has
continued on one level or another all the way up
to college. But now, I really am beginning to know
what I feel and to act on it cautiously, at the same
time trying to be open to what is going on.

Hopefully, this caution will slowly change to increased freedom
of expression in words or behavior as his awareness grows. Like
many students, he realized that "you can't change when you are
threatened." Students cannot learn when they are overwhelmed
by anxiety. A safe environment allows for more relaxed reflection and unforced adaptation.

Awareness grows when students allow the feelings to per-
colate, accepting their existence rather than denying them or
distracting attention from them. For some students, the layers
of armor are thick, having been donned as survival mechanisms
during years of family unhappiness. Feelings may need to reach
intense levels before they can be noticed. One student traced
her struggle with "conflicting inner voices":

When I was about eleven or twelve, the comfortable security of my childhood started to slowly
crumble as my parents became less content with
their own lives and less able to cope with the stress
of working and raising five kids. As the years between ages eleven and eighteen progressed, the

atmosphere at home got progressively worse. Mom and Dad were both drinking way too much and couldn't be counted on to be coherent after 6:00 or so. They were both terribly unhappy, Mom especially, and there was a *lot* of unexpressed anger and misery floating through the air. Yet no one ever talked about anything; we all kept bopping through our lives outside the home as if we were perfectly happy, trouble-free people.

And this led to the development of a clear pattern in my own behavior: completely ignoring or denying any unhappiness within myself. It was a behavior that had been modeled for me by masters from a pretty young age and one that I thought was "normal" and good.

When I happily left home at eighteen, I carried this habit of going through life as a happy, completely "put-together" person with me. But the next several years were difficult for me. In addition to not facing the inner terrors that dwelled within as I went forth into the real world, I had severed my emotional ties with my parents four or five years earlier and knew that I couldn't rely on them for emotional support of any kind. As I tried to build a new life for myself, I found myself being fiercely independent (as I had also been taught was "good"), to the point of extreme isolation and solitude. And for a few long years I was a very, very unhappy person, unable to acknowledge or face my depression — yet always maintaining a happy facade — and feeling desperately alone, unsupported, and afraid [graduate student].

This student becomes more aware of the conflicting messages inside her head as she reflects on her past. From a relatively safe distance, she can see how critical self-talk can make negative feelings worse. In this case, one part of the self said, "You are alone, unhappy, and frightened, and you can't handle it." Another said, "You should be strong. You can handle this. If you admit you're unhappy, you'll dissolve. Keep going!" A rationalizing voice said: "You're lucky to be out here on your own. Others are so much worse off than you! Really, you're having the time of your life." All of these sound like variations on an internalized parental voice, which can persist in all of us, no matter how long we have been away from home.

This student was able to analyze why the pain was there and to see what action she could take to resolve the problem. She also learned that sometimes there was nothing she could do to change the situation. She had to accept it as it was or remove herself from it. By the time she reached graduate school, she was able to say: "I think I'm more honest with myself about my emotional response these days. If I'm feeling depressed or unable to cope, I still tend to analyze a lot, but I let myself feel whatever I'm feeling. And really, with such a finely honed talent for denying my fears, I hate to let go of it completely — it can be useful when facing unavoidably scary situations." Like the previous student, she tries to use her analytical skills, but also realizes that feelings do not need to lead to action — they just need to be felt. She has also acknowledged her growing honesty with herself and reframed denial from a negative habit to a positive strategy.

In reflecting, the student above recalled much unexpressed fury in her home. Many students have never seen anger expressed directly and appropriately. They may not be aware of their own tendencies to be aggressive until a catalyzing experience brings it out. It may be a heated debate in the student senate that becomes personal. It may be a first encounter with a rival, fueled by too much alcohol. It may be a date with someone who appears docile enough but later becomes offensive verbally or physically.

By improving communication and observation skills, students in close relationships can minimize misinterpretations of the behavior of others by explicitly checking out ambiguous signals. They can also learn about factors that, in combination, can lead to problems. Alcoholics learn to spot warning signs for relapse by using acronyms like HALTS (hunger, anger, loneliness, tiredness, and seriousness). Potential abusers and victims can also learn to be cautious when certain predictors appear. For example, do friends condone the dehumanization of women or boast about conquests? Is there hostility toward women, or a need to feel powerful and dominant? Is there a perceived insult or pent-up frustration? Did traumatic events occur in the past? Are erotic magazines, films, posters, or books in evidence? Are alcohol or drugs being used? Malamuth and Briere (1986) proposed a model showing how these originating and situational variables can interact to produce aggression. Peterson and Franzese (1987, p. 226) conclude that sexual abuse is "part of a web of interlinked factors." From their survey of college men, they conclude that "there is a positive relationship between the tendency to abuse and the acceptance of rape myths, downplaying of sexual assault as a problem, and rather traditional views of women's role in American society." Women need to realize that the traditional norms of acting patient, compliant, and accepting may put them at risk (Muelenhard, Friedman, and Thomas, 1985).

Adding new frames of reference can also help awareness. For example, Lopez (1986) reports that both depressed and nondepressed students face similar psychological stressors (such as academic and financial pressures), but depressed students were more likely to have a negative view of their families. While they may have good reasons for these negative views, a reframing process might make a difference (for example, "My parents did the best they could, knowing what they knew" versus "My parents were insensitive jerks"). By exploring their past hang-ups with parents, some students can change resentment to amusement or balance skewed negative memories with a more balanced view and, in so doing, free themselves from leftover emotional burdens.

> My mom was always sending me articles she cut
> out about women who did amazing and creative
> things. She'd say, "This woman reminds me of you."
> Mary Tyler Moore reminded her of me. Marlo
> Thomas reminded her of me. And so on. She gave

me a belief in myself, that I could do extraordinary things. The hook with her was that she was a very traditional Italian Catholic who expected me to live according to her principles. In the world according to Mom, women did not have sex until they were married. Even married people didn't French kiss. No one drank liquor until they were twenty-one. And no one touched marijuana.

I became more and more a disappointment to my mother. She wanted me to marry a Catholic man with a professional job, have kids, and work part time at some creative job. The men I chose were never quite right. My jobs were embarrassing. When I was director of rape relief, she wouldn't even tell her friends what I did. So while her love did some very positive things for me, it came with a price tag. Guilt and shame. The feeling of letting her down was always present [graduate student].

The ability to affirm the validity of one's own feelings, despite parental resistance, is an essential step in identity formation. The process of naming the patterns and owning responsibility can be painful but liberating, and for older students, college can be the vehicle for seeking a new life.

I was very much in love with my first husband. I became the perfect housewife, mother, and friend. While he attended college, I cooked, cleaned, and supported him in every way possible to make his life easy and successful. I gave to him my heart and soul, and from my childhood still sparked those thoughts that people could truly live happily ever after. The "fall" arrived when my husband's best friend informed me that my husband was having an affair with another student.

I was shattered emotionally. I had depended on my husband for all of my own happiness, and I felt that my heart would break. It was at this point that my trust level regarding love and happiness evaporated, and I came to believe that nothing lasts forever. Along with hatred for women (that is, my mother), I developed an anger toward all men.

During the next five years, I wandered with no direction, trying to escape the pain of my seven-year marriage and the new awakening of my childhood scars that had never truly healed. Finally with the help of one close friend, I began counseling. I remember the first time that my counselor tried to reach out to me with a hug and how I pushed her away with so much anger. To love somebody meant pain, and my defenses were very high.

I spent a year in counseling looking at my childhood, accepting and learning how to forgive my parents. My trust level toward women and men began to return and I felt good about myself. I decided to enter college. During this period I fell in love with a man, against the wishes of my friends and counselor. They felt I needed more time, but I was feeling lonely and enjoyed the excitement that being in love brought into my life. I married him a year later.

It was not a good marriage, but I was blind and felt that with time things would get better. I struggled against believing that my husband would never change. I thought if I helped him (caretaking, parenting), he would want to change because he loved me. I continued to struggle for five years. In my heart and mind, I didn't want to be a failure. I continued to go to school. Classes and books I read spoke truths to me. I started to realize he would never change. The victim/rescuer cycle reigned supreme in our household until one day I had just plain had enough. It's been lonely without him, but it's different this time. Now I have the tools to know the difference between what's good for me and what isn't [graduate student].

Increasing Integration

The above statement reflects the beginning of integration. It is a gradual process, helped along by relevant books, counseling, and painful experiential learning. Integration involves the ability to exercise flexible control, so that feelings do not take charge but instead add depth and texture to self-expression. By testing through action or symbolic behavior, students can gradually learn how to regulate the intensity of feelings. They can learn when to withdraw and reflect on a situation of high drama. They can broaden their repertoire of verbal and nonverbal responses and begin to exercise conscious choice about when and how to express feelings. They can detach from interactions and watch their own self-talk, observing how it leads to irrational or self-deprecating patterns and how it can be changed. They can develop new frames of reference that serve as guidelines for behavior and meaningful beliefs that put events into perspective. An adult student's statement illustrates the importance of new cognitive structures:

> One year my life fell apart. My oldest son (sixteen) had run away from home. My youngest son (ten) was having stomach problems. The dog was allergic to the grass, the cat had hurt his foot, and my husband was in Vietnam. The straw that broke me was my best friend dying of a heart attack. I had what is commonly called a nervous breakdown. I believed all of the above was my fault. From this experience, I learned many things. They are: (1) I did the best I could, (2) I'm not responsible for everyone, (3) there are some things you have to accept because you can't change them, (4) the only one you can change is yourself, and (5) it is better to bend than to break. I am still learning every day to accept life as it is, not how I want it to be. [What helped?] I had a lot of support from family, friends, and my doctor. I remember one statement the doctor made: "I'm glad we finally found you — the person

who is causing all the troubles in the world." This
helped me realize I didn't cause wars, poverty, and
all the other problems around me [senior].

Learning the skills to succeed academically can foster integration. For example, techniques have been developed to help
students manage test anxiety. Traditional behavior modification approaches, such as conditioning, systematic desensitization, gradual habituation, guided imagery, and relaxation have
been successful (Siegel, 1986; Edelmann and Hardwick, 1986;
Koapp and Mierzwa, 1984; Kuhlman, 1982). Practitioners have
used hypnosis to aid positive imagery and tension release (Cerio,
1983). They have also helped students learn problem-solving
techniques to counter domestic pressures (Mayo and Norton,
1980), self-control techniques to improve study habits and control anxiety (Spurr and Stevens, 1980), and study skills (Annis,
1986).

Some students are chronically anxious. Spielberger (1972)
found that students suffering from "trait anxiety" have a sense
of self that is easily threatened by performance demands or other
problems of living. They tend to perceive a large number of
situations as dangerous or threatening. Educators can help students to reduce anxiety by creating a relatively safe environment and structuring classes so as to minimize surprises. For
example, Davidson, House, and Boyd (1984) demonstrated that
permission to retake a test one or two times improved scores
and decreased test anxiety. A study by Saigh (1985) found that
students in an experimental group subjected to unscheduled assessment (pop quizzes) were significantly more test anxious and
dissatisfied with the course, even though their performance on
the tests was not significantly different from that of the controls.

Destructive, confrontational behavior is uncomfortable
for most of us. Anger Management 101 is not in the curriculum, but perhaps it needs to be. Lerner (1985) proposes that
managing anger should not be done by trying to get rid of it,
doubting its validity, or directing it at another person. Yet these
are standard responses. The more challenging goal is to understand why it is occurring and work on changing one's own atti-

tudes and behaviors. Students can learn that silent submission, blaming, complaining, and emotional distancing are "management styles" that do not work. They can learn, through assertiveness training, counseling, modeling, or disciplinary procedures, how to restrain the tendency to turn anger into aggression or accusation and to ask, What is the real issue here? Why am I feeling so strongly? What do I really want? What will solve the problem? They can learn to adopt a calm, direct, and specific communication mode, rather than suppressing anger or indulging in put-downs. They can also learn to live with the anxiety aroused when they begin to express valid resentments, to take a firm stand, confront questionable behavior, or set boundaries in relationships. Acceptance of responsibility for anger and exercising conscious choice about the time, place, and method of expression are the key to integration.

Students can also learn to channel anger or frustration into constructive action. For example, in 1988 the board of directors of Gallaudet University — a university for the hearing impaired — appointed a hearing president who could not use sign language. The students responded by forcing the school to close until the president-elect and the board chair resigned and a hearing-impaired person was appointed. Anger flared on many campuses when war in the Persian Gulf broke out in 1991. Students mobilized peaceful sit-ins and teach-ins, and many faculty transformed classrooms into safe places to vent intense feelings of all kinds. Other instructors behaved as if nothing unusual was happening and expressed uneasiness about directly addressing students' feelings. Advisers of student organizations can play a critical role in helping impassioned students decide how to turn a whirlwind of strong feelings into effective action. Sometimes this can entail the difficult lesson that what is needed is to look within the self rather than trying to force change on an oblivious organization or an unwilling friend. The following anecdote illustrates the integrative process that can emerge out of frustration:

> I have been committed to several missions — for example, against the war in Vietnam, against police

brutality in inner-city Chicago, against rape and pornography, and in support of black studies classes, welfare rights, the women's movement, children's rights, and so on. Probably the ones that have most fundamentally changed me are the antirape and antipornography movements. I made a conscious choice to stop making speeches about pornography a couple of years ago. It was too upsetting to learn that people I knew read pornography. I saw a lot of pornography and read the stories of many of its victims and it made me ill. I was filled with rage and hurt and anxiety. I remember trying to talk to my friend Beatrice about Linda Lovelace's book, *Ordeal*. I told her what Linda had said about *Deep Throat* and expressed my outrage and pain that this woman was living in a world that allowed movie theaters to show a movie of her being raped. She had no power to stop it. Beatrice said, "But *Deep Throat* is a good movie . . . she's probably making that up just to make money." I just couldn't stand getting into these discussions with people I knew and liked. And I hated the "support" of fundamentalists. Once I was shouted off the stage at a fundamentalist church for "that women's libber garbage." I decided that this work was hurting me more than it was helping to change the world. It seemed apparent that I needed some time to go inside myself and heal the hurts that were there before I could try to transform the world. . . . I used to think cloistered nuns were weird and useless. Now I wonder if they don't have a good idea [graduate student].

Integration can also be strengthened by an influx of positive emotions. Feeling good is the antidote for depression. Love can uplift at any age, although it can unravel scholarly pursuits, as this adult learner reports:

After being alone for five years, following the breakup of a thirteen-year marriage, for the first time I was attracted to another man. I had resigned myself to planning my life as a single person. I was actually irritated and frustrated by the reawakening of my emotions and really fought and denied the reality of the situation. Finally, we agreed to meet for a cup of coffee. As this was the first date I had accepted since my divorce, my kids were merciless at teasing me about the encounter. I insisted that he was only someone with similar interests and that it would be nice to have a male friend, while inside I was terrified of my interest in this man.

It was intense from the start. We left the coffeehouse and drove through the tulip fields and walked on the beach. We talked like we had known each other for a long time. We had this urgency to catch up on each other's lives and thoughts. There was a frustration that we hadn't met earlier, as we found we had gone to the same schools, grown up within a couple of miles of each other, and knew a lot of the same people. When we held hands as we walked along the beach, my whole body responded to his touch, and the anticipation of being open and vulnerable both terrified and thrilled me. School, work, family, and friends all were put on the back burner as we plunged into this relationship, hardly being able to stand being apart. We were exhausted from the late hours we were keeping, and I frantically tried to cram studying into the few hours we weren't together. . . . I felt unconditionally loved for the first time and was truly transformed. I went from a kind of a practical, hair-in-a-tight-bun, brown Oxford, neutral observer of life to a vibrant participator, as I literally "let my hair down" [graduate student].

This student is experiencing the other polarity in Koestler's (1967) scheme—the self-transcending emotions. As he says, "Rage is immune to understanding; love of the self-transcending variety is based on understanding and cannot be separated from it" (p. 88). Rather than driving toward action, these self-transcending emotions move us toward tranquility, surrender, or catharsis. "You cannot take the mountain panorama home with you; you cannot merge with the infinite or dissolve in the universe by any exertion of the body; and even in the most selfless forms of love and communion each individual remains an island" (p. 273).

Koestler proposes that these observations are in keeping with the character of the bifurcated autonomous nervous system. In contrast to the sympathetic system, which galvanizes the body into action to cope with anger or fear, the parasympathetic division does not move toward focused action. When the sympathetic division unleashes its adrenalin, it acts directly on the body as a whole, as the pedals of a piano affect all the notes sounded, amplifying the force of the chords. In contrast, the general action of the parasympathetic system is inward directed, calming, and cathartic. Like a focused performer carefully striking separate keys, this system acts locally on specific organs. Its function is to counteract and complement the fight-or-flight excitations, to lower blood pressure and pulse rate, to neutralize excesses of blood sugar and acidity, to facilitate digestion and the disposal of body wastes, to activate the flow of tears, and to surrender to feelings or experience identification rather than taking action to separate and protect the self. As Koestler puts it,

> Listening to Mozart, watching a great actor's performance, being in love or some other state of grace, may cause a welling up of happy emotions which moisten the eye or overflow in tears. Compassion and bereavement may have the same physical effect. The emotions of this class, whether joyous or sad, include sympathy, identification, pity, admiration, awe, and wonder. The common denominator of these heterogeneous emotions is a feeling of participation, identification, or belonging. In other words, the self is experienced as being part of a larger whole, a higher unity — which may be Nature,

God, Mankind, Universal Order, or the Anima
Mundi; it may be an abstract idea, or a human
bond with persons living, dead, or imagined. . . .
In these emotional states the need is felt to behave
as a part of some real or imaginary entity which
transcends, as it were, the boundaries of the individual self; whereas when governed by the self-
assertive class of emotions the ego is experienced
as a self-contained whole and the ultimate value
[p. 54].

Whether one is twenty, forty, or sixty, colleges provide
wonderful environments for developing increasing capacities for
passion and commitment through intelligent behavior. Studying
the arts, humanities, and sciences provides ample opportunities for wonder and inspiration. In social sciences classes, comparative religion courses, human services internships, or volunteer work, students can find sources of hope and courage. In
order for colleges and universities to be true learning communities, more of these self-transcending feelings are needed. Sensitivity and caring must counteract alienation and competition.
Neither students nor staff will let down their guard or feel free
to enter into conflict, if the fear of reprisal overshadows the search
for truth. We need programs that celebrate our common humanity and vulnerability as well as our cultural differences. We
need teaching methods that balance connection to the subject
with objective distance, that balance dissection and analysis with
continuity and synthesis.

Mentors are needed to help students go through the emotional tribulations of modern life. Barker (1989) cites the tale
of Dante, lost in a dark wood and blocked in his ascent to the
light by a marauding beast. As happens for those on the hero's
journey, magical help appears in the form of Virgil, who comes
from another dimension to guide him. But instead of pointing
the quickest way to heaven, Virgil tells Dante to descend and
go through hell and then climb the seven-story mountain of pur-
gatory before returning to Eden, which is surrounded by a wall
of flame. Dante endures the pains of the detour and the fires

of purification and transformation. He cannot see ahead, but he goes forward only because of the mentor's urging and because he can hear singing on the other side of the fire. Mentors can provide vital encouragement, tools for staying on course, and reminders that there is music playing somewhere, even when everything seems to be going up in smoke.

FOUR

Moving Through
Autonomy Toward
Interdependence

Psychosocial theorists like Erikson (1968) and Blos (1967) emphasize the importance of separation and individuation in the development of identity. While separation involves a physical distancing, individuation means becoming one's own person and taking increasing responsibility for self-support. It is possible to do one without the other. Some students go away to college but continue to live at home psychologically. Other students live with parents but use the college environment to define personal goals and values that are truly their own. Older students may have left home long ago but never developed self-direction. Perhaps they took whatever job came along or wandered from one passing interest to another. They go to college ready to become newly autonomous, searching for realistic purposes and meaningful achievements. Other mature students have followed career paths, raised families, and managed their lives with independence but enter college in order to change directions or start afresh. For them, development may entail clarifying goals, reordering priorities, and asking family members to support them as they redefine themselves.

115

Cognitive theorists like Perry, Kohlberg, and Gilligan see development as increased ownership of well-thought-out opinions, beliefs, and judgments, more confidence in articulating and acting on guiding principles, and greater tolerance for other points of view. This involves the will to question social conventions and parental injunctions and resist the pressure to blend into the crowd. Belenky, Clinchy, Goldberger, and Tarule (1986) chart the shifts from received knowledge and subjective knowledge, as women became more aware of their feelings and thoughts and find their own voice.

Loevinger (1976) describes the critical transition from the conscientious stage to the autonomous stage in her model of ego development. Individuals in the conscientious stage have a growing sense of personal choice and responsibility for forces affecting their lives. They are no longer at the mercy of fate. They begin to measure achievement by an emerging set of internal standards. At the autonomous stage, these standards are clearly identified, even though inherent conflicts and complexities may also have become more apparent. The transition from conscientious to autonomous is marked by a heightened appreciation of personal uniqueness and a concern that "one can remain emotionally dependent on others even when no longer physically or financially dependent" (p. 22).

Gilligan (1982) and Douvan and Adelson (1966) call our attention to the difference in focus between males and females. In their view, adolescent males push for autonomy through separation, individual rights, and playing by the rules, while adolescent females define who they are through their attachments to others, seeking ways to preserve harmony rather than fight for competitive advantage. Kegan describes the tension between the need for autonomy and the need for inclusion, proposing a spiral of evolutionary truces between the two, with overall movement toward healthy interdependence.

Josselson (1987) conducted a fascinating longitudinal study of identity development in college-educated women, interviewing sixty subjects from four different universities in 1971. Twelve years later, she interviewed thirty-four of them again. Two themes ran through the lives of these women. One was the theme of distance from home, both physical and psychological (p. 169). A second theme was interconnection with others. Using the concepts of *agency* and *communion,* she says, "Communion is central to female development, and women are likely to opt for preserving attachment before pursuing their agentic needs. For many women, success in communion, in relationship, is itself an expression of agentic needs for assertion and mastery. The problem of separating is the problem of not only becoming different but of becoming different and maintaining connection at the same time" (p. 171).

With these concepts in mind, we can say that moving through autonomy toward interdependence involves three components: (1) emotional independence — freedom from continual and pressing needs for reassurance, affection, or approval from others; (2) instrumental independence — the ability to carry on activities and solve problems in a self-directed manner, and the freedom and confidence to be mobile in order to pursue opportunity or adventure; (3) interdependence — an awareness of one's place in and commitment to the welfare of the larger community.

The first step toward emotional independence involves some level of separation from parents, increased reliance on peers, authorities, and institutional support systems, and growing confidence in one's own self-sufficiency. Cognitive skills are needed for self-determination. Students strengthen this volitional part of the self through practice at choosing, deciding, deliberating, reflecting, planning, and judging (Dearden, 1972, p. 461). Learning to think critically and independently, discriminating between external "shoulds" and internal "wants," and defining meaningful and realistic goals lead to confidence in personal judgment and more focused action. When students can rely on their own ability to get the information they need, move toward goals of their own choosing, and navigate from one place to another, physically and psychologically, they can function as responsible adults with the will to survive and succeed.

In contrast, Josselson (1987) describes subjects with the lowest level of ego development (those in the identity diffusion group). Some seemed to suffer from "atrophy of the will" (p. 143), were unable to define a consistent direction, drifted along without either crises or commitments, and felt that they had so little control over their lives that there was no point in trying to plan anything. Others worried about the meaning of life and experimented with drugs, sex, and fringe religious groups but remained fragmented, disorganized, and unclear about their own standards and beliefs. Still others carried scars of early psychological trauma, borderline personality characteristics, and other recurring problems that blocked autonomy. They searched for ways to heal the earlier wounds. "Impulsive, avoiding guilt at all costs, they were unable to make identity commitments because of the instability and unreliability of their capacity to organize and integrate their experiences" (p. 142).

Autonomy implies mastery of oneself and one's powers. In addition to becoming free from the dictates and interferences of others, one must also be free from disabling conflicts or contradictions within one's own personality (Gibbs, 1979, p. 119) and free from the obsessive desire for an external savior or rescuer. Some progress in the management of emotions is needed for movement along this vector, since the only way to find what fits is to explore and experiment, and this often involves guilt and anxiety. Letting go of the old dependencies involves a grieving process. Sometimes anger accompanies a break with others. Learning to speak more assertively requires freedom from fear and self-consciousness.

The growth of autonomy in college students has been researched in a variety of ways during during the past thirty years. General increases in students' freedom from the influences of others have been documented in both large-scale, nationally representative studies and smaller-scale, single-institution studies, according to Pascarella and Terenzini (1991, pp. 214–218). "Few psychosocial traits have received more attention, and the evidence — from whichever decade — consistently indicates changes along this personal dimension during the college years" (p. 215). They report numerous studies of changes in students' locus of control that found increases in students' sense of control over what happens to them and a decline in their sense that the world is controlled by luck, fate, chance, or other external forces. Nine studies were identified that addressed changes in independence from family and peers, with six reporting statistically significant increases in autonomy in relationships with parents between the freshman and senior year (p. 217). Studies of independence from peers produced mixed results. For example, two studies reported a decline in independence from peers among freshmen (Newcomb and others, 1970; Heath, 1968). Hatch (1970) found this to be true only among women, while the men in her study increased in independence from peers. Two other studies found statistically significant increases on peer independence scales, with increases in independence from family exceeding those relating to peers (Nelson and Johnson, 1971; Nelson and Uhl, 1977).

Earlier studies by Beecher, Chickering, Hamlin, and Pitkin (1966) and Chickering (1967) reviewed Goddard students' records. They looked for evidence of increasing autonomy and interdependence over a four-year period. Since the questions they used to assess students provide some more specific ways to describe development along this vector, we include them here. They used a dimension called Venturing to describe students who were open to new experiences, willing to initiate things, and able to confront questions and problems and to disagree. The following questions were used to assess this dimension:

1. How much does the student speak up in class? How ready is he to express his own ideas and join the battle? Does he brood and maintain a stoic silence or does he externalize his feelings and ideas?

2. How easily does she communicate with the instructor? How free is she to disagree?

3. To what extent does he engage in study or other activities to tackle perceived weaknesses or liabilities?

4. How frequently does she speak of lack of self-confidence, of fears that restrict her activities (reverse scoring)?

5. To what extent does he seek out new, challenging, or unusual work-term or summer experiences? To what extent is the work term used to engage in new experiences or to test new skills or attitudes?

Average ratings on these five questions increased over the four-year period, with most change occurring during the first two years. Ratings dipped temporarily at the third semester, possibly indicating a period of recovery or quiescence after the difficult adjustments of the first year.

The Goddard study of resourcefulness and organization is relevant to the self-sufficiency component (Beecher, Chickering, Hamlin, and Pitkin, 1966; Chickering, 1967). Questions were designed to gauge whether students could be efficient and practical at carrying out activities on their own, working out intermediate steps to a goal, knowing when they needed help and how to get it, and knowing how to make good use of available resources. Faculty used four questions for rating students on this variable:

1. How freely does the student make use of a wide range of resources for learning?
2. How well does he make plans, follow through on them, or modify them consciously and judiciously and then carry through?
3. How well does she discover or develop new ways of going at matters of concern to her?
4. To what extent is he able to handle a variety of responsibilities and sustain good effort and performance in relation to all? How well is she able to avoid being overwhelmed or snowed under at the end of the semester or at other times, when several obligations seem to coincide?

It was hypothesized that average ratings for these questions would increase. Despite the large standard deviations, the differences between the first and fourth semesters and the first and seventh semesters were well beyond those which might occur by chance. Steady growth occurred during the first two years and then tapered off during the last two years.

Interdependent students were defined as nonpunitive and nonhostile. They were also seen as attuned to the whole and aware of their place in it and responsibilities to it. The following questions were used in the Goddard study (Beecher, Chickering, Hamlin, and Pitkin, 1966; Chickering, 1967) for rating the students:

1. Is the student ready and able to work with others on community affairs such as recreation events, community government, house business, and so on?
2. Does the student pull together with others well on the work program? To what extent is he conscious of his role in a broader work program context, when such a relationship exists?
3. Does she seem to be aware of the relationship between her own behavior and community welfare in general?
4. Is the student tolerant of differences in behavior or in point of view on the part of other students and faculty members?

Change over four years showed a slight overall increase, with the sharpest jump occurring during the third semester. Fourth-semester ratings were about as high as those for the seventh semester. These data were consistent with other observations that participation in cocurricular and community activities increases sharply during the second year and then levels off.

We will try to bring some of these research findings and abstract principles into focus with examples from students' self-reports and further discussion of the three components of this vector.

Emotional Independence

Pearson (1986, p. 4) uses six archetypes to describe the journey of individuation: "The Innocent lives in the prefallen state of grace; the Orphan confronts the reality of the Fall. The next few stages are strategies for living in a fallen world. The Wanderer begins the task of finding oneself [sic] apart from others; the Warrior learns to defend oneself and to change the world in one's own image; and the Martyr learns to give, to commit, and to sacrifice for others. The progression, then, is from suffering, to self-definition, to struggle, to love."

The road to emotional independence begins with disengagement from the parents, proceeds through reliance on peers and role models, and moves toward a balance of comfort with one's own company and openness to others, without the need to cling. During the first weeks, college students may feel the excitement of newly acquired freedom. But it is the independence of a hog on ice. The territory is new and slippery, and without familiar footholds, clumsy thrashing or bewildered immobility is likely to occur. Free from accustomed restraints or outside pressures, students can engage in random activity or rigid adherence to behavioral standards from days gone by. The dominant impression is instability. There is a conspicuous lack of coordination and little observable progress in any direction.

This student reports on the universal experience of leaving the family comfort zone behind:

> A shift from dependence to independence occurred as I returned from Africa to attend university in Canada. My parents returned to Zimbabwe, and I more or less had to fend for myself. Previous to this, I had a comfortable support system (family). While this was valuable, I never really appreciated it until I was forced to be on my own. Learning a new culture and discovering how to be responsible and independent represented a developmental turning point. The stress and anxiety initially experienced soon tapered off as I became more comfortable in this new setting and . . . [I] realize[d] that change had occurred. [What helped?] Initially I didn't find any person who helped the process, although as I reflect, there were probably a number of people who would have gladly assisted. A roommate in the university who was going through the exact same experience helped in that we were able to bond and observe the world through the same eyes. Peers' ability to relate was the most important activity for assisting me. A mixture of adventure, discovery, and delight accompanied by a

deep sense of loss, isolation, and loneliness made
for a rollercoaster experience [graduate student].

Seeing no adult helpers on the horizon, this student turned to
his roommate, but the adjustment was not painless. Another
student recounts a similar process, acknowledging the value of
a tolerant response and an accessible leadership experience:

My big changes have taken place over the past three
years. The event that caused it all was going to college. I went to a small high school where I was a
big fish. I felt very alone and lost when I came to
college. The past three years here have been a real
growing time. I went from being cocky and loud
but insecure, to quiet, withdrawn, and depressed,
and now I'm feeling confident and more expressive
but more aware of and sensitive to others and how
I affect others. Three major events were: (1) going
to college but living at home, which left me feeling
alone; (2) moving out, which gave me more social
contacts and confidence; (3) becoming an R.A.,
since this has given me a great support network and
confidence in myself. My friend also helped me by
accepting most of me and helping me with the not-
so-hot stuff. He's allowed me to grow and to be a
jerk sometimes [junior].

In some cases, parents have paved the way for the development of autonomy by encouraging it at home and by helping
young people develop the skills to manage anxiety and uncertainty. Early exposure to choice making may help. For example,
DeMan (1982) investigated the relationships between parental
practices and levels of anomie, self-acceptance alienation, and
self-esteem. (*Anomie* is a condition of uncertainty about what
to believe and how to act, which may lead to increased anxiety
and deviant behavior.) He tested sixty middle-class university
students age twenty to twenty-four. Twenty students came from
families that encouraged exploration of different norms and

values before finalizing their own. These reported fewer anomie feelings than students from more restrictive families. Apparently this early exposure to options led not to confusion but to greater self-confidence in decision making.

Adolescent rebellion may occur, no matter how well meaning the parents, as a means for breaking psychological shackles. A two-year-old fell into the water. "Help! Help!" his mother called. "Save him! My son, the doctor!" If such a son escapes drowning at two, he may still be fighting for air at twenty. Rebellion may be the only way out. When children more frequently followed parents' footsteps and were more constrained to do so, a vigorous leap was sometimes required to escape an unwanted existence. But now rapid change makes the world of parents seem obsolete. Constraints are few. The possibility of becoming like the parents is more remote. With less need to wrench away, the disengagement can happen simply and quietly.

> One change I remember was in developing autonomy from my parents. I remember realizing, while at my parents' house during a vacation, that no longer was I looking to my parents for permission to do things. I was just telling them what I had decided to do. I was also referring to the university as "home" instead of "school." I moved from a dependence on my parents' opinions to a reliance on my own values and opinions. I believe this occurred early in my sophomore year when I was applying for R.A. experience. [What helped?] The important things were being away from home in a college residence hall environment, having a student leadership position in the hall, making the decision to put myself through college, working as a peer adviser, and feeling that my work spoke for itself [graduate student].

On the other hand, some parents may help the process along by creating distance. Disengagement and devaluation can be mutual. Some parents have little use for children who have become young adults, especially if they continue to be a drain on family resources. While parents may have enjoyed bringing them up, they may experience less pleasure in watching them hang around indefinitely or move away and build a different life elsewhere. Under such conditions, adolescent devaluation of parents may be reciprocal, especially if parental needs are not met and togetherness is strained.

The challenge for younger students in developing autonomy may be compounded when the home environment is unsupportive.

> In my freshman year, I very much wanted to leave home but was also very afraid, since I had been involved in a legal case involving my family and I felt "persecuted" by members of the community. I spoke with a counselor, who reassured me that my perceptions were valid. This assurance that I could see things correctly — even if they were very negative — gave me the confidence to "leave home" and continue my studies. In other words, having my feelings validated by an adult I trusted allowed me to move from being uncertain and dependent to greater certainty and independence [faculty member].

This confirmation that "I can trust my own insights and feelings" is tremendously important in developing autonomy. So is the discovery that "I can experience as well as manage threatening emotions":

> I have always been an anxiety-ridden person — full of fear about so many things in life — fear of authority, the unknown, failure, and so on. Now I find myself so much less in that modality. It's wonderful! Now I think about how I will deal with any crisis-type situation from a positive rather than a negative perspective. Like, last week I sent four payments for bills all to the wrong companies! I

thought about the worst that could happen and experienced absolutely no anxiety or fear at all. [What
helped?] A family crisis precipitated going to a
counselor. During the therapeutic process, I felt
every emotion along the spectrum—sad, happy,
relieved, ecstatic, vulnerable, trapped, freed, and
worthwhile [junior].

This student turned to a counselor. Others may seek out
other supportive adults. Parents may be disappointed when their
daughters and sons spend vacations at the homes of college
friends. But this adoption of other parents can serve as a kind
of replacement for the home being left behind. When the visitor and friend talk about the vacation, opportunities exist to compare perceptions and sharpen awareness of differences. The visitor may return with glowing memories of the host family's
warmth and high principles. But the friend may return disillusioned and angry, having seen subtle instances of hypocrisy or
phoniness on the part of family members. For example, a guest
enjoyed refreshments in his friend's home. The host, however,
was shocked when his mother accepted compliments about cook-
ies he knew she didn't bake.

Parents' attempts at control or protection may increase
the importance of supportive advisers, inspiring teachers, and
helpful internship supervisors:

I had little self-confidence in what I felt and believed, having had a very dominating father. Being a student and having jobs that were not growing experiences didn't help my self-image. Being
in this academic program and having a good internship supervisor is changing the way I feel about
myself. I feel more confident in my own opinions,
apart from my father, and feel I can establish autonomy in my life. I also have a wonderful feeling
of being able to contribute to the community. [What
helped?] My supervisor helped a lot, but mostly it
was my self that established the change in my self-

> view. I was able to go across barriers that I thought
> were impossible to cross in my work situation. By
> going ahead and doing the work despite what I felt
> about myself and my abilities, I gained in confidence.
> Inspiration also came from my classes [junior].

This type of observation recurs in students' self-reports. It is almost as though an emerging part of the self takes risks and learns to do things that an older part could not imagine. Both are referred to as "my self," even though sometimes the student does not yet identify with the new self ("it was my [more autonomous] self that established the change in my [earlier] self-view"). This student's older self felt stifled by a dominating father, but the emerging one moves forward freedom. To continue her development, she must own this new self, instead of seeing it as a mysterious visitor.

Parents may be reasonable in setting limits and moderating them as maturity increases. Yet no matter how reasonable the expectations or how conventional the family norms, new ideas from "learned" professors may constitute a foreign element.

> I had no ideas in high school, only facts. When I
> went to the university, I was thrilled with what I
> was being taught. There was Plato and John Dewey,
> and an art professor who talked about art as expe-
> rience. We would go to museums and try to recre-
> ate how the artist painted and how the sculptor
> sculpted. Even cleaning strawberries or washing the
> dog could be an aesthetic experience, he said. When
> I discussed these fabulous ideas, my father called
> it a bunch of baloney. He attacked the ideas on in-
> tellectual grounds, but as far as I was concerned,
> the profs knew everything. And as authorities, they
> were much less punitive. By the time I was a junior,
> he was convinced that the school was a hotbed of
> "Communist ideas" and threatened to stop paying
> my tuition. So I got a scholarship in case he was

> serious about it, and that made him feel guilty, and
> he did pay for my senior year, despite the subver-
> sive environment I was in [returning adult].

This statement shows the interplay of emotional and instrumental autonomy in a family power struggle. In this case, the lustrous image of the professors was beyond tarnishing, not because of their superior knowledge but because she *felt* differently about them. They were interested in discovering, not controlling. The father's opinion was the shackle to be broken, regardless of its content. In the meantime, the daughter moved toward instrumental autonomy, represented by the scholarship to pay her own way.

Perry and other cognitive theorists have described changes in students' view of themselves as learners and in their perception of instructors as authorities. A multiplistic thinker comes to see a professor not as someone who "knows everything" but as one authority among many, possessing as many flaws as a parent has. Many of us who, as teachers, administrators, counselors, and family friends, have experienced close relationships with freshmen and sophomores, have found ourselves on a pedestal. But as these idolaters move toward more realistic perceptions of their parents, so also do they perceive us more realistically. We find ourselves less frequently flattered and more often portrayed in stark and revealing terms. Students may become disillusioned, or, if we are lucky, they may humanize their image of us.

Disillusionment can trigger the movement toward autonomy, regardless of age. It comes when we discover that whatever we put our trust in—leaders, mentors, authorities, institutions, political parties, philosophies—falls short of our ideal. Pearson (1986, p. 27) calls this "the Fall." It's an event that causes Innocents to become Orphans:

> The Orphans' story is about a felt powerlessness,
> about a yearning for a return to a primal kind of
> innocence, an innocence that is fully childlike,
> where their every need is cared for by an all-loving

mother or father figure. This yearning is juxtaposed against a sense of abandonment, a sense that somehow we are supposed to live in a garden, safe and cared for, and instead are dumped out, orphans, into the wilderness, prey to villains and monsters. It's about looking for people to care for them, about forgoing autonomy and independence to secure that care; it's even about trying to be the all-loving parent — to their lovers, or children, or clients, or constituencies, anything to prove that that protection can be or is there. After the Fall comes the long and sometimes slow climb back to learning to trust and hope. The Orphan's task eventually is to learn self-reliance [p. 28].

Students with this orphan mentality can show up in our offices and classrooms regularly. They may have had rifts with parents, partners, employers, social service agencies, or other authority figures. They may be looking for quick fixes or role models who can restore their faith in a flawed system. It is a challenge to offer them support without increasing their dependence. Pearson (1986, p. 14) describes essential tools for helping people move toward autonomy: (1) an individual or group that shows genuine concern and that will not exploit or augment their dependence; (2) an opportunity to tell and retell their personal experiences in a way that overcomes denial ("retelling how painful it was before they were saved, stopped drinking, became a feminist, etc."); (3) an analysis that moves the locus of the blame outside the individual; and (4) encouragement to begin to talk about taking responsibility for their own lives, once it is established that they are not at "fault."

Some students move toward emotional autonomy with the help of a recovery program. Colleges can support this by providing information, assessment, referral, and support services for students dealing with substance abuse. When recovery outside the classroom connects with relevant content inside the classroom, this cocurriculum can powerfully influence development.

"I quit drinking and taking drugs and began to work
a twelve-step program. I moved from being an emotional, spiritually bankrupt individual to being a
childlike person experiencing recovery. I know a
significant change has occurred because I am counseling addicts and alcoholics rather than living in
sickness. [What helped?] Members of AA initially,
and then professors at the university helped me gain
new knowledge to arm myself against relapse. One
of my core classes enlightened my spirit by exploring how I relate to others and the world" [junior].

This student articulates an inner movement from emptiness toward wholeness. Temporarily relying on someone outside themselves — a higher power, counselor or adviser, the group,
the movement, the church — can help people learn the skills of
taking charge of their lives and also of getting appropriate help.

Orphans may believe that they have put their lives
in the therapist's, priest's, or guru's hands, and that
belief provides the security to start moving and putting their lives in order, but it is critical that they
make decisions themselves and carry them out.
Later they can look back and see that they did it
themselves. Remember Glinda the Good Witch in
The Wizard of Oz, who tells Dorothy at the end of
her journey that she could have gone home anytime
she wanted to? Dorothy asks why she did not tell
tell her that before, and Glinda explains that Dorothy would not have believed her. First she had to
convince her that there was a Great and Powerful
Wizard who could fix things for her. In journeying
to find him, Dorothy developed and experienced her
competence, so that ultimately she was able to understand that it was she who killed the Wicked
Witch, and it was her own power that would get her
home. Until she had experienced these things, however, she would have felt too powerless to proceed

except under the illusion that she was about to be rescued [Pearson, 1986, pp. 40–41].

Those who felt safe and loved in their families of origin are less likely to fruitlessly search for perfect teachers, lovers, or escape mechanisms. In fact, they may never disengage, emotionally or psychologically, from parents at all. Josselson's initial research (1973) applied Marcia's (1966) categories of identity formation to college women. The *Foreclosures* were preoccupied with security, which was founded in an intense and early attachment to one or the other parent. Unlike the *Moratoriums,* who left home "sometimes dramatically and always guiltily, in search of absolute rightness that eluded them," and the *Identity Achievements,* who "could rework their childhood selves in a comfortable way, defining a path for themselves that they felt they had truly chosen" (Josselson, 1987, p. 33), these women "represent a form of growth through identification rather than individuation. That is, they grow by taking in, ever more completely, aspects of their adored parents rather than through self-discovery and increasing differentiation" (p. 62). All of the Foreclosures had difficulty forming peer relationships. Many had parents who were distrustful of the outside world and who believed that only family could really be counted on. When a preoccupation with security blocks identification with peers or role models or links students with rescuer figures who reinforce dependence, autonomy can stall.

Parental support may continue through college and into graduate school, even if students are married. Finkelstein and Gaier (1983) assessed the impact of prolonged student status and economic dependence in late adolescence. They compared small groups of independent nonstudents and economically dependent male students at different ages and found that prolonged student status tends to foster emotional dependence, decelerate the progress of vocational identity formation, and have negative repercussions for the identification of "who one is" physically, morally, personally, and socially, even though overall level of self-esteem was not affected.

Emotional autonomy can be a challenge for older students

as well. Many adults who successfully run corporations and households can revert to nervous, passive learners when they return to school. At least their life experience may give them an edge in clarifying priorities and trusting their instincts.

> I took a job to teach after completing my degree. But I quit just before school started because I knew in my heart I really didn't want to teach. Instead of saying "I should do this because . . . " I chose to do this because it felt right from within. It was as if a huge weight of others' expectations had been lifted. I felt self-assured that I could find something to do that I wanted to do and that I could support myself in the process. [What helped?] Several teachers had affirmed me as a capable person with intelligence. My internal feeling was one of rightness strongly felt [student affairs staff member].

The shift from "should" to "want" and the reference to the kind of feeling-knowing from within typifies movement toward emotional independence. Whether young or old, people new to college tend to feel inadequate and need direction about how to function in the new system. Success in college requires freedom from fear — of not knowing what to do or where to go, of making a mistake, of being less than perfect. Many adults must also contend with family members or partners who are threatened by their return to school. By acknowledging their fears and proceeding in spite of them, students gradually replace anxiety with assurance.

Instrumental Independence

Instrumental independence has two major components: (1) the ability to carry out activities on one's own and to be self-sufficient, and (2) the ability to leave one place and function well in another. Emotional and instrumental independence are linked and mutually facilitating. This sophomore illustrates how increasing self-assurance enables him to work at home and elsewhere, without needing constant confirmation of his acceptability and without fear of being enmeshed at home:

> My family was very close, but before, I was always
> really afraid to voice opinions, to feel, you know,
> to show any true feelings that I had about things
> because I felt there was something wrong with it,
> for saying I don't want to do this or that. But now
> I feel that much more sure of myself that I think
> when I go home if a situation arises I can present
> myself in a fashion that will show them I am some-
> body who has given a lot of thought to things, and
> that I have my own things I want and that I want
> to try. I can still be part of their things, more or
> less. I could go and work for my father if I wanted
> to now and still not have to worry about being stuck
> for the rest of my life [sophomore].

Goldscheider and Davanzo (1986) use the term *semiauton-omy* to denote living separately from parents but not yet being established in a truly separate household with all its accompanying responsibilities. They refer to military service and residence hall living as typically transitional roles culminating in adulthood. Moore and Hotch (1983) identified steps in the leaving-home process for traditional-age students. These included personal control, economic independence, graduation, establishing one's own residence, physical separation, school affiliation, dissociation, and emotional separation. The data suggest that the most important indicator of parent-adolescent separation for these students is establishing personal control, which entails reducing parental control, assuming responsibility for their own decisions, feeling mature, and doing things for themselves.

Disengaging from parents can be hampered when insufficient opportunities exist to develop instrumental independence. Students may never learn to manage money, furnish an apartment, cook from scratch, or manage time if everything is dictated or provided. Colleges may leave instrumental independence out of the curriculum, offering instead only academic problems and theoretical discussions with no chance to experiment. If prescribed ways of solving problems are spelled out and advisers are always standing by to bail students out, there will be little incentive for taking initiative.

To survive at college, students need to grasp responsibility for planning and producing their own work in an orderly way.

> In my first year at the university, I learned that no one could do the job for me. I came from a small-town high school where I had lots of support and encouragement from teachers and family. All of a sudden, I was thrust into a university that was ten times the size of my hometown. The supportive group was no longer there, so I had to learn how to be my own support. The feelings that accompanied the change were despair and helplessness. I learned that if I didn't write the paper myself, it wouldn't get done. I learned not to procrastinate and to break tasks into manageable "chunks." I didn't actually realize that a change had occurred until I was in my second year. I noticed a change in my study habits and an improvement in my marks. My own persistence helped me go on. I couldn't give up since there was so much riding on my graduation [faculty member].

Students may be forced to develop good discipline and time management because they must hold jobs while attending college. White and Hood (1989) report on the use of the Developing Autonomy Inventory (DAI), which consists of ninety items and is composed of six subscales: Mobility, Time Management, Money Management, Interdependence, Emotional Independence–Peers, and Emotional Indepence–Parents. Using this inventory to assess a sample of 255 students at a large Midwestern university and 25 from two small Bible colleges, they found that students who held part-time jobs during college possessed a greater ability to manage their time and money than students who were not working. In addition, students who had strong time-management skills tended to have high grade-point averages and rated educational progress in college as substantial or exceptional (p. 258).

Instrumental autonomy increases as students of all ages gain intellectual competence. Harrison (1978) proposes teaching principles that can encourage self-directed learning. These include giving students the greatest possible choice at all points, reducing anxiety by providing a clearly articulated conceptual framework wherever possible and relating all the learning activities and resources to it, and supporting students up to the point where they can move ahead independently. Explicit norms — such as, "It is all right to initiate anything; it is all right to withdraw or withhold one's own energy and resources; the unexamined activity is not worth doing" (p. 162) — can also foster autonomy.

Some educators are becoming more adept at changing their methods as their students demonstrate greater autonomy, rather than applying one set of principles to all students. Brundage and MacKeracher (1980) suggest that all adults, when they enter a new learning experience, begin with dependent behaviors. But their four-stage model describes a progression toward instrumental autonomy from the perspective of the learning facilitator (pp. 54–55):

(1) *Entry stage.* The entry is triggered when learners enter a situation that presents a high degree of novelty, uncertainty, or unfamiliarity. It may entail personal stress or a perceived threat to the self. Students may become disoriented and interpersonally inhibited. They may defend themselves by using inappropriate behavior, act as an observer without making a commitment to participate, appear to be dependent or counterdependent, or communicate largely through monologue. Learners at this level tend to rely on external standards to guide behavior and to make assumptions based on past experience that may or may not be relevant. Support for students at this stage is best provided by creating a reliable environment, standardized and explicit behavioral norms, and clear consequences for behavior.

(2) *Reactive stage.* Learners move into the reactive stage when they perceive themselves as acting independently or when they perceive the environment as unreliable and unsupportive. They often express negative feelings, engage in conflicts and arguments with others, express the feeling that the group is disorganized and confused, and prefer to carry out individual activities within a group setting. Support is best provided by encouraging expressions of individual feelings and opinions and not demanding strict adherence to standardized behavioral norms.

(3) *Proactive stage.* When learners feel more confident about themselves as accepted and acceptable members of the group or actors within the situation, they discover and eventually accept the individuality of others involved. Learners tend to engage in fewer arguments and individual activities and to involve themselves in more cooperative, mutual activities and dialogues. They make attempts to understand others in relation to themselves and to develop shared norms. Support can best be offered in the form of encouraging collaborative behavior and giving descriptive and immediate feedback.

(4) *Integrative stage.* Learners integrate the others' perspectives with their own; they develop a balance between themselves and others and between working at group or individual tasks and maintaining relationships with others. They may also integrate perspectives that involve multiple standards of behavior, interpretations of experience, and sources of information. Support is best offered when teachers or others encourage students to develop internal standards, openly share information about themselves and their feelings and values, willingly act as colearners, and value both individual and group activities.

As students experience their critical thinking ability and find the courage to express their own thoughts, they discover a new part of the self, which can be "amazing," as this former adult student reports:

> The turning point in my life was making the decision to return to school. After completing one year at a community college, I realized that I could converse more freely with others than previously — that I finally had something to say. The old way of thinking was that my opinion didn't matter because I was a wife and mother with no formal education after high school. I learned to listen and to adopt the opinions of those around me. I went from that way of thinking to being able to say, "I disagree with you . . . " and offered another side to the conversation. I was amazed at myself when I did this and actually felt surprised and shocked each time

my brain went against my old way of thinking.
[What helped?] The important thing that helped
me was the supportive community college experience. They had mechanisms and people in place
to help older, returning and largely female students.
They had activities that combined young and older
students together. They had remedial programs
available, though I never had to take one. They
had convenient hours for registration, counseling
appointments, classes, and student activities. Just
as important were the students with whom I attended classes. They received support and passed
that support on to me. It was a chain reaction that
spread throughout the college community. It caused
a chain reaction in me to transfer to the university
for completion of my B.A. and to seek further education, to have career goals, life goals, and personal
goals [student affairs staff member].

Again we see the split between the developing part of the self,
which in her consciousness is not "I" but "my brain," and the
less developed way of thinking or feeling (that she had nothing
important to say). She is aware of the new pattern and, in observing the chain reaction, moves toward full ownership of her
increasing autonomy.

Learning to think objectively is another tool and an indicator of growing instrumental independence. This student acknowledges the value of professors' respect for her life experience and the caring environment provided by the university:

I had been an elementary school teacher for ten
years, and, moving to a new province, found that
my qualifications were not sufficient to work there.
I felt competent, although I was always trying to
improve; I did not feel a need to go back to the
university, but was forced to become a student
again. This changed my life and my thinking. A
whole new world of academia was opened to me

and my life has been a series of challenges and exciting experiences since then. I knew a change had
occurred when I found myself arguing objectively
(at least I thought I was objective) with others who
had only subjective viewpoints. At first I discounted
subjectivity. Now I realize its great importance.
And so the cycle continues! One professor in particular helped that process, although the entire program was organized to provide challenge and support. Each person in the class was respected. I felt
my ten years of experience were valued. I moved
from a focus on the young child to the new world
of secondary and postsecondary education. Knowing I had that support and open communication
enabled me to take that jump. Had I felt threatened, I think I would have remained in elementary education. Sharing, caring, and practical experiences were a major part of this program [faculty
member].

In finding the words to argue objectively, she frees herself from
the bounds of subjectivity, which she first devalues and then
reclaims. Perhaps another test would have been her ability to
disagree with authority figures as well as peers.

Instrumental independence involves literal mobility — the
ability to leave one place and get to another, to leave a bad situation and arrive safely at a better one. Erikson (1963, p. 11)
talks of *Wanderschaft*, of youth's "craving for locomotion . . .
expressed in a general 'being on the go,' 'tearing after something,'
or in running around." Comments from a graduate illustrate
this pattern:

I spent the summers of my junior and senior years
in France. The first summer I worked for the Uni-
tarian Service Committee and the second I attended
the University of Dijon. My work with the service
committee in the foothills of the Pyrenees did not
prohibit me from going to Biarritz to gamble on

weekends, and in six sojourns I won about $500 with a system for roulette. We had ten days to travel at the end of the summer and after about six I wound up in the casinos of Nice. The first night I won and the second I lost everything but my train ticket to Rotterdam and my boat ticket to Hoboken. Black came up fifteen times in a row and I ran out of capital. But I worked off my hotel bill, shared the nuts and cheese with some Italian peasants on the train to the boat, and hitchhiked from Hoboken to the loving wallets of my fraternity brothers at college.

Through these experiences I found I was happy and healthy, and indeed I enjoyed the challenges involved. And most important, I realized that with few beginning resources I could go to Hong Kong if I wished. And that was the way I thought of it at the time. I guess Hong Kong carried connotations of magic, romance, and faraway places. Somehow that realization carried great force [graduate].

Much of the aimless travel, the carelessness about advance planning, and the spontaneous arrangements for eating and sleeping provide the trial-and-error foundation for a growing capacity to travel confidently. Those of us who worry about students blithely setting off on some adventure, without much of an itinerary or the apparent sense to cope with unplanned difficulties, may need to step back and wish them well. When an individual cannot risk, cannot work alone, or cannot come and go as needed or desired, development of autonomy is limited. On the other hand, drifting and impulsivity, or travel experiences that become traumas instead of learning experiences, may postpone development. Josselson (1987, p. 164) reports that her subjects in the *Identity Diffusion* group remained like Pirandello characters, ready to move on a whim or act on impulse, but without the inner resources for determining whether the expression of the impulse makes sense for them or serves any real purpose.

Despite the new environment and the distancing from parents, younger students may remain stuck in their shyness, ensconced in their residence hall room or returning home every weekend. Students who travel across the country to college or take advantage of study abroad programs may blossom more rapidly. Returning adults also need to learn the ropes and understand how they fit into the new academic system. Gaining interpersonal competence can help them to meet new people, speak up in class, interact with faculty, and redefine relationships with family members.

Autonomy, the independence of maturity, is secure and stable. Students who have it display coping behaviors well coordinated to personal and social ends. They see parents for what they are, middle-aged persons neither omniscient nor omnipotent. Nettlesome feelings about parents are resolved sufficiently for a more adult-to-adult relationship to emerge. Reliance on peers, nonparental adults, and occupational and institutional reference groups fosters awareness of interconnectedness with others.

Interdependence

The recognition and acceptance of interdependence is the capstone of autonomy. It cannot be experienced until a measure of independence has been achieved and a sense of one's place in the community and global society has been awakened. One cannot move very far toward personal goals without bumping into other autonomous beings. With the growing knowledge that every action has an impact on others and that freedom must be bound by rules and responsibilities, individuals moving toward interdependence learn lessons about reciprocity, compromise, sacrifice, consensus, and commitment to the welfare of the larger community. The need to be independent and the longing for inclusion become better balanced, as does the sense of when to ask for help or go it alone. Grandiosity becomes tempered by reality. Hard lessons bring the acceptance of those things that cannot be changed. Interdependence means respecting the autonomy of others and looking for ways to give and take with an ever-expanding circle of friends.

A heightened appreciation of their own autonomy helps students to recognize others' needs for authenticity. Younger students may discover that parents cannot be dispensed with without continuing pain for all. In fact, parents can turn out to be welcoming ports in a storm. Freedman (1962), studying Vassar undergraduates and alumni, found that early rebellious independence, skepticism, and condemnation were replaced by more realistic evaluation and increased understanding and warmth. Perhaps Mark Twain provided the first self-report on this change. "When I was a boy of fourteen, my father was so ignorant I could hardly stand to have the old man around. But when I got to be twenty-one, I was astonished at how much he had learned in seven years" (Flesch, 1957, p. 195). Finding the courage to ask for needed assistance is also a mark of interdependence:

> In many cases, I have been nonassertive. Recently I had to ask my mother for tuition. She has always paid my sister's tuition, but I said I wanted to pay my own, only because I felt bad about taking money from my parents. Normally, I would have found a way to make ends meet, if it meant getting another job or whatever. I thought a lot about it and decided I would ask my mother for help. I would pay her back when my financial aid came in. She made me, I mean I made me feel bad about asking and I told her that if she couldn't afford it I'd understand, but if I ever needed her help, now was the time. I have always fought for my independence, so it was very hard for me to swallow my pride. I felt guilty and even a little ashamed that I had to ask for money. But I felt the need to say, "You've always helped my sister, and although I appreciate your letting me be independent, you shouldn't try to make me feel bad for needing help." This class — and the work we've been doing on assertive communication — was the vehicle for the shift. Before, I would have just shut down and not said a thing and hoped it would work itself out [junior].

This student was able to acknowledge her independence as well as her request for assistance, without being overwhelmed by guilt or self-condemnation. She weighs her decision, and as an adult negotiating with another adult, offers to pay her mother back. While the attempt at assertiveness is awkward, she invokes the principle of fairness and gives her mother notice that she will not be made to feel bad for making a reasonable request. Like many students, this one spirals back through the trials of managing emotions when unexpected barriers are encountered, but she has integrated enough interpersonal competence and felt sense of worth to carry on bravely.

Many students today are looking out primarily for themselves. Autonomy may be well developed, but sensitivity and patience lag behind. They may mask anxiety by appearing to be uninhibited or may spout off or act out, oblivious to the negative impact on others. Students may suffer from "entitlementarianism," demanding service, berating staff who do not deliver quickly enough, even threatening legal action. They may impose their wishes on less assertive peers or camp out in the offices of nonconfrontive advisers. Shy students may whisk on and off the campus, receding back into the back row of classes, becoming friends with no one. For students as well as others, development involves learning that nonassertive or aggressive behavior affects everyone around them. To reach their goals, they must learn courtesy, engagement, and cooperation.

College experiences that involve students in group decision making and learning communities help counteract these tendencies. Students willing to get involved in cocurricular activities have laboratories for learning about interdependence.

> I found a new, stimulating challenge before me in the form of a new [student] government and in the greater amount of independence granted to the student body. I took an active interest in writing our house plan, as I feel these small houses are an excellent opportunity for all of us to work constructively toward the particular goals we choose for ourselves. I honestly believe that it is up to each of us to perform consistently as conscientious, concerned

members of a community that is ours for the making; if we fail to assume our responsibilities, then
we have no right to demand the privileges of self-
government. By doing my share, I naturally expected others to do theirs, and consequently I saw
how very much of an interdependent community
we are, for if a few links gave way, the whole chain
collapsed [student].

Colleges can help students see that they are part of a larger
whole, that they cannot receive benefits from a social structure
without contributing to it, and that they cannot ride roughshod
over others without facing a judicial process. In the same way,
learning experiences that illuminate connections between past,
present, and future and between neighborhood, nation, and
planet can encourage students to feel the importance of their
own recycling habits, purchasing patterns, voting choices, and
travel plans. A mark of development is the ability to consciously
find a place in the larger whole and to preserve or enhance it
for the next inhabitants.

Growing awareness of world events, economic shifts, political upheavals, and unexpected crises reminds us of our limits
and heightens our appreciation of supportive relationships. As
Loevinger (1976, p. 23) says, "The Autonomous person . . .
typically recognizes the limitations to autonomy, that emotional
interdependence is inevitable. He will often cherish personal ties
as among his most precious values." As students mature, they
sharpen their identity and purpose through connections they
form with others. Growth occurs when relationships of reciprocal
respect and helpfulness are developed with parents and peers
and when mutually satisfying interrelationships are sustained
through vagaries of distance and disagreements. Strengths and
weaknesses in self and others are recognized. Conflict within
self and with others can be acknowledged and handled. Action
becomes focused and sustained. From a base of awareness and
inner harmony, students discover the gifts they can offer to the
world.

Going to college is a rite of passage. Some institutions
mark its significance with convocations that preview commence-

ment ceremonies. Those with higher degrees are set apart by ceremonial colors on their hoods and gowns, emblems of their successful passage through the trials and revelations of the curriculum. Success in college requires the growth of autonomy, which involves a transformation of self. Time in a community of scholars demands recognition of interdependence with those beside us, ahead of us, and behind us. Joseph Campbell (1988, p. 124) reminds us of the deep significance of this individualizing process:

> The spiritual sense of this adventure can be seen already anticipated in the puberty or initiation rituals of early tribal societies, through which a child is compelled to give up its childhood and become an adult — to die, you might say, to its infantile personality and psyche and come back as a responsible adult. This is a fundamental psychological transformation that everyone has to undergo. We are in childhood in a condition of dependency under someone's protection and supervision for some fourteen to twenty-one years — and if you're going on for your Ph.D., this may continue to perhaps thirty-five. You are in no way a self-responsible, free agent, but an obedient dependent, expecting and receiving punishments and rewards. To evolve out of this position of psychological immaturity to the courage of self-responsibility and assurance requires a death and a resurrection. That's the basic motif of the universal hero's journey — leaving one condition and finding the source of life to bring you forth into a richer or more mature condition.

Campbell saw the connection between the journey toward self-reliance and the return of the hero, transformed by trials and revelations, to revitalize the community. Learning to use strengths and act on values enriches the society. When students struggle to define their best selves, rather than succumbing to passivity or alienation, they fulfill their own potential and renew the world around them, one corner at a time.

FIVE

Developing Mature
Interpersonal
Relationships

"The paradoxical needs for self-assertion and union, with their accompanying dangers of isolation and annihilation, continue throughout the life cycle" (Josselson, 1987, p. 16). The ability to develop mature relationships involves rebalancing these needs for autonomy and attachment — moving from distance to closeness in some cases and from intimacy to separation in others. In college, students find a new constellation of potential friends and acquaintants. They discover people different from themselves as well as peers that share common experiences. Attractions can be passing or powerful and can lead to the rewards of enduring warmth or the sorrows of hurt and rejection.

Relationships are connections with others that have a profound impact on students' lives. Through them, students learn lessons about how to express and manage feelings, how to rethink first impressions, how to share on a deeper level, how to resolve differences, and how to make meaningful commitments. Students may already have developed some interpersonal skills and may have gained an awareness of the importance of interdependence. But success in building time-tested relationships that enhance growth and sustain us throughout life requires other kinds of skills and attitudes.

At the heart of this vector are the following components: (1) tolerance and appreciation of differences and (2) capacity for intimacy. Both require the ability to accept individuals for who they are, to appreciate and respect differences, and to empathize. Tolerance implies a willingness to suspend judgment, to refrain from condemnation, and to attempt to understand an unfamiliar or unsettling way of thinking or acting rather than to ignore, attack, or belittle it. Tolerance enables students to bridge gaps, to be objective, to transcend boundaries by gaining a clearer view of unknown customs and values, and to understand how labeling, stereotyping, or discrimination can diminish community. This broadening of awareness and experience leads to an appreciation of cultural diversity and a comfort with people from all walks of life.

Sensitivity to people from other cultures needs to move beyond intellectual understanding. One fearful resident speculated that a visiting student from Africa had been exposed to AIDS. Soon the rumor reached the visiting student, whose enthusiasm about studying in the United States quickly turned into shock and defensiveness. He got a blood test and publicized the results, trying to prove to his hallmates that he was not infected. But the gulf could not be bridged. The student's spirits fell, and he left for home. His hallmates needed more than tolerance, information, and objectivity. They needed the communication skills to initiate dialogue, the courage to challenge prejudice, and the commitment to reach across barriers created by unfamiliarity.

It is not easy to see persons as they are, to respond to them as individuals instead of as representatives of a stereotype. Nor is it easy to respond with warm, open, and respectful friendliness instead of with anxiety, defensiveness, or artificiality. White (1958) used the phrase "freeing interpersonal relationships" to describe one of his four major "growth trends" for young adults. "Social interaction becomes more free not only from neurotic trends but also from the impulsive inconsiderateness and egocentricity of youth" (p. 343). In his view, growth involves learning not to be so immersed in our own behavior or so intent on the impression we are making that we disregard the people around us. It involves developing the capacity to interact, to respond in a way that recognizes and honors the others' responses. "My" agenda then merges into "our" agenda. Developing mature relationships means not only freeing ourselves from narcissism, but also learning to choose healthy relationships and making lasting commitments based on honesty, sensitivity, and unconditional regard.

Increased capacity for intimacy involves a shift in the quality of relationships with partners and close friends. The shift away from too much dependence or too much dominance toward an interdependence between equals, with a larger space around each person and wider-ranging freedom of movement and behavior. People developing along this vector become more able to see partners clearly, with all their flaws and strengths, rather than distorting the view with rose-colored glasses. Unconditional regard pervades interaction, and the intrinsic rewards of being together keep the connections intact. Openness leads to greater candor, better communication, and more trust. Healthy intimacy — expressed in both sexual and nonsexual ways — provides nurturance for both parties. Movement along this vector also involves a growing ability to differentiate between relationships that are consistently nurturing, despite occasional difficulties, and those that are toxic and demeaning. Students become more selective, directing more energy toward relationships that provide enjoyment, companionship, and growth and backing away from those that do not. When partners become overcontrolling or overdependent, there is a will to confront the problem or back away. When this change has occurred, close feelings persist despite sharp disagreements. Stability and loyalty endure through crises, distance, and separation.

Pascarella and Terenzini (1991) reviewed research on the relationship between college attendance and interpersonal relations and on changes in authoritarianism, dogmatism, and/or ethnocentrism. They defined *ethnocentrism* as "an individual's tendency to view social interactions in terms of in-groups and out-groups, where in-groups are seen as dominant and perceptions of individuals' characteristics are determined on the basis of stereotypic positive or negative images of the groups to which they belong" (p. 218). They cited eighteen studies conducted between 1970 and 1988, some of which were large scale and nationally representative and others, smaller scale and based on a single institution. These studies found consistent increases in the maturity of students' interpersonal relations and in non-authoritarian thinking and tolerance for other people and their views (p. 257).

A number of researchers have used the Student Development Task and Lifestyle Inventory (SDTLI), which has a Mature Interpersonal Relations (MIR) scale. For example, Winston, Miller, and Prince (1987) used the SDTLI to study undergraduates at twenty colleges in the United States and Canada and found average increases of 22 percentile points. The scale assesses students' relationships with the opposite sex, mature relationships with peers, and tolerance (the capacity to respond to others as individuals rather than stereotypes). The SDTLI asks students to answer true-false questions about intimate relationships based on actual dating partners, spouses, or romantic relationships within the past twelve months. High scorers agree that they regularly discuss or make plans on how they will spend time together, frequently talk about what each is seeking from the relationship, know where they stand in the eyes of the partner, can resolve major disagreements, can tell their partner things they do not tell others, and are open about sexual needs and desires. The sense of equality and interdependence is indicated when students agree that they have helped a partner achieve a personal goal and that they see their partner's successes as their own. All of these are appropriate benchmarks for growing capacity for intimacy.

Other researchers have used the Social Extroversion scale of the Omnibus Personality Inventory to investigate students' social and interpersonal interactions. These studies generally found stability or slight declines in students' reporting that they sought out social activities and derived pleasure from being with people (Chickering, 1974b; Brawer, 1973; Hatch, 1970; Kuh, 1976; Yonge and Regan, 1975). If Social Extroversion is a personality preference, as literature on the Myers-Briggs Type Indicator suggests, we should not expect much change. Rather than representing a measure of approach or avoidance, Pascarella and Terenzini (1991, p. 223) speculate that a shift toward introversion may reflect "an increase in students' interpersonal maturity, in their selectivity of friends, and in increased intimacy with that smaller circle of close friends," which is consistent with our theory.

In reviewing research on changes in students' sociopolitical attitudes, values, and views about sex and gender roles, Pascarella and Terenzini (1991) again find consistent movement in the direction of humanitarianism, altruism, political tolerance, and liberalism. "Without exception, the nature and direction of the observed changes involve greater breadth, expansion, inclusiveness, complexity, and appreciation for the new and different. In *all* cases, the movement is toward greater individual freedom: artistic and cultural, intellectual, political, social, racial, educational, occupational, personal, and behavioral" (p. 326).

Another body of research and theory deals with gender differences as they affect capacity for intimacy and its relationship to autonomy and identity. Erikson stressed separation and individuation. Others said we must look at both sides of the process: both the autonomous part and the relating self. Miller (1976, p. 83) proposed that a "relational self" is central to women's development, since "women's sense of self becomes very much organized around being able to make and then to maintain affiliations and relationships."

Josselson's longitudinal study (1987) sheds light on the role of relationships in women's development. She found that the main function of the relationship for those she called the Foreclosures was the satisfaction of dependency needs. They looked to marriage for the security they assumed they could never find within themselves. They wanted to rely on the partner to provide love unconditionally and forever, taking care of the person as their parents did. She found that given a satisfactory partnership, such women did quite well, but she wondered how they would confront separation or widowhood, since the relationship was the internal foundation for existence. Those with more self-defined identities looked to relationships for self-validation and support. Feeling more whole and differentiated, they wanted to be cared about rather than cared for. They were more able to acknowledge and respond to their partners' individuality and to cope with change, take risks, experiment with their own capacities, and shape the relationship to meet their needs (pp. 180–181).

Josselson's description of mature relationships echoes the two components of this vector—tolerance of the other's uniqueness as well as a capacity for intimate sharing and reciprocity between two relatively autonomous individuals. Both topics will be discussed in more detail.

Tolerance and Appreciation of Differences

We can focus on two different arenas for developing tolerance, an intercultural and an interpersonal context. The basic mechanism is the willingness not to judge or condemn based on how others differ from us—not to leap to a negative interpretation of others' behavior based on ignorance. To increase tolerance means not simply to grit one's teeth and bite one's tongue in the company of those we disagree with, nor to use filtering devices to screen out contrasting values and behaviors that might threaten our own assumptions. If our need for safety is too great or the stereotypes too ingrained, bias prevails despite varied experiences and new information. Development involves reassessing assumptions about people we do not know. It means moving beyond initial disapproval or impetuous labeling to try to understand the basis for the difference, and even to appreciate how it is a contributing part of a larger whole.

Now that multicultural communities are growing, academic institutions have a responsibility to equip their graduates with tolerance and empathy as essential survival skills. Colleges and universities across the country have in fact recognized the increasing diversity of the population, both on campus and in the nation. They have acknowledged that the lives and contributions of women and non-Europeans have been underrepresented in the curriculum. Some faculty have tried to broaden the range of readings to include more women and minorities.

Others have added requirements of so many credits of non-Western or minority cultures. For example, the University of California at Berkeley is establishing an "American Cultures" course requirement. The College of Wooster has a freshman seminar entitled "Difference, Power, Discrimination: Perspectives on Race, Gender, Class, and Culture." "Taught by 35 professors in different sections, the course is meant to teach the campus's 480 freshmen to think and write critically, while introducing them to vexing questions about discrimination and inequality" (Heller, 1992, p. A33). Some critics rail against restructured curricula and added course requirements as an erosion of the hallowed foundation of higher education in Western civilization. Nevertheless, a growing majority agree that students have lived in the splendid isolation of their ethnocentric attitudes for too long. Colleges are beginning to challenge them to become citizens of the world and sensitive members of a unified, but multicultural society.

Bennett (1986) gives us one approach to describing the growth of intercultural tolerance. His developmental model describes movement from ethnocentric states, which involve stages of resistance to cultural diversity, to "ethnorelative" states. The focus is on how people experience cultural differences:

Ethnocentric States

I.   *Denial of Differences.* Cultural differences are not recognized, due to isolation or intentional separation. When "outsiders" are encountered, there is a tendency to dehumanize them. If their behavior differs from the norm, it may mean they are deficient in intelligence or personality, or the significance of the difference may be denied ("They have their ways, and we have ours"). Avoidance, segregation, and protection of one's own territory can produce defensiveness and feelings of fear and anger.

II. *Defense Against Differences.* Differences are acknowledged but disliked. The greater the difference, the more negative the evaluation. Negative stereotypes of the other group are presented as "the truth." Definitions of what is "good," "right," and "acceptable" do not include actions or feelings that people have not experienced, or if they have experienced them, these values or modes of behavior are simplistically categorized as inferior. In the evolutionary scheme, the observers' own group is at the apex. Therefore, there is a tendency toward social or cultural proselytizing of "underdeveloped" cultures. *Reversal* can occur, which is a tendency for people to see another culture as superior while denigrating their own.

III. *Minimization of Differences.* Rather than pointing out the differences between themselves and the diverse group, people focus on the many similarities we all share. The basis of commonality is defined in ethnocentric terms ("Everyone is essentially like *us*"). While noticing differences in dress, customs, ceremonies, and life in other countries, travelers still assume that all people are basically alike physiologically, all subordinate to a particular supernatural being, religion, or social philosophy and living in cities or towns that are "not very different from ours."

Ethnorelative States

IV. *Acceptance of Differences.* Rather than finding fault with those who are different, people accept and enjoy diversity. Interest grows in the underlying causes of the differences. Cultural relativism replaces dualistic thinking and cultural differences are seen as viable alternatives in organizing human existence rather than as superior or inferior.

V. *Adaptation to Differences.* Individuals develop communication skills that can enable intercultural communication and become more effective at using empathy, or frame-of-reference shifting, to understand and be understood across cultural boundaries.

VI. *Integration of Differences.* Bicultural or multicultural frames of reference become internalized. Identity becomes more "marginal" to any particular culture, or people may think of themselves or be thought of by others as "citizens" of many nations.

Increasing tolerance begins with identifying one's own biases and proceeds with a growing understanding of how stereotypes are created and perpetuated. Regardless of the particular subgroup they examine, students can learn tolerance by studying the dynamics of intolerance. For example, Rockland Community College has developed a course requirement called "Pluralism and Diversity in America." Interdisciplinary teams are participating in organized and individual professional development activities to create a shared developmental experience for all students. The goals of the course also shed light on components of intercultural tolerance [Wilder, Sherrier, and Berry, 1991, pp. 2–3]:

1. The students will demonstrate through papers, essays, group or individual projects, and class discussions their understanding of:
    a) The role of stereotypes in intergroup human relationships
    b) The impact on human behavior of communication and language
    c) The effects of the demographic changes that are taking place in the United States
    d) The necessity for Americans to take full advantage of the existing and growing diversity of this society
    e) The ways in which various aspects of culture (art, music, literature, media, performing arts, institutions) enrich our understanding of pluralism and diversity
2. The students will acquire and refine (through readings, class discussions, and experiential exercises of projects) and subsequently demonstrate on both objective and essay examinations their knowledge of:
    a) Definitions of the concepts of race, ethnicity, culture, acculturation, class heritage, gender, religion, minority group, and dominant group

b) Definitions of racism, sexism, prejudice, and discrimination

c) The processes through which discrimination develops

d) The principal demographic characteristics of the United States population

e) The major policies of the "dominant" group toward "minority" groups

f) The major responses of "minority" groups toward a "dominant" group

g) The values, beliefs, attitudes, and culturally-determined responses to basic life issues of the various groups that make up the United States population

In the absence of such structured learning experiences, students can find many campus opportunities to learn about cultures and social classes, especially when living arrangements or student activities foster positive contact. International student program coordinators can play a key role in arranging discussion groups among students from different countries or organizing exchange programs with other colleges. However, merely coming into contact with students from different cultures may not improve tolerance and empathy. For example, a colleague told of some American students who took a group of Japanese students to get ice cream. They were appalled when the Japanese students refrained from individually choosing from among the enticing array of flavors. Instead, they went into an extended huddle until they all agreed on vanilla. American students could not conceive of that way of thinking, even if they had acquired an intellectual awareness of the Asian value of consensus over individuality.

In the same way, students may observe persons with unusual idiosyncrasies, with unfamiliar disabilities, or with transient or more lasting emotional disturbances and have a heightened level of interpersonal intolerance as a result. The following exchange between an instructor and student is illustrative:

Student: I don't know if the administration knows about her and why they allow her to stay here if she is seriously disturbed. But she is not functioning too well, from what I observe.

Instructor: What do you observe?

Student: Well, I have her in one of my classes. She will come, and maybe for an hour in the beginning of [a three-hour class] she will sit and watch. If she says something, it takes her about five minutes to get up a sentence, and her voice is very weak. Most of the time people can't hear her anyway. At least she tries. She gets upset very easily. If there is any kind of disturbance or discussion with tension involved in it within the class, she will get up and leave. Sometimes she'll run out of class, and once the instructor had to go out and see what was wrong. . . . In the dining hall, . . . she sat with us at breakfast one morning and she just sat for about two minutes with the salt shaker in her hand, just holding it, looking at just nothing. I got really scared. You know, I mean, a person like that I don't know . . . what good is it doing her to be here?

Instructor: Are you afraid she would do something to you?

Student: No, not me. I just wonder what is wrong. Does she have some kind of mental condition? . . . I'm torn between feeling responsibility to help her and at the same time feeling that it isn't — not really wanting to do it, and I don't.

Instructor: You don't want to? Why?

Student: I just don't want to take the time.

Instructor: That's a good reason. I think one reason she has continued to be here is that it is hard

> to think of a better place for her to be. . . . I think
> you are right in observing that she is having diffi-
> culty functioning here and that she has things to
> deal with that make it difficult for her to operate. . . .
> There is about as much potential for her develop-
> ment here as there is anywhere else, and the col-
> lege should enable her continued presence long
> enough so that she has substantial opportunities to
> test the possibilities for her that reside here. Sec-
> ond, . . . her continuation should be enabled as
> long as there really isn't a drastic drain on the com-
> munity, as long as her presence doesn't severely
> hamper other students. I agree that it is, well, a
> burden in the sense that it is a kind of presence that
> other people would rather not have to deal with or
> respond to, just as other kinds of persons are a bur-
> den in quite a different way. Persons who may be
> much more disruptive, for example. At the same
> time, her presence is a kind of education for other
> people, and I would encourage most anyone to get
> to know her.

The instructor reframes the student's intolerant response by
affirming that the other student is worth getting to know. While
recognizing the validity of the wary advisee's ambivalence, he
helps her see the college as a positive environment and her presence as an educational contribution.

Little research has addressed the impact of relationships
on the development of broad-mindedness and identity. It seems
obvious that the experience of getting to know someone "different" as a human being and fellow student cannot help but loosen
rigid cultural stereotypes. The chance to interact with supervisors and faculty members who serve as role models for open-
mindedness, honesty, and appreciation of differences can help
reduce students' anxiety and challenge them to examine their
values. When the theory and practice of broad-mindedness converge, students shift from being frightened or judgmental to
acknowledging that different patterns of behavior can comple-

ment their own and add spice to the homogeneity, as this student reported:

> One of the many developmental turning points occurred for me during my experience as a resident director. This was my first job in which I supervised other people as well as being supervised myself. I gained two main things from this experience: (1) knowledge of my strengths and weaknesses, which helped me to develop confidence in my ability, and (2) a broader, more tolerant understanding of the ways in which people and organizations function. I moved from feeling insecure and uncertain (and often defensive) to feeling more self-assured and in control. I learned that I didn't have to be in control of everything, right about everything, and so on, but could consciously choose not to be "in charge" and defer to other people. [What helped?] My colleagues and direct supervisor helped my process of development. Some of my colleagues shared their insight and acted as role models, while others behaved as role models of a "less desirable" way of being. I learned by observing their struggles or discontent or mistakes. My supervisor was very influential in my development, . . . and I was challenged to develop areas that I had not used before in order to work effectively with him. We spent many frustrating hours, but I feel it was a very rewarding and rich experience [graduate student].

This student identifies three factors that fostered greater maturity: role models who shared their insights, the opportunity to observe firsthand the struggles of others, and the challenge to develop new ways to interact.

While a person can adopt an intellectually tolerant attitude toward others by simply refraining from judgment, empathy must be felt and must be grounded in what has already been experienced. White (1981, p. 161) says that "we can share, with a joy of our own, the joy of someone blessed by sudden good fortune. We can participate in the elation of a victor or in the happiness of someone whose life and work are prospering. We can be angry when a friend is angry at an injustice, and surely, as every child so painfully knows, we can be anxious when we sense that those around us are anxious. Very obvious is the distress we experience when another person gives evidence of acute distress. Cries of pain have an almost primitive power to upset us."

White calls empathy "the affective root of humanitarian concern" (p. 160). He recalls that Alfred Adler brought altruism back into psychological discourse, giving it the name *Gemeinschaftsgefühl,* or feeling for humankind, which he believed would naturally supplant self-interest and the urge toward superiority. Allport (1961, pp. 283–285) regards self-love as an inescapable part of our nature but says that "only self-extension is the earmark of maturity." He believes that we can extend the sense of self by valuing the interests or welfare of another person as highly as our own interests. This is the kind of empathy that generates caring, whether it is for a loved one or a stranger. College seems to help it along. Pascarella and Terenzini (1991, p. 277) cite twenty-five articles as "abundant and consistent" evidence that altruism, humanitarianism, and sense of civic responsibility increase during the college years. White (1981) says that empathy emerges early in life. If the mother is anxious, the infant tenses. If a nursery school chum gets bruised, fellow toddlers get sore. And

> during adolescence . . . there is often an abrupt expansion of empathy. The growth spurt in abstract thinking and generalization makes it possible at this point to project one's sympathies onto a global canvas. Parents may be startled to hear their children suddenly espousing, often with considerable information, the cause of an emerging third world nation or the rights of an oppressed minority. Parents may wonder what ideas the teachers are putting into their children's heads, but this underestimates what

the children's heads are now able to do for themselves. Allowing that the generalizations may be
hasty, we must still see them as a phase in the growth
of humanitarian concern [p. 162].

New friends, work experiences, and messages that altruism is
a duty can foster the growth of empathy. Students take up the
causes of new friends. They work in a new environment and
learn the problems of those who inhabit it. They watch parents
contribute to charities, volunteer their services, or extend a helping hand. Intrinsic rewards come from participating in volunteer efforts, political campaigns, fundraising drives, or cocurricular activities celebrating other cultures. Concrete information
about the living conditions of those less fortunate, the ways that
institutions can perpetuate sexism, racism, and classism, and
the histories of oppressed groups can feed the fire of commitment. Development is fostered by those who can help students
channel their anger effectively and work within the system, or
just outside of it, to replace dramatic but empty gestures with
substantive change. For many students, the pressure to just get
through the semester can preclude learning tolerance and empathy. Yet every student will need these qualities to succeed in
the world.

Developing empathy means going beyond the motions of
helping as an obligation, beyond giving in order to be liked by
others. It means acquiring the staying power to continue caring even when there is no quick fix, when there are irritating
opponents, and when the news media bombard us with problems too numerous to do anything about. "The decision to care,
even at the cost of self-sacrifice, is a choice . . . for life and against
despair. It also is the dominant spiritual lesson people have been
working on for thousands of years," as Pearson says (1986, p.
103). She notes that

We see this kind of ennobling sacrifice not only in
people who die to save others but also in those who
spend their whole lives helping them. I think of famous examples, such as Mother Teresa of India;

but I also think of the many people who take jobs
that in our society are not very rewarding in terms
of pay or chance for promotion, simply because they
care. They may be working in daycare facilities,
in homes for the aged, in community organizing,
or in many other places that make such a difference in the lives of people. Few may know who they
are, but they daily make the world a better place
to be in [p. 105].

Appropriate caring sharpens and defines the self, feels compatible with our identity, and is an outgrowth of who we are.

In *Civilization and Its Discontents* ([1930] 1961), Freud observed that people who are aware of the differences of others
and can be accepting of them have learned to control their aggressive instincts. The management of emotions like anger and
fear, together with the development of other kinds of interpersonal competence, seem to be prerequisites for moving beyond
intolerance. On some level, developing individuals have realized that aggression only escalates rather than reduces tensions
and threats. They have realized that separation of self from people who are different is neither possible nor desirable. They have
reached a level of maturity that places more emphasis on the
common good than on their own personal safety or superiority.
They have gained an ability not only to accept and respect differences, but to be interested in exploring them further and to value
the fact that those differences exist. In this way, the "social atom"
that constitutes the relational self expands outward to take in
not only the student's intimate partners, friends, colleagues, and
acquaintances, but also members of the larger community, the
country, and the world.

Capacity for Intimacy

Growing tolerance, empathy, and openness to people multiply
the possibilities for deep connections. Many alumni recall less
about the content of their college courses than about the vibrant
experiences with the people they met at college. Romantic inter-

ludes, shared adventures, and creative collaborations stay in our memory. Rewarding partnerships and long-term friendships formed between classes become lifetime treasures.

Erikson (1950) saw intimacy as the central developmental task for eighteen- to twenty-two-year-olds. Younger students, leaving behind the old roles in the family and community, can enter a kind of "psychosocial moratorium"—a condition of role suspension removed from the demands of parents and not yet restricted by the responsibilities of earning a living. For once, students can just be themselves rather than the banker's son or the doctor's daughter. Weathersby (1981) contends that most traditional-age college students start out at the conformist or self-aware stage of Loevinger's model of ego development. At the conformist stage, interpersonal style is dominated by a concern with belonging and by a tendency to try to be "nice" to everyone. As Weathersby says, "A student at the Conformist Stage would be concerned with appearances and social acceptability; would tend to think in stereotypes and clichés, particularly moralistic ones; would be concerned about conforming to external rules; and would behave with superficial niceness. Emotions would be described in undifferentiated terms that betray little introspection. Group differences would be perceived in terms of obvious external characteristics such as age, race, marital status, and nationality. There would be almost no sensitivity to individual differences" (p. 53).

With all parties on their best behavior, infatuation or idealization can occur. As they spend time together, students have more opportunity to share and explore. Acceptance, trust, and reciprocal caring may deepen their capacity for intimacy— "the willingness and ability to commit oneself to close affective relationships for their own sake" (Douvan, 1981, p. 191). Students develop mature intimacy when the relationship is valued for itself, when both persons can be whole and authentic, when love and loyalty allow for growth and experimentation. This form of relating is free of roles and game playing, free of normative judgments and power struggles.

Sustaining intimacy involves self-awareness, spontaneity, some measure of self-confidence, and ongoing work on support and communication. Douvan feels that higher education should encourage the capacity for intimacy for two reasons: "The ability to enter into and sustain such relationships is a major vehicle for increased self-understanding, in terms of one's motives, values, future plans and aspirations, and interpersonal style. These self-understandings have instrumental value on the job and in the home and the community. More importantly, such relationships are themselves major sources of satisfaction and fulfillment. Without them one's life is empty; without the capacity to sustain them one's life is filled with pain, frustration, or loneliness" (p. 192).

Students must usually deal with a variety of pitfalls in order to cultivate the capacity for intimacy. When the attraction is returned, infatuation can quickly lead to fusion, or at least longing for incessant contact and exclusivity. This heady obsession seems to recur no matter what a person's age is. Symbiosis flourishes to the point of needing to be literally "in touch" as much as possible. In some cases, it is almost as though the reality of one's own existence was in question as soon as the object of affection was out of sight. Schedules are arranged to permit maximum closeness. Other friends fade into the background. Sometimes classes and homework go by the wayside. Students may also fuse with a group, spend all their time hanging out together, and even take on the characteristics of the group, forgetting that they exist as separate beings.

Kegan (1982) described this fusion process in his model of the evolving self at stage 3, where the "interpersonal" self *is* its relationships. Rodgers (1990, p. 40) describes the developmental dilemmas here:

> For many students, nothing is as influential as the peer group, for "who they are" is defined by their relationships in these groups. Therefore, in a property damage situation in a residence hall, the self would rather help pay the damages than risk disapproval of the group by reporting the person actually responsible. . . . Students at Stage 3 cannot settle or resolve conflicts between different but im-

portant interpersonal relationships. For example, the peer group and parents may have different norms on the issue of drinking alcoholic beverages before being of legal age. The student may behave one way with peers and another way at home. In each case, the student behaves according to the norms of the group, even though they are inconsistent. If these two worlds come together, however, such students often report feeling sad, wounded, or incomplete, but not angry at their friends or parents. They may become depressed and express their depression as feeling lonely, deserted, betrayed, and strained. The tension behind the depression results from being both vulnerable to what peers and family think of them and yet feeling selfish and uncaring if they begin to put themselves and a new set of values first.

To increase emotional autonomy, students must shift identification from their relationships to their internal frames of reference—to their "institutional selves," which have a kind of ideology or rudimentary identity. Sometimes the only way to shift is to break off the relationship. Josselson (1987) found that the loss of a relationship brought about the most dramatic examples of growth and change in her sample of college women. For her interviewees, ending a partnership meant more than losing a loved person: "It is, more deeply, the loss of a precious fantasy, the belief that someone else will be there to perform psychological functions, to soothe distress, to structure time, to stabilize and to reassure, to make one feel worthwhile. Having to learn to take over these functions for oneself seems to be growth promoting for women. Here, growth refers to increased internalization, increased ability to stand alone, to set individual goals, to be aware of who one is" (p. 180). Josselson emphasized that it is not whether one has a partnership that is significant, but how the relationship is used for inner psychological functioning. Those women who were leading "fully interdependent lives" were in some cases more content and no less psychologically healthy than those who were unattached, but she found that by and large, they had done less exploration with the self and were less sharply defined as persons (p. 180).

Students moving along this vector may be continually reassessing their level of dependence and making adjustments to stop the fusion from returning.

> I became more and more aware that I had been "taking care" of my husband's business things— going through the messes and straightening them out. I found I did not feel good after these times.
>
> I stood back, allowed the messes to accumulate, and eventually he went through them himself. It took much longer, but I felt better! [What helped?] I had someone point out that I was doing this; I became aware that I was being codependent. While I did the work, I was angry at him. When he started doing the work, I felt better about him and myself [freshman].

This student needed a self strong enough to risk rejection and a clearer sense of the boundary between herself and her husband before she could establish a new level of equality with her partner. She was able to register her discomfort, stand back, and identify the limiting pattern. In so doing, she moved toward Kegan's interindividual stage (stage 5).

The relationship might have gone differently if the student had kept quiet about her discomfort and allowed resentment to build, or if she had tried to control the other's behavior with threats or punishments, as another student reports having done:

> My old way of thinking would have to be described as sexist and one-sided. I thought mostly about how I could change the actions of others. I had a belief in a fantasy lifestyle—if I lived a certain way, the person I loved would see things my way. And if they didn't change because I wanted them to, there

was something wrong with them. There was an incident where I was very angry and physical towards a loved one, and through legal intervention and a lot of reflection I was able to understand that people don't change other people. Each individual is responsible for his or her own life. I no longer demand things to be my way and have let go of suspicions and self-doubt about others and loved ones. They are what they are and I try to respect their choices [graduate student].

Capacity for intimacy also involves making oneself vulnerable. Greater self-disclosure is a risk. Making greater investments in the relationship produces anxiety. What if it does not work out? What if the other leaves me? What will my friends think? What if I do not live up to the other's expectations? What if he or she does not live up to mine? Relationships can trigger the subconscious tripwires of unexamined longings and expectations and activate ingrained parental or religious teachings or stored images from romance novels. It takes effort to unravel the real dynamics from the fears and fantasies. This student writes eloquently of the traps she discovered and the insights that came with personal growth work:

I think that, like most of us, I have spent time searching and hoping for the one "true love" to come riding in on a white steed and sweep me away. I have learned through experience, however, that love in its most real and true sense takes damn hard work and that it can be sweeter and more satisfying than the outer reaches of my imagination.

Love for me has been both an agony and an ecstasy. I never received the kind of love and support I wanted from my family. Consequently, my early attempts at relationships were often overly dependent and controlling in trying to fill the voids left by my family. My vision of love was that it could and would provide me with the self-esteem and wholeness that I was lacking and so deeply desired. I usually began relationships completely exuberant and totally enamored. Needless to say, the partners I selected never lived up to my expectations, no matter how hard I tried to make them. This process seemed to occur with friends as well as lovers. Either my own disillusionment caused me to leave the relationship or my forceful control resulted in pushing [people] away from me. I was so desperate in wanting to feel loved that when I got into a relationship, I thought if I didn't hold on tightly that love would slip away. In the end, I would be heartbroken because I felt I had tried so hard at making it work and was still unsuccessful in securing what I most desired.

I think my view of love was that it was some sort of commodity. Everyone wanted it, so there wasn't much to go around. If I didn't play the right games, I would never earn it and never experience it. I would guess that part of this thinking came from a fundamentalist Christian perspective that God loves you but only if you behave according to certain dictates prescribed by the church. Love was not free-flowing, infinitely abundant, and nonjudgmental, but was only appropriate when it adhered to strict measures laid down in advance by holy men. It also meant that if love failed, it must have been a sign from God that it was not meant to be. It was an easy escape hatch for ignoring my own failings and my own insecurities in the break-up process. Each time I would get on my knees and pray and cry and sometimes feel comforted and more often not. I continued to believe that if I just prayed long enough and hard enough, my obedience would be honored by being sent the right lover, to love forever.

Then one day when I was praying fervently, sobbing to the depths of my soul, and contemplating putting an end to my life, I stopped to listen first to the silence and then to my own small voice. That voice was telling me that I was looking for comfort and fulfillment in all the wrong places. It could not come from other people or from some external intervention. It had to come from myself. . . . This realization, combined with the incredible work I have done in therapy, has transformed my ability to give and receive love. Love for me now means complete acceptance of whoever that individual is right now. Including myself. That's very hard sometimes. It also means giving the respect and freedom to allow individuals to define for themselves who they are, what they want, when they want it, and how they're going to get it. Love means offering support without expectation of return. Love means accepting the ways an individual loves you back. And probably most important, love means working on your own unintegrated parts that get in your own way and that get in the way of others. It means finding a process of individual development that keeps you safe and continues to challenge you to move beyond [graduate student].

This report identifies steps that must be taken if development is to occur: (1) relinquishing the need to control and the need to depend on the other as the sole basis for one's happiness; (2) understanding the frames of reference that shape our assumptions—for example, that love has to be earned or expressed in some preordained way; (3) realizing that current friends and lovers are often sought out as antidotes for past hurts and therefore saddled with old baggage that does not belong to them; (4) building systematic self-examination into the process, so that we do not project our own unfinished business and outdated images onto the other or stifle them with our needs for constant reinforcement.

Capacity for intimacy rests on openness. Students must reveal themselves and see their partners clearly, imperfections and all. Unconditional regard can be blocked when students constantly compare others to a standard of perfection.

> My parents divorced recently. I had always pictured them as "perfect." This brought me to the realization that nobody is perfect, and this especially applies to me. I have started new friendships that are lasting, whereas in the past they didn't grow because I had always compared them to my parents. [What helped?] What is helping through this process is individual and group support and counseling sessions. These sessions are helping me take a look at myself, at what I can change in myself to become more comfortable with who I am. There are a lot of feelings affiliated with this change, but the most significant one is trust in myself [junior].

Comparison with parents may occur on a different level. Some students look for partners as unlike their parents as they can find but are surprised to find themselves acting out familiar dramas from earlier days. Unconsciously casting the partner in the role of the critical parent or all-knowing caretaker and oneself as the helpless victim or suffering martyr perpetuates inequality and game playing. Students can make important breakthroughs when they realize that they are acting out family or cultural scripts.

> The death of my first husband was the turning point. My old way of thinking was the image of Beaver Cleaver's mother, trying to be the perfect mother and dependent on Husband for that image. After going through the grief process, I enrolled at community college during the time that the women's rights movement started. I owe my independence to that time. I knew a change had occurred when I took my children to California to decide if we should live near my parents. After six weeks, we returned because I knew that I had changed from

being the dutiful daughter to being a responsible woman who happened to be a mother, too [junior].

Women face societal conditioning about deferring to the male partner, sometimes at the expense of their own selfhood. Many return to college as a result of some interpersonal upheaval, such as a divorce or the departure of the last child. Relationships that remain intact will also be affected as women take on new roles as students. Many experience a constant state of guilt and exhaustion in trying to balance their family's needs with their own. As Douvan (1981, p. 199) says,

> These women return to school seeking a new autonomy, and for the most part they find it — that is, they learn to test their own competence, to set their own intellectual and vocational goals, to pace their own efforts, and to take responsibility for their own intellectual work and products. They do these things, all in all, extraordinarily well. What they do not apparently grasp or learn nearly as well, judging from their guilt — is to make legitimate demands on others or to credit the interdependence of all human activity. And their failure to learn these lessons reflects directly on the educational system. We in higher education perpetuate the myth of total individual autonomy and rarely teach students the nature and significance of interdependence.

Friends can provide invaluable support and comfort by offering positive feedback and encouragement, as this student reports:

> As a teen and as a young woman, I tended to be a damsel in distress, a follower, a child looking for completion and validation from males. I did not lack strength or brains or ambition; I simply didn't recognize or believe I had these things. Better to marry well. I did marry early and, as is usually the case, with hasty actions. I did it poorly. That poor

choice was gradually clarified in a realistic definition of myself to myself. My thirtieth birthday
present to myself was to take control of my life, determine my own path, and set my own standards.
[What helped?] My friends (women) helped me by
recognizing my destructive dependency and by having the belief in me that I didn't have in myself.
The actual experience was the thirtieth birthday,
which I dreaded. I saw my life as a zero. I had no
clue where I was going. I prepared for that day with
much dialogue and introspection with the help of
my friends. Our motto became, "Men come and
go, but your girlfriends are always there" [gradu-
ate student].

Males may have more difficulty forming friendships, especially with other men. "Except in heterosexual friendships,
the male's competitive orientation tends to interfere with intimacy. Since all men are potential rivals, the exposure of vulnerability to another man carries the danger that that vulnerability will come back to haunt one — that the 'friend' may in some
future competitive situation call on and use it to his own advantage" (Douvan, 1981, p. 203). Closeness between males is
also discouraged by homophobia. Men are more likely than
women to equate warmth and closeness with sex and to look
for an erotic component when a strong emotional connection
exists.

Students may face diapproval if they feel attracted to
others who do not fit someone's norm. Intimacy with same-sex
partners or persons from different racial or ethnic groups, social classes, or religions can result in learning or trial by fire —
or perhaps both. While interracial dating is much more com-
monplace than it used to be and tolerance for gay and lesbian
relationships seems to be increasing, universal social acceptance
is not yet a fact. Incidents of gay bashing and racial attacks still
plague some campuses or their surrounding communities, where
conservative groups continue to mount adversarial campaigns.
Faced with the reality of attraction to someone their parents or

friends might not approve of, students must come to grips with whether to end the relationship, deny that it is happening, pursue it secretly, share it with a few trusted friends, or decide not to hide it from anyone. Defining one's sexual orientation may take years, as this former student reports:

> All my life I wanted to be happily married, preferably to a minister. When I met B. at the university, he fit the bill perfectly. We were very compatible, and soon we were engaged. It seems odd to look back on, but for several months while I was engaged, I was also involved with a woman. She was my dearest friend from childhood, and we connected on a very deep, emotional level, very different from the relationship with my fiancé. Hugging and holding her seemed very natural and comforting, and slowly the psychological intimacy grew to include physical expressions of love. I didn't question it, but I didn't talk about it either. It never occurred to me that it was a lesbian relationship. For me, the word was so negatively charged with terrible images that of course it did not apply to me. It took me many years to finally accept a recurring pattern of preferring intimacy with women, and even longer to begin letting close friends know that this was true [faculty member].

In this case, capacity for real intimacy was blocked, while superficial commitment to her fiancé was reinforced by fantasy, compatibility, and parental and societal approval. The more powerful bond was only partially acknowledged, and it was not until much later that she accepted the same-sex connection as a persistent orientation.

When physical intimacy enters the picture, whoever the partner may be, other tests of character arise. Sexual intimacy for today's students involves greater danger than ever before. Development in this area involves becoming informed about sexually transmitted diseases, safe sex, and ways to set clear boundaries. Information alone does not necessarily change behavior, as a number of studies have found. For example, Walters (1992) surveyed 180 undergraduates about their knowledge of AIDS and their sexual behavior. After receiving information on the nature of AIDS and its routes of transmission, 29 percent reported changing risky behaviors to safer ones. But 12 percent increased their risky behavior.

Growing capacity for intimacy involves responsibility, respect, and honesty. It is a challenge to put the brakes on the body's arousal process and consider consequences. It is not always easy to communicate what feels comfortable, to take precautions, or to get further information before proceeding with sexual intimacy. When the relationship is solid and consensual and based on equality and genuine caring, it becomes a springboard for further development as well as a source of deep fulfillment.

Students with increasing capacity for intimacy learn to balance time with friends, time alone, and time with a partner. Their relationships are reciprocal and interdependent, with high levels of trust, openness, and stability. Deriving great pleasure from shared activities, they enjoy spending time with partners and friends. They learn to anticipate the needs and preferences of those they care about, coming to know what surprises and delights their partner. They can be direct in confronting others about something they do not like and in resolving disagreements. They take responsibility for their own behavior rather than giving others too much power. They do not need to apologize constantly for their behavior or appearance, do not feel hemmed in by possessiveness, and do not succumb to jealousy about the partner's close friendships with others. But they will not stay in a toxic relationship indefinitely. They are willing to end it if it cannot be transformed. They take the initiative to make new friends, becoming more discriminating as they focus attention on relationships that nourish and enrich all aspects of the self. They extend themselves in order to maintain and honor existing friendships and continue to work on their own growth. In so doing, they bring their most authentic and integrated selves into communion with others.

SIX

Establishing
Identity

At one level of generalization, all the developmental vectors could be classified under "identity formation." Establishing identity certainly involves growing awareness of competencies, emotions and values, confidence in standing alone and bonding with others, and moving beyond intolerance toward openness and self-esteem. Erikson (1959, pp. 92–118) recognized all of these in describing adolescent identity formation:

> It is important to understand intolerance as the necessary defense against a sense of identity diffusion, which is unavoidable at a time of life when the body changes its proportions radically, when genital maturity floods body and imagination with all manner of drives, when intimacy with the other sex approaches, . . . and when life lies before one with a variety of conflicting possibilities and choices. . . . It is difficult to be tolerant if deep down you are not quite sure that you are a man (or a woman), that you will ever grow together again and be attractive, that you will be able to master your drives,

that you really know who you are, that you know
what you want to be, that you know what you look
like to others, and that you will know how to make
the right decisions without, once and for all, committing yourself to the wrong friend, sexual partner, leader, career. . . . Psychologically speaking,
a gradually accruing ego identity is the only safe-
guard against the anarchy of drives as well as the
autocracy of conscience. . . . An increasing sense
of identity, on the other hand, is experienced pre-
consciously as a sense of psychological well-being.
Its most obvious concomitants are a feeling of being at home in one's own body, a sense of "knowing where one is going," and an inner assuredness
of anticipated recognition from those who count.
Such a sense of identity, however, is never gained
nor maintained once and for all. Like a "good conscience," it is constantly lost and regained, although
more lasting and economical methods of maintenance and restoration are evolved and fortified in
late adolescence.

As we noted in Chapter One, Erikson believed in a blueprint that dictated a sequence of development for the ego's components. His epigenetic principle suggests that the life cycle has
a universal sequence of challenges or crises, and as each is resolved, we gain another form of ego strength (trust, initiative,
industriousness, intimacy, and so on). However, he warned social scientists not to think of these crises as "resolved" once and
for all. He knew that the hazards of existence force a continual
process of integration and that we struggle, progress, and regress
in trying to maintain equilibrium. He suggested the term *favorable ratio* — for example, of basic trust over basic mistrust. Enough
of the key tasks will hopefully be achieved at the critical life stages
so that when we experience setbacks, we have a reservoir of skill
and knowledge that tides us over until we can rebound.

Some researchers have tried to operationalize Erikson's
concept of ego identity (Bourne, 1978a, 1978b). James Marcia's

approach has been one of the most widely used. Others have focused on Loevinger's ego development theory and on studies of self-esteem and gender roles. Marcia (1966, 1976) built on Erikson's proposition that the definition of identity was the most important goal of adolescence. He saw it as consisting of two psychosocial tasks. The first is the experience of a "crisis" or turning point characterized by the potential to go either forward or backward in one's development. Competing alternatives also had to be present. Like Erikson, Marcia did not view a crisis as a physical or psychological emergency, but as a stimulus (or challenge); the nature of the response to the challenge determines the direction of development. The second task is "commitment," or making choices about occupation, religious or spiritual direction, and political and sexual values. According to Prager (1986), crisis leads to differentiation and individualization, while commitment is assumed to result in stability, continuity, and comfort. Marcia (1966) proposed four styles of coping with this identity resolution process:

Identity-diffused: No identity crisis has been experienced, and no commitments have been made consciously to any particular career directions or belief systems. Like students in Perry's multiplistic stage, all positions are seen as more or less equal.

Foreclosed: No identity crisis has been experienced, but commitments have been made; these tend to conform to parents' values or conventional social norms without much question or examination.

Moratorium: A conscious search is underway, but not all the alternatives have as yet been understood or evaluated.

Identity-achieved. The crisis has been endured, and meaningful commitments have been independently made.

Pascarella and Terenzini (1991) cite fourteen studies based on Marcia's model, including cross-sectional designs and short- and long-term longitudinal designs. With one exception, research supports shifts toward identity resolution and achievement during varying periods of college attendance (p. 164). Estimates of the magnitude of the change vary widely across studies, with the effects of colleges being greatest in the vocational area. Twenty other studies, many of which have been based on Erikson's model, have produced consistent evidence of student development in positive directions (p. 165). For example, Constantinople (1969) conducted a cross-sectional and longitudinal study of 952 students over four years at the University of Rochester, using a measure of Erikson's fourth, fifth, and sixth stages of psychosocial development (industry versus inferiority, identity versus identity diffusion, and intimacy versus isolation). Significant increases in the successful resolution of identity issues occurred from the freshman through the senior year.

Josselson (1987) used Marcia's theory in her longitudinal study of identity formation in college women. She noted that Marcia explored college students' crises and commitments by looking at occupational choices and religious and political ideology, as Erikson suggested. After interviewing college students, Marcia and his co-workers found that they could divide subjects into the four identity categories fairly reliably, especially with male subjects. Schenkel and Marcia (1972) added sexual values and standards as another arena for crisis resolution, and in so doing, got the same level of reliability in categorizing women, for whom identity decisions regarding religion and sexual values were more predictive of overall identity status than were decisions about occupation or political ideology (Josselson, 1987, p. 32). Josselson's interviews confirmed this difference in focus.

> Among the women whose lives we have considered here, the watershed issues of identity tend not to be political or occupational, but social and religious. They internalize the central priorities of their mothers as the issues to feel the same or different about. As college-age, late adolescents, these women judge their distance from their families by whether and how much they carry on family religious traditions, whom they choose as friends, what sexual values they adopt, how they dress, whether and when and whom they plan to marry. These are the pivotal points of negotiation in the separation-individuation drama [p. 172].

Josselson uses the term *anchoring* as a metaphor for the connecting processes that counterbalance separation. In her subjects, anchoring could be seen in four areas: primary family, husband/children, career, or friends (p. 175). Those who anchored in their primary families (the Foreclosures) found meaning and satisfaction in carrying on traditions that brought them security and comfort as children. They chose partners based on their likelihood of fitting in to the primary family. Others formed new families and found partners who supported their talents and interests. Work was of secondary importance for these women. "The relational web, with their new family as the center, is the anchor" (p. 176), and they were deeply involved in pursuing avocational interests, taking part in crafts and sports, redecorating their houses, developing couple friendships, and facilitating their children's growth. A third group anchored in productive work in a nondomestic sphere. Those who defined themselves in this way typically had mentors who took a personal interest in their careers, as well as significant others who also validated the importance of their work. A few chose to anchor in friendships, but this was done only when other anchor points had been rejected or were unattainable.

"Identity is an amalgamation of these anchor points," says Josselson (p. 178). While recognizing that each person's process of identity formation is unique, she sees one major difference between the groups as college seniors—how they came to feel about themselves: "The history of both positive/rewarding and negative/punishing transactions with others becomes internalized and later structuralized as the superego. The child, until adolescence, has an inner agent of the parents determining when she is good and when she is bad. The developmental problem of adolescence is to shift the inner psychological balance so that the superego has less power and the ego—the reality principle— has more" (p. 187). Josselson reports that the Foreclosures in her study had harmonious, gratifying relationships with their families and got lots of praise for being "good girls." The Identity Achievements apparently did not submit as willingly to superego messages, valuing competence for its own sake rather than for the approval it earned from others. They also had more tolerance for the anxiety and guilt that occurred when they did not meet their own or others' standards. The Moratoriums tended to swing back and forth between trying to please an approving superego and battling it or denying its existence, and the Diffusions, "lacking the building blocks that the other statuses are trying to rearrange. . . . are questing for parts of the self that they failed to develop at earlier times of their lives" (p. 188).

Loevinger (1976) sees ego development as a more global process that includes changes in impulse control, character development, interpersonal style, conscious preoccupations, and cognitive style, as part of a unified but dynamic whole. A number of studies have used Loevinger's sentence completion tests to measure movement from the conformist stage to the conscientious stage, through the self-aware level. Movement through the stages is away from conformity to group norms and societal rules, toward greater self-awareness as alternatives are recognized, toward complex reasoning, and toward a growing sense of responsibility to internalized standards.

Research on ego development has produced mixed results. For example, Redmore's (1983) four-and-one-half-year study of fifty-seven pharmacy students found a significant increase in ego development, but it was primarily among the men in the sample; women's scores did not change over the period of the study. In a second study in the same report, Redmore also found a statistically significant increase in ego development over four years among forty students in psychology classes at two community colleges. Adams and Fitch (1982), using a cross-sectional sample of freshmen, sophomores, and juniors, found that 22 percent of their students showed gains in ego development one year later, 17 percent regressed, and the majority (61.4 percent) showed no change over the year. After analyzing over twenty-five studies, Pascarella and Terenzini (1991, p. 170) conclude that "there is insufficient evidence to indicate reliable gains in ego development during the college years." They speculate that since Loevinger's model is more global than Marcia's, perhaps it is attempting to describe psychosocial structures that are more resistant to change, or it may also be that "the relative stability of ego status is a function of attenuated variance in the measures currently in use."

A third element of identity, self-esteem, refers to people's overall level of satisfaction with themselves, based on how the "real" self stacks up against an "ideal" self. Coopersmith (1967) defines self-esteem as the evaluation of self that individuals make and customarily maintain. It expresses an attitude of approval or disapproval and indicates how much people judge themselves to be capable, significant, successful, and worthy (pp. 4–5). It differs from self-concept, which, like the sense of competence referred to in Chapter Two, involves people's comparison of their performance with that of others. As Pascarella and Terenzini (1991, p. 175) say,

> In contrast to studies of change in students' academic and social self-concepts (studies that typically ask students to compare themselves with other students), studies of self-esteem examine students' generalized judgments of their own worth or merit, evaluated not in terms of their position relative to others but with reference to an internal, personal standard. While studies of changes in students' self-esteem adopt various measurement schemes, an individual with high self-esteem is typically characterized as having feelings of worth, being able to do things as well as others, having a number of good qualities, having much to be proud of, having a positive attitude toward oneself, feeling useful to others, feeling self-confident, and being satisfied with oneself.

Citing eight studies of self-esteem in college students, which relied on nationally representative samples and applied sophisticated analytical techniques, Pascarella and Terenzini conclude that the studies consistently indicate increases in students' self-esteem during the college years.

Pascarella and Terenzini also cite Wylie's (1979) comprehensive and rigorous review of the developmental literature on *self-regard* (a term she uses interchangeably with *self-concept*), which clearly suggests that changes in self-esteem are not related to age (p. 182). They add that

Some evidence does indicate that the "search for identity" is a far more common practice among college students than among similarly aged young people or in the general population. Moreover, it appears to be a process common across institutions. No differences were found in the rate of "questing" among students at the University of California, Los Angeles, and one British and two Australian universities . . . . It is worth remembering, however, that if identity development is defined as the simultaneous achievement of an identity in the occupational, religious, political, and sexual realms, then it remains a relatively infrequent occurrence during the traditional college years [p. 183].

In conclusion, Pascarella and Terenzini lament the tendency of researchers in this area to focus on the structural characteristics of identity and ego development, noting that "few studies have examined the processes of such development, and even fewer analyze characteristics of the higher educational setting that might be related to identity or ego development change" (p. 189). Reviewing studies of ego development within majors and the effects of participation in experimental learning programs on ego development, they say: "These studies present such different findings, vary so widely in their designs and samples, leave so many relevant variables uncontrolled, and make up such a tiny body of literature that one can conclude only that nothing is yet known about the effects (if any) of academic curriculum or major on identity or ego stage development during the college years." However, they cite several studies indicating that the people — faculty and peers — with whom students come into contact play an important role in changes in identity and ego development during college, with peers having a greater impact than anyone else. "These studies suggest that it is the diversity of individuals (particularly other students) that developmentally challenges students' conceptions of themselves and that requires adaptation and commitment to certain attitudes, values, beliefs, and actions" (pp. 189–190).

Based on theory and research, we could conceptualize identity development primarily as resolving crises. By facing them and making their commitments, young adults build a strong ego and gain high self-esteem; periodic reconstruction occurs throughout adulthood. But that frame of reference is no small umbrella; it covers a multitude of diverse events and activities. Such inclusiveness makes its application difficult when concrete decisions must be made concerning curriculum, student services, student-faculty relationships, and other matters of educational policy and practice. It also makes it difficult to see some less global components of growth. This is why the other six vectors were carved out for more discrete treatment.

With identity thus broken down, what remains? The primary element is that solid sense of self, that inner feeling of mastery and ownership that takes shape as the developmental tasks for competence, emotions, autonomy, and relationships are undertaken with some success, and that, as it becomes firmer, provides a framework for purpose and integrity, as well as for more progress along the other vectors. Erikson (1959, p. 89) calls it "a sense of ego identity"—the accrued confidence that one can maintain inner sameness and continuity. It is that "fuller, richer establishment, compounded of bodily sensations, feelings, images of one's body, the sound of one's name, the continuity of one's memories, and an increasing number of social judgments delivered through the words and behavior of others" (White, 1958, p. 332).

Josselson (1987, pp. 12–13) describes identity as "a dynamic fitting together of parts of the personality with the realities of the social world so that a person has a sense both of internal coherence and meaningful relatedness to the real world." We propose that one way to view the components of this solid sense of self is to focus on the following attributes: (1) comfort with body and appearance, (2) comfort with gender and sexual orientation, (3) sense of self in a social, historical, and cultural context, (4) clarification of self-concept through roles and life-styles, (5) sense of self in response to feedback from valued others, (6) self-acceptance and self-esteem, and (7) personal stability and integration. While other theories also stress vocational and ideological commitments, we will address these two dimensions in Chapters Seven and Eight.

Identity establishment then becomes grounded in answers to the following critical questions that correspond to the components just listed:

1. How comfortable am I with my physical being and my appearance?
2. How comfortable am I being a male or a female? How do I feel and express what is culturally defined as "masculine" and "feminine"? What is my persistent pattern of sexual attraction (sexual orientation)?
3. Where do I come from? Who are my people? What were their values and traditions? What have they passed on to me? How do I feel about my family of origin and my ethnic heritage? Do I define myself as a part of a family group, a racial group, a religious tradition? How do I define myself as a member of a specific culture among many cultures? How do I define myself within a social and historical context?
4. What roles best fit my sense of self—at work, at play, at home? What roles are genuine expressions or extensions of myself, helping me to define more sharply who I am? What kind of life-style do I feel comfortable with?
5. How do others see me? Am I accepted and valued by others? How do I deal with feedback? Do I usually anticipate positive recognition from others who count or expect disapproval or nonrecognition?
6. How much do I accept and value myself—my competence, emotional health, relationships, and thought processes?
7. How stable and clear am I about who I am and what is important? How accurately do I see my strengths, preferences, and limitations? Am I confident that I can stay on course and weather the storms of life?

We will briefly discuss each of the components listed earlier, with special attention to new models of identity development for homosexual and minority students. We will then return to the intriguing question of how to conceptualize the self in a way that organizes these components into an identity.

Comfort with Body and Appearance

Adolescence inevitably brings increased attention to the body, and self-consciousness is heightened when students arrive at college. Younger students who are already in good physical condition may become fitter, especially if they are involved in athletics, take physical education courses, or use the track, swimming pool, or weight room. Some institutions have initiated wellness and preventive health care programs, declared themselves smoke-free campuses, or organized on-site assessment programs for cholesterol levels, alcoholism, HIV, and other health problems. College apparently has a salutary effect on physical health. Pascarella and Terenzini (1991, pp. 541–543) cite numerous studies indicating that the more extensive people's college education is, the less likely they are to smoke and the likelier they are to use health services and to be healthier and live longer.

While the campus may provide an environment conducive to maintaining health and fitness, many students do not take advantage of it. They overeat, encouraged by dining halls with unlimited helpings, or skip meals because their class schedules do not coincide with cafeteria hours. Some struggle with eating disorders, alcohol and drug abuse, too little sleep, or too much junk food. Students who do not feel healthy and attractive may find themselves in a downward spiral of diminishing self-esteem unless they lose weight, build muscle, or accept a less-than-perfect body. While complete satisfaction with looks is rare, an important component of a positive identity is a friendly attitude toward one's body and an ability to take care of it. Constant self-criticism and self-consciousness breeds inner turmoil that ties up energy and blocks development.

Appearance also becomes a matter for conscious concern and decision. Some students aim to enhance strong points with careful dress, and to modify, compensate for, or at least disguise weak ones. While the sense of self is unclear, presentation of self remains an issue. Some superficial comfort may come from dressing according to others' tastes or images. Other students may stick to their own style on principle, especially if they have achieved some measure of autonomy. Still others may view college as a time to adopt a new style. They realize that the move from work or home to the college environment allows them to make some change in their appearance. Students with a limited income may find it a struggle to create a new wardrobe, especially when job interviews require a professional appearance or when new relationships offer a night on the town.

College provides an incentive to experiment, a host of new people for comparison, and a supportive environment for improving health and appearance. Development comes with increasing awareness of one's body as a vehicle for expression and enjoyment, and the realization that despite its limitations, the physical body in which one resides is the only one available as a vehicle for living and must be accepted and nurtured.

Comfort with Gender and Sexual Orientation

Issues of sexual identification interact with concerns for bodily appearance and self-presentation. Exploring what it means to be a man or a woman and coming to terms with the styles and roles appropriate for each is an absorbing and complex task, especially in this society, where gender-role stereotyping has constrained behavior. There is more freedom now than in earlier times to explore styles of dress and ways of behaving. Androgynous figures appear more often in movies and concert halls. Students are exposed to a broader array of images, roles, and relationships for men and women than ever before.

Some students may be uncomfortable with their biological gender because they have been conditioned to believe that biology is destiny, and certain social or occupational roles are automatically prescribed by male or female reproductive systems. Colleges and universities may help students feel comfortable with their gender by exerting a liberalizing effect on gender-role attitudes and values. Numerous studies have been done on changing attitudes toward women. With few exceptions, the studies conclude that students become increasingly more egalitarian in their views of gender roles, educational and occupational opportunities, and distribution of responsibilities in marriage and family relations (Pascarella and Terenzini, 1991, pp. 282–283). Furthermore, education seems to have a more pronounced effect on those views than do age, race, husband's income, religion, marital status, work history, age at marriage, or other variables (p. 294).

Courses that focus directly on gender roles, stereotyping, and equal opportunity issues can foster reexamination of values. When a class was asked to write about their earlier images of males and females, one student wrote:

> The very subtle, very unconscious message I got about playing the female part was based on my mother's and sister's models. From my mother I learned that women are the stronger, more socially skilled, more competent half of a marriage but that they always defer to the husband. On one level, my mother was very confident and outgoing and could juggle six thousand things at once, but at the same time, her identity and needs always came second to Dad's. Not unusual for that generation, I suppose, and definitely how I thought men and women throughout the universe interacted. From my sister . . . I learned that women are sweet and sensitive and kind and full of selfless, nurturant love for all living things [graduate student].

This student associates a number of positive qualities with being a female — strength, competence, generosity, nurturance, confidence, and sociability. She may look to other female role models and add more valuable attributes. She also implies a knowing that bonding with a male partner need not mean subordinating her needs or identity to his.

Despite the opening up of options for both genders, some students may be uncomfortable with their biological gender because they identify psychologically or emotionally with the opposite gender. Some may eventually get sex-change operations in order to match their perceived gender with a male or female body. As research produces more insights about hormonal dynamics, brain structure, and prenatal experiences that influence feminine and masculine patterns of behavior, greater understanding of gender identity formation will follow.

Comfort with one's gender is different from comfort with one's sexual orientation. Gender does not necessarily dictate to whom one is attracted. Students discovering an attraction to the same sex face an additional developmental challenge—dealing with the stigma of "abnormality." Yet the American Psychological Association has removed homosexuality from the *Diagnostic and Statistical Manual of Mental Disorders* and added a new category—ego-dystonic homosexuality disorder—for individuals who *themselves* reject their sexual inclinations and wish to become exclusively heterosexual (Bootzin and Acocella, 1988).

The proportion of college students who are gay, lesbian, and bisexual is as unclear as is the percentage of the larger population. Recent research has called into question the findings of Kinsey, Pomeroy, and Martin (1953) that 10 percent of men between sixteen and fifty-five are more or less exclusively homosexual for periods of up to three years. Data from France, Britain, Canada, Norway, and Denmark, as well as surveys conducted by the Battelle Human Affairs Research Centers and the University of Chicago, indicate a range of 1 percent to 4 percent (Painton, 1993). According to Hyde (1986), perhaps 25 percent of men and 15 percent of women have had some homosexual experience.

Whatever the numbers, students face discrimination, harassment, and rejection if they experiment. As many as 30 percent of the teenagers who eventually commit suicide identify themselves as gay or lesbian, according to a study by the National Institute of Mental Health (Adams, 1989). For heterosexual students, college may provide the first exposure to openly gay individuals and with it, the chance to further entrench stereotypes or to develop new tolerance and respect.

Evans and Levine (1990) have reviewed several models

of gay identity development, including focus on increasing acceptance of the label and involvement with the gay community; or focus on "coming out" and the progression from self-acknowledgment to identifying oneself as gay to an expanding circle of people. Other researchers have studied differences in identity formation for males and females. Marmor (1980), for example, found that the experiences of lesbians are more similar to those of heterosexual women than they are to those of gay men. Marmor and other researchers found that (1) women tend to develop a lesbian identity later than men develop a gay identity, (2) women tend to develop a lesbian identity before becoming sexually active, (3) emotional attachment is more important to women than sexual activity, (4) women seem to be less threatened by homosexuality than men, and (5) sexuality tends to be more contextual, relational, and fluid for women than for men.

Cass (1979) has developed a model of sexual identity formation that, like Marcia's, appears to involve a linear, stage-based approach:

Stage 1: Identity Confusion. The person becomes aware of thoughts, feelings, or behaviors that could be homosexual in nature. Self-disclosure is rare, and self-questioning occurs. If the person has positive feelings about the desirability and meaning of the behavior, movement to Stage 2 occurs.

Stage 2: Identity Comparison. As self-perceptions are reconciled with behavior, conflict with others' perceptions of the self increases and social alienation must be dealt with. Negative experiences may lead to foreclosure and self-hatred. Positive experiences may increase contact with homosexual others, while a public image of heterosexuality is maintained.

Stage 3: Identity Tolerance. Increasing tolerance of one's private self-image, and empowerment based on contact with the gay community, lead to conflict about one's public image.

Stage 4: Identity Acceptance. Contacts with the gay or lesbian community tend to validate individual homosexual identity. Selective disclosure increases with heterosexual others. This stage may become a comfortable place to stay, or if the incongruence remains high, the conflict may push them into stage 5.

Stage 5: Identity Pride. Because there is a conflict between self-perceptions and others' perceptions, individuals at this stage become angry with heterosexual society. This may cause a narrowing of contacts to those with a shared sexual orientation, and a devaluing of the heterosexual mainstream. Negative responses from heterosexual others can entrench the alienation, while positive responses challenge this view.

Stage 6: Identity Synthesis. The frustration of stage 5 recedes, and the individual finds that values may be shared with both homosexual and heterosexual others. Incongruence declines, and sexuality becomes one part of the total identity, rather than the main determinant.

As Evans and Levine (1990, pp. 53–54) point out, progression through these stages may not be so linear in real life. Yet they feel that Cass's work provides the most comprehensive overview of the homosexual identity development process to date. As with heterosexual or bisexual individuals, development proceeds through awareness, exploration, and acceptance.

Sense of Self in a Social, Historical, and Cultural Context

Whereas it may be possible to conceal one's sexual preference, students of color are bringing more visible heterogeneity to America's campuses. While every student's self-definition is shaped by genetic predispositions, family norms, cultural traditions, and experiences as a member of a majority or minority ethnic group, little research has been done on minority student development. How is the identity of an African-American student affected by the legacy of racism? How does a Native American student balance membership in the life of the tribe, where he or she may literally have a different name and a different perspective on time, nature, and the American Way, with life in a campus population of predominantly middle-class white students? Which reference group does an Asian American student identify with—parents who may value conformity, humility, obligation, and emotional restraint, or peers who value individuality, autonomy, and expressiveness? How do traditional Hispanic norms about community, religion, family, and gender roles affect students' evolving sense of self?

One Mexican-American student reflects on her family history as context for her own identity development:

> My parents were both born and raised in a small farm village in Mexico. My father came from a family of eleven children. They lived in "town" and were the "men" of the village. They were all boys. My mother lived on a farm with her four sisters and five brothers. She never went to school past the third grade. Her father was killed when she was thirteen years old, so her mother needed all their help to run the farm. My father's family was a completely patriarchal family. The boys basically could do whatever they chose to. Each one of them had their own horse to show off in the village (there were no automobiles there). My mother's family was probably the same until her father was killed. My grandmother never remarried and was in control of her family.
>
> One day, my dad, who was about seventeen years old at the time, was riding his horse to the train station. He saw my mother, who was eleven years old, and saw how beautiful she was and at that point decided he was going to marry her someday. About three years later, my dad decided that he could not live with his father and brothers any longer. They were all basically alcoholics and promiscuous. My father came to the United States illegally to work in California, Texas, and even Michigan. Somehow he ended up in Walla Walla, Washington. There he met a really good Christian farmer who befriended him and opened his home to him. He got his papers together and became a legal resident.
>
> He returned to Mexico at twenty-four and courted my mother for about a month, and they were married. He set out to come back to the United

States and work so he could bring his new family up legally. Several years later, he brought his wife and three children up to Washington. My parents realized then how difficult it was to raise children with such a low income. They both worked — my father at a lumber mill and my mother as a laborer in a factory. Basically, we were very poor. My parents never took government help even though they were eligible. They set out to do it alone. . . .

When I began a Head Start program, my mom would always make sure I looked really nice. She would take time to brush my thick hair and braid it and make sure I had nice clothes on that sort of matched. I think my mom took a lot of pride in how we looked. I still do, too. . . . While my parents insisted on an education, they put more emphasis on working hard at a job. I see that pattern to this day. I can "skip" a class when I don't feel particularly well, but I will not skip my paying job [junior].

In this student's story, we see the rich threads of her heritage woven together into a sense of self that values hard work, a neat appearance, loyalty to family, and upward mobility through education. She is aware of her roots in a poor village, a large family with its blessings and curses, and a patriarchal culture, yet she retains the image of women who were strong and attractive and of a father who risked a great deal to find a new life. These images all contribute to her own sense of who she is and can be.

Some research has been done on African-American identity development. For example, Branch-Simpson (1984) conducted psychosocial biographical interviews with black male and female college students and analyzed the content for developmental themes. She found many areas of overlap with the vectors presented in our theory. Creamer and Associates (1990, p. 66) note that in Branch-Simpson's model, a religious and spiritual identity was prominent in the developmental processes described by black students, and that for both men and women, identity is achieved in relationships with extended family. Role models are black humanitarian figures or family members. One African-American student recalls his father's impact on the development of his ethnic identity but otherwise the absence of visible role models:

> I grew up in "the Projects," across from the polo grounds where the Giants played. I had lots of friends and was happy at school until the fifth grade, when we moved to Jamaica, Queens. I felt displaced and never really made friends with my peers in junior high or high school, many of whom were Jewish. I set the pattern of staying apart from others, and that has remained throughout my life. I still hold back from total commitment, perhaps for fear of losing myself or being disappointed.
>
> My father was vocal about civil rights. He encouraged me to participate in a protest about lack of blacks on construction crews. I noticed that Jews didn't have to do this protesting and felt more set apart. One day in the seventh grade, I was talking about Hannibal. We were studying him in our history class. My father said, "Did you know that Hannibal was an African?" My only image of Hannibal was Victor Mature. I was shocked to hear of another possibility.
>
> I got no exposure to black writers in college. We only read Dickens, Dostoyevsky, and Conrad. I remember wondering, sometime in my freshman English class, "What does *Lord Jim* have to do with *me*?" Out of a thousand students in this Midwest college, there were about seventy black students. But there was a black community and church where a lot of us went. It reminded me of living in two worlds — going to the predominantly white high school and then taking the train back to the black neighborhood. I had the opportunity to study abroad in either Ghana or England. I went to London

because I didn't know about anything interesting
going on in Africa. I listened to Hyde Park leftists
and got to meet Sartre. He became a hero for me,
as did Henry Miller, Simone de Beauvoir, and
Anaïs Nin. I returned to my senior year with much
more interest in academics but continued to wonder,
"Are black writers really as good?" [graduate student].

Other studies have examined self-concept issues and variables critical to the academic success of African-American students. Research by Gloria Johnson-Powell (Mabry and Rogers,
1991) and others suggests that black children absorb negative
images early in life. One study of preschoolers showed that 76
percent of the black children chose a black doll as "bad." The
study, by Hopson and Hopson (Mabry and Rogers, 1991), also
showed that when black preschoolers were asked whether they
would like to play with a black doll or a white doll, 60 to 78
percent chose the white doll. Johnson-Powell's research suggests
that black children prefer black dolls until about the age of five.
Then, she says, they begin to be aware of their racial differences and to perceive those differences as negative.

Sedlacek (1987) reviewed research concerning black students on predominantly white campuses over a twenty-year
period and cited confidence and self-esteem as critical variables
for black student success. Seven other variables were also identified, each having aspects unique to black students when compared with others. These included realistic self-appraisal, management of racism, demonstrated community service, preference
for long-range goals over immediate needs gratification, availability of a strong support person, successful leadership experience, and nontraditionally acquired knowledge.

While Pascarella and Terenzini (1991) lament the absence
of studies dealing with identity formation among students of
color, they conclude that Cross's model has attracted more research attention than any other (p. 25). W. Cross (1971) proposes that black identity takes shape by passing through five
stages:

Stage 1: Preencounter (or prediscovery). A person's world-view is a Euro-American perspective, with an emphasis on assimilation and integration into the white world.

Stage 2: Encounter. An experience forces a rethinking of blacks' place in the world and catalyzes a reinterpretation of initial views and beliefs. The assassination of Martin Luther King, Jr., is given as an example.

Stage 3: Immersion-Emersion. The individual searches for a new sense of self as a black person. This involves a turning inward and the feeling that everything of value must be black. After immersion in a "world of Blackness," which is oversimplified, racist, and "either/or," the individual emerges and begins to exercise more control.

Stage 4: Internalization. The individual can continue in this mode, remaining fixated at Stage 3, or can form a superficial internalization of a black identity, but without an active commitment to making improvements in the community.

Stage 5: Internalization-Commitment. Serious personal commitments are made to political and sociocultural reform in the community.

After reviewing studies undertaken to operationalize this theory, as well as studies producing conflicting evidence about students' degree of subscription to various black ideology positions, Pascarella and Terenzini (1991) conclude that the available evidence appears to support the construct validity of W. Cross's model, but further research is needed to clarify whether changes in identity status are related to college attendance, to the racial/ethnic mix of students at the institution attended, or to sociocultural and economic conditions external to postsecondary educational institutions (p. 168).

Excessive allegiance to a group identity, when it leads to separatism, may serve to isolate black students from the kinds of social and academic contacts, experiences, and environments that can foster social and academic development. Just as Cass's model included a "gay pride" stage, W. Cross's also includes an immersion in the world of "blackness." Atkinson, Morten, and Sue (1983) suggest a five-stage model of minority identity development, which they feel is generic for ethnic groups: (1) conformity stage: preference for the values of the dominant cultural system, (2) dissonance stage: confusion and conflict regarding the dominant cultural system and their own group's cultural system, (3) resistance and immersion stage: active rejection of the dominant system and acceptance of their own cultural group's traditions and customs, (4) introspection stage: questioning the values of both the minority and the majority cultures, and (5) synergistic articulation and awareness stage: developing a cultural identity that selects elements from the values of both the dominant and the minority cultural groups.

Like the models presented above, our theory proposes that a positive identity is enhanced by an awareness of one's cultural background, an immersion in the social world of one's ethnic group, a valuing of the rituals, traditions, and artifacts of one's extended family or adopted network, and a sense of one's lineage. Knowing "who I am" rests in part on knowing "where I came from" and on pride in the character or accomplishments of one's ancestors. This awareness may eventually lead to a conscious choice to depart from some cultural traditions. However, a sense of one's roots in a particular cultural, historical, and social context is needed in order to locate oneself in context, and to appreciate the values and traditions of other cultural groups.

Clarification of Self-Concept
Through Roles and Life-Style

Movement into a gay life-style that includes only the most superficial encounters with heterosexual others or insulation within one's own ethnic group may be a normal component of identity development. Similarly, identifying oneself primarily as a basketball player, a student leader, a socialite, or a future lawyer may be a comforting response to the anxiety and pressure that characterize many college environments. We agree with the researchers and theorists cited above, however, that basing one's identity solely on one dimension of self establishes a limited foundation. Adopting any particular role or pattern of living may be helpful if it provides learning experiences and meaningful achievements and relationships, but it is a trap if staying in the role takes precedence over seeking more diverse experiences and more challenging settings.

In today's society, identity in terms of a prescribed role or lifestyle is no longer a given. Young persons no longer experience a unified and internally consistent framework of beliefs, behavior, and adult roles that they can assimilate almost automatically. Adults no longer rely on uninterrupted careers. The executive laid off in a recession, the lumberjack displaced by spotted owls, the autoworker replaced by robots, the farmer evicted by bankruptcy, or the parent facing an empty nest must again ask, "Who am I?" apart from the roles they have played. Now conflicting and mutually exclusive messages about what constitutes a satisfying life offer a smorgasbord of ingredients from which identity must be constructed and reconstructed. Mary Catherine Bateson (1989, pp. 2–4) speaks of composing a life as an improvisatory art rather than a stubborn struggle toward a single goal:

> Today, the materials and skills from which a life is composed are no longer clear. It is no longer possible to follow the paths of previous generations. . . . Just as the design of a building or of a vase must be rethought when the scale is changed, so must the design of lives. Many of the most basic concepts we use to construct a sense of self or the design of a life have changed their meanings: Work. Home. Love. Commitment [p. 2]. . . . A good meal, like a poem or a life, has a certain balance and diversity, a certain coherence and fit. As one learns to cope in the kitchen, one no longer duplicates whole meals but rather manipulates components and the way they are put together. The improvised meal will be different from the planned meal, and certainly riskier, but rich with the possibility of delicious surprise. Improvisation can be either a last resort or an established way of evoking creativity. Sometimes a pattern chosen by default can become a path of preference [pp. 3–4].

Development in terms of life-style and role taking involves both the ability to make commitments and the ability to improvise. It flourishes with the growth of a sense of self that has continuity despite changes in the environment. It involves a growing ability to discriminate between those cognitive constructs that are no longer needed and those that should be kept and treasured, between the role that stifles the self and the role that stretches it, and between the commitment that one makes out of obligation and the commitment made out of personal choice. One must also stay attuned to the inner direction that comes from somewhere deep in the self. We cannot "settle down" when the urge to be free is strong, without feeling uneasy. Likewise, there is a felt readiness to put down roots and take our place in the community, as this faculty member describes:

> An important turning point was a decision to buy a home for myself. When I was married, I owned a home, but it was primarily for my wife's benefit. I did not want the trappings of settlement, commitment, financial obligations, and so on. In a way, I didn't want to grow up but rather to play for the rest of my life. My divorce allowed and forced me to take more responsibility, to mature and develop a more stable approach to life to build from, because no one else would do it for me. These changes gradually occurred over several years, until one morning I woke up and said, "I want a house," which also meant settlement, responsibility, and so forth. The experience that catalyzed the shift was wanting "roots," a place to make my own, "nest-building" impulses, perhaps. Feelings of self-confidence and clarity accompanied the process [faculty member].

Perhaps this comment illustrates the epigenetic principle at work. The part of the self that wanted roots came into the foreground; the urge to roam receded. Becoming a home owner can then be authentic, as opposed to being a role played for someone else's sake.

Development brings experience with a variety of roles and life-styles and the search for a satisfying combination. In college, students try out the role of student, leader, participant, or observer in different ways. Work opportunities lend clarity about vocational roles. Relationships offer the chance to play out various dramas. When students take up residence on or near the campus, their changes in life-style are inevitable. Fluctuations in income bring about leaner or more opulent lifestyles. As students experience such changes, they begin to solidify self-definitions and coping skills.

Sense of Self in Response to Feedback from Valued Others

Erikson (1968, p. 165) proposes that identity involves not only a sense of well-being, a feeling of being at home in the body, and a realistic self-assessment of assets and liabilities, but also "an inner assuredness of anticipated recognition from those who count." One problem for the evolving self is that those in the immediate neighborhood may not be affirming, especially if we are remodeling in a way that does not look right to critical egos nearby. If mutuality does not exist, there may be reciprocal negation, or

> The denial on the part of others to take their place in my order and to let me take mine in theirs. Nothing in nature, in all probability, resembles the hate which this arouses. . . . Foremost among the complexities of human life is communication on the ego level, where each ego tests all the information received sensorily and sensually, linguistically and subliminally for the confirmation or negation of its identity. The persistent effort, then, of jointly ordering these processes into psychosocial "territory" of trusted mutualities and defined reciprocal negations is what we mean by a "group ego"; and I have indicated the further complication that the boundary of this territory runs right through each constituent ego, dividing it into a positive and a negative identity [pp. 219–220].

This component is slightly different from the development of interdependence, which involves balancing autonomy with connectedness. Regardless of how well autonomy and interdependence have been achieved, we define who we are in part by discovering who we respect, how they feel about us, and how to deal with reactions that do not confirm our self-image.

Pike (1985) suggests a handball metaphor to illustrate part of the process. We discover who we are in relation to the outside world by putting forth actions, feelings, words, or thoughts, as a handball player throws out a ball against a wall. We observe reactions of others; we watch how the ball bounces back. The more we throw and observe it bouncing back, the better we learn about controlling the action. If the wall against which we are throwing is warped, we coordinate our functioning accordingly. Later, we travel to other neighborhoods and throw against other walls, and when the ball does not bounce back the same way, we feel confused and uncoordinated. The ego, busily at the controls of incoming sensory data, may develop into a censor or rationalizer in order to preserve a positive image for the self. It may discount the new walls, or explain away the unexpected bounce-back, instead of helping the self see the real circumstances and adapt. But when the odd bounce-back repeats itself, or when the gap between earlier learning and current reality becomes too great, the censoring and rationalizing no longer work. We may then experience a breakdown—physical, emotional, or mental—or sometimes a breakthrough to a new definition of self and others. The breakthrough may be an understanding of why others form judgments about us, an ability to detach emotionally from the evaluator and see the feedback offered as information that can be used or discarded, or a decision to move to a more compatible environment.

When we are clarifying identity by trying out new roles, we may do so with warm support from others or in spite of their contempt. While acclaim may make life easier, following our star in the face of others' resistance can also build character. We may have experiences that evict us from the familiar neighborhood, as this former student did:

> In high school I was "busted" for pot. The change was from my identity as one who fit in, a good person, an athlete, a conformer to a person with less constraint on what I chose to do and be. [What helped?] Being suspended (a public display meant loss of public persona). I was ostracized by my previous peer group. Support from people who mattered most to me and knew me well and said, "It does not matter about this. You are still a good person" [student affairs staff member].

Both the ostracism by this student's previous friends and the confirmation of his essential goodness by those who mattered most helped solidify this student's identity.

Development involves an ability to update our self-concept based on information from others. In college, students weave together the feedback from grades and test scores, coaches and directors, and friends and loved ones and form a fairly accurate picture of how others see them. A sense of adequacy and self-acceptance emerges when feedback is not only consistent but specific about where students are doing well and how they can improve.

Self-Acceptance and Self-Esteem

Studies cited earlier in this chapter attest to the growth in self-esteem among college students. Self-esteem involves a generalized judgment about personal value or merit. Research indicates that students tend to develop a more positive sense of their academic and social competence, but also develop a stronger sense of self-worth, based not on comparisons with other students' performance, but on internal, personal standards.

This student expresses her relief as she begins to accept and value herself:

> A change has occurred in my self-perception. The "old" way was to look at myself with a sense of disgust, to be supercritical of my outward as well as

inward self. The "new" way is to focus on the more
positive attributes and characteristics that I possess
and to lift the burden of perfection off my shoulders. The only way that I know a significant change
has occurred is by hearing my inner dialogue to
reflect a more positive attitude and to notice how
one change in perception about myself initiates a
series of changes. [What helped?] Two people have
played significant parts in the process of my change.
Both listened to me—I mean really listened. Both
allowed me to speak uninterrupted and without
judgment. One person was a professional and the
other a friend. The experience that brought on this
shift in me was separation, both physically and emotionally, from my estranged husband. With a change
in marital status, there were so many feelings to deal
with that it became an overwhelming experience.
The feelings I received from interacting with these
two people were feelings of being important, feelings of being accepted, feelings of being cared for
in a very special way [graduate student].

This statement captures an essential shift from a perfectionistic
and overly critical attitude to a self-affirming one.

Movement along this vector is marked by greater self-confidence, faith in one's abilities, feeling useful to others, knowing
that one has valuable qualities and is basically a good person.
It also involves a willingness to acknowledge weaknesses and hear
constructive criticism, and a counterbalancing power to change
self-deprecating inner messages to more supportive self-talk.
Without a core of self-love, students tend to look to others to fill
the inner emptiness. With a growing sense of self-worth, a peaceful inner self can move toward stability and integration.

Stability and Integration

An earlier study by Goddard College faculty focused on personal stability and integration (Chickering, 1967). It suggests

a pattern that development of identity may take during the college years. According to the definition developed by the faculty, students high on this dimension knew the kind of person they wanted to be and had a sense of balance and perspective. They tended to see things whole, with a well-ordered set of values. They had sorted out what was important to them and were aware of their own strengths and weaknesses. They were relatively at ease dealing with problems concerning academic work, future vocation, partnership, and family life. Not that such problems ceased to exist or that these students resolved all of them, but their level of anxiety and concern about such matters was relatively low. A faculty team assessed students' records each semester, noting the students' level of reliability and responsibility on work programs in relation to other responsibilities undertaken, level of personal stability and integration, comfort with the kind of people they were now, and comfort with their past behavior.

The pooled ratings of all graduates for each semester indicated substantial and fairly regular change over a four-year period. A sharp rise occurred from the first to the second semester; further acceleration took place in the seventh semester. Perhaps the first semester presents a kind of "culture shock" that demands greater responsibility and stability, and as students settle into the campus routine, familiarizing themselves with new knowledge, new friends, and new freedoms, comfort with self increases. A higher level of personal organization and integration is also required for the transition from college to the adult world.

In examining components of identity, we also need to consider the concept of self. Who or what is the self that observes, learns, and decides? If the self is an integrated system, who is in charge of coordinating it? Who organizes the facets of personality into an integrated whole? There are no easy answers. Various theories about the parts of the self have been in vogue at different times. Freud gave us three aspects of personality: the id, ego, and superego. Berne (1961) gave us the parent, adult, and child ego states. Wegscheider (1981) proposed six parts of the self—the physical, emotional, mental, social, volitional, and spiritual. While these models, and others like them, have emerged from clinical settings, not college campuses, they nevertheless offer some insight into the related concepts of ego, self, and identity and how they may interrelate.

Erikson (1968, p. 217) is eloquent on the subject of the "I" that observes its various selves:

> What the "I" reflects on when it sees or contemplates the body, the personality, and the roles to which it is attached for life—not knowing where it was before or will be after—are the various selves which make up our composite Self. There are constant and often shocklike transitions between these selves: consider the nude body self in the dark or suddenly exposed in the light; consider the clothed self among friends or in the company of higher-ups or lower-downs; consider the just awakened drowsy self or the one stepping refreshed out of the surf or the one overcome by retching and fainting; the body self in sexual excitement or in a rage; the competent self and the impotent one; the one on horseback, the one in the dentist's chair, and the one chained and tortured—by men who also say "I." It takes, indeed, a healthy personality for the "I" to be able to speak in all of these conditions in such a way that at any given moment it can testify to a reasonably coherent Self.

In Erikson's view, this "I" is more conscious than the preconscious selves, which become conscious when the "I" makes them so, and when the ego agrees to it. The ego is another part of the self which we cannot observe directly. We are conscious only of its work, for it manages to do for us, as the heart and the brain do, what we could never "figure out" or plan consciously. Erikson (1968, p. 218) sees the ego as "an inner 'agency' safeguarding our coherent existence by screening and synthesizing, in any series of moments, all the impressions, emotions, memories, and impulses which try to enter our thoughts and demand our action, and which would tear us apart if unsorted and un-managed by a slowly grown and reliably watchful screening system."

Identity cannot evolve, in this view, unless an ego also evolves. After studying the interaction of external societal demands with biological development, and the internal ordering of those experiences, (ego functioning), Erikson proposed that there was also an "I" that exists, apart from the unconsciously operating ego. Several writers have used the same metaphor to conceptualize the evolution of identity (Pike, 1985; Pearson, 1986). Emily Dickinson ([1890] 1983) may have been the first:

XXVI

The props assist the house
Until the house is built,
And then the props withdraw —
And adequate, erect,
The house supports itself;
Ceasing to recollect
The auger and the carpenter,
Just such a retrospect
Hath the perfected life,
A past of plank and nail,
And slowness — then the scaffolds drop —
Affirming it a soul.

At the risk of oversimplification, let us visualize a house to represent the structure of the individual, the person's identity. It has a first floor, second floor, basement, and attic. The owner of the house is the person's self, the I that looks out on the world. If we agree with Erikson, this consciousness is not the same as the ego, which is an unconscious function. Aspects of this metaphor have been adapted from concepts presented by Pike (1985).

Before we are ready to own it, our parents build the house for us. They use a familiar blueprint, based on what they feel the new owner will need. They decorate and furnish it, based on their tastes, thoughts, and belief systems. They paint it their

emotional colors. They store treasures and junk in the basement.
The house is an extension of a particular family's group identity. It is also designed according to the styles of the neighborhood and the zoning laws of the community. Conforming to
these preferred styles, the initial structure reflects the values of
the ethnic and socioeconomic background of the family. In fact,
the basement rests on a solid foundation of thousands of years
of human evolution. The owner has an inheritance — the accumulated experience, the collective unconscious, and the genetic
predispositions forged over centuries of adaptation.

Certain equipment comes with the house. Wiring, plumb-
ing, and thermostats help the house function fairly well without a lot of management, which is desirable since the owner
does not understand how everything works. The owner spends
much of childhood downstairs, in a living room and a den. The
living room is the "body self," symbolizing physical activity,
where behavior patterns, genetically wired for adaptation to the
external world, are stored. It is really a suite, which includes
a dining room, a bedroom for sleeping, and later, sex, a play-
room, a workroom, and spare rooms for pursuing valued activities, such as music or exercising. That area is decorated with
furniture, paintings, and objects that symbolize norms about
eating, drinking, playing, working, family rituals and ceremonial
behavior, and values connected with achievement, status, gender
roles, and life roles — all related to observable behavior and, in
this model, the development of physical and manual competence.

The den is the place where emotions are registered and
expressed. Perhaps it contains a large organ, which appears to
play by itself in a broad range of chords, volumes, and tones.
The term *den* implies a connection to our animal lineage, with
its instinctive patterns of rage, fear, and desire and its drive
toward fight or flight. In fact, some dens are inhabited by a top
dog and an underdog, subsystems that Perls (1969) identified.
One speaks with a dominating, critical, blaming voice; the other
is placating, submissive, rationalizing. These characters actually think that they can run the house in the early stages of development, before the owner has discovered the ability to hear
them for what they are and quiet them down. The top-dog voice

is related to the critical part of the superego and the urge to control others. The nurturing part lives upstairs.

Different emotional energy characterizes the room on the second floor, over the den. We can call it the "heart center." It is a place for calmness and detachment, for receiving self and others with acceptance and appreciation. The room is warmed by pictures of friends and loved ones, and perhaps inspirational readings. In this room, the self and others can be nurtured, affirmed, and renewed. In order for self-esteem and mature relationships to develop, the owner has to spend time here, relaxing in its comfortable furniture, listening to its soothing music or reassuring motivational tapes, and learning that sometimes people and experiences must simply be allowed to go on in their own way, without attempts to change, protest, condemn, or push away.

Across the hall, above the living room, is a "head center." It is full of complex data processing equipment, video screens, tape recorders, keyboards, and devices for designing, storing, and measuring. It contains sophisticated mechanisms for receiving and classifying sensory input, for analysis and association, and for short and long-term memory. The mainframe computer, connected to all the other rooms, controls and enhances conscious viewing and decision making, once the owner learns how to use it. This high-tech equipment has many complex, automatic functions. Somewhere inside, an executive is at work, managing key elements of the process. This is the ego. It does not own the house, although sometimes it wants to, especially if the owner is trying to interfere with its control. It may resemble Hal in the film *2001,* the computer that spoke calmly to the crew, made sure everything was running smoothly, and sometimes outwitted the pilots in order to maintain itself.

Erikson's theory (1968, p. 208) is relevant here. In attempting to sort out the components of *identity,* he acknowledges using the term in three ways: "At one time it seemed to refer to a conscious sense of individual uniqueness, at another to an unconscious striving for a continuity of experience, and at a third, as a solidarity with a group's ideals" (p. 208). The ego's job is to screen, test, and match against stored familiar patterns and ideals and to synthesize the incoming data from the other rooms in the house — the impulses, impressions, emotions and needs. In so doing, the ego tries to maintain a coherent sense of self, or "continuity of experience." It provides the frame of reference that structures the way we see the world. This job keeps the ego very busy. It is always in motion, as impulses and reactions are constantly being registered. Yet its goal is equilibrium. Jane Loevinger (1976, p. 58) uses two metaphors for the ego: a gyroscope, whose upright position is maintained by its rotation, and an architectural arch, which provides thrusts and counterthrusts to maintain its own shape and to support the whole building.

In our house metaphor, establishing identity involves, first, becoming more familiar with all the rooms, furniture, and equipment, as well as the neighborhood. It involves understanding the particular patterns of behaving, feeling, thinking, and relating that have been built in ahead of time and becoming aware of the cultural heritage passed down through the generations. It involves noting the expectations or hopes of one's group; there may be family portraits on the walls or trophies on the mantelpiece that symbolize their ideals. Through this exploration, the new owner finds answers to the question, "Who am I?"

Establishing identity involves some knowledge that the *I* is a tip of an iceberg, some recognition that our behavior, thoughts, and feelings can be affected by forces we are not normally aware of. Ideally it also means locating, exploring, and refurbishing some of what is in the basement (the unconscious). It is usually dark down there, and we tend to avoid descending the stairs. It is full of junk, treasures, and mysterious creatures. Messages from the basement may be received when we dream, undergo hypnosis, or react strongly to another person or life experience, signaling that we may be projecting outward some unclaimed part of the self. If we are actively engaged in discovering who we are and decoding those obscure messages, we become curious about what is hidden, and choose to descend, flashlight in hand. We may then find that an imagined monster is really a harmless mouse or that an old curiosity is a valuable possession.

The attic is the spirit, the realm of intuition, a repository for universal principles, the boundary between what we can know and what is beyond human understanding. In our youth we are given descriptions of what is up there, and we form our beliefs accordingly. In this culture, the message from the group psyche is usually, "You don't need to actually visit the attic. It just finishes the house." There may be ministers or teachers in the neighborhood who articulate belief systems, but they may or may not have actually visited the attic. Forming an identity involves reexamining belief systems about a larger reality, about our place in the universe, the meaning of life and death, and our purpose for being here. It involves making our own journey upstairs.

At some point, we wake up to the fact that we actually own the house. We can refurnish, redecorate, even completely remodel it. Like a traveler coming back with souvenirs from faraway places, the increasingly more selective self chooses what to add, change, and throw out. Then the identity structure begins to fit the evolving consciousness that resides there. We have seen the precursor of this discovery in student reports that seemed to have difficulty locating the owner's position. An old way of thinking or acting conflicted with a new, more conscious self coming into view. Later the *I* will become identified with an adult who can activate thinking skills, listen to feelings, mobilize the body, and use intuition and inspiration creatively.

Knefelkamp, Widick, and Parker (1978) say that the establishment of identity seems to require (1) experiences that help people clarify their interests, skills, and attitudes; and (2) experiences that aid individuals in making commitments. In their chapter on Erikson, they state that "the formation of identity is fostered by an environment which allows for (1) experimentation with varied roles; (2) the experiencing of choice; (3) meaningful achievement; (4) freedom from excessive anxiety; (5) time for reflection and introspection" (pp. 6–7). To these we can add: (6) interaction with diverse individuals and ideas; (7) receiving feedback and making objective self-assessments; and (8) involvement in activities that foster self-esteem and understanding of one's social and cultural heritage.

In earlier eras, the principal task of education was "socialization," and the problem of individuals was to learn the attitudes, actions, and skills necessary for a satisfying and productive fit with "society." The symphony had a clearly stated theme and rhythm. The types and positions of the instruments were settled. To contribute, one had merely to choose a standard instrument, learn to play it, and practice the part. In the global society of the twenty-first century, where change is the only certainty, not socialization but identity formation becomes the central and continuing task of education. With a firm sense of self as artist — as performer, composer, improviser, and conductor — tomorrow's graduates will not be bound to a single instrument. They will be equally at ease with the classics and the avant garde. Regardless of the roles they assume or the demands of the performance, they will know how to bring forth their best talents and contribute to the greater whole. And if need be, they can go out and form their own ensemble.

SEVEN

Developing
Purpose

Progress along the first five vectors generates a variety of answers to the question, "Who am I?" A host of critical questions get tentative answers. What can I do well? What do I feel, and why? How do I manage and express my feelings? Who am I, apart from my role as son or daughter, parent or worker? Who am I, as a partner, friend, or lover? How do I respond to people who are different? How comfortable am I with myself—with my body, my gender, my heritage? This growing clarity provides a foundation for looking ahead and answering new questions. Where am I going? What are my goals and ideals? What kind of life do I want to lead as I complete my college experience?

Developing purpose entails an increasing ability to be intentional, to assess interests and options, to clarify goals, to make plans, and to persist despite obstacles. Miller, Galanter, and Pribram (1960) shed light on how plans and purposes guide behavior. Seeking to fill the theoretical vacuum between cognition and action and noting that "the will seems to have disappeared from psychological theory" (p. 11), they consider the role of imagination and the hierarchical structure of behavior. They observe that often we imagine what our day will be like and make broad, flexible decisions. For example,

> As you brush your teeth you decide that you will answer that pile of letters you have been neglecting. That is enough. You do not need to list the names of the people or to draft an outline of the contents of the letters. . . . You take one and read it. You plan your answer. You may need to check on some information, you dictate or type or scribble a reply, you address an envelope, seal the folded letter, find a stamp, drop it in a mailbox. Each of these subactivities runs off as the situation arises — you did not need to enumerate them while you were planning the day. All you need is the name of the activity that you plan for that segment of the day, and from that name you then proceed to elaborate the detailed actions involved in carrying out the plan [p. 6].

Miller, Galanter, and Pribram point out that knowledge, action, and evaluation are essentially connected by a plan, which is a hierarchy of instructions for carrying out specific activities. The brain comes equipped with mechanisms for organizing sequences of behavior, for initiating each step in the sequence, for gauging progress toward a target. A purposeful self must learn how to use that equipment. A plan becomes a map for moving from the current situation to a more desirable one, for altering the status quo, for composing a life. It becomes a kind of servomechanism, a grid for measuring achievement, and a prod for mobilizing further effort to close the gap between the condition we are in and the target we want to reach.

To have a good plan, we must first have an image of a desired outcome. This image has to be plucked or constructed from knowledge accumulated about the self and the world — a private representation or everything learned. Facts, observations, and beliefs affect our picture of the goal. One problem is that our image or cognitive representation of experience can only be based on past events and past reactions. In terms of visualizing a future role or life-style, it is hard to plan a way to live if we have not seen it before. The pull of the familiar is strong. "Habits and skills are Plans that were originally voluntary but that have become relatively inflexible, involuntary, automatic. Once the Plan that controls a sequence of skilled actions becomes fixed through overlearning, it will function in much the same way as an innate Plan in instinctive behavior" (Miller, Galanter, and Pribram, 1960, p. 82). Furthermore, "The construction of these integrated strategies for skilled acts through long practice and repetition has a further consequence for the kind of planning that the adult human can do. The construction of these subplans enables a person to deal 'digitally' with an 'analogue' process" (p. 90). Like the typist who first learns letter habits, then word habits, then phrase habits, each subplan is mastered and turned over to the muscles, freeing more energy for higher mental processes without having to formulate each step verbally, symbolically, or digitally as a beginner would. We can then look beyond the trees to the forest. Attention is freed to concentrate on meaning, to pursue questions that engage our curiosity.

The paradox is that we must build up a certain amount of digital competence in order to get to the analogue perspective, and having glimpsed the next horizon, we may need to become a beginner all over again, mastering the basics for moving in a new direction. An alternative to becoming a beginner again is to continue to use our tried-and-true skills. We look competent but never go anywhere. For some, this may be a life purpose. In *My Dinner with André,* Wally listens to André's enthusiasm for a life "in which each day would become an incredible, monumental creative task." He replies that he does not feel the need for anything more challenging than earning a living, paying his bills, staying home with Debby, and reading Charlton Heston's autobiography (Shawn and Gregory, 1981). It takes an act of will to move beyond past patterns and seek purposes that take us into the unknown.

When colleges provide flexibility and encouragement for students to pursue their own interests, imagination and intentionality can provide tremendous motivation. Murphy (1960, p. 100) saw this dynamic at Sarah Lawrence College, and we believe it still holds true:

> Some students express surprise and pleasure at their new ability to work thoroughly and intensively in an area that seems important to their purposes and for the sake of greater thoroughness at the points where thoroughness is most needed, and to deal with other materials more casually. This flexibility is most satisfying where it occurs in connection with increasing clarity about one's goals, plans, vocational aims, interests, and educational purposes. Some students reflect a change from thinking about educational values in absolutistic terms to a way of thinking which is more relevant to the meaning of each piece of work in terms of their own purposes.

Developing purpose requires formulating plans for action and a set of priorities that integrate three major elements: (1) vocational plans and aspirations, (2) personal interests, and (3) interpersonal and family commitments. It also involves increasing intentionality in exercising personal will on a daily basis. To be intentional is to be skilled in consciously choosing priorities, in aligning action with purpose, in motivating oneself consistently toward goals, and in persevering despite barriers or setbacks.

Vocational Plans and Aspirations

Finding our vocation is more than just securing a job. Vocations can include paid work, unpaid work, or both. We discover our vocation by discovering what we love to do, what energizes and fulfills us, what uses our talents and challenges us to develop new ones, and what actualizes our potentials for excellence. If it pays the bills too, all the better. But poet Wallace Stevens sold insurance by day, so he write on his own time.

The employment structure in our culture is limited by the times we live in. It presses people toward specialization, glamorizes monetary success, and rarely requires employees to ponder the long-term contributions of their labor. College students during the 1970s and 1980s shifted their emphasis from the 1960s goals of self-actualization and social change to securing their own future. The proportion of freshmen who said one of their life goals was "being well off financially" increased from 39.1 percent in 1970 to 75.6 percent in 1987. In contrast, the proportion of students who said they wanted to "develop a meaningful philosophy of life" dropped from 82.9 percent in 1967 to 39.4 percent in 1987 (Dodge, 1991). These statistics come from the Higher Education Research Institute at the University of California, Los Angeles, which surveyed more than six million freshmen from 1966 to 1990. The report's authors say that the cycle may be reversing, however. In recent years, they have noted sharply declining interest in business careers and majors and more interest in bringing about change and in helping others.

Today's younger students may be caught in a bind if their purpose is to graduate and move into middle-class prosperity. They know that a college degree used to guarantee this, at least for some segments of the population, but 65 percent of eighteen- to twenty-nine-year-olds surveyed by *Time*/CNN feel that it will be harder for their group to live as comfortably as previous generations. "While the majority of today's young adults think they have a strong chance of finding a well-paying and interesting job, 69 percent believe they will have more difficulty buying a house, and 52 percent say they will have less leisure time than their predecessors. Thus the monetary motivation for higher education may be questionable. Asked to describe their generation, 53 percent said the group is worried about the future" (Cray, Curry, and McWhirter, 1990). While earning power is important, young workers also want job gratification, stimulation, personal contact, and a chance to learn leading-edge technology (Cannon, 1991). Apparently, the majority no longer believe that an undergraduate degree will give them what they need to reach their career goals. As of 1990, 53.1 percent of freshmen plan to prepare for graduate or professional school, versus 34.5 percent in 1971.

Commenting on today's students, Astin says, "The saddest thing of all is that they don't have the quest to understand things, to understand themselves" (Cray, Curry, and McWhirter, 1990, p. 60). They apparently value external validation, through grades, performance evaluations, and constant feedback from supervisors. They also expect an environment that supports their personal growth, affords them flexibility and access to decision making, and restores the sacredness of work-free weekends. The *Time*/CNN poll found 58 percent agreeing that "there is no point in staying in a job unless you are completely satisfied" (Cray, Curry, and McWhirter, 1990, p. 59). The pool of entry-level workers will decline by 500,000 per year in the immediate future, so it may be that these young graduates will be able to move around in search of these ideals. On the other hand, a tight economy may bring on the painful discovery that good jobs of any kind are hard to find, let alone those that are "completely satisfying."

Adding to the problem for younger students is the increasing complexity of today's society. Jobs can be so technical or esoteric that students cannot visualize them, yet most colleges cannot afford the staff or equipment to teach robotics or fiber optics or histology. Without skilled assistance, younger students may remain at sea in terms of purpose. Choosing academic goals based on hazy images of high pay or glamorous work may lead to a first-class berth on the Titanic.

Older students may be better acquainted with the realities of the job market, the consequences of stumbling into a job, and the fact that early rewards may evaporate. One former student reports:

> I had completed several years of part-time university studies right after high school. Unsure of my career goals, I felt as if I was floundering. An opportunity to join the city police as a constable became available and I made the decision to join in a matter of days. The training and camaraderie

were my support, and for two years I was satisfied with my position. As I entered the third year of this job, I began to have serious questions about fulfillment, lack of personal growth, and career advancement. After months of frustration with this career [and] criticism from colleagues who could not believe someone would not be satisfied with the challenges of the job, I resigned and returned to the university [faculty member].

Many working adults are returning to college to upgrade job skills, change careers, or survive unemployment. Others may have been raising children or doing volunteer work when they became interested in higher education, as this adult learner reports:

The major change that occurred for me was that I went from being a person with three years of college education who, in twenty years, had never had any desire to go back to school, to a person enrolled once again, and on my way to a bachelor's degree. In fact, I'm applying for graduate school. The decision to go back to school was an instantaneous flash of desire to become qualified to do a kind of work I've always wanted to do. [What helped?] I was sitting in a guardian ad litem monthly training session, which featured an advocate from the victim/assistance unit of the prosecutor's office. She was asked what kind of educational backgrounds people doing that work have. The answer was a hodgepodge of backgrounds, but all included a bachelor's degree. I realized I could do advocacy for a career by getting my degree and that the degree could be in almost anything I'm interested in. It was the return of a long-buried dream [senior].

Whether they are younger or older, students frequently change their occupational plans during college. Feldman and

Newcomb (1969) estimated that between one-third and two-thirds of all students change their career choice during college. Astin (1977) agrees, but he also finds that initial career choice at the beginning of college tends to be the single best predictor of career choice at the end of college and of the actual entry-level job. Whether the career choice changes or stays the same, development of purpose involves an increasing level of clarity about what one wants to do, or at least about the next step in the process (which may well be graduate school). Pascarella and Terenzini (1991, p. 425) find a small but reasonably consistent body of evidence that students develop more mature levels of thinking about or planning for a career as they proceed to senior status. They define career maturity as the ability to acquire accurate information about job opportunities, training requirements, and financial returns, to formulate career plans, and to reach a degree of certainty about one's career choice.

The extent to which higher education helps this process along is uncertain. Greater maturity may come with aging, regardless of college attendance, as Healy, Mitchell, and Mourton (1987) have suggested. Students who remain undecided about career direction may be less likely to persist toward degree completion and therefore would not be included in research samples. Several researchers have found indirect evidence that the degree of uncertainty about one's academic major tends to be positively linked to withdrawal from college (Bucklin and Bucklin, 1970; Demiutroff, 1974; Newton and Gaither, 1980). Again we find a reason why actively assisting students with goal clarification should be a high priority for college and university personnel.

Students who work with career counselors, take career exploration courses and workshops, arrange internships, and discuss future plans with their instructors are much more likely to identify future directions. The power of conscious planning and self-assessment becomes immediately apparent when compared to a more serendipitous approach, as this student reports:

> I enrolled in a career exploration course that included abilities/aptitude testing. The results changed

how I viewed myself and my career goals. I moved from lack of confidence to an active exploration of options. My old approach was what I call "the little bell strategy." I'd wander around and it was as though a little bell would ring in my head when something came along, and then I'd impulsively decide to do it. For a while I'd be swept along in the novelty, but then boredom would set in. But I'd be afraid to move out and explore on my own because I was afraid of losing the security of a paycheck. Eventually I'd see another opportunity and the little bell would go "ding" again. I never stopped to consider in a serious way what my life's work could be. [What helped?] A counselor helped me to see this pattern — to affirm my need for variety and to challenge my overriding concern with security. The concrete assignment to do informational interviews and to formulate plans helped in counteracting my anxiety [graduate student].

Clarifying personal interests is a major step in this process. The freedom to take courses that inform and extend those interests is essential. College may be the one time in life when people can sample new fields of knowledge, pursue familiar topics in more depth, test hunches about career possibilities, discover new capabilities through experiential learning, and leave comfort zones to do a novel class assignment or partake of cocurricular options.

Two student evaluations of their undergraduate experience illustrate how career development can be enhanced by a balance of structure and independent work. Though the first is from the 1960s and the second is from the 1990s, we believe they illustrate relevant principles. The first is by Alan, who indicated on his admission application to Goddard College that his chief interest lay in the outdoors, forestry, wildlife management, hunting, and boating. During his first two years, he took an array of liberal arts courses, such as Individual and Society, Modern Literature, Contemporary Africa, Small Community

Life, Visual Arts, Contemporary America, Introductory Psychology, Literature of Social Relations, and some science courses. Reviewing his first two years, he wrote:

> I began these past two years not knowing exactly in what direction I was heading, but I knew that one of my primary aims in coming to college was to find out where my real interest lay. I undertook an investigation of a variety of subjects, which I feel has proved beneficial, in that it has not only broadened my experience but has also enabled me to grasp and develop a partially hidden interest and ability.
>
> Thus, in the last year or year and one-half, I have concentrated my efforts in the field of conservation — specifically conservation of forests, wildlife, and water. I consider these three resources to be interrelated and of equal importance. . . . I wish to expand on the basic knowledge . . . using such resource aids as the following: the county forester and other forest and state personnel, Hawk's Hill Demonstration Woodlot, the Soil Conservation Service, the Fish and Game Department, and the Water Resources Board. . . . I expect that much of my study will be on an independent basis, but I also expect to engage in some group studies.

Alan's third- and fourth-year coursework included Economics of Labor, Game Management, World of Animals, Studies in Literature, Soils and Resource Planning, Ecology, Natural Resource Policies, Dance, and Anthropology. He reported that "I worked harder, and longer, and more independently than I have previously." His senior study project — to which he devoted his last semester — was titled "Conservation as a Way of Life." Of this work, he said:

> I feel that this has been one of my best semesters, both socially and academically. I feel that I have

met most all of my commitments to the college and
to myself quite successfully. I had no roommate this
semester, which I think was a definite advantage
for me. I spent more time "at the desk" than I have
in the past and was able to do more reading. . . .
There have been significant changes in my life since
I first arrived on campus. I felt that perhaps I was
better equipped for college life than many were at
first, but I also realized that I had much to learn
in the way of living with others and developing my
personal and academic responsibilities. Goddard
gave me the leeway to make many decisions. I made
them — some good, some not so good — but on the
whole, I think that I made the right ones for myself. I had no particular field of study in mind at
first, so it seemed to me that I should pursue a program of a general and broad nature. After all, I
had come to a liberal arts college. I did this, in fact,
by registering in a wide variety of courses. I enjoyed this type of program, for I touched on many
unfamiliar subjects that I was able to gain an interest in. . . . Being in Vermont, being from a farm
and country background, and always possessing an
interest in nature and the natural environment —
all were significant factors in my decision to concentrate my academic efforts during the last two
years in the study of conservation. Of course, I did
not limit my study to conservation alone, but I did
take a number of courses in conservation and resource management. I am well satisfied to have
"majored" in this area. I am not nor could I be considered a well-rounded conservationist at this time.
Nevertheless, it is a start.

These comments reveal much about the clarification of
vocational plans and aspirations. First, when such plans have
meaning, they serve to carry forward interests, values, and a
way of life that have been rewarding in the past — in Alan's case,

his enjoyment of the outdoors, his concern to be a socially responsible person, and the general satisfactions he derives from a rural existence. Second, when plans become more clearly formulated, learning becomes organized in relation to them. Greater time and energy are invested in such activities, sometimes at the expense of other significant interests, among which, for Alan, were the position of fire commissioner and his participation in community government. Third, the importance of study not directly or only tangentially related to future professional plans is recognized more clearly. Thus, Alan could take courses in literature, dance, and anthropology.

Spohn's (1960) study at Sarah Lawrence supports the implications of Alan's record. Spohn found that students who show no interest in some kind of work after college do not, on the whole, become deeply enough involved in their college work to derive a clear direction for it; their personal interests and inclinations may remain lively, but they are not strong or deep. When students were rated on the intellectual level of their work, flexibility, and objectivity, those with no vocational interest scored lowest (pp. 139–140).

Some students enter with clearly defined interests and are supported in their efforts to individualize their degree programs, despite the haziness of a future career path. Our second student, Lisa, graduated from Fairhaven College (an alternative college within Western Washington University) in 1990. Her senior evaluation paper includes highlights of her developmental journey. She begins by sharing the context for her education — broad goals and beliefs, family heritage, and life experience:

> Prior to designing the concentration in native cultures and nutrition, I became aware of my desire to actively participate in social changes involving native communities. I wanted to become familiar with contemporary, local, native culture. . . . I made the assumption that social change can be mediated through foodways. The process of enculturation has robbed the indigenous populations of healthy social constructs by usurping control of their

lands. . . . My personal assignment is to participate in the exchange of food and culture concepts between the dominant society and Native American communities.

I show an affinity for being of service to people, and from my father I inherit an interest in food and health. He taught me how to bake whole wheat bread, introduced me to hypnosis and self-help books, and kept a stern eye on my eating behaviors. I carry with me a truckload of cookbooks, nutrition guides, and diet books. My interest in the subject of food is as old as I am, yet I had to look deeply to discover it as a worthwhile area of study. From my mother, I may have acquired the attitude that if it's not difficult and arduous, it's not worthwhile. The difficulty in this is not always being aware of my limitations.

From 1982 through 1986, I worked at a salmon processing plant in southeast Alaska. During this time I befriended a Tlingit family. In the course of this relationship, I was informally adopted into the Bear Clan of Hoonah. I learned how to fish for salmon and halibut and how to dry halibut and smoke sockeye; I enjoyed chum caviar, herring roe, seal oil, and dried kelp. My romantic stereotype of native culture clashed with the reality of a culture in transition. I heard rumors of child molestation, suicide, and social conflict. I watched the fishermen throw their garbage into the sea. I saw icons of Christ and pictures of Jesus. Some people abuse the earth because they think it is worthless; other people neglect it because they believe it is invincible. Both peoples have lost an appreciation for the creative process — for applying human systems to the natural world.

She then describes her process for deciding what courses to take, based on her broad purpose:

I used the course list for nutrition majors as a selection guide and discovered relevant science, psychology, and home economics classes. Then I eliminated management classes pertaining to large institutions like hospitals; to me they're the antithesis of an ethnic orientation to health. By the time I completed the necessary requirements, the nutrition program was no longer geared toward giving students registered dietician status. Although eager to hold this professional title, I took advantage of the circumstances to concentrate on Native American cultures. I was often accosted by the question, "What are you going to do when you graduate?" In a frustrated mode I would suggest social work, secretly hoping I could work on the Lummi Reservation, yet secretly fearing that social work defeats the real purpose of this study. When I applied for work-study, the director could only point me to volunteer work at a day-care center. Needless to say, I was having difficulty trying to justify my education in terms of a career. Eventually I no longer felt a need to do so.

Lisa cares more about what she is learning than about justifying the utility of it, trusting that one step will lead to the next step; she uses her immediate purposes to consciously structure her reading assignments and relies on faculty members who seem to understand her individual goals:

I trusted my adviser to guide me in my independent studies. He encouraged me and seemed aware of the significance of food to culture. The first book he recommended was *Wild Rice and the Ojibway* by Thomas Vennum, an admirable model of the food and culture relationship. The independent studies in Native American cultures provided a general and theoretical foundation. As a consequence of my own interests, they included perspectives on politics, law, and history, including the critical perspective, which

engaged new ways of looking at these subjects. . . .
I concentrated on three cultural groups — Ojibwe,
Navajo, and Lummi of the Northwest coast. I discovered the various food adaptations (for example,
wild rice, sheep, and salmon), traditional life-styles,
and current sociopolitical dilemmas. I tried to analyze the writer's methodology as well as to be evaluative about the content. My impressions formed the
essence of essays on ethnohistorical texts and library
resource materials. An exciting book by William
Cronan showed how resources (climate, geography,
and flora and fauna) coexist with people to create
cultures. An example of an interdisciplinary approach to history, this book was also important for
introducing the concept of aboriginal societies im-
pacting their environment. These groups enhanced
resource availability and subsistence methods with
land management practices (like burning under-
growth, for instance).

Like many students, Lisa reveals that self-directed learning was not easy, but her intellectual curiosity and commitment
to excellence outweigh her fears:

The independent study experience was frightening
at first. I didn't realize I couldn't fail. I became my
own worst enemy, paralyzed by self-condemnation
and procrastination. At the same time, I was fueled
by enthusiasm for the subject matter. Library and
research skills developed. It took a lot of courage
to read the professors' comments on my essays. I
avoided it for days. Sometimes I knew what was
wrong (I wanted to correct myself). The feedback
has manifested a writing conscience. Improvements
in my writing came slowly. They are evident in organization of material, presentation of details,
grammar, paragraph structure, and development
of ideas. . . .

One of the highlights of my academic career was the field trip to Northern California, a part of a course called Native American Religious Freedom. Our mission was to talk with people involved in a court case that debated the rights of Indians to sacred land. Aside from the excitement of personal contacts, I made thrilling discoveries about the gulf between reality and documentation, the difference between law and history, between history as it is experienced and as it is taught, between law as it is in process and how it appears on paper, and once again the importance of the individual and the danger of generalizations.

The sense of fulfillment is tangible in this student's words. Having a mission in the broad sense of an overriding purpose and in the narrow sense of a concrete assignment provides the vehicle for further discoveries—the indirect payoffs of being fully engaged in any learning project that has personal relevance.

When students are required to write their own educational goals, reflect in writing on what they are discovering, or apply for senior division status, as Alan did, they move from passive to purposeful learners. As Alan said, "When the time came for senior division applications, I had to do some serious thinking as to what I thought I should do with my college education; what I should make of it, and what it would lead to." Few students have the option to design their own degrees. Most choose from those already listed in the catalogue. Students who have made tentative vocational choices and enrolled in a technical or professional program may have a clear path of required courses. Development for less decided students involves actively considering career alternatives and choosing courses related to career plans or emerging talents—not because they are easy courses, taught by a popular instructor, recommended by friends, or offered at a convenient time. A hallmark of development is increasing engagement with coursework and cocurricular activities, which are valued as relevant to career goals or at least valued as stepping-stones to higher-level professional training.

On a deeper level, identifying a life purpose or a sense of one's personal mission may take years of experience and reflection. It may be intuited or vaguely defined in college, for example, as a desire to help people, cure disease, create art, design buildings, or nurture children. These early intimations may be idealistic, but they may also be dreams worth pursuing. A career becomes a true vocation when the work itself brings happiness. Joseph Campbell (1988, p. 91) gave this advice to his students:

> If you follow your bliss, you put yourself on a kind of track that has been there all the while, waiting for you, and the life that you ought to be living is the one you are living. Wherever you are — if you are following your bliss, you are enjoying that refreshment, that life within you, all the time.

Personal Interests

Clarification of vocational plans and aspirations exerts a stabilizing force. When choices have real meaning, increased time is spent on study and other exploratory or preparatory activities. As commitment increases, role considerations begin to be felt. Somehow those activities that were so enjoyable when one was younger are not as appealing now that graduation is approaching. Now a meeting of a professional association may have more attraction than rugby tryouts.

Indeed, it is not surprising that students with the most diverse, rich, and meaningful interests often seem to vacillate most about future plans. It is difficult to recognize, and more difficult to accept, that every affirmation is 90 percent renunciation, that every choice to do one thing is a choice not to do nine others. It is hard to give up becoming a good skier, an accomplished musician, or a creative skit producer in order to pursue a profession. It is hard to give up reading fiction, walking on the beach, talking with friends, building with wood, or watching television. All avocational and recreational interests provide satisfaction and stimulation. Who wants to surrender them for the abstract, unexperienced rewards that may reside down some vocational path? Small wonder that many secure, able, and creative students put off such decisions and spend their energy keeping as many balls in the air as possible.

Interest in dating and socializing, which begins in high school or even earlier, reaches full force during college. A blossoming relationship means less time for activities formerly of interest. Stamp collecting may just have to go. Even with maximum goodwill, flexibility, and energy, whenever two persons spend substantial time together, some interests will get lower priority. True, new interests may emerge as a result of the friendship, but because both must find some satisfaction from them, the net effect is reduced diversity. And as the relationship persists, those interests that both people share and find most satisfying become increasingly stable.

Other avocational interests may be discovered in elective courses, in faculty interactions, in nonrequired reading, and in travel abroad, as this Fairhaven College student writes:

> Yet another surprise at Fairhaven was the nature of student-faculty interaction. In my observations of academia, seldom had I seen exceptions to the hierarchical relationships between students, faculty, administration, and staff. Mutual sharing and participation in the learning process was a welcome surprise. . . .
>
> For years I had wanted to draw but lacked the confidence to lay down a line and begin. In contrast, I had become quite assured in matters of the mind and escaped from the nagging artist within to an intellectual playground. During my junior year, I tentatively peered into the world of art through books, and with some trepidation, I picked up a pen and began to draw. I then began to study art history and in my last quarter undertook an independent study project titled "Creating." This was the culmination of a year's experimentation with different artistic mediums. Drawing with pen and ink and writing

poetry were extremely empowering—I felt very much a beginner but gained much confidence in the fact that I had finally begun to explore a world previously closed to me by my own fears. . . .

The same quarter I picked up the Tao and a pen, I enrolled in an anthropology class on Mexico and central America in preparation for a study abroad stint in Mexico. The class gave me a broad understanding of sociopolitical and historical facets of Latin American culture and prepared me for my senior project. I used Latin America as a foil for better understanding United States culture. . . . I followed pretrip research with a three-month home stay in Mexico, studying the culture and language. After returning, I volunteered with a local group, Central American Refugee Assistance. I was a companion to refugees awaiting hearings in Canada and planned and organized a successful fiesta for refugees and their American host families. Other projects included research and presentation of the Cinco de Mayo holiday to all grades at the Bellingham Cooperative School and volunteering with a local low-cost health clinic, instructing women migrant workers on self-administering breast examinations. . . .

Fairhaven has given me tools that will ensure success as I define it: confidence; respect for all that exists outside myself, including that which I don't understand; an inquisitive and questioning mind; understanding the importance of creating; expression of my own creativity; willingness to risk; appreciation for diversity; resourcefulness. Although Fairhaven was most beneficial in its nontraditional approach, I am thankful for having spent two years on main campus in a mainstream environment. Experiencing both has made me wary of extremes and careful in making judgments. I no longer believe any one way to be the only way [graduating senior].

Whether these interests will be incorporated into this student's identity and long-term priorities remains to be seen, but for now, evidence of development is clear. She has discovered drawing, poetry, art history, cross-cultural awareness, and humanitarian concern.

Some students find a guiding purpose for their personal lives through religious or spiritual development. Involvement with campus ministries, prayer groups, or religious organizations can bring about transforming redefinitions of purpose, as this student reports:

> The most significant change in my adult life (to this point) was my conversion to Christianity. My "old" way of being or thinking was present oriented and self-centered. I sought to meet my own needs and was reluctant in considering others. I viewed my environment as the challenge to overcome—to fulfill immediate wants or needs. I eventually realized a lack of purpose in my life and sought out more significant meaning to my own life and life in general. "Where was I going?" and other future-oriented questions became the central issue in my life. This change was evidenced in my everyday decisions to live as a Christian and, more specifically, to seek education to further my goals. [What helped?] What may have contributed to this process was a lack of satisfaction—of deeper meaning—in my life. Feelings of despair and confusion elicited my search for a more relevant existence. The exposure to Christian teachings fulfilled that need [graduate student].

Personal commitments of time and energy must be made during the college years. Whether they involve letting go of some pastimes and adding new ones, sacrificing some social contacts for deeper relationships, joining a church or questioning the teachings, playing harder or playing less, greater intentionality is needed. College may be an ideal place to experiment, but as homework assignments pile up and senior status signals an end to the scholar's life, students must inevitably become prioritizers.

Interpersonal and Family Commitments

Considerations of life-style and family also enter the equation. As intimate relationships increasingly involve the question of marriage or partnership and as education and vocational exploration draws to a close, clarification of long-range goals, intermediate steps, and immediate requirements become more urgent. It is difficult to construct a plan that balances life-style considerations, vocational aspirations, and avocational interests. Many compromises must be made.

One response to this difficult task is to continue searching for the right path. Robert Frost pondered the possibilities of the road untaken, but he did so while progressing down the other. For some students, the main thing is to avoid the fork. For others, it is to travel a short way down it, maintaining a state of indecision and noncommitment and then returning to the crossroads and trying some of the others.

Josselson's (1987, pp. 108–114) description of Millie portrays this Moratorium phase where testing and searching go on indefinitely, with no firm identity in sight. Millie entered college wanting to be a nurse like her mother. Finding that she did not have the temperament for it, she switched majors three times, first applying for physical therapy but being turned down because of poor grades, then trying psychology, which made her "get too much into myself," and finally settling on biology. She spent two summers working in a nursing home and thought about working in cancer research. However, frog dissection in her physiology class put an end to that. She wished she had prepared for teaching, but it was too late. Feeling tied down by school, she thought about traveling, being a waitress, and generally learning more about life before settling into a routine. Raised a Catholic, she stopped going to church rather than deal with its "hypocrisy." She was apathetic about politics and uncertain about sexual standards, having slept with a man she loved and hoped to marry but who later became abusive. He was, like her father, a strong, authoritarian figure who attempted to control her through ridicule. She left college with no clear sense of what roles she could move into, and over the next few years, continued to drift from a low-paying lab job, to collecting unemployment benefits, to driving a taxi, to a clerical job in a hospital. There she took computer courses in order to move up (pp. 114–115).

There are many students like Millie. They may return to college to gain job skills, or lay the foundation for a new lifestyle after experimenting. For example, this student was embarking on a new direction by enrolling in a community college counseling course. Having tried two extremes, she was planning a new route:

> In the late 1970s, I was living a "hippie" lifestyle I had always wanted to live, in a teepee in northwest Montana. I was for peace, love, and equality, and was spending all my time doing diapers by hand, growing our food, preparing it on the wood cookstove, and hauling water (get the picture?) while he sat around getting stoned, thinking, and talking (with other males only, of course) about "heavy" subjects. After I had had enough, I moved to town, bought a house (with running water), started a business, was very successful in a short period of time, joined the chamber of commerce, and became a materialistic, capitalistic American. But that's another story. I'm better, now that I'm back in college. I think I moved from a very extreme, stagnant life-style to one that allows me more room to do, to be, and so on. I knew a significant change had occurred the first time I pushed a button and the heat came on in the house. [What helped?] In a silly way, the most important person who helped to get me together was an old friend of the family—someone I'd long felt was a twit. She'd come up to the teepee for tea (probably

> herbal) and started talking about a current event
> (political) that I literally didn't have a clue about.
> It frightened me how far I'd regressed—that I
> couldn't even hold my own in a conversation with
> her. It occurred to me for the first time that this
> "free" life I'd always wanted was in its own way very
> restrictive. So I went overboard in the other direc-
> tion for a while. Now I just shave my legs when
> I want to [freshman].

Many returning adults are ready to make commitments in order
to move into more desirable social or economic environments.
Their firsthand knowledge of low-paying, rootless life-styles is
highly motivating.

Students who face several forks in the road as graduation nears will need to decide whether to go on alone or form
partnerships, work or seek further education, or move away or
stay put. Other decisions include whether to rent an apartment,
purchase a house, or perhaps move back in with parents temporarily. Student loans come due; credit cards are a temptation, especially if a new residence has to be furnished or a new
baby is on the way. The newly employed must again confront
the issue of dress and appearance, of a new environment, of
first-time professional and social contacts. The time before and
after commencement is a prime time to ask the following questions: What is my purpose? What is really important? What
do I have to have, and what can I live without? This transitional period can be traversed more easily if the individual will
has been strengthened and the overall ability to think purposefully has increased.

Intentionality

The Goddard faculty studies of Goal-Directedness and Full Involvement, Motivation, and Persistence (Beecher, Chickering,
Hamlin, and Pitkin, 1966; Chickering, 1967) bring this pattern into focus. Goal-directed students were defined as those who
had conscious and fairly well-defined goals that were meaningful
to them, who had developed an ability to see the relationships

between their purposes and other aspects of their lives, and whose studies had increased in focus and depth through their relationships to personal goals. Eight questions to make this definition more specific were used as a basis for rating student records, which consisted of student self-evaluations and instructor comments. The questions were as follows:

1. Is the student's program planned with reference to a clear goal or purpose?
2. Are courses or independent studies evaluated in terms of their helpfulness or contribution to a larger purpose?
3. Are objectives for study explicitly related to more general plans or purposes?
4. Is there recognition of gaps in knowledge or skills in relation to purpose?
5. Are efforts made or plans formulated to deal with gaps or weaknesses?
6. Are there general expressions of feeling lost, at loose ends, without any purpose or direction? (reverse scoring)
7. Do plans for the Nonresident Work Term reflect concern for some general plan or purpose?
8. How solid does the final commitment seem?

The average ratings on these eight questions increased each semester, with the sharpest increase occurring in the fourth semester, during which application was made to the senior division based on clearer specification of future plans. When colleges require reflection, exploration of alternatives, and planning, vocational plans and aspirations take shape more quickly.

The faculty also defined "purposeful students" as well motivated and working for their own satisfaction. They had the energy and determination to keep at a job. They were willing to tackle routine or difficult jobs congruent with their purposes and could overcome obstacles. They persevered in spite of mistakes or difficulties. They could sustain effort in the face of distractions and seek out, in addition to academic work, extra activities related to their goals. This variable was called Full Involvement, Motivation, and Persistence. The questions used for rating student records were the following:

1. In general, how well motivated, persistent, and fully involved is this student?
2. What is the general level of effort reflected in preparation for classes, work on papers, and in relation to other kinds of responsibilities?
3. How consistent, steady, and regular is the student's output?
4. How great is the student's interest, enthusiasm, and intensity of involvement in his or her work?
5. How good is attendance in relation to the general expectations and nature of the class?
6. What is the level of participation as compared to that which seems to be usual or satisfying for the student?

Again ratings indicated that change occurred over the four-year period. Ratings dropped during the fifth semester, after admission to the senior division, but recovery was strong during the sixth and seventh semesters.

Vocational plans and aspirations become increasingly clear for most students as they move through college. Purposes important to the student become stronger. This increasing strength and clarity influences the areas of study selected and the reasons for the students' choice, the amount of energy they give to study and other preparatory activities, and the nature of their engagement with other aspects of the college experience. Purposes need not be highly specific, nor must commitment be absolute. Sufficient clarity of direction must exist to plan the next destination, even though the whole itinerary may not be clear.

Purpose works on a deeper level than goals, objectives, and activities. Purpose and integrity are interrelated. Bender (1989) created a self-directed learning project designed to counteract what she called the "tyranny of lists." An accomplished artist and therapist, she valued accomplishments and results. She pursued her daily goals and activities with great intensity, believing that what really mattered most in life was being independent and having many choices. As a result, her life had pattern, but it resembled a crazy quilt. Drawn by the order and serenity of quilts made by the Amish, she found a way to live for several weeks in an Amish community in Brimfield, Iowa. Her book *Plain and Simple: A Woman's Journey to the Amish* tells about her experiences and what she learned about how to bring purpose and unity into her life.

She realized that there were many things she did not have choices about: "the decent and loving family I was born into; the social, religious or economic circumstance of that family; or to be 5'10" tall, have brown hair, a thin frame, a hearty constitution, or a questioning nature" (p. 131). She realized that she had tried to achieve without first knowing who she was or what really mattered. She reclaimed her past and stopped working so hard to change herself, trusting that she had everything she needed inside and did not have to choose between one part of herself and another. She also realized she did not have to be judged by a label that placed people in status-based hierarchies. She remembered her host making vegetable soup and saying, "It's not right for the carrot to say I taste better than the peas, or the pea to say I taste better than the cabbage. It takes all the vegetables to make a good soup!" (p. 130).

She learned to value both process and product, to honor all work, both ordinary and unusual, and to practice single-minded focus. Rather than trying to stand out by creating prize-winning art, she worked with no plan, creating an empty space or "fertile void" for intuition to come through. "The Amish often leave a space, a seeming mistake in the midst of their well-thought-out plans, to serve as an opening to let the spirit come in" (p. 136). She simplified, removed what was superfluous, saw what was essential, and realized that accepting limits and making a commitment to do her best at what she did well brought greater freedom.

A strong commitment to a value or belief can determine purpose. If one believes it is important to be authentic, to be patient, to be conscientious, then developing or embodying that quality can become one's purpose. Values constitute important frames of reference that add depth to purpose and context to action. Beliefs give us images of how the world is and should be. In clarifying purpose, we must therefore go beyond what is merely interesting and find an anchoring set of assumptions about what is true, principles that define what is good, and beliefs that provide meaning and give us a sense of our place in the larger whole.

EIGHT

Developing
Integrity

Developing integrity is closely related to establishing identity and clarifying purposes. Our core values and beliefs provide the foundation for interpreting experience, guiding behavior, and maintaining self-respect. Students bring to college an array of core values and beliefs — that is, assumptions about what is right and wrong, true and false, good and bad, important and unimportant. Younger students may have acquired these assumptions from parents, church, school, media, or other sources. Older students bring life experiences fraught with moral dilemmas, unanswered questions, and hard lessons. Regardless of age, developing integrity involves reviewing personal values in an inquiring environment that emphasizes diversity, critical thinking, the use of evidence, and experimentation. It may involve an affirmation of values that have ongoing relevance, a search for new ways to interpret complex realities and reconcile discordant perspectives, or a substantive shift away from old values. Throughout this examination, students explore the links between values and behavior. They observe themselves and the people around them, constantly assessing and comparing. They struggle with the gaps between belief and practice, between words and deeds, between ideals and flawed actualities.

Movement toward greater integrity involves efforts to bring behavior into alignment with a personally valid and internally consistent set of values.

In discussing the concept of integrity, it is important to differentiate between the content of values and the processes used to apply them. For example, Barron (1963) pointed out that people can be rigid, dogmatic, and closed to evidence contrary to their beliefs whether they are liberals or conservatives, believers or disbelievers. He identified four different patterns, which he labeled fundamentalist belief, enlightened belief, fundamental disbelief, and enlightened disbelief. Fundamentalist believers and fundamentalist disbelievers had in common low ratings on flexibility and adaptability, even though the particular beliefs they held were dramatically opposed.

A student may arrive with traditional religious beliefs, conservative political views, or self-righteous social judgments and continue to voice those beliefs tenaciously until graduation. Does this indicate a high level of integrity? Another student may enter college with cynicism and materialistic values, even believing that it is not wrong to lie, cheat, or bully others to get ahead. If the student leaves college with self-serving values intact, having plagiarized or intimidated as a result of those values, would that also be a kind of integrity?

From our perspective, movement toward integrity means not only increased congruence between behavior and values, but also movement toward responsibility for self and others and the consistent ability to thoughtfully apply ethical principles. We propose that maintaining rigid beliefs without openness to new information and without the ability to seriously consider other points of view before taking a position is not the same as the development of integrity, for then there is no real choice making, no moral conflict. There is only the foregone conclusion of the rightness of one's own position. Likewise, clinging to selfish values that justify hedonistic or exploitative behavior or submitting to internal rules that demean or deny one's own best interests or the welfare of others does not constitute integrity.

Developing integrity involves three sequential but overlapping stages: (1) humanizing values—shifting away from automatic application of uncompromising beliefs and using principled thinking in balancing one's own self-interest with the interests of one's fellow human beings, (2) personalizing values — consciously affirming core values and beliefs while respecting other points of view, and (3) developing congruence — matching personal values with socially responsible behavior.

Humanizing Values

A student who goes through college can conceivably do so from a completely detached point of view, treating everything as an intellectual exercise without allowing critical questions to sink in. The student may continue to hold dogmatic beliefs, whether they are rooted in religious tradition, pure scientific rationalism, or unexamined prejudice. A faculty member in an Education program reported a student in one of her classes who adamantly insisted on his right to a politically incorrect perspective — that whites were genetically superior to other races. The instructor was in a quandary about how to deal with this future teacher. Should she respect his right to believe in racial superiority, hoping that his behavior in the classroom would be nondiscriminatory, or should she hold him to a standard of demonstrated multicultural sensitivity before allowing him to move on? The student solved the teacher's problem by dropping out, but the department continued to discuss the difficult issue of which values it should be consciously imparting and how to evaluate the professional ethics of its graduates.

Most students do experience changes in their values during college. Pascarella and Terenzini (1991) review extensive research conducted on attitude and value change among students since the publication of Feldman and Newcomb's *The Impact of College on Students* (1969). Findings on students' changing social, political, and religious values have special relevance to integrity. Pascarella and Terenzini (1991, pp. 277–279, 283) find "abundant and consistent" evidence of movement toward greater altruism, humanitarianism, and social conscience, more liberal political stances, more interest in social and political issues, more involvement in the political process. They also find more social, racial, ethnic, and political tolerance and greater support for the rights of individuals, for due process, and for gender equality with respect to education, employment, and family roles. Along with these shifts toward increasing openness and "other-person" orientation, the literature published since 1967 consistently reports statistically significant declines in religious attitudes, values, and behaviors during the college wars.

These findings are consistent with Perry's (1970) model of intellectual and ethical development, which describes students moving away from dualistic, black-and-white thinking and becoming more liberal as they are increasingly exposed to alternative perspectives. White (1958) uses the phrase "humanizing of values" to describe the same process. He calls attention to Piaget's (1932, p. 353) work, which "demonstrated a trend from a literal belief in rules, almost as if they had an independent physical existence, to an attitude of relativity, in which precepts were perceived in relation to the social purposes they were designed to serve." Sanford (1962, p. 278) calls this change the "liberalization of the superego" or the "enlightenment of conscience."

For many college students, humanizing values is like urban development. Old structures are torn down, blown apart, or otherwise demolished — and the demolition frequently is carried out at the same high level of indiscriminate fervor and ponderous momentum that recently has destroyed many fine and sound buildings of former times. Misery and misgivings are the lot of nearby inhabitants and distant admirers. But remodeling is in order, and for some college students, blasting is the only way to prepare the building for new structures better able to carry the increased traffic and new modes of existence. Some students break free by moving dramatically to the opposite frame of reference, at least temporarily:

> I was raised in a religious family that taught me that either everything bad that happened to me was punishment or was some trial or test by God that I had to endure. Even though I rejected this long ago, I still felt as if I were a victim, as if someone was always looking over my shoulder. It took the

horror of war to make me realize that it wasn't God inflicting pain, but that we did these horrible things to ourselves, or they happened by accident. I woke up one morning in a foxhole and the someone looking over my shoulder was gone. I knew that I was now in control of my life. Then I tried just about everything I wasn't supposed to do to test my new-found freedom, to see if in fact I would be punished. I felt free, as if a great weight or black cloud had been removed from my life and I could take risks without fear of going to hell. I set about making my own heaven [senior].

This veteran brought his value issues into the campus setting. Having rejected a vindictive image of God and having tried all the forbidden fruits, he was searching for a new foundation of beliefs. He learned from experience that neither fear of punishment nor unlimited gratification was acceptable, and so he set about taking personal responsibility for counteracting the pain around him. His choice was to intern in a human service agency.

Disillusionment with authorities can also launch a new search, as this student reports:

I used to have some very strong, definite feelings about religious worship. Although I felt many forms of worship might be valid for others, I did not allow that flexibility for myself. A very unpleasant experience caused me to do some "soul searching." I felt like an orphan for awhile. I moved to a broader concept of religion and worship. I knew that a significant change had occurred when my emotions no longer felt bruised. I came to a new level of acceptance of myself and others. [What helped the process?] A person in authority committed acts of immorality and exhibited a lack of ethics. The experience was not one event but a long chain of events. I had feelings of disappointment, grief, outrage, fear, and abandonment [junior].

This student took time to sort through her experiences and re-define her religious beliefs and practices, spurred on by the hypocrisy she observed and by her strong feelings.

Others may make an intellectual change in response to challenges presented in class, as this former student writes:

> I was taking a theology class as a freshman in col-lege and was presented with "bold" alternatives to understand and interpret the creation story—pri-marily to understand it as a myth. My life up to that point was characterized by asking many ques-tions but arriving at few answers. To those in my fundamentalist background, those questions were annoyances but not insurmountable problems. In my shift to some answers to those questions, I moved away from fundamentalism to a more broadly based and responsible manner of critical thinking. [What helped?] The professor was very bright and respon-sible, yet in a sophisticated way he was somewhat irreverent. I was troubled by the dilemmas that this posed for me in terms of my belief structures, but something about the information and the self-assur-ance of the professor encouraged me to embrace this new way of thinking [student affairs staff member].

These self-identified turning points all illustrate the hu-manizing of values. Just as Perry observed students becoming more relativistic in their thinking—that is, more attuned to con-text, to evidence, to the particular situation, to how this fits into a broader picture—so J. W. Fowler (1981) proposed a model for spiritual development that moves toward multidimensional approaches to life and truth. In the earlier developmental stages, moral rules and religious teachings are interpreted literally. But if the stories are seen to contradict each other or if the teach-ings contradict life experience, literalism breaks down. New teachers may be found, but sooner or later, interpreters are bound to differ. As students deal with tensions between ancient traditions and new ideas, conformity and questioning, guilt and freedom, self-interest and unselfishness, they slowly recognize the need to take responsibility for defining their own positions, to commit to beliefs that ring true to their deepest selves, while remaining open and tolerant.

A graduate student reflecting on her journey from China to the United States recounts her spiritual development, illustrating the humanizing process with vivid memories:

> Obedience governed my behavior during childhood and adolescent years. As a child, I liked to run and feel carefree. This free spirit was quickly put to an end by adults who thought that running was unladylike. In school when a teacher assigned a lesson to be memorized, I would spend numerous hours reading the text aloud until I could recite it by heart. Failure to complete an assignment could mean physical punishment, which was permissible in China. . . .
>
> When we lived in Bangkok, my father returned to the Catholic faith. An Italian priest who once worked as a missionary in China became our family priest. Father X. taught me the French language. He helped me to secure a scholarship from a Catholic college in the United States. His dedication to his mission and his kindness inspired me greatly.
>
> When I arrived at college, the sisters patiently helped me to pronounce English words and to adjust to the new culture. The need to create a new home and the wish to express my appreciation of the nuns led me to baptism. For a few years, I studied the Church doctrines. I followed the rules conscientiously. In the chapel I listened to the beautiful Gregorian chants. I whispered to the statue of Christ hung above the candles: "Are you a man or a god? Why is the Christian god so domineering and controlling?" I longed for the folktales from my homeland that teach human values.

It was not easy to leave the Catholic church. Disappointing the nuns who had nurtured me during my difficult years in America was unbearable. Heaven and hell were insignificant compared to that. Besides, in a totally Catholic environment, giving up the church membership was socially unacceptable. As a cousin of mine, a Franciscan nun, said, "Catholicism is not a passing whim to be discarded lightly."

I searched for a new identity in California. I met people who were very much in tune with the American traditional values, individuals who participated in the civil rights and the antiwar movements, young people who sought meaning through religious cults, new life-styles, free sex, or the use of hallucinogens. Once I visited a commune whose members grew their own food and built solar shelters. A writer friend of mine found spiritual renewal in her literary work. My artist cousin protested the Vietnam War through his art and films.

I learned that people found their religion in different forms: human creativity, commitment to a cause, a cult, group experience, or an established church. My nun cousin was absolutely correct that Catholicism should not be a passing whim, because spiritually she was very much a part of the Catholic Church. But when I saw that religion appears in various forms, I bade Catholicism farewell. Today I believe that religious freedom must include respect for individuals' autonomy, for faith must come from within, not from an external authority that practices control and indoctrination [graduate student].

Thus, freedom and autonomy became deeply felt values for this student, as did appreciation for whatever form of spiritual expression she encountered. The exploration process began with obedience to preordained rules but evolved when discomfort and awareness led to a journey of discovery. What stands out is not the validity of textual teachings, but the human connection to those in the church who nurtured her as well as to those she encountered in the counterculture.

Often it is pain or conflict that catalyzes the humanizing process. One absolute standard clashes with another. Interpersonal relationships offer fertile grounds for values exploration. For example, this student describes the difficulty:

> I felt myself becoming less and less emotionally involved. The dilemma developed as I realized that I was becoming emotionally less committed, but he wasn't. And even though my feelings about him were fading somewhat, I found the warmth and security of the relationship hard to give up. So . . . what to do? Should I be completely honest and end the relationship as soon as I knew that I wasn't willing to commit to it long term, if I knew that a long-term commitment was what he wanted? Or should I just stay quiet and let my silence hide the truth while I hung onto the companionship and security the relationship offered? Was it dishonest to do that? Was it misleading? Was it fair? What guidelines was I supposed to follow in this situation? What were my responsibilities to him and to myself? [graduate student].

We may wonder whether these values issues can surface at all if students are not as aware of their feelings as this student was and are not able to manage them to some extent. Integrity requires the ability to detach, to withhold judgment, while staying in touch with persistent feelings and asking the kinds of questions she asked. It is easy to suppress discomfort, especially if acknowledging it might lead us to leave the church, the family, or the relationship. This student is clearly looking for a standard that feels right to her, and she seems to feel confident about expressing her feelings, should she choose to do so. Many unassertive students do not even acknowledge this choice. One student wrote her reactions to Carol Gilligan's book *In a Different Voice: Psychological Theory and Women's Development* (1982):

Gilligan says that the women she studied often made
moral decisions by acting so that no one would be
hurt. They assessed the morality of action based
on its appearance in the eyes of others, rather than
on the realities of its intention and consequences.
I can truly relate to these patterns. So much of my
life was dictated by the church and by my feelings
of powerlessness. I always tried to make decisions
that would reduce conflict (rather than act on what
was true for me), so as not to cause problems with
my family. I wanted approval and caring from my
family and peers, and the whole idea of self-assertion meant being selfish and therefore deserving of
condemnation. I would feel guilty if I did something for me. I now am aware of this, and even
though I still feel some guilt when I make a decision with myself in mind instead of everyone else's
feelings, I feel positive about my progress. I can
no longer carry the burden of making everyone else
happy at my expense [graduate student].

For many students, the power to express what one sees,
feels, and wants and the obligation to care about others are mutually exclusive concepts. This student is asking, like some of the
women in Gilligan's study, "whether it is selfish or responsible,
moral or immoral, to include her own needs within the com-
pass of her care and concern. . . . In separating the voice of the
self from the voices of others, the woman asks if it is possible
to be responsible to herself as well as to others and thus to reconcile the disparity between hurt and care. The exercise of such
responsibility requires a new kind of judgment, whose first demand is for honesty. To be responsible for oneself, it is first
necessary to acknowledge what one is doing" (Gilligan, 1982,
pp. 82–83).

A developmental change has occurred when students can
get beyond polarized ways of thinking to a new synthesis that
incorporates both honesty and caring, both power and empathy, both rule and exception. This former student reports the
synthesizing of diverse cultural attitudes:

I worked with a small group of Japanese students for a period of six weeks. During this time I had a lot of fun but didn't realize until after the students left and another group came and went that I had changed my attitude about the American culture and different cultures. It was the first time that I realized that our culture's way of doing something wasn't necessarily the best way of doing things, and more than that, the values that I had always had were being questioned (by me). The first year I moved to an opposite extreme—that I didn't like American culture very well. The following year I made some new discoveries that neither was "better," just very different, as were many other cultures. This prodded me into the desire to learn more about other cultures. I didn't know at the time that this change was occurring, but now that I look back, it's easy to see the changes that took place [student affairs staff member].

The shift from *either/or* to *both/and* signifies that a humanizing of values is happening. This involves a reflection and reassessment process leading to an insight that the earlier belief no longer tells the whole story or that the unyielding assumptions need softening. It may entail letting go of things or people we formerly embraced and tolerating the kind of ambiguity that constantly appears in human experience.

Personalizing Values

While students are more likely to report the dramatic ethical conflicts when asked to reflect on developmental turning points, most of the movement toward integrity is gradual. Like the student quoted above, they may not realize that a lasting change has occurred until they reflect on it. The basis on which values rest, the ways they are held, and the force with which they operate in daily life may be of more importance—within limits—than the particular values held. In a democratic society with many different cultures, where cultural pluralism is itself a value, and where all citizens have a right to their own convictions as long as others are not damaged, the most significant contribution a college can make may be to increase students' tolerance for diverse values while encouraging them to affirm their own principles.

Humanizing values does not mean anything goes. It means modifying values and beliefs to include more humane frames of reference, balancing the ethic of care with the ethic of justice, and learning to apply principles flexibly based on analysis and understanding. Depending on the situation, it may be best to be subtle or direct, unyielding or conciliatory, irate or ironic. The realization that fundamental rightness, unchanging meaning, and unfailing advice do not necessarily exist in the external world can lead to deep anxiety. Perry (1970) observed that some students react by temporizing, retreating, or escaping. They may postpone or avoid a commitment, hoping that the light will dawn sooner or later. Others may regress to more dualistic reliance on external authority; tired of uncertainty and confusion, a career counselor who can prescribe the right job and even place them in it can offer much relief. Some may escape by dropping out or adopting positions of permanent uninvolvement or alienation.

Most students proceed to work on some kind of internalized and more solid supporting structure, a framework of principles and commitments. At first this foundation is suitable for some circumstances and not others, and even then it may wobble. But with time, testing, and redesigning, a broader and more stable platform is built. Gradually, beliefs become less tenuously held. They provide a more comprehensive basis for judgments about the actions, policies, and personality characteristics of others and provide implicit and explicit criteria for one's own behaviors and choices.

This is the development of what Smith (1963) calls self-requiredness. Values are "owned up to." They are accepted as part of oneself and as what one stands for. They are consciously held and can be articulated. As a result, they also can be challenged and can be modified in light of further experience or new evidence from the experiences of others. It is like acquiring and maintaining a new wardrobe. Not only is it necessary to keep things clean and pressed, but worn and outmoded items must be replaced. Usually such replacement occurs piecemeal and does not tax the budget. But occasionally change in circumstance or personal characteristics may require extensive outfitting, accomplished at considerable cost and strain to personal economy.

For example, this Fairhaven College student reports a major shift in her cultural and educational values and her growing efforts to personalize her own standards for action:

> I began my undergraduate education immediately following twelve years of private school instruction and was instantly overwhelmed by university culture. I remained in an academic trance, unstimulated and alienated by large classes, the typical mode of presentation, and the usual methods of evaluation until my second year of college. This frustrated my burgeoning intellectual curiosity; academia seemed to be a door to worlds of discovery and knowledge, yet the normative pedagogy and evaluation methods were blocking the way to the knob. I maintained an above-average GPA in that first year not because I was learning a tremendous amount, but because achieving good grades was an interesting challenge and a way to exercise and strengthen my memory.
>
> In my fourth quarter, I enrolled in a political science class called Poverty, Minorities, and Government. Its content provoked, disturbed, and shook my cultural foundations. For perhaps the first time, I was introduced clearly and intensively to concepts like ethnocentrism and colonialism and the nature of power relationships manifest in the world. I became aware of the implications of my status as a white middle-class woman and U.S. citizen. Much of what I had learned previously about my country and cultures was revealed as being only part of a complex picture. . . .

Another first in the class was recognition from the professor. I became more than a number, one of the hundred student faces he saw daily. We had a number of exchanges, orally and in writing. This was very satisfying to me. I glimpsed for the first time a different way of "doing school," wherein I as a student was a significant individual instead of a number, interacted consistently and face to face with professors, and was encouraged to question and respond with my ideas rather than simply memorize and regurgitate someone else's. It was his commitment to students' learning, combined with my thirst for knowledge, that motivated me to turn the knob on that academic door. . . .

I enrolled in three Fairhaven classes. Though it was a radical change from my previous education, I was ripe for Fairhaven's methods of teaching and expectations of self-motivation. I craved to learn, to explore without restraint the new worlds and perspective opening up to me. Initially, the shift from traditional to alternative education was difficult. If my cultural foundations were shaken in the Poverty, Minorities, and Government class, they were shattered—and rebuilt in different form— during my first quarter. Fairhaven was the first time in my schooling since grade two that I was expected to perform in my own way, encouraged and trusted to direct my own learning. Among other things, the past two years have involved a slow process of rediscovering what "my" way is. . . . Dr. K. played a significant role by taking the time to carefully edit and respond to my writing. Never before had anyone so forthrightly challenged my assumptions about the world and the nature of truth. This provoked much introspection and examination of my beliefs and worldview [graduating senior].

College staff members can be of great assistance by inviting students to find their own way—of acting, communicating, and performing in the world. This requires personal dialogue and time to reflect, as well as an opportunity to consider both subjective and objective knowledge in constructing one's own answers to life's important questions. Multiple-choice tests do not help this process, nor does experiential learning without reflective observation. Mezirow (1991) differentiates between reflection and "introspection" or "nonreflective action." Stimulated by a problematic situation, reflection is "the process of critically assessing the content, process, or premise(s) of our efforts to interpret and give meaning to an experience" (p. 104). It involves not just thinking consciously about our actions but reaffirming or changing the value-based belief systems used to make meaning. This process goes beyond merely correcting a misinterpretation. It "is more likely to involve our whole sense of self and always involves critical reflection upon the distorted premises sustaining our structure of expectation" (p. 167).

The following report signals another facet of the personalizing process. This student identifies the "distorted premises" by reflecting on the beliefs that have kept her from being successful:

> I began my education with the relatively simple goal of preparing myself to pass the state massage licensing boards. I had informally been doing various kinds of healing work for years, for free, and felt it was time to learn more, to become more proficient, and to be able to be paid for something I enjoyed and was able to do well. Although it took much longer than I anticipated, I did pass the boards with flying colors. I have become a good massage therapist and am slowly beginning my business. Learning to do massage was the easy part; overcoming my personal barriers to success is still difficult. . . .
>
> Because I decided to stay with my education after passing the state test, I found the opportunity to take some classes in women's studies and to immerse myself in the supportive, introspective community of this college. I was able to look at the self-sabotaging behavior that manifested when I came

close to finishing something, succeeding at something I felt was important. I battled futilely against
my resistance, not quite understanding that resist-
ing resistance only compounded it. I struggled with
all the judgments of my culture, my subcultures,
and my personal neuroses:

- Money is the root of all evil; I shouldn't have
  any.
- Suffering is good and more suffering is better.
- You can't enjoy your work; work and life must
  be separate.
- I don't deserve to be paid.
- I must give up my power, especially to males.
- Healing should always be free.
- I don't know what I'm doing, and what if some-
  one finds out?
- I'll fail anyway; better quit before someone no-
  tices I'm really trying.

And now I have to deal with the judgment
that I chose the healer's path because I am a female,
conditioned by society to be self-sacrificing, "loving too much," or even "codependent." The more
I overcome my own inner judgments and barriers
to open the way to my inner voice, the more it
seems others drape and enfold me with their truths,
and once again I find myself losing touch with my
own truth, my voice, my power [graduating senior].

To develop integrity, this student must reframe each of these
beliefs, based on ethical principles, logic, and evidence. She has
made an excellent start by naming them and realizing that they
serve as psychological shackles.

To personalize values is to engage in what Kohlberg called
"principled reasoning." Kohlberg (1971) organizes six stages of
moral development into three broader levels. At the preconventional level, moral decisions are based on obedience to rules,

cultural labels of good and bad, the power of rewards and punishments, or mutual interests ("You scratch my back and I'll scratch yours"). At the conventional level, conforming to the expectations of one's family, group, or nation is seen as valuable in its own right, and individuals strive to please others, show respect for authority, and do their duty. At the postconventional or principled level, an individual effort is made to define moral values and principles valid apart from the groups that hold them. This cannot occur until a clear awareness of the contextually relative nature of morality exists; in other words, people must be aware that ethics are constructed by human thought rather than proved by objective justification. Then, aside from what is agreed to through majority vote or the rule of law, right action is a matter of personal values, negotiated agreements, and more abstract, universal principles, like justice, equality, fairness, respect for individual persons, and the Golden Rule.

As noted in Chapter One, Gilligan (1982, 1986a) has criticized Kohlberg's scoring system for using justice-oriented dilemmas that place care-oriented responses at a lower developmental level. She points out that this model handicaps women, since she and her colleagues have found that about 80 percent of women prefer the "care voice" (viewing moral dilemmas in terms of relationships and the needs of others) and about 70 percent of men prefer the "justice voice" (emphasizing the effects of moral choice on the self and evaluating action based on rules and principles of fairness).

While the debate continues about the applicability of Kohlberg's model for women, it has been the most widely used theoretical framework for researching the influence of college on moral development, according to Pascarella and Terenzini (1991, p. 336). For example, they cite Rest and associates (p. 339), who synthesized data from over fifty published and unpublished cross-sectional studies that used the Defining Issues Test (DIT), representing over 5,700 subjects and 136 different samples. Average scores based on responses to moral dilemmas tended to increase about ten points at each level of education as a student progressed from junior high to senior high to college to graduate school. According to Pascarella and Terenzini,

"Remarkably similar results were reported in other cross-sectional studies, which showed that upperclassmen or seniors tended to give greater preference to principled moral considerations in making moral decisions than did underclassmen or freshmen" (p. 339). Studies in Hong Kong, Korea, Iceland, the Philippines, and Australia were also cited, again indicating that "subjects who were older and who had completed higher levels of formal education (through college) tended to attribute more importance to principled moral considerations on the DIT than subjects who were younger and not as well educated" (p. 340).

Whether the DIT or the "Moral Judgment Interview" (MJI) was used, Pascarella and Terenzini conclude that

> The overwhelming weight of evidence . . . suggests that extent of principled moral reasoning is positively associated with level of formal postsecondary education and that students generally make statistically significant gains in principled moral reasoning during college. . . . We infer from the body of evidence that *a* major (if not *the* major) change that takes place during college is a movement from conventional moral reasoning toward postconventional moral reasoning. It would also appear that the greatest gains in principled moral reasoning occur during the first or the first and second years of college. The latter conclusion is tentative, however, because it is based on a small number of investigations [p. 343].

One could argue that measures based on Kohlberg's theory would naturally produce higher levels of postconventional reasoning, since colleges, like other institutions, tend to perpetuate the dominant value system, including the "justice voice" and the male point of view (if there *is* one). On the other hand, postconventional reasoning can also invoke the "care voice," the Golden Rule, and other universal values. The research appears to support the proposition that students increasingly clarify their personal values, apart from those held by peers, family, and society. They move through a rule-oriented, legalistic way of thinking toward a preference for more abstract principles and confidence in their own interpretations. Once students have achieved greater clarity, the next challenge is to use those principles consistently to guide behavior.

Developing Congruence

For Carl Rogers (1961), congruence is the peak of personhood. The congruent person achieves an accurate "matching of experience, awareness, and communication" (p. 339). Authentic persons are without facade. Where they stand is clear to others, and more important, is clear to themselves. Erikson's (1950) description of integrity is consistent with Rogers's. He says that "it is the acceptance of one's one and only life cycle and of the people who have become significant to it as something that had to be and that, by necessity, permitted no substitutions. It thus means a new, a different love of one's parents, free of the wish that they should have been different, and an acceptance of the fact that one's life is one's own responsibility. It is a sense of comradeship with men and women of distant times and of different pursuits, who have created orders and objects and sayings conveying human dignity and love" (p. 143).

Life constantly offers us opportunities to test our congruence by behaving according to espoused values. Argyris and Schön (1974) conducted revealing research with educators and administrators who said they believed in honesty, openness, and collaboration. They asked subjects to record or reconstruct important dialogues with colleagues and then analyzed their behavior. The incongruity between what they *said* they did and what they *actually* did usually came as a complete and unpleasant surprise to them. One minister found, to his dismay, that in trying to organize a church protest against the bombing of Cambodia, he was unwittingly acting just like President Nixon by trying to railroad his congregation and withhold information from his church board. Rather than being open and collaborative, he controlled the agenda, unilaterally defined the goals, tried to control the process and the outcome, distorted facts, and suppressed feelings.

This pattern was termed the *mystery-mastery strategy,* since initiators seek to put a veil of mystery over their own intentions and to master others (Torbert, 1981). Argyris and Schön found that this strategy was characteristic of virtually all the professionals in their graduate courses, whatever their fields. It is a style that students observe in every classroom and every meeting where leaders have not adopted an inquiring strategy that maximizes valid information, invites others to make informed choices, and promotes truly mutual commitment. Honesty and good communication take much practice, and it is easy to self-delude without skilled observers who can confront our blind spots.

Many students know perfectly well what they "should" do, but faced with real-life pressures and temptations, they revert to what is most comfortable or self-protective. Sometimes they can rationalize violations of ethics, but if the relentless voice of conscience combines with support for reform, congruence can be restored, as this story illustrates:

> Like many college graduates, I left the university with several thousand dollars of debt. I had nine months to acquire a job and begin paying off the loans. Instead, I abandoned that responsibility and borrowed more money to go to graduate school.
>
> I had no idea what it meant to be in debt for that much money. I had received paychecks through previous summer and school employment, but that gave me no sense of what it meant to take part of every paycheck to pay off a loan. My father "protected" me from learning the details of monetary responsibility. I used to see him working on his bills at the kitchen table. When I would ask him to show me what he was doing, he would brush me off and say, "Don't worry about it until you have to."

Nevertheless, I had every intention of paying back my loan. When I did land my first real job, I set up arrangements to pay $50 a month on my loan. I did that for two years. Then I moved to another city and after two months acquired a job as a bookseller. I did not tell the bank about my move. Although they had my family's address, I was essentially lost in their records. I was making less money and welcomed the reprieve, although I still intended to pay my debt.

After a year I got a job as a file clerk in a city attorney's office. It was not a lot of money, though I probably could have afforded to begin paying on my loan again. But somehow the bank did not track me down. I knew it was wrong not to pay back the loan, but I was looking out for what was best for me. Starting payments on my loan again would trap me, I felt, into a job I did not want. I had pangs of guilt for several more years, and I moved to another area of the country, into a university setting again, for work and graduate school.

The federal government began to crack down on defaulted loans. Increasingly, I became nervous about getting caught. I also felt that my social group would not approve of my behavior (one of my close associates being the director of financial aid) and had an increasing sense that it was unethical for me to not pay. It finally dawned on me that my nonpayment was hurting college students today, making it harder for them to get student loans. I paid back my debt in full, with interest [graduate student].

Here we see all three levels of Kohlberg's model apparently coming together — the preconventional fear of punishment, the conventional concern with peers' approval, and the principled reasoning that "I need to feel good about myself by honoring my commitment, and in so doing, help others." The student's approach reflected Hemingway's loose definition of ethical behavior: "What's moral is what feels good after. What's immoral is what feels bad after." While immediate circumstances made it easy to escape and short-term financial relief felt good, the ongoing disparity between the moral imperative and the dodging behavior finally forced closure.

Researchers have produced an impressive body of evidence to suggest positive, systemic links between principled moral reasoning and what might be considered moral behavior among college students. Pascarella and Terenzini (1991, p. 363) report a variety of studies showing statistically significant positive associations between principled moral reasoning and resistance to cheating, resistance to peer pressure, resistance to unlawful or oppressive authority in the Milgram "shock experiment" paradigm, and civil disobedience. It was significantly and positively linked with "whistle-blowing" on corruption, keeping contractual promises, political and social activism, nonaggression, and helping behavior.

Students may have an easier time determining their obligation to keep promises and act on injustices than in applying moral principles in complex relationships. Sexual attraction seems to be the great confounder of earlier vows. One regretful student writes:

> While in my high school days, I somehow came up with a moral code for my life. It consisted of three rules: I would not use drugs or alcohol, I would not smoke, and I would not have sexual intercourse before marriage. Knowing the effect of drugs and nicotine on the body and not liking the party scene made it easy to live by the first two rules. The third was part of my Christian belief system, that sex should occur in the context of mutual commitment, for life.
>
> However, being of sound mind and body and being a nineteen-year-old sophomore, sexual temptation became a moral dilemma. I was a resident

aide when this relationship took place with a woman who had authority over me. She was one of those women who turned my head. The first time I saw her, I thought, "Wow! She's pretty!" I never believed I'd ever get close to her because of her age, position, and station in life. We started out as great friends, and the feelings grew stronger. I was so amazed by our caring for one another and proud that this woman could care for me. I wanted to express my caring through physical intimacy, but since it was not only wrong but also supposed to be some kind of mystical happening, my impulses caused fear, anticipation, and excitement.

The decision to have intercourse was made, despite reservations, more by my emotions and glands than my brains and my beliefs. I knew it was going to have to be a hush-hush thing, and this secrecy, though exciting in its own weird way, ate at me. My friends had the satisfaction of being open with their lives, but not I. This hurt me and frustrated me deeply. The physical part of our relationship became too much of a focus, and I became jealous of her with other guys and fearful of losing her.

Now I view this as a loss of personal integrity and one of the biggest mistakes I've made. While I loved this friend with all my heart, I know I messed up. The toughest thing remains that I was hypocritical to what I say I believed and didn't discipline my behavior. I felt selfish and guilty. I never looked at women in the same way again. I had to confess to my fiance that I was not a virgin, and this became a very difficult issue to work through before our marriage [graduate student].

This student achieved congruence after disobeying his own rule and learning from the consequences. His renewed commitment to Christianity has been sharpened by reflecting and judging himself. Other students may have a positive experience with sexual intimacy, and finding no accommodations within church teachings, feel forced to depart. These struggles also have implications for college friends who become confidants, as this student recalls about a friend's dilemma:

> Joan and I were friends in high school. We played basketball together, lived in the same residence hall during our freshman year, and as sophomores got together for lunch or a movie about once a month. At the end of our sophomore year, she confided to me that she had fallen in love with her female roommate and was feeling very guilty about their physical interaction. Joan was a staunch, conservative Christian. She, in fact, had "led me to the Lord." She was sure that God was going to send her to hell for her actions, and worse, that if her parents found out, they would stop paying her tuition.
>
> At my encouragement, Joan decided to talk to her roommate and put a stop to their physical involvement. Apparently it didn't work. The following fall, they were living together as lovers. I challenged her as a Christian to get out of the relationship and pray for forgiveness and healing. She said that she knew what was right for her and if I couldn't accept her for who she was, she didn't want my friendship.
>
> When Joan was home for Christmas, her mother read a letter from the lover. Joan was devastated with guilt. She talked to her parents' pastor and agreed that her homosexual behavior was an immature stage of rebelliousness. She got back on track in living a Christian life-style, going to church each Sunday, and living a model, stereotypical life. She even went out with men a few times. She told me that she found a new sense of freedom and joy in Christianity and that she felt bad about how earlier she had rejected it.
>
> Later that spring, Joan confided to me that

she had fallen in love with her female Bible study teacher. They had had a long talk, admitted their love, recognized that they both had gay tendencies, but because they respected the laws of God and the church, they firmly believed that with Christ's assistance they could overcome this challenge.

In June, Joan went to work as a research assistant in graduate school. She became friends with a number of feminists and gay activists. She stopped going to church. Later she was seen on television marching hand in hand with her lover in support of gay rights. We had one last talk. Joan explained to me that she still loved God but she could no longer deny all of who she was. She had talked to a pastor about being gay and remaining in the church, but he forced her to make a choice. Her choice was to accept herself as gay, to feel good about no longer hiding a very vital and important part of her life, and to define for herself what her own spirituality meant for her. I couldn't accept this very well and haven't really talked to her since that night [graduate student].

When congruence dictates that we leave friends, family, or reference group, the conflict can be traumatic. While her friend faced the hard choice between life-style and church, this student's values dictated a break in the relationship. For both, this resolution of belief and behavior may be temporary. Affirming more conventional value systems is still the easier route. Facing up to past transgressions requires more courage. Redefining moral and spiritual codes to bring them into harmony with one's own reality is the riskiest path.

At least in a college setting, one is more likely to find a variety of meanings and an array of companions for each of the paths. Pascarella and Terenzini (1991, p. 365) conclude that an essential function of the college in fostering principled moral reasoning is to provide a wide range of intellectual, cultural, and social experiences. On page 366, Pascarella and Terenzini state:

College experiences in which an individual is exposed to divergent perspectives (for example, living away from home, intellectual interactions with
roommates) or is confronted with cognitive moral
conflict (such as courses presenting issues from
different perspectives) were reported by students as
having a salient influence on their moral development. Also consistent with Kohlberg's expectations
are students' specification of the importance of interactions with upperclassmen in residential facilities (that is, exposure to more advanced stages of
moral reasoning) and assuming new personal responsibilities, such as social role taking. . . . However, it would appear to be the extent to which an
individual takes advantage of these opportunities,
particularly those having an intellectual or academic
content, that is the key determinant of growth in
moral reasoning during college.

Relationships exert a powerful influence on developing integrity.
As the student reports in this chapter have illustrated, relationships provide the context for broadening perspective on right
and wrong, for dealing with moral conflicts, for making difficult
choices about what is true and what is best. Integrity involves
using the will and dealing with the emotions, like guilt or anger,
that sometimes arise when choices upset loved ones. Death and
sex are topics not usually dealt with in college curricula, but
both are crucial to students of all ages, and the significance of
both is deeply affected by the shared interpretations of an individual's reference group.

Vandenberg (1991) questions moral development theories
that spring from "cognitive-structural models." For example, he
proposes that both Piaget and Kohlberg saw development in
terms of acquiring scientific or logical concepts about the physical and social world. Progress involves greater use of principled reasoning, "formal operations," and empirically based concepts. This perspective has little room for existential concerns
about death, the mysteries of nature, the role of religious prac-

tices, and the power of beliefs as "fervent hopes." Magical thinking, animism, synchronicity, and spiritual beliefs are not given
much credit as ways to explain or interpret reality. In fact, from
a traditional epistemological viewpoint, mature adults should have
outgrown things like childlike faith and an interest in unfathoma-
ble mysteries. Vandenberg disagrees:

> Research . . . indicates that some religious adults
> in the United States who are fully capable of for-
> mal operational levels of causal reasoning also har-
> bor magical notions of causality. . . . The beliefs
> that characterize many religions contain magical
> thinking and animism: belief in resurrection from
> the dead, immaculate conception, the power of
> prayer to a personal God who is capable of interced-
> ing in the general order of things, miracles, and
> events as rewards or punishments for personal trans-
> gressions. . . . We are enshrouded in mystery; lurk-
> ing beyond the reach of logic and epistemology are
> fundamental existential issues. It is our existential
> predicament—our being thrown into an uncertain
> universe that is beyond our understanding—that
> serves as the wellspring for religion, mysticism, and
> other nonrational forms of thought that coexist with
> formal operational thought in the modern mind
> [p. 1280].

Individuals can affirm core values and beliefs in a number of ways. The use of principled reasoning and empirical evidence is one way. Other ways have been suggested by existentialist philosophers, psychotherapists, and writers, including
Dostoyevsky, Kierkegaard, Nietzsche, Heidegger, Sartre, Buber,
and more recently Viktor Frankl, Rollo May, and Irvin Yalom.
Earlier existentialist traditions in Europe emphasized the negative dimensions of human existence—meaninglessness, isolation, and sterility—and asserted that personal freedom and
responsibility were important tools for counteracting these forces.
Corey (1991) notes the Danish philosopher Kierkegaard's idea

that without the experience of *angst* — a combination of dread and anxiety — we may go through life as sleepwalkers. "Many of us, especially in adolescence, are awakened into real life by a terrible uneasiness. Life is one contingency after another, with no guarantees beyond the certainty of death. This is by no means a comfortable state, but it is necessary to our becoming human. Becoming human is a *project*" (p. 175). Contemporary existentialist thinkers preserve an emphasis on human mortality, noting that anxiety is a normal consequence of an awareness of mortality. They also stress the need to strive for identity and relationship as antidotes to aloneness and to find the courage to search for meaning, since meaning is not automatically bestowed on us. Without an internally derived value system, life can become meaningless, especially when despair and suffering descend on us.

Frankl's compelling book *Man's Search for Meaning* (1963) describes the growth of integrity under the most adverse circumstances. Having begun his clinical psychotherapy practice prior to World War II, Frankl (1963) observed and experienced the truths expressed by existentialist writers while imprisoned in the concentration camps at Auschwitz and Dachau from 1942 to 1945. There he learned firsthand that everything could be taken from a person but one thing: "the last of human freedoms — to choose one's attitude in any given set of circumstances, to choose one's own way" (p. 104). He learned that no matter how terrible the loss, whoever was still alive had reason to hope, because "health, family, happiness, professional abilities, fortune, position in society — all these were things that could be achieved again or restored. After all, we still had all our bones intact. Whatever we had gone through could still be an asset to us in the future. [As Nietzsche said,] 'That which does not kill me, makes me stronger'" (p. 103). Frankl portrays the power of the will and the mind to transcend suffering:

> I remember a personal experience. Almost in tears from pain (I had terrible sores on my feet from wearing torn shoes), I limped a few kilometers with our long column of men from the camp to our work site. Very cold, bitter winds struck us. I kept thinking of the endless little problems of our miserable

life. What would there be to eat tonight? If a piece of sausage came as an extra ration, should I exchange it for a piece of bread? Should I trade my last cigarette, which was left from a bonus I received a fortnight ago, for a bowl of soup? How could I get a piece of wire to replace the fragment which served as one of my shoelaces? Would I get to our work site in time to join my usual working party or would I have to join another, which might have a brutal foreman? . . .

I became disgusted with the state of affairs which compelled me, daily and hourly, to think of only such trivial things. I forced my thoughts to turn to another subject. Suddenly I saw myself standing on the platform of a well-lit, warm, and pleasant lecture room. In front of me sat an attentive audience on comfortable upholstered seats. I was giving a lecture on the psychology of the concentration camp! All that oppressed me at that moment became objective, seen and described from the remote viewpoint of science. By this method I succeeded somehow in rising above the situation, above the sufferings of the moment, and I observed them as if they were already of the past. . . . Emotion, which is suffering, ceases to be suffering as soon as we form a clear and precise picture of it.

The prisoner who had lost faith in the future — his future — was doomed. With his loss of belief in the future, he also lost his spiritual hold; he let himself decline and became subject to mental and physical decay. Usually this happened quite suddenly, in the form of a crisis, the symptoms of which were familiar to the experienced camp inmate. We all feared this moment — not for ourselves, which would have been pointless, but for our friends [pp. 94–95].

Frankl created *logotherapy* as a way to help people find a meaning in life by becoming aware of the hidden *logos* of their existence. *Logos* is a Greek word that denotes "meaning." By choosing a value and holding it before us as a beacon, we can transform an ordeal into an achievement. In Frankl's case, it was love as ultimate and the highest goal. "I understood how a man who has nothing left in this world may still know bliss, be it only for a brief moment, in the contemplation of his beloved" (p. 57). The values that sustain us through good times and crises may be discovered on the way to someplace else. They may be based in feeling, not fact, in faith, not intellect, and in the ability to give ourselves completely to whatever we are doing. Corey (1991, p. 183) says, "Paradoxically, the more rationally we seek it, the more we are likely to miss it. Yalom (1980) and Frankl are in basic agreement on the point that, like pleasure, meaning must be pursued obliquely. Finding meaning in life is a by-product of *engagement,* which is a commitment to creating, loving, working, and building."

Lewis Carroll ([1865] 1962, p. 111) wrote that "everything's got a moral, if you can only find it." The meaning of learning experiences is not always apparent. Once we discover it, it often takes time and effort to apply it. Achieving congruence is a lifelong task. Traumatic experiences may sorely test or shatter long-standing convictions. Few have the strength of Job. Faith, responding to doubt, must be renewed and reworked. Past behaviors that serve us well become ineffective or damaging. Close friends who supported our earlier image may leave us. New sources of strength must be discovered or developed, and new relationships that enable love and hope to flourish must be built. Research has documented the key role colleges play, with their catalyzing intellectual, cultural, and social experiences, in fostering principled moral reasoning, in helping students define goodness, truth, and quality, and in encouraging them to actualize their highest ideals.

By tempering rigid beliefs, becoming open to other interpretations, weighing evidence and experience, and claiming ownership of a meaningful set of principles, students humanize and personalize values and thus develop integrity. Greater ability to behave congruently comes when standards are applied to one's own behavior. Meaningful beliefs can be based on reason, faith, or intuition, but for development to occur, these beliefs must contribute to the good of all as well as sustain the individual in times of crisis.

PART TWO

Key Influences on
Student Development

Our basic proposition is that human development should be the organizing purpose for higher education. That proposition rests on the knowledge, based on decades of research, that community colleges and four-year institutions *can* have significant impact on student development along the major vectors addressed in Part One. This is not to say that all institutions have positive impacts or make significant contributions. But it is clear that educational environments do exist and can be created that influence students in powerful ways. Part Two addresses seven key ingredients for encouraging human development, with a chapter devoted to each: (1) institutional objectives, (2) institutional size, (3) student-faculty relationships, (4) curriculum, (5) teaching, (6) friendships and student communities, and (7) student development programs and services. It concludes with a chapter suggesting ways to create and sustain educationally powerful environments.

In 1969, when the first edition of this book was published, we posed these ingredients of influence as "hypotheses" based on the evidence available then. The substantial evidence that has accumulated since then consistently validates those hypotheses. Since none of the hypotheses posed have been rejected, it is tempting to give up the language of hypothesis and move to simple assertion. But we resist that temptation. We stick with it not because the supporting evidence is weak or uncertain, but because there is much more to be learned. A hypothesis is primarily a theory or supposition tentatively adopted to account for certain facts and to shape the investigation of others. Although the general directions of change and sources of influence we identify are strongly anchored in research, we are a long way from understanding the intricate interactions among (1) students in their infinite variety, (2) psychological, sociological, and environmental ingredients in all their complexity, and (3) developmental outcomes across the full spectrum of human potentials. We were lucky that the first edition of *Education and Identity* provided a conceptual framework that helped others pursue some of these interactions. We hope that this revision, building on research since then, does the same.

For clarity and succinctness, we state our hypotheses baldly. We drop those ubiquitous terms "in general," "tend to," "probably," and "under normal circumstances" that educators and behavioral scientists use to protect their rears and obscure their meanings. Though we may seem to be dogmatic, we do have strong convictions and strong concerns about strengthening higher education's contributions to individuals and to society. It is just such concerns that drive our work. But we also encourage you to insert your own qualifiers, "yes buts," or elaborations that move our thinking toward greater accuracy and relevance.

Clear and Consistent Objectives

Hypothesis: Impact increases as institutional objectives are clear and taken seriously and as the diverse elements of the institution and its programs are internally consistent in the service of the objectives.

Of course it is not the simple statement of objectives that has an impact. Every college catalogue contains such statements. But where objectives are taken seriously, institutional impact is strengthened in three ways. First, policies, programs, and practices tend toward greater internal consistency. When faculty members sitting on ubiquitous committees make decisions in terms of commonly shared and explicit institutional objectives, then the various parts fit together with greater coherence and integration. The developmental impact of one element less frequently runs counter to another. Second, clear objectives help students make more explicit their own reasons for attending the college and their own purposes while there. The objectives help them use time and energy more directly in the service of those objectives they value. Third, it is important to be explicit about objectives because they contain within them strong value commitments. No institution is without commitments. Often they are absorbed unwittingly by students as matters not to be questioned. At some institutions, for example, the success ethic, rugged individualism, personal achievement, self-denial or conservative morality, and future-time orientation are among the dominant values assumed; at others, such values as sociability, a relativistic moral attitude, conformity, or a hedonistic present-time orientation is left unquestioned. Unconscious learning seals off these matters from conscious control and modification. Enter rigidity and dogmatism. When objectives are explicit and when the attendant values are overtly expressed, they can become the object of examination, disagreement, and challenge. Then the learning that occurs makes for more conscious and flexible integration of these values with other components of personality and behavior.

As institutional objectives remain salient and are clearly expressed, a distinctive atmosphere develops. It develops not only out of the conscious effort of those who stay with the institution for some time; more important, it develops because prospective students and prospective faculty who support the objectives and their modes of implementation are accepted and retained. Through this process, a community of shared values, which sustains its members and influences those who join, comes into being.

Institutional objectives are thus of primary importance. Not only do they influence the emphasis given to one vector relative to another — for one college competence is most important, for another integrity, for a third autonomy and purpose. But their clarity and the internal consistency with which they are implemented largely determine whether any substantial development will occur or whether the student, subject to opposing forces, remains fixed or changes only in response to other external pressures.

Institutional Size

Hypothesis: As redundancy increases, development of competence, mature interpersonal relationships, identity, and integrity decreases.

Barker and Gump (1964) use the term *redundancy* to describe the situation where the number of persons for a given setting exceeds the opportunities for active participation and satisfying experiences. When people are superfluous because of excessive numbers, redundancy exists; if three runners end up on second base, two are redundant. Redundancy is one person driving from behind the wheel and another from the back seat, three persons to change the tire, or four to diagnose the engine failure. It is ten players per tennis court, a thousand golfers per golf course, ten thousand visitors per city park. And when redundancy occurs—when increasing numbers cause decreasing individual participation and satisfaction—forces operating for personal development diminish.

As redundancy sets in, the activities and responsibilities of those who do participate become more specialized and those with marginal qualifications are more quickly and more completely left out. A hierarchy of prestige and power develops, and evaluation shifts from an emphasis on the fit between abilities and the requirements of a job to an emphasis on how one person compares with another. Rules and standards for conduct become more formalized and rigid.

Under such conditions, the opportunities to cope with significant problems become more limited and challenges to existing skills and knowledge are encountered less frequently. Experience becomes less varied and self-testing more restricted. The range of different people to be dealt with in contexts important to one's own life decreases, and situations provoking examination of values and consideration of the consequences of one's actions have to be faced less often. Thus, development of competence is more limited except when provided by special ability or special interest; the development of identity, mature relationships, and integrity are fostered less than is the case when the ratio of people to settings is smaller.

Conceived in these terms, institutional size therefore sharply affects institutional impact. For as the number of persons outstrips the opportunities for significant participation and satisfaction, the developmental potential of available settings is attenuated for all.

Student-Faculty Relationships

Hypothesis: When student-faculty interaction is frequent and friendly and when it occurs in diverse situations calling for varied roles and relationships, development of intellectual competence, sense of competence, autonomy and interdependence, purpose, and integrity are encouraged.

The first step in moving through autonomy toward interdependence is redefining relationships with parents. After this step is taken, support of nonparental adults and peers is sought and idolization and idealization of warm, sensitive teachers and other adults occurs. Thus accessible adults, open enough to be known as real human beings, can have substantial impact, whether they be advisers, custodians, or professors. With them, the actions and reactions learned during childhood and habitual with parents or other authorities can be reexamined, and alternative behaviors can be tested. New modes of relationship with people in authority and with institutional expressions of authority can be developed. Movement from dependency or rebellious independence toward relationships of mutual respect can occur. Areas of interdependence can be recognized. Space for an autonomous existence can be carved out of the larger context. By demonstrating varied life-styles and value orientations, such adults can also help foster development of purpose and integrity. In them, students can see more clearly the rewards and frustrations of varied vocations and avocations, of varied marriage and family relationships. Of course, as Adelson (1962, p. 414) points out, a teacher may also serve as an "antimodel," as a lodestar from which the student sails away as fast as possible, saying, "Whatever he is, I will not be; whatever he is for, I will be against." But teachers who are such a force for repulsion also provoke development.

Curriculum

Hypothesis: An educationally powerful curriculum encourages the development of intellectual and interpersonal competence, sense of competence, identity, purpose, and integrity.

Curriculum, properly understood, includes the full range of activities and investments that a student's college experience comprises. We use the more restricted and conventional definition: "the courses of study offered by an educational institution." But we need to recognize that "course of study" involves both process and content. When faculty debate curricula, they generally focus on content; those debates seldom address four critical criteria for content selection. In our judgment, content should:

1. Be relevant to students' backgrounds and prior experiences
2. Recognize significant dimensions of individual differences among students
3. Create encounters with diverse perspectives that challenge preexisting information, assumptions, and values
4. Provide examples of, opportunities for, and activities that help students integrate diverse perspectives, assumptions, and value orientations

Selecting content based on these criteria will help foster the dimensions of development hypothesized above.

But the force of the "hidden" curriculum needs to be recognized as well. This curriculum resides in the assumptions and orientations that underlie curriculum and teaching and in the student behaviors and interactions that result. Palmer

(1987, p. 22) clearly articulates the dominant assumptions underlying most curricula: "Objective, analytic, experimental. Very quickly this seemingly abstract way of knowing, this seemingly bloodless epistemology becomes an ethic. It is an ethic of competitive individualism, in the midst of a world fragmented and made exploitable by that very mode of knowing. The mode of knowing itself breeds intellectual habits, indeed spiritual instincts, that destroy community. We make objects of each other and the world to be manipulated for our own private ends." He does not advocate throwing out objectivity, analysis, and experimentation but calls for "a capacity for relatedness within individuals — relatedness not only to people but to events in history, to nature, to the world of ideas, and yes, to things of the spirit. We talk a lot in higher education about the formation of inward capacities — the capacity to tolerate ambiguity, the capacity for critical thought. I want us to talk more about those ways of knowing that form an inward capacity for relatedness" (p. 24).

Another kind of hidden curriculum exists. This curriculum involves how the student learns, not just what is learned. The professors' rhetoric may call for critical examination of diverse ideas, for creating one's own analyses and syntheses, for originality and developing one's own perspectives. But often, wittingly or unwittingly, evaluation and grading emphasize getting the right words in rote order or simple memorization for multiple-choice exams. Students quickly spot the disparity. They deliver what gets the best grade.

As Astin's (1991) research indicates, it is the behaviors provoked by the curriculum that have most impact, not the content. Among the most significant variables are (1) the amount of interaction and cooperation among students and between students and faculty, (2) the hours devoted to studying, (3) an institutional emphasis on diversity, and (4) a faculty that is positive about the general education program.

Curricula that recognize our four criteria for content and that strengthen interaction and cooperation among students and between students and faculty can make powerful contributions to key vectors of student development.

Teaching

Hypothesis: When teaching calls for active learning, encourages student-faculty contact and cooperation among students, gives prompt feedback, emphasizes time on task and high expectations, and respects diverse talents and ways of knowing, the following qualities are fostered: intellectual and interpersonal competence, sense of competence, mature interpersonal relationships, autonomy, identity, and purpose.

Intellectual competence does not just happen. An uneducated mind may be sufficient for trial-and-error behavior, but education is required to develop analytical, synthetic, and creative abilities. Evidence indicates that different teaching practices produce different kinds of cognitive operations and therefore may foster different kinds of intellectual competence. The differential effect of lectures versus discussion classes in most settings is well documented. Lectures are superior for the transmission of information (Barnard, 1942), either quite specific in nature or integrated in a way not otherwise held. Discussion classes provoke more active thinking than lecture classes (Bloom, 1953), and several experiments have demonstrated that active learning is more efficient than passive learning (McGeoch and Irion, 1952). Group discussion provides experiences in integrating facts, formulating hypotheses, amassing relevant evidence, and evaluating conclusions. When information encounters intellectual or emotional resistance, discussion can reveal the source so it can be examined and dealt with. And group membership can contribute to changes in motivation and attitudes because it is often easier to effect change with a group than with a single individual (Lewin, 1952). Research concerning student-centered teaching is also relevant. In ten of eleven studies reviewed by McKeachie (1962), greater changes in ability to apply concepts, in attitudes, in motivation, or in group membership skills were found for discussion techniques emphasizing freer student participation than for discussion with greater instructor dominance.

Evaluative procedures also influence cognitive behavior. When grades are based on memorization of details, students memorize. When grades are based on integrating diverse materials and applying principles, students will try to develop such abilities. Meyer (1936) and Terry (1933) found that an upcoming essay exam leads to study emphasizing the organization and interrelationships of facts and principles, while an upcoming multiple-choice exam leads to memorization. Dressel (1958) observed that the need to cover large masses of material leaves little time to reflect on the meaning, interrelationship, and applicability of the knowledge being gained. And even the able student often is reluctant to think independently, partly because such efforts are time consuming and difficult, but also because they apparently contribute little to better grades.

Sense of competence is also affected. Thistlethwaite (1962, p. 313) found that curricular flexibility, controversial instruction, informality, and warm student-faculty contacts characterized colleges "outstandingly successful in encouraging undergraduates to get the doctorate in humanistic fields." Davis (1964) found that intellectually elite colleges significantly underproduced graduate students in science and blames the competitive grading practices that restrict faculty encouragement to those few A students at the top of the curve — even though all the students may have an aptitude for science.

Teaching also has implications for developing the emotional and instrumental independence necessary to move through autonomy to interdependence. When teaching completely specifies what will be studied, when learning involves memorizing information and developing only the content and skills deemed important by the teacher, and when grades depend on absolute conformity to these requirements, emotional and instrumental independence do not flourish. These qualities are fostered when students can help define key areas of content and competence to be pursued and when objectives for learning are established collaboratively, taking account of individual interests and motives within general parameters set by the curriculum and course. Such development is strengthened when students must cope with diverse tasks that have consequences for themselves and when they must identify, find, and get to whatever resources are needed to achieve the objectives. It is also strengthened when they are asked to participate in defining the products or behaviors that will be evaluated, the methods to be used, and the criteria to be applied in making judgments about whether the desired learning has occurred.

But most teaching does not involve students in shaping course objectives in ways that recognize their priorities, in helping identify appropriate resources, and in specifying the products, processes, methods, and criteria required for effective evaluation. Instead, a limited set of skills and competencies is called on. A trip to the library and use of the card catalogue fill the demands for mobility, search, discovery, and learning resources. That is why successful course achievement adds so little to the coping abilities needed beyond the classroom. And that is why college grade-point averages show so little relationship to post-college success, satisfaction, and social contribution.

According to Erikson (1950) and Sanford (1966), development of identity is fostered by varied experiences and roles, meaningful achievement, and relative freedom from anxiety and pressure. Few colleges offer these conditions. Grading systems and detailed requirements work directly counter to the sampling and self-testing through which self-definition proceeds. High academic pressures make thinking for oneself risky. That all-important index of worth, the grade-point average, makes venturing into areas of weakness dangerous. Meaningful work can counterbalance a narrow role. But most college work is meaningless to most students. Observe student-taught courses and programs of study in "free universities." Teacher behavior, learning activities, student role, content, and evaluation depart markedly from the usual curriculum, lectures, and examinations.

Interpersonal relationships also are affected. Competitive grading pits one person against another. Grading on a curve means that your good grade makes mine more unlikely. And the problem is amplified if we are both training for the same kind of work, both in the same department shooting for graduate fellowships, assistantships, and other significant goodies. It is not so much that close friendships are precluded but that they have to carry such a burden. On the other hand, when the emphasis is on cooperative effort to complete complex tasks with excellence, then diversity of skill, perspective, and insight become valuable and the orientation is toward sharing and toward knowing different persons and being able to work with them. Then more wide-ranging friendships and easy relationships become possible and valued. Clinging together in couples and cliques becomes less necessary.

Friendships and Student Communities

Hypothesis: When students are encouraged to form friendships and to participate in communities that become meaningful subcultures, and when diversity of backgrounds and attitudes as well as significant interchanges and shared interests exist, development along all seven vectors is fostered.

The personal connections developed during college can have lifelong ramifications. Whether relating as casual acquaintances, classmates in a small-group discussion, teammates, roommates, club members, best friends, or committed partners, students often learn more from each other than from teachers. Dialogue clarifies values and purposes. Caring brings up dependency issues and an array of feelings to explore and manage. Mutual enjoyment stimulates shared adventures and the discovery of new interests and skills. Recognition from others bolsters self-esteem.

Communities on campus can include informal reference groups, residence halls, student organizations, and classes that emphasize student connections to each other and to content and process. Once a student identifies with a particular group, it becomes both an anchor and a reference point, influencing behavior and thinking powerfully if older ties to family and friends have loosened and if the group supports the individual's goals.

Residence halls can provide ready-made communities for students. Because the college can vary the mix of students, place trained student staff members on site, organize developmental activities, and alter the arrangement of rooms and furniture so as to balance privacy with interaction, residence halls have great potential for fostering development of competence, management of emotions, autonomy and interdependence, and mature interpersonal relationships. They can also inhibit development if they are operated *in loco parentis* or create an overly protective environment with few intellectual and social challenges. By applying developmental principles in programming, governance, architectural design, size of units, and matching of students, college administrators can amplify the positive aspects of residential living.

Student culture can affect the development of identity and purpose by encouraging wide-ranging exploration or curtailing it. The sense of self is strengthened by encountering different kinds of people and situations, observing their reactions, trying out different roles with varying degrees of investment and receiving useful feedback. But when the community validates a limited set of roles, development of identity suffers. Too little feedback or reflection time and too much passivity or premature commitment to a single alternative can countermand growth. When friendships and the intimate exchanges that accompany them are valued and promoted, identity and purpose become clearer. When the culture inhibits personal or cross-cultural connections, or assigns second-class citizenship to certain types of students or relationships, stereotypes are reinforced.

Learning communities involve innovative restructuring of curriculum by linking courses around a common theme and enrolling students in cooperative groups. Encouraging students to work together and explore engaging interdisciplinary topics enhances development by helping students to care, not only about their own work and each other, but also about what they are learning. By balancing "separate knowing" (objective analysis, debating positions, weighing evidence) with "connected knowing" (honoring feelings, personal experiences, and subjectivity), ideas can be shared as works in progress. This requires trust, support, and a nonjudgmental attitude in listeners, who, like midwives, help emerging insights struggle into being. For this collaborative approach to succeed, classmates need to know each other relatively well and must be able to tolerate their individual opinions and remarks.

For optimum development, the community, whether it takes the form of residence hall unit, sorority or fraternity house, student organization, or informal circle of friends, should have the following characteristics:

1. It encourages regular interactions between students and provides a foundation for ongoing relationships.
2. It offers opportunities for collaboration — for engaging in meaningful activities and facing common problems together.
3. It is small enough so that no one feels superfluous.
4. It includes people from diverse backgrounds.
5. It serves as a reference group, where there are boundaries in terms of who is "in" and who is "out." It has norms that inform those with different roles, behaviors, and status that they are "good" members or that what they are doing is unacceptable.

Student Development Programs and Services

Hypothesis: When student development professionals define themselves as educators working collaboratively with faculty to apply student development theory, they increase the direct and indirect impact of programs and services on students' movement along all vectors.

Those responsible for helping students enter an institution, move through it, and exit successfully have been called "student personnel administrators," "student services staff," or "student affairs administrators." This vocabulary conveys an image of supervisors moving "personnel" through the system or of staff dispensing services to consumers. These terms may have been appropriate when staff members were seen as administrators shepherding individuals through the system, dispensing financial aid, issuing transcripts, or enforcing conduct codes. They evolved from faculty wardens living in colonial colleges with students aspiring to the ministry, molding students' character through prayer, indoctrination, and strict supervision. When colleges became more secular, these staff members became enrollment managers and deans charged with maintaining discipline. Later they transcended the trend toward specialized administrative functions and redefined a profession grounded in a concern for "the whole student" and in a growing body of theory and research on student development. They proactively defined themselves as equal partners with faculty in educating students. Yet often their actual status and mission did not match these aspirations, and they continued to be seen as service providers somewhat extraneous to the educational mission of the college.

During the past thirty years, research and theory on student development have continued to provide a foundation for the profession. We recommend that administrators of student programs and services redefine themselves as educators and refer to themselves as "student development professionals." Staff members well versed in theory and skilled in applying developmental principles can have profound influence on individual student growth and on an environment that intentionally provides a mix of challenge and support.

Knefelkamp (1974) identified one reason why the potential of student services had not been realized: administrators and faculty members continued to view student services as ancillary to the real work of the institution. After analyzing theorists and critics since 1950, she concluded that the profession itself stopped short of practicing what it preached. It "recognized the interrelationship between the intellectual and the affective but consistently failed to enter both areas of the student's life" (p. 31). Instead, it focused on learning outside the classroom — in workshops, small groups, and one-to-one interactions — as the solution. Yet those who are knowledgeable about student development, student characteristics, and individual differences have much to offer faculty. The opportunities for collaboration and communication are many. The 1984 Traverse City Statement *Toward the Future Vitality of Student Development Services* (American College Testing Program, 1985), drafted by student development leaders at two-year colleges, affirmed "integrating student development into the educational experience" as one of seven major goals. It specifically emphasized "collaboration with faculty and other campus educators to incorporate student development concepts into the college mission, academic program competencies, co-curricular programs, and ultimately, course objectives" (p. 5). To be effective, student development professionals must also understand faculty priorities and feelings and find ways to enhance their effectiveness and satisfaction.

All colleges have cultures and climates. Student development professionals play a major role in how the parts function, how the pieces fit into a larger whole. How do the publications look? How well do bulletin boards provide information and market services? Does the layout of the place invite student interaction? Are the offices designed to invite students in? Are the policies, calendars, and directories "user friendly"? Are student success stories featured in area newspapers? Does the student newspaper inspire pride and keep the campus up to date? Are receptionists skilled at interacting with students? Have advisers been trained and supported in work with groups that need special help? Does the registration process convey chaos or orderly efficiency? The questions are endless, but it is obvious that students can be frustrated or supported by every part of the system. Using student development concepts to evaluate everything done outside the classroom can facilitate both large and small changes. Together, they add up to a lively, inviting, stimulating, friendly place that fosters student success.

Creating Educationally Powerful Environments

Hypothesis A: Educational environments that have powerful impacts on human development *can* be created.
Hypothesis B: We know enough about the key principles and ingredients for such environments to tackle that challenge.

Sound research, dating back to the 1920s and 1930s, indicates that educational environments that encourage key dimensions of human development can be created and sustained. That research also indicates some of the key principles and characteristics of such environments.

The most important principle recognizes that any environment is a *system* or a totality of interacting parts. An educationally powerful environment coordinates all elements — awareness of students' precollege characteristics and background, admission, orientation and advising, curriculum, teaching, and evaluation, cocurricular activities, norms concerning relationships among students and between students and faculty, facilities — so that they are internally consistent with regard to desired outcomes. In many institutions, different parts of the system conflict with other parts and thus neutralize potential sources of influence on students. So the starting point is to undertake an analysis that examines institutional policies and behaviors for their internal consistency with regard to objectives for student learning and development important to the institution.

The second principle is to examine existing assumptions. When Einstein was asked how he got started on his theory of relativity, he said, "I questioned an axiom." President Kennedy urged us to "forgo the comfort of opinion and bear the discomfort of thought" (Schlesinger, 1965, p. 238). Our own posture should be the same.

The other chapters in Part Two identify major sources of institutional impact on students and describe ways they can be shaped to maximize such impact. As our first "system" principle makes clear, these sources are highly interdependent. If no clearly agreed-on institutional objectives exist, there is no basis for examining and coordinating the system. If institutional size is such that students are redundant, all forces for change are minimized. If curriculum and teaching leave students as passive receptacles for predigested information and treat them all alike, then few students will be affected. If strong friendships and student communities are not created, those major opportunities for personal identification and involvement will be lost. If student programs and services do not have clearly defined educational purposes, their potential contributions will be diminished.

Three other principles must help shape these interdependent parts:

1. Integrate work and learning.
2. Recognize and respect individual differences.
3. Remember that significant learning and human development involve cycles of challenge and response, differentiation and integration, disequilibrium and regained equilibrium.

Creating and sustaining such an environment requires committed leadership and an appropriate organizational culture. Eight elements characterize high-quality institutions that are themselves "learning organizations." These organizations

1. Clearly define core values, mission, and vision.
2. Emphasize an ethic of quality.
3. Make people their prime resource.
4. Learn from the people they serve.
5. Emphasize autonomy and entrepreneurship.
6. Orient toward action.
7. Analyze strengths and weaknesses.
8. Invest in professional development.

These ingredients suggest the leadership and organizational culture we need in order to create and sustain educational environments that contribute powerfully to human development.

NINE

Clear and Consistent Institutional Objectives

At most colleges, process has taken over, leaving purpose to shift for itself. Objectives rarely surface when questions of policy and practice are raised. Faculty and staff seldom ask whether the activities and experiences offered by the college environment actually facilitate academic and personal development. Often the only person concerned about objectives is the catalogue writer, who raises a question every two or three years when it is time for revision. Consciousness of purpose has given way to deference to tradition and authority or uncritical acceptance of current practice. Innovation and experimentation, if they occur at all, are often undertaken or borrowed with no apparent thought to institutional objectives.

Need for Objectives

Boyer (1987, p. 2) found a pervasive absence of clear and consistent objectives and defined the issue as a central concern: "During our study we found divisions on campus, conflicting priorities and competing interests that diminish the intellectual and social quality of the undergraduate experience and restrict the capacity of the college effectively to serve its students. At most colleges and universities we visited, these special points of tension appeared with such regularity and seemed so consistently to sap the vitality of the baccalaureate experience that we have made them the focus of this report."

At most institutions, administrators and faculty as well as students are caught in the machinery. The main thing is to keep it running smoothly. Squirt oil where it squeaks. If that does not work, replace the part or redesign it until it functions again. Comfort becomes the prime criterion. For administrators, it is a smoothly functioning institution, a shiny image, solid financial security. For professors, it is minimal teaching and maximum time for professional advancement and personal interest, two office hours per week to keep individual students at a safe distance, lectures that can become books and articles. For students, it is freedom to study as much or as little as they are inclined to do, time for social pleasures, and good grades earned with little effort. The assertions may be exaggerated, but the basic point is not — comfort does not always accompany significant development; institutional purposes are not always best realized when things go smoothly.

As Boyer (1987, p. 3) emphasizes, "Scrambling for students and driven by marketplace demands, many undergraduate colleges have lost their sense of mission. They are confused about their mission and how to impart shared values on which the vitality of both higher education and society depends. The disciplines have fragmented themselves into smaller and smaller pieces, and undergraduates find it difficult to see patterns in their courses or to relate what they learn to life."

Some institutions can be clear about their mission but not clear about what that mission implies for student learning and development. Typical mission statements include eloquently formulated goals. For example, some goals related to student development are included in this mission statement from an energetic public institution that aims to become a "university of the twenty-first century" (George Mason University Board of Visitors, 1991, p. 1):

The University will be an institution of international academic reputation providing superior education enabling students to develop critical, analytical, and imaginative thinking and to make well founded ethical decisions. It will respond to the call for interdisciplinary research and teaching not simply by adding programs but by rethinking the traditional structure of the academy.

The University will prepare students to address the complex issues facing them in society and to discover meaning in their own lives. It will encourage diversity in its student body and undergraduate, graduate, and professional courses of study that are interdisciplinary and innovative. The University will energetically seek ways to interact with and serve the needs of the student body.

Though more effective than most, statements like these remain abstract about outcomes for students. They provide an excellent point of departure, however, for identifying much more specific objectives.

The president of the university whose mission was just described clearly articulates the distinctive characteristics of this forward-looking institution contrasting new directions with earlier constraints (Johnson, 1986):

Two distinct models of the university come to mind. One is the classical image of the ivory tower, divorced from surrounding events, indifferent to materialistic values, immersed in activities of the mind, detached from all worlds but its own. The other is the interactive university, alert to trends in the society, be they international, national, regional or local, and sensitive to the potential symmetry in the relation between the university and its many constituencies; oriented to service in the broadest sense, which includes teaching and research; rubbing shoulders with potential consumers of the university's human and intellectual products; immersed in the turbulent environment; and honoring multiple faculty roles inside and outside the institution, with regard to influencing the future . . . [pp. 14–15].

After all, much of the structure and organization of a modern American university bears the marks of the industrial era, of the factory system. Indeed, it was that great gulping expansion when industrial America capitalized the machine amplification of human muscle that the undergraduate college, the academic department, the graduate school, and professional training formats were all invented. Indeed even the semester hour credit was an invention of that period, and perhaps a significant one, since a moment's review reveals the factory model: quality standards for input materials; a process which is synchronous, serial, and uniform; output which is standardized and graded. While other institutions in our society, including our current factories, have customized their services and products, universities remain locked in an organization which is an artifact of an age now gone [pp. 12–13].

An *interactive* university must also be *interdisciplinary* if it is to have educational programs that respond to local, regional, national, and international needs. Knowledge packaged according to discipline-based departments does not address complex social issues. Individual faculty talent must be *distributed* across departments and schools. Teaching and learning must occur in residential units, the library, and the university center, as well as in classrooms and faculty offices. Education, research and service cannot go forward on a single comprehensive campus but must be created and carried out collaboratively in diverse locations in the region and elsewhere.

These approaches—interactive, interdisciplinary, and distributed—and the innovative new programmatic elements they drive have attracted creative and talented faculty members and administrators as well as external political and financial support for new ventures. The three words pervade oral exchanges, printed material, new program proposals, and task forces concerned with institutional development. But they have not yet led to equally clear and visible objectives for student learning and development. No similarly shared language exists among faculty members, administrators, and student services professionals about key outcomes for students, appropriate for the twenty-first century, that would be consistent with this powerful institutional orientation.

That absence was dramatically illustrated by a proposed new general education core that resulted from three years of hard work by a highly competent and concerned faculty committee. Each of the new courses articulated its own objectives, but the proposal omitted any indication of general objectives that the core intended to fulfill. The problem hit home when a university task force was charged with creating the conceptual basis for a new university center that would integrate a core library with a diverse set of student activities, facilities for student-faculty interaction, and eating and recreational spaces. The only way to arrive at some sense of the core objectives was to analyze those mentioned for individual courses and look for overlap among them.

Impact of Clear Objectives

The basic point is that clear and consistent objectives, stated in terms of desired outcomes for learning and personal development, are critically important in creating an educationally powerful institution. These should not have to be deduced from course descriptions. They should be explicit and compelling. They should be defined by the members of the college community, taken to heart by campus leaders, and invoked as guides to decision-making.

Research evidence, dating back to Newcomb's (1943) detailed study of Bennington College, indicates that clear and consistent objectives make significant contributions to student development. Bennington College started in the late 1930s with a clearly defined philosophy and with a program consciously designed to be consistent with it. A liberal sociopolitical viewpoint was pervasive. Daughters of Republicans, curiously enough, came to the college. Upon graduation many were, in today's jargon, activists; they held strong liberal beliefs and worked for

them. Those who most identified with the dominant orientation
of the college changed most. They enjoyed most prestige on
campus, while those who maintained more conservative beliefs
were less popular. The converted liberals more often than not
married men who were similarly inclined, joined organizations
congruent with their interests, and generally created, or moved
into, conditions that sustained that orientation. So twenty-five
years later, their views were relatively unchanged (Newcomb,
Koenig, Flack, and Warwick, 1967). The few institutions that
Jacob (1957) found to influence student values had their own
prevailing atmosphere where teachers with strong value commitments were accessible to students and where students' value-
laden personal experiences were integrated with the general
educational program.

Clear and salient objectives make for internally consistent policies, programs, and practices. Such objectives reduce
the frequency with which the developmental impact of one component runs counter to that of another. Thus, if development
of purpose is a key objective, curricular requirements, teaching styles, and evaluation procedures can be coordinated accordingly, and the resulting arrangements will differ from those
where intellectual competence has higher priority.

Clear objectives also help faculty members operate as individuals in ways more congruent with each other. Most of us
have little control over our routine behavior. Our manner of
teaching, our ways of responding to students, and our allocations of time and energy are all pretty well built in. To modify
them in response to differing purposes and differing student
needs and characteristics is enormously difficult. It requires a
high degree of self-consciousness and unremitting efforts at self-
correction. With clear institutional objectives, which we can be
consciously attuned to, such self-correction has a chance to operate and in time may enable modification of our own behavior.

As Heath (1968, pp. 242–243) has pointed out in his study
of Haverford, "A community that has an ideal or vision has,
in effect, expectations of what its members are to become. . . .
When such expectations are consistently expressed in all structures and activities of the institution, then different communal

experiences may mutually reinforce one another. It is rare that a specific type of educational experience is very significant in a person's life, as our data so clearly show. Rather, it is the coherence, the consistency, the 'atmosphere' of one's environment that makes its impact upon development." Thus, for example, a college that aims to develop interpersonal competence could generate such specific objectives for students as understanding others, participating in groups, expressing thoughts and feelings, and appreciating cultural differences. It could identify opportunities for students to develop through working on group projects, sharing ideas and talking with friends about their backgrounds, taking classes and workshops that emphasize interpersonal communication, volunteering for a leadership position, or joining a student organization.

Institutional clarity and commitment generate similar clarity and commitment on the part of students, leading not only to increased efficiency but also to higher levels of motivation. Salient institutional objectives keep alive for students their reasons for being in college, and for being at that particular college. They can then organize time and energy more consciously to reach those objectives they value. Furthermore, when institutional objectives are explicit and widely shared, students teach each other; thus, whether the objective is development of intellectual competence or development of tolerance or identity, conversational content and patterns of relationship become organized around those goals.

Boyer (1987, pp. 59–60) illustrates his research finding as follows:

> At a large public university, we asked an associate dean about institutional goals. She pointed to the front flyleaf of the university catalog and read a statement that emphasized vaguely worded references to "usable skills," "the expansion of knowledge," and "improvement of the quality of life."
>
> A faculty member at the same institution said the university's goals are meaningless to faculty and students: "I'll bet you a thousand dollars if you asked

students, 'Do you know what the university's goals are for you?' they would give you blank looks." We asked and they did. Even the student body president, who might be expected to have a better idea of such things, said: "If there are any goals around here, they haven't been expressed to me."

In contrast, several institutions we visited seem confident of their objectives. One middle-sized college defines its mission as follows:

> The college stands for an education that will give each student the skills of communication, the ideas and principles underlying the major areas of modern knowledge, the understanding that learning is a continuous lifetime process, and the courage and enthusiasm to participate in the creation of a better world.

At an urban, church-related university in the West with nearly six thousand students, the statement of purpose stresses the following convictions: "To pursue truth, to strive for excellence in teaching and learning and in scholarly endeavors, and to improve and enrich the community which the University serves and from which it draws its support."

An administrator at the institution said, "I think the distinctive dimension of our university is the religious emphasis. I think there's something distinctive about the people who come here. A graduate of our university will bring certain moral and religious values with him." What we found impressive was not the printed statement but the way the goals were talked about during the day-to-day decision making. This university had a clear idea of what it was trying to accomplish.

As the passage from Boyer illustrates, when institutional objectives are taken seriously, in time another factor begins to operate. Because the objectives are those of "the college," they can be perceived as somewhat outside and beyond any particular student. We can thus become identified with them and develop missionary zeal; our own self-interest is tied up with our realization of the college objectives and the same realization on the part of others. Under such conditions, campus visitors may frequently be exhorted to modify their behavior and orientation to agree with the particular objectives, and the virtues of the institution in fostering integrity, social concern, breadth of perspective, highly developed cognitive skills, or whatever the dominant objectives may be are persuasively extolled.

When faculty and students have taken the objectives seriously, they come to pervade various aspects of the institution, affecting parietal rules, academic and nonacademic expectations and requirements, student-faculty relationships, and admissions criteria. This then leads to a third phenomenon — self-selection by prospective students and faculty members, which adds momentum and provides for self-perpetuation. Thus, in time, a community of shared ideas and goals becomes a reality sustained by processes of self-selection, which operate with increasing force and subtlety. The evidence for student self-selection when institutional objectives are clear and pervasive is abundant and unequivocal (Astin, 1964; Pace, 1962; Stern, 1964; Alverno College Faculty, 1992; Loacker, Cromwell, and O'Brien, 1986; Mentkowski and Doherty, 1983).

Alverno College gives us an excellent example of the power of clearly articulated objectives taken seriously. Alverno describes the eight abilities it wants its students to develop (Schmitz, 1992, p. 5):

1. *Communication:* The competent communicator habitually makes meaningful connections between self and audience, with well-chosen words and with and without the aid of graphics, electronic media and computers.
2. *Analysis:* The competent analyzer is a clear thinker and a critical thinker. She fuses experience, reason, and training into considered judgment.
3. *Problem Solving:* The competent problem solver gets done what needs to be done. The ability overlaps with and uses all other abilities.
4. *Valuing in Decision Making:* The responsible decision maker is reflective and empathic in approaching the value issues in her life. She habitually seeks to understand the moral

dimensions of decisions and accepts responsibility for the consequences of actions taken in all facets of her life. She understands and is sensitive to a variety of perspectives and experiences in making her own decisions.

5. *Social Interaction:* The competent interactor knows how to get things done in committees, task forces, team projects, and other group efforts. She elicits views of others and helps reach conclusions.

6. *Global Perspectives:* The person who takes multiple perspectives articulates interconnections between and among diverse opinions, ideas, and beliefs about global issues. She makes informed judgments and tests out her own position.

7. *Effective Citizenship:* The effective citizen develops informed choices and strategies for collaborative involvement in community issues.

8. *Aesthetic Response:* The aesthetically responsive person articulates an informed response to artistic works which is grounded in knowledge of multiple frameworks and exposure to a variety of artistic forms. She is able to make meaning out of aesthetic experiences and to articulate reasons for her choice of aesthetic expression.

Like every college, Alverno expects a student to learn a certain amount of subject matter. It posits that a student is best prepared for the future with a combination of subjects that includes the arts and humanities, the sciences, and the social sciences.

But as valuable as it is, this knowledge alone is not enough. Woven through all classes are activities that help students integrate it with successively higher levels of sophistication in each of eight abilities. A history course, for example, helps a student analyze and communicate historical knowledge. A science course includes among its goals the formulation and solution of scientific problems. The eight abilities give backbone to Alverno's curriculum, uniting it with a common purpose for teaching and an organizing framework for learning.

Students choose a course for both the subject matter and the abilities it offers. At the beginning of each course, a student "contracts" to advance in several of the eight abilities. Faculty have defined six levels of sophistication for each of the eight abilities. To graduate, a student must advance to the fourth level in all of them, and to the fifth and sixth levels in those specified by their major. Progression toward a degree is based on in class as well as external performance-based assessments. For example, developmental levels for two of the abilities which have particular relevance for our vectors are listed below (Alverno College Faculty, 1992):

4. *Develop facility in making value judgments and independent decisions.*
   Level 1 — Identify own values.
   Level 2 — Infer and analyze values in artistic and humanistic works.
   Level 3 — Relate values to scientific and technological developments.
   Level 4 — Engage in valuing in decision making in multiple contexts.
   In majors and areas of specialization:
   Level 5 — Analyze and formulate the value foundation/framework of a specific area of knowledge, in its theory and practice.
   Level 6 — Apply own theory of value and the value foundation of an area of knowledge in a professional context.

2. *Develop global perspectives.*
   Level 1 — Assess own knowledge and skills to think about and act on global concerns.
   Level 2 — Analyze global issues from multiple perspectives.
   Level 3 — Articulate understanding of interconnected local and global issues.
   Level 4 — Apply frameworks in formulating a response to global concerns and local issues in majors and areas of specialization.
   In majors and areas of specialization:
   Level 5 — Generate theoretical and pragmatic approaches to global problems, within a disciplinary or professional context.
   Level 6 — Develop responsibility toward the global environment in others.

Alverno's Office of Research and Evaluation found that graduates consistently develop these abilities. In addition, every student must fulfill the requirements for a major and a support area. "Annually, over 90 percent of Alverno's graduates put their degrees to work in areas related to their college major within six months of graduation. Nearly 30 percent of Alverno's graduates eventually pursue graduate studies after earning their baccalaureate degrees" (Schmitz, 1992, p. 5).

Alverno's clearly articulated objectives and the thoroughness with which they pervade the academic program, the general educational climate, its assessment program, and its institutional research demonstrate the educational power of such arrangements. They illustrate Pascarella and Terenzini's synthesis of research and comments concerning its policy implications (1991, p. 655).

> We have already noted that the effects of specific within-college programs, conditions, or experiences consistently appear to be smaller than the overall net effect of college. This is no surprise, since it is probably unrealistic to expect any single experience to be a significant determinant of change for all students. Nonetheless, this conclusion implies that the enhancement of the educational impact of a college is most likely if policy and programmatic efforts are broadly conceived and diverse. It also implies, however, that they should be consistent and integrated. There appear to be only a few specific programmatic or policy levers that administrators can hope to pull and produce a significant effect across the campus. Indeed, it may be potentially more productive for faculty, administrators, and researchers to conceive of the environment of any given campus not as unitary and global but rather as an amalgam of many diverse subenvironments, each of which has an influence (Baird, 1988). Furthermore, while the impact of any single subenvironment may be small or modest, the cumulative effect of all

subenvironments—if they are mutually supportive—
can be substantial.

Thus, instead of singular, large, specially
designed, and campuswide programs to achieve a
particular institutional goal, efforts might more pro-
fitably focus on ways to embed the pursuit of that
goal in *all* appropriate institutional activities. For
example, while special speakers and campuswide
meetings may be one way to increase racial tolerance, it may be even more effective if awareness
of and sensitivity to the issue permeate the selection of course content; the cultural activities of the
campus (such as speakers, plays, concerts, art shows);
student admissions and faculty and administrator
hiring and reward systems; committee appointments; selection of trustees; swift and unambigu-
ous responses to activities or incidents that are ra-
cially tainted; and so on. In short, rather than
seeking large levers to pull in order to promote
change on a large scale, it may well be more effective to pull more small levers more often.

Clear objectives concerning student learning and development, widely shared and emphasized in oral and written communications, help ensure internal consistency between the "small
levers." The particular vectors of development affected, of course,
will depend on the particular emphasis of a given institution.
For one college, competence is most important; for another, integrity; for a third, autonomy and purpose. But it is the clarity
and consistency that determine whether development will be
fostered. In their absence, conflicting forces and ambiguous messages may immobilize students, leaving them passive, uncom-
mitted, and inarticulate about what they have gained from their
college experience.

TEN

Institutional Size

Institutional size interacts with institutional objectives. Not surprisingly, colleges with clear and salient objectives are usually small. For while small size is not a sufficient condition for clarity of purpose, it seems to be a necessary one. The diversity of people and functions — spanning research and service as well as teaching — that characterizes large universities makes it almost impossible to formulate clear-cut objectives for student learning and development. Even when the college of arts and sciences has considerable autonomy, clearly articulated purposes rarely characterize the language, thinking, and conversations among faculty members, and students across diverse disciplines. Agreed-on outcomes for student learning and development shared by the colleges of business administration, engineering, and education, as well as arts and sciences, are typically nonexistent.

Several developments have driven institutions toward increasing size during the last thirty years. First, the legacy of World War II created enrollment pressures and growth opportunities during the 1960s. Second, a public policy shift took place

Note: This chapter draws heavily on Thomas and Chickering (1983).

in the late 1960s from a meritocratic to an egalitarian orientation toward higher education. Increasingly, Americans assumed that everyone had a right to postsecondary education, not just the best and the brightest. Consistent with this policy shift, the federal government made a basic decision to fund students through grants and loans rather than to fund institutions. The hope was that by increasing student choice between diverse public and private institutions, market considerations would create pressures for educational quality. A third element has been escalating costs combined with economic declines, which have significantly affected both public and private institutions. But perhaps the most insidious force driving increased size is the way public institutions are funded. Formula funding based on full-time equivalent student enrollment dominates public funding. This means that the only way a public college or university can get increased resources for new programs and a few discretionary dollars for innovation and change is by increasing enrollment. This constellation of forces has interacted with a general social assumption that "bigger is better" and with an impulse toward empire building shared by many educational leaders. Thus, it is not surprising that colleges and universities, as well as many other social institutions, have seemed to grow beyond human scale.

Perhaps Schumacher (1973, pp. 65–66) puts the issue best:

> In the affairs of men there always appears to be a need for at least two things simultaneously, which, on the face of it, seem to be incompatible and to exclude one another. We always need both freedom and order. We need the freedom of lots and lots of small, autonomous units, and, at the same time, the orderliness of large scale, possibly global, unity and coordination.
>
> What I wish to emphasize is the duality of the human requirements when it comes to the question of size: there is no single answer. For his different purposes man needs many different structures, both small ones and large ones, some exclusive and

some comprehensive. . . . Today we suffer an almost universal idolatry of giantism. It is therefore
necessary to insist on the virtues of smallness — where
this applies.

The question of scale might be put in another
way: what is needed in all these matters is to discriminate, to get things sorted out. For every activity there is a certain appropriate scale, and the
more active and intimate the activity, the smaller
the number of people that can take part, the greater
is the number of such relationship arrangements
that need to be established. . . . What scale is appropriate? It depends on what we are trying to do.

Myths and Realities Concerning Institutional Size

Sale (1980, p. 39) asserts that in higher education, as in a number
of other areas, "human scale" is appropriate whether we are referring to business, government, or education. Human scale is "a
scale at which one can feel a degree of control over the processes
of life, at which individuals become neighbors and lovers instead of just acquaintances and ciphers, makers and creators
instead of just users and consumers, participants and prota-
gonists instead of just voters and taxpayers."

Several obvious developments that occurred in colleges
and universities in the wake of the burgeoning enrollments of
the 1960s support the views expressed above. Many institutions
created advocacy offices and other support services designed to
counter the escalating depersonalization and bureaucratization.
Student protests decried this depersonalization. The buildings
constructed then, with their high-rise dormitories, libraries, and
classrooms, stand as brick-and-mortar testimony to the attempts
to realize savings in construction and administrative costs through
substantial increases in unit size. Sale (1980) catalogues the
human problems that seem to be inherent in such structures,
noting that "it is true that the bigger the skyscrapers become,
the more costly, less efficient, less adaptive, less safe, and usually
the more hideous they are." And Sale's observations are sup-

ported by the high crime rates and vandalism associated with high-rise urban development apartments as well as with similar college and university structures.

Sale (1980, pp. 311–318) cites five major myths and provides evidence concerning the contrasting realities:

1. *Larger units are more economical.* In fact, there seems to be a curvilinear relationship between size, costs, and productivity. "There seem to be no clear connections between the economics of scale of a particular plant and the success of that company" [p. 311].

2. *Larger units are more efficient.* In fact, large scale corporations or large scale institutions are less efficient in energy use, in use of raw materials, and notably, in the use of human resources. They also generate more waste. And "wastage" in higher education is greatest at the largest public institutions. Indeed a number of studies have indicated detrimental consequences resulting from increased unit size.

3. *Larger units are more innovative.* In fact, most significant inventions during the 20th Century have come from individual inventors operating completely on their own or autonomously within institutions. Most educational innovations have occurred in small colleges rather than large universities.

4. *Larger units provide goods and services at a cheaper price.* In fact, costs of production, advertising, promotion, and packaging result in higher prices.

5. *Larger units are more profitable.* In fact, findings repeatedly demonstrate that as corporate size increases profit rates decrease or remain constant.

Definition of Appropriate Size

One of the most useful conceptual frameworks and some of the most powerful data concerning relationships among size, human experience, and developmental consequences come from the work of Roger Barker and his associates. Their studies of differences associated with school size are particularly pertinent. Barker (1964) begins by looking at the interaction among three variables: numbers of "settings," varieties of settings, and numbers of persons per setting. A "setting" has two major components: behavior and the objects with which behavior is transacted. The behavior and objects within a setting are organized in nonrandom fashion, and the boundaries of a setting are usually quite clear. The people who inhabit a setting are often interchangeable, while the setting remains fairly constant. A living room, for example, is a behavior setting. It differs in expected behaviors and objects from a kitchen or a bedroom. Living room behavior across families is more similar than living room and kitchen behavior within the same family. Similarly classrooms, campuses, factories, production lines, and playgrounds are all settings. Table 10.1 presents findings concerning variations in settings, varieties, and people for schools of differing size. The table shows that as schools increase in size, the number of people increases much faster than the number of settings or varieties of settings. In the smallest schools, there

Table 10.1. Size, Settings, and Students.

School	Community Population	School Enrollment	Settings	Students per Setting	Varieties of Settings
Otan	199	35	60	0.58	29
Dorset	169	45	58	0.78	28
Walker	450	83	96	0.86	31
Malden	507	92	78	1.18	33
Meadow[b]	—	113	94	1.20	32
Midwest	781	117	107	1.09	33
Vernon	1,150	151	98	1.54	29
Haven	2,907	221	154	1.44	36
Eakins[c]	551	339	139	2.44	34
Booth	3,004	438	218	2.01	39
University City	23,296	945	312	3.03	36
Shereton[c]	4,739	1,923	487	3.95	41
Capital City	101,155	2,287	499	4.58	43

[a]Adapted from Tables 4.1 and 4.3, pp. 42 and 49, Barker and Gump, 1964.
[b]Meadow was two miles from the nearest town; it served two towns.
[c]High school that served several communities in addition to the one in which it was located.

were about two *settings* for each person; in the largest school, there were more than four *persons* for each setting.

What are some of the consequences of those differences in school size for the experiences and learning of the students? Here are some of the key findings:

Students in small schools held an average of 3.5 responsible positions per students (as members of play casts, officers of organizations, members of musical groups, and members of athletic teams); students in large schools averaged 0.5 responsible positions per student. Put differently, on the average, in the large schools every other student held a single position; in the small, each student held three or four positions. Furthermore, students in small schools held twice as many *different kinds* of responsible positions as those in large institutions.

Students in small schools received twice as much pressure to participate or to meet the expectations of the school as those in large ones, and academically marginal students in small schools received almost five times the pressure to participate as those in large institutions.

Self-evaluations of students in small schools were based on the adequacy of their contributions and on their level of competence in relation to the job requirements; self-evaluations of students in large schools were based on comparison with others.

Students in large schools exceeded those in small schools in satisfying experiences related to vicarious enjoyment of others' activities.

Students in small schools exceeded those in large schools in satisfying experiences related to developing competence, to being challenged, and to engaging in important activities.

Students in small schools tended to achieve relatively limited development in a wide variety of areas, while those in large ones tended to achieve greater development in narrower or more specialized areas.

As we have noted, Barker and Gump (1964) use the term *redundancy* to describe the condition where the ratio of persons to settings becomes unfavorable. In general, redundancy occurs when the number of inhabitants of a setting leads to decreasing opportunities for satisfaction and participation for each individual.

Six general consequences seem to be associated with increasing redundancy:

1. A smaller proportion of the "inhabitants" actively participate.
2. The activities and responsibilities of those who do participate become less varied and more specialized.
3. Persons with marginal ability are left out, ignored, and actively denied opportunities to participate.
4. Evaluation of performance shifts from how well a person's abilities actually fit the requirements for participation for a given position or for an area of responsibility to how good one person is compared to another; in educational terms, evaluation shifts from *criterion-referenced evaluation* to *norm-referenced evaluation*. Furthermore, as numbers increase and put pressures on the need to discriminate, judgments are made on the basis of increasingly fine distinctions.
5. A hierarchy of prestige and power develops.
6. Rules for conduct, definitions of appropriate behaviors, and standards for performance become increasingly formalized and rigid.

These findings are consistent with the results of studies of the effects of size in factories, public agencies, discussion groups, and other task groups. They are also consistent with the research synthesized by Sale and with the observations by Schumacher quoted earlier.

Some of the things that happen as the ratio of people to settings changes are illustrated by the experiences of the senior author with baseball. In my early childhood, I lived in a neighborhood where there were five other boys about my age, and we all liked to play baseball. Fortunately for us, there were three younger brothers and two younger sisters among these families; in addition, there were two fathers and one mother who were energetic if not athletic. Out of this assortment of talent we used to construct baseball games. This baseball setting had several salient characteristics:

We were all in action most of the time. Each usually had a lot of territory to cover, and you often had a chance to hit.

Sometimes a teammate would have to come out on base and run for you so you could go to bat.

We seldom played the same position in two consecutive games, or even within the same game. Different individuals pitched, caught, or played right field, depending on who was available. If another player came home from a piano lesson, positions would shift to accommodate that person's particular capabilities. We evaluated players on the basis of what they could do and how well they could do it; assignments were made and accepted accordingly. We would press into service whoever was available and willing. Visiting peers and adults were vigorously enjoined to play. No small child was spared.

We played by rules never heard of in the majors, and seldom by the same rules twice. Where we could hit the ball, whether a team "caught for itself," which team covered home plate — these and other regulations were modified with impunity to suit our purposes. Even within an inning, the rules would change; the pitcher would have to move up halfway and pitch underhand to the younger brother, for example.

At age eleven, I moved downtown. In this new neighborhood of about twenty-five boys, enough players were usually available "for a good game." This setting differed strikingly from the other.

In the field or at bat we stood or sat around a lot. Specialists developed. A few were good pitchers and did little else. One boy loved to catch and always did. First base and shortstop were usually nailed down. A hierarchy of leadership developed. The rules were standard.

Younger siblings and inept parents were never included, and some peers with marginal skills were usually relegated to being spectators when "we had enough" players. And some were punished severely even when they were able to play. I can clearly recall the tension that developed when two places needed to be filled and four or five persons were left. Not being chosen was painful, but being chosen last was not much better.

After a while, I entered a college along with about three hundred others and played some baseball there. These seemed to be the salient characteristics of the college baseball setting:

Competition was severe. Most people did not get to play at all, and coaching was reserved for those already highly skilled. Evaluation was comparative, and choices were made on the basis of rigid distinctions. A good hitter could always play. Exceptional skills in some other area sometimes could counterbalance mediocre hitting, but lack of that particular skill ruled a person out.

Only infrequently did players move from one position to another, and each developed the skills associated with his position to a high degree. Both a formal leadership hierarchy with a captain and co-captain and an informal hierarchical structure of prestige and power existed.

The dynamics that underlie these results are quite straightforward. It is not surprising, therefore, that they are consistent across a wide range of settings. Behavior settings offer a variety of satisfactions and opportunities that individuals find attractive. When the number of people is small, each person has more opportunities to participate and derives more satisfaction from the experience. In task-oriented settings, some functions impose obligations on the participants. When few people are available, each participant has to assume more responsibilities and each becomes the focus for more obligations. Under such conditions, individuals become more aware of the importance of their own participation and that of others. Thus, feelings of loyalty or responsibility are added to the initial intrinsic satisfactions that attracted the individuals to the activities in the first place.

In addition to these internal or personal forces, if the setting is important as part of a larger context, external pressures will increase as the number of participants diminishes. There will be more invitations or demands, and the social rewards for contributions will increase. At the same time, requirements for admission or for certain kinds of positions will become more liberal. Thus, people who usually might only be spectators will be pressed into service; reticent followers more often will find themselves in leadership roles. In this way, those who under circumstances of overpopulation might be seen as unsuitable or marginal will find themselves in demand.

The appropriate size of an institution, then, is determined by examining the numbers and variety of settings, the ranges of activities and responsibilities required, and the numbers of persons needed to carry out those activities and responsibilities effectively. In short, the appropriate size is the size that avoids making individuals redundant. If the institution's purposes are educational, or if the organization providing goods and services is also concerned about creating a developmentally challenging environment, the ratio of person to settings and the associated activities should be such that each person experiences (1) a reasonable level of demand and (2) a sufficient variety of challenges. Furthermore, the ratio should be such that they and others are aware of their contributions and such that they have frequent opportunities to develop new areas of competence and understanding.

Size and Its Effects on Institutions and Students

The findings and perspectives of Schumacher, Sale, and Barker and Gump provide a useful background for research on higher education. The implications for institutional policies, practices, and organization of the relationships they identify between size and student development can be captured in a phrase—"the need to disaggregate." Pascarella and Terenzini (1991, p. 654) put the implications this way:

> To a certain extent, all of the preceding discussion boils down to the issue of psychological size. . . . A number of steps have already proven effective in increasing student engagement and reducing the psychological size of larger institutions by affording opportunities for students to become involved with smaller groups of individuals, some of whom may be like-minded while others are not. Such downsizing can include cluster colleges and other purposeful housing arrangements, architectural alterations, academic organizations (for example, honors programs, discipline-based clubs, peer tutoring programs), cocurricular activities, work-study and other on-campus employment programs, intramural athletics, and so on. . . .

Whatever form engagement might take, however, students should be helped *early* in their academic careers to find academic and social niches where they can feel that they are part of the institution's life, where friendships can be developed, and where role models (whether student or faculty) can be observed and emulated. Because of the interconnectedness of areas of change noted earlier, the simple fact of involvement, as long as it is educationally productive, may be as important to educational changes as the specific areas of involvement.

As we look at higher education research, we need to recognize a fundamental point. In their literature review, Pascarella and Terenzini (1991) repeatedly note that the effects of size are "indirect," and though often statistically significant, "small." These observations are not surprising, especially with reference to recent research, when most colleges and universities by the 1980s had grown to a scale where students were "redundant." Although these campuses may have a different atmosphere, whether there are 5,000 or 50,000 students probably does not make much difference in the basic dynamics concerning involvement and participation. Competition for available positions for teams, clubs, and other student activities, opportunities for taking on leadership roles, the degree to which students know, and are known by, a significant portion of the faculty, administrators, and student services professionals — all these variables change dramatically once institutional size reaches such a scale. Thus, when so many institutions are so big and have such a rigid structure that students are redundant, it is not surprising that size effects are indirect and small.

Nevertheless empirical studies do demonstrate relationships between size and (1) institutional ethos and sense of community, (2) student involvement and participation, (3) faculty concern for students, and (4) persistence and retention.

Institutional Ethos and Sense of Community

Relying on twenty years of research concerning relationships between college characteristics and student development, Heath

(1981) documents the significance of a clear institutional ethos defined as discernible character, identity, and climate. Smaller institutions find it easier to establish and maintain a clearcut identity, which, in turn, communicates more clearly to students what the institution stands for, the values it holds, and the outcomes it desires for its graduates. Students selecting such an institution are more likely to achieve a good fit between their objectives and those of the college, to find their motivation reinforced, and to more actively take advantage of the educational opportunities provided. These dynamics have been documented in a number of studies. Eddy (1959, pp. 143–144), reporting on his study of college influence on student character, says, "The potential of the environment is measurably increased by a feeling of community. And that feeling appears to begin where it should—in common understanding and acceptance of commonly shared goals." Jacob's (1957) survey of research concerning the effects of college on attitudes and values found little influence except at a few institutions where a distinctive climate prevailed.

Sharp differences in institutional ethos and associated values sometimes exist. Chickering's (1971) longitudinal study of student development at small colleges (those with fewer than 1,500 students) examined graduates' perspectives on the most and least desired outcomes. Sometimes these were in direct contrast. For example, graduates of one institution listed as the most desired traits: being "educated in the liberal arts within the context of a Christian world view," "committed to Christ," and "activated by Christian ideals in the various pursuits of life"; the students desired least to be an "independent member of society," to "recognize and accept feelings as relevant to decisions," and to be "educated in the traditional liberal arts." Graduates of another institution listed as most desired: having "understanding of self as an individual and as a member of society," being a "constructive and creative member of interdependent society," and being "able to recognize and develop own creative potentials"; they desired least to be "educated in the liberal arts within the context of a Christian worldview," "committed to Christ," and "dedicated to Christian service." Regardless of whether one agrees with the particular characteristics desired, clarity of purpose and institutional character have an obvious impact on what the graduates themselves identify as valuable goals. That is why research by Chickering, Astin, and others finds that many "podunk colleges"—small, poor, little-known institutions—often turn out to foster more substantial student development than larger, comprehensive, well-supported institutions with elaborate facilities, strong research productivity, and high-powered faculty.

In days of rapid change and economic stringency, such institutions also have a good prognosis for survival. On the basis of his research, Heath (1981, p. 93) hypothesizes that "those colleges that will adapt healthily and effectively to the demands of the future are more accurately and reflectively aware of themselves, empathetically responsive, internally coherent, stably resilient, and autonomously distinctive." So a clear institutional ethos not only has solid consequences for student development, it has survival value as well. These qualities are much more readily achieved in institutions or in subunits with fewer than 2,000 students than in large, complex units facing the typical problems of poor internal communication, lack of organizational coherence, cumbersome decision-making processes, and multiple agendas (Gallant and Prothero, 1972).

Student Involvement and Participation

Astin (1977) reports that the small, often single-gender private college had the most widespread effects, primarily because of student involvement and opportunities for participation. According to Pascarella and Terenzini (1991, pp. 379, 380),

> That attending a large institution (or a large public institution) has an inhibiting influence on different dimensions of social involvement or integration during college is consistent with a substantial body of evidence. This evidence indicates that the inhibiting influence persists even when controls are made for salient student precollege traits, place of residence during college, and other institutional characteristics. . . . Furthermore, such evidence is also

consistent with the theoretical notion of redundancy in social settings. . . . Thus, student isolation and anonymity would be most likely in more populous institutional settings. Conversely, as institutional size decreases, it presents the student with a more psychologically manageable setting in which opportunities for social involvement and integration are enhanced.

In institutions with underpopulated settings, all participants will know one another more fully. They will have more numerous and more diverse opportunities to work and play together and more challenges to develop healthy cooperative relationships. In large overpopulated settings, the proportion of the community known and the level of information about fellow community members become much more limited (Wallace, 1966). Depersonalization escalates. Students create subcultures that insulate them from more general identification with the institution and its purposes and values.

Faculty Concern for Students

Bayer (1975, p. 557) found that "size was the attribute most highly correlated with the criterion: the larger the institution, the less was the concern for the individual student." Pascarella (1980, p. 563) noted that "present evidence suggests that institutional size is negatively associated with amount of student-faculty nonclassroom contact." Numerous studies have found that the quality and frequency of student-faculty contact are key variables in student development. Admiration of faculty is associated with higher grade-point averages. It also affects graduate school aspirations, since faculty encouragement is a major influence in going on to graduate school (Davis, 1964). On the basis of his multicollege research, Thistlethwaite (1959, p. 189) describes the faculty member who stimulates graduate study: "He does not see students only during office hours or by appointment; open displays of emotion are not likely to embarrass him; students need not wait to be called upon before speaking in class;

in talking with students he frequently refers to his colleagues by their first names; students don't feel obligated to address him as 'professor' or 'doctor.'"

Of course, there are many faculty members who share these characteristics in large, comprehensive institutions. The problem is that the institutional ethos does not usually support substantial interaction with students. Most important, as Astin's work (1963) has made clear, faculty attention is usually reserved only for the best and the brightest students. Those average or marginal students who would be most helped by the friendship, support, and encouragement of key faculty members seldom have the courage to seek them out and are seldom recognized by the professors themselves.

Persistence and Retention

Numerous studies demonstrate that persistence and retention are highest where students have a keen sense of involvement, have frequent informal contacts with the faculty, and experience a caring attitude on the part of the institution and its staff. A comprehensive report concerning retention identified "inadequate student faculty contact, lack of faculty care and concern, and inadequate academic advising" as three of the top five negative campus characteristics in relation to retention (Beal and Noel, 1980). Conversely, the report's authors found that the top positive characteristics were "caring attitude of faculty and staff, high quality of advising, and student involvement in campus." Pascarella and Terenzini (1991, p. 391) say, "The weight of evidence is quite clear that both the frequency and quality of students' interactions with peers and their participation in extracurricular activities are positively associated with persistence." Obviously, it is difficult to have much influence on students if they do not stay with us long enough to experience what we have to offer in any significant way. Thus, the fundamental consequences concerning retention are basic to all the other variables concerning institutional characteristics and student experiences.

Institutional Size and Student Development

The general evidence concerning relationships among institutional size, institutional characteristics, student involvement with peers and faculty, and student participation in extracurricular activities is substantial and clear. Because of these relationships, it makes sense that size has consequences for student development. The implications seem particularly powerful for development of competence and sense of competence, mature interpersonal relationships, identity, and integrity.

Competence and Sense of Competence

Astin's multi-institutional research shows a clear advantage for small institutions in student achievement, competence, and sense of competence. Compared to counterparts at large institutions, students at small colleges are more involved in academic studies, honors programs, and athletic activities. They interact more with the faculty concerning their studies. They evidence greater achievement in leadership skills, journalism, and athletic ability. Smith and Bernstein (1979) note that many small residential institutions, by virtue of their curricular coherence and shared educational experiences, foster communication among students concerning intellectual issues. And it is through just such informal discussions and debates that critical thinking skills are sharply honed. Pascarella and Terenzini (1991, p. 626) say, "Indeed, in some areas of intellectual development, such as critical thinking, . . . it is the student's breadth of involvement in the intellectual and social expertise of college, not any particular type of involvement, that counts most."

Once size increases to a level where students are redundant, evaluation shifts from a focus on how one's competence matches up against particular tasks or responsibilities (criterion-referenced evaluation) to how good one is compared to a large number of peers (norm-referenced evaluation). Then, by definition, a high proportion of students come out "average" or "below average" even though they may perform well when measured against some external criteria. These circumstances of competitive, norm-referenced evaluation can be very hard on sense of competence. As self-evaluation comes to be based primarily on comparisons with others, it is difficult to see oneself as competent. Those who are better in the areas to which one aspires are highly visible; there seem to be so many of them up there in front. Those less skilled are invisible and their presence carries little force. The steep pyramid means only a few can be on top. The rest of us struggle along, frequently using as much energy to cope with feelings of inadequacy as to cope with the tasks at hand.

Sense of competence flourishes when opportunities for achievement comprise a wide range of challenging tasks and responsibilities and when it is possible to work with a diverse range of people in accomplishing significant tasks. When the emphasis is on who can do the job and who is willing to undertake it, where esteem and respect derive from successful completion of significant tasks rather than from relative standing, we can learn where our real competencies lie. But as such opportunities become more constrained and one is precluded from diverse activities and recognition by increasingly tough competition, a broad-based sense of competence is hard to sustain. Astin's research (1963) concerning differential college effects on the motivation of talented students to obtain the Ph.D. degree documents these dynamics. Institutional size was the second most important variable that had a negative effect on Ph.D. aspirations. The most important variable was the percent of males, which is consistent with the negative effects engendered by highly competitive environments.

Development of Identity

Although we do not have direct empirical evidence, development of identity is likely to be more constrained under conditions of redundancy. If opportunities for active participation and involvement are limited, so are the opportunities for the kinds of self-discovery, or "resonance testing," through which a full and rich sense of identity may come about. If people only rarely have a chance to get behind the wheel — and if then they can only drive on a country lane, in sunshine, with an automatic transmission — not much development occurs and they may feel uncomfortable in facing other conditions. Of course, a similar result occurs if they drive only through snow and mud with smooth tires in a car without a heater.

The response to the combination of limited opportunities and competitive pressure is often observed. In secondary schools, students too often rely on either beauty, brains, or athletic prowess as the center of their self-esteem, as the core of their being. In college, students may adopt more particular roles: the nerds, the activists, the party goers, the Greeks, and others. However, when opportunities are many and varied and when competitive pressures are lessened, people can range more widely. The increased range of vicarious experiences available to the person in the overpopulated setting may somewhat compensate for the decreased opportunities for more active participation, but they do not provide the experience of self-testing on which a sense of identity ultimately is built.

Development of Mature Interpersonal Relationships

Under conditions of redundancy, freeing of interpersonal relationships is less likely to occur. In-groups and out-groups develop and assume greater force. Relationships become more hierarchical. Increased competition for entry into attractive settings may generate personal animosities. Other people whose peculiar ideas and behaviors match with one's own are more numerous, and it is thus easier to avoid those whose life-styles are incongruent. As a consequence, stereotypes and biases that students bring to college from earlier years more frequently remain untested, and they do not experience the cooperative working contexts in which such attitudes might be examined and modified. This narrowing of the range of contacts, which probably occurs with increasing overpopulation, may be primarily responsible for the large number of students who go through college relatively untouched. For it is basically the significant personal relationships that have an effect, whether with students or with faculty. And when these relationships become highly self-selective, it is less likely that change, liberalization, or enrichment will occur. Increased institutional size and the correspondingly reduced opportunities for human encounter and working relationships may contribute powerfully to sexism, racism, and other forms of intolerance in our colleges and universities.

Development of Integrity

Evidence also suggests that under conditions of redundancy, development of integrity will be more limited. Astin (1977) reports that small institutions seem to foster a greater degree of altruism and intellectual self-esteem (or sense of competence); large institutions encourage increased liberalism, hedonism, and "religious apostasy." The most striking difference was between the altruism found among students at small institutions and the increased hedonism found at large institutions. Note that these findings are highly congruent with Barker and Gump's findings (1964) concerning the positive effects of underpopulated settings on sense of responsibility and on the importance of individual contributions to community activity and needs.

The development of integrity involves two steps. The first step requires clarification of the values to which people are committed and that provide the major organizers for their words and deeds. The second step involves achieving congruence and internal consistency between word and word, word and deed, deed and deed. Clarification of values occurs when people must make choices that influence the lives of others and where the effects of those choices are observable. The context may be a committee to consider residence hall rules, or a hall meeting to deal with a problem of noise or stealing, or an honor system. Value choices reside wherever decisions must be made regarding the living conditions in the college community; in underpopulated settings, the opportunity for each individual to confront problems and to think through alternatives occurs more frequently. Similarly, where there are few individuals, the impact on the behavior of each is significant and observable. Students working with a group of five or ten others, or living in a house of twenty or thirty, quickly see the consequences of their choices for the lives of others.

Limited size carries particular force for the development of congruence. When the totality of a student's behavior is visible to many others who share classes and parties or sit on committees and in general meetings, it is difficult to talk one kind of life and live another. Thus the development of congruence is significantly related to institutional size and organization.

Institutional size has implications for other aspects of student development, but those described are probably the ones most affected. The basic point is that as redundancy occurs, less development is fostered. Redundancy takes place when increases in the number of inhabitants lead to decreasing opportunities for participation and satisfaction for each individual. As redundancy sets in, the activities and responsibilities of those who do participate become more specialized, and those with marginal qualifications tend to be left out. A hierarchy of prestige and power develops, and evaluation shifts from an emphasis on the fit between abilities and the requirements of a job to an emphasis on how one person compares with another. Rules and standards for conduct become more formalized and rigid.

Under such conditions, the opportunities to cope with significant problems become more limited and challenges to existing skills and knowledge are encountered less frequently. Experience becomes less varied and self-testing more restricted. The range of different people to be dealt with in contexts important to a person's own life decreases, and situations provoking examination of values and consideration of the consequences of an individual's actions less often have to be faced. Thus, development of competence is more limited except when supported by special ability or special motivation. The development of identity and the development of a personal value system are fostered less under conditions of redundancy than they are when the ratio of students to settings is smaller.

Taylor (1964) postulated the law that "people tend to disappear when huddled together in large numbers." A corollary is that when students are redundant, institutional impact is feeble. Until colleges and universities disaggregate in ways that create human-scale units for learning and involvement, their contribution to student development will continue to be limited.

ELEVEN

Student-Faculty
Relationships

After relationships with peers, relationships with faculty members are most important for students. Structural arrangements can support or inhibit the form and frequency of interpersonal contacts, but it is people who affect people. We hypothesize that when faculty are committed to creating quality learning experiences, when they are consistent in showing respect, caring, and authenticity, and when they are willing to interact with students in a variety of settings, then development of competence, autonomy, purpose and integrity is fostered. Pascarella and Terenzini (1991, p. 620) report that "A large part of the impact of college is determined by the extent and content of one's interactions with major agents of socialization on campus, namely, faculty members and student peers. The influence of interpersonal interaction with these groups is manifest in intellectual outcomes as well as in changes in attitudes, values, aspirations and a number of psychosocial characteristics."

Because of their influence on students, faculty should use their positions with a clear focus and intentionality. Faculty can encourage student development — as scholars and teachers, mentors, role models, and skilled listeners. They can strengthen their

316

influence by grounding their interactions in a basic understanding of developmental theory and by refining their interpersonal skills. This responsibility extends far beyond the traditional role of classroom professor. It goes beyond credentials and academic knowledge to the character of the person. While the role of faculty is key, administrators, support staff, librarians, teaching assistants, and custodians all can contribute to student development. What they say and do, and *how* they say and do it, can make a critical difference. Competence is fostered first by the example of those in teaching or leadership roles, second by the expectations they convey, and third by the encouragement they offer. When all three are present and balanced, they have the maximum affect.

This chapter explores faculty impact on classroom learning, on career aspirations, educational goals, and personal and occupational values. It examines ways that faculty can influence autonomy and integrity through nonclassroom interactions, as well.

Influential Faculty

Raushenbush (1964), Thistlethwaite (1959, 1960, 1962), Davis (1964), and Heath (1968) portray influential faculty not as therapists or buddies, but as experienced professionals, intellectually alive and capable, pursuing problems and sharing experiences with those still testing their competence. They take students seriously. They respect students' developing skills and life experiences, while both student and teacher work to refine them. While course content varies, students mature intellectually as a direct result of inspiration, discipline, example, and style. Baxter Magolda (1992, p. 294) makes this point nicely: "Contradicting the sense that authority is omnipotent is also essential. Teaching students that knowledge is not absolute and that authorities can disagree creates the possibility that students can learn in ways beyond collecting authorities' ideas. Sharing with students how we as educators form our own perspectives, and that our ideas are often in disarray before we arrive at a coherent view, makes the thinking process accessible. As long as instructors do not reveal the difficulties inherent in learning, students will not perceive that their struggles to understand are part of that same process."

Research confirms the importance of establishing rapport with students, offering specific and consistent feedback, presenting information with skill and clarity, and effectively structuring the way time is used in class. Providing stimulation in the form of challenge, inquiry, and an invitation to integrate and apply what has been learned is also important (Pascarella and Terenzini, 1991, p. 619). Various studies point to the importance of *engaging* or *involving* students (Pace, 1974; Astin, 1985; Boyer, 1987; Kuh, Schuh, Whitt, and Associates, 1991). While students may ultimately bear the responsibility for involving themselves in academic pursuits, the faculty member who speaks with passion and invites active learning, who adapts the structure of the class to the interests and abilities of the students, and whose articulate dynamism has students looking forward to every class does much to awaken dormant cognitive skills. With an engaging teacher, students learn that beyond the content lies the power of the knowledge-seeker. As Daloz (1986, p. 232) says, "Although our students may take a while to recognize it, what is important about our minds. . . . is not what is in them but how they operate. What we model for our students is not our knowledge but our curiosity, the journey, not the destination. As teachers, we recognize that we are channels through which information flows, configuring itself into certain patterns they may name 'knowledge.' However, the tradition we keep is not the knowledge itself but the capacity to generate it."

Yet many instructors do not model competence in the classroom. Few have studied teaching methods, learning theory, or intellectual development. Few elicit student evaluations at regular intervals, receive feedback from peer observers, or arrange to see themselves on videotape. Computerized ratings generated at the end of the semester give some indication of whether the instructor was prepared well, graded fairly, or encouraged critical thinking, at least from the students' subjective point of view. Once instructors receive tenure, the impetus to seek feedback and reflect on teaching often disappears, unless it is self-generated. But a college commitment to professional development can encourage such activities. For example, the staff at the Center for Instructional Development at the University of Washington conducts over two hundred small group instructional diagnosis (SGID) sessions for faculty members who wish to receive midcourse feedback from their students. On a prearranged day, in the absence of the instructor, the facilitator asks students to form groups of four to six people and reach consensus about what helps them learn and what improvements they would like to suggest. After eliciting reports from the small groups and clarifying their comments, the facilitator summarizes the feedback in individual meetings with the instructor, highlighting themes and helping the instructor to understand student perspectives, whether or not they agree with them (White, 1991).

Without this kind of thoughtful and specific feedback, faculty members develop a hazy sense of how effective they are in the classroom. They may persist in styles that do not fit well with students' needs or make assumptions about standards, grading practices, or students' abilities without checking these against reality. Colleges need to invest in more systematic assessment of teaching behaviors and their consequences for students. And individual teachers need to invest in their own teaching competence. Unless this occurs, students will continue to meet many more professors leaning on traditional methods and assignments than competent, vigorous professionals reaching for increased effectiveness.

Perhaps more opportunities exist for faculty to engage and inspire students in performance-oriented classes, engineering or design work, and athletics. Faculty who have demonstrated their artistic, mechanical, or athletic ability have many opportunities to model, coach, and oversee projects that mix theory and practice. For example, at Western Washington University, a team of automotive engineering students worked with their teachers to design and race a solar-powered car. Faculty members worked closely with students, from the theory to the design to the road test and to national and international competition. This kind of teamwork leading to inventive solutions, tangible rewards, and travel opportunities can have significant impact on the students' identity and purpose, as well as on their competence.

Opportunities to model interpersonal competence for students may arise in smaller seminars, interdisciplinary learning communities, or courses on counseling or interpersonal skills. But too many college buildings hold only large classrooms or lecture halls, filled with rows of passive, listening students. In four-year institutions, emphasis on research and publishing dominates the reward system and may block opportunities for positive relationships.

Kuh, Schuh, Whitt, and Associates (1991, pp. 174–175) document a discouraging trend. They found two faculty cultures: "student-centered faculty members — those who are committed to involvement with undergraduates (they tend to be older, tenured faculty), and those who are not involved with undergraduates out of class (often younger faculty or cosmopolitan scholars)." Furthermore, they found that the number of student-centered faculty members whose primary commitment is to the institution and to the welfare of undergraduate students is shrinking (p. 176). Newer faculty are warned about spending too much time on teaching-related activities, let alone meeting individually with students. When tenure time approaches, the list of publications is what counts. Beyond that, time spent on curriculum development, individual advising, or work with student organizations is not part of the official workload.

Faculty can have great influence on student development when they make themselves available to students outside class. Pascarella and Terenzini (1991, p. 620) state that "the educational impact of a college's faculty is enhanced when their contacts with students extend beyond the formal classroom to informal nonclassroom settings." They reported that the extent of informal contact with faculty is positively linked with a wide range of outcomes, including "perceptions of intellectual growth during college, increases in intellectual orientation, liberalization of social and political values, growth in autonomy and independence, increases in interpersonal skills, gains in general maturity and personal development, educational aspirations and attainment, orientation toward scholarly careers, and women's interest in and choice of sex-atypical (male-dominated) careers" (p. 620).

Given these outcomes, it is amazing that so little is known about the contribution of out-of-class experiences to learning and development. Students spend most of their time doing things other than attending class (Wilson, 1966; Boyer, 1987; Kuh, Schuh, Whitt, and Associates, 1991). Adult learners may be much more engaged in working, parenting, and trying to maintain their sanity. Boyer (1987) estimates that only about forty-eight hours of a typical college student's week are spent in class or studying. That leaves seventy hours unaccounted for (if you subtract fifty hours for sleeping). If some of those hours are spent being actively involved, students are more likely to be satisfied with their social life, living environment, academic major, contact with faculty, and the college overall. Most important, they are more likely to persist through graduation (Kuh, Schuh, Whitt, and Associates, 1991; Kegan, 1978; Astin, 1977; Kapp, 1979; Pascarella and Terenzini, 1981).

Student-Faculty Interaction

Kuh, Schuh, Whitt, and Associates (1991, p. 174) delineate some characteristics of student-faculty interaction, outside class, in "involving colleges" — those whose students are actively engaged:

- Contact is "after class," through extending points made during class discussions; these contacts sometimes evolve into conversations about personal or career concerns and issues. The interactions are encouraged by the availability of benches or clusters of chairs in the hallways of classroom buildings or accessible departmental lounges.
- During these contacts class material is often related to "real world" matters such as learning through cooperative education and internships.
- Other contacts usually focus on major-related activities or clubs, undergraduate research, or undergraduate teaching assistantships.

- A few contacts are initiated by faculty, and they sometimes evolve into a mentoring or sponsoring relationship with undergraduate scholars who have potential to become faculty members.

Kuh, Schuh, Whitt, and Associates further point out that even when college officials thought that it was a myth that its faculty cared more about students than at other institutions, the faculty *believed* that this was so, as did the students.

Pascarella and Terenzini (1991) echo the importance of students' *perceiving* that faculty care about them. Summarizing the research concerning college impacts on cognitive skills and intellectual growth, they find that students who reported the greatest cognitive development were also most likely to perceive faculty as being concerned with teaching and student development and to report developing a close, influential relationship with at least one faculty member.

This close, influential relationship has been eloquently described by Daloz in *Effective Teaching and Mentoring* (1986). K. Patricia Cross, in her foreword, puts the term in context by referring to the kind of mentoring that occurs in business, where a more experienced person helps a protégé move up the corporate ladder. "There is not much question about the goals, and the mentor clears the way, gives some travel tips, and smooths the bumps. Occasionally the mentor helps the protégé develop the necessary skills to navigate an especially difficult turn in the road, but by and large, the mentor concentrates on providing a map and fixing the road rather than on developing the traveler" (p. ix). In academia, the goal is less clearly defined. It may involve initial plans to complete a degree, transfer to another institution, or gain job skills, but unexpected opportunities and discoveries alter the journey. "In exploring previously unknown byways that are revealed to them as they travel, they discover goals never before considered and satisfactions not previously experienced. The mentor of adult learners is not so much interested in fixing the road as in helping the protégé become a competent traveler" (p. ix).

Daloz describes mentors as guides who "lead us along the journey of our lives. We trust them because they have been there before. They embody our hopes, cast light on the way ahead, interpret arcane signs, warn us of lurking dangers, and point out unexpected delights along the way" (p. 16). Consider this relationship between Jean, a student, and a faculty mentor:

> The term *mentor* had only recently come into [the professor's] vocabulary, but she liked it. It had a reciprocal, two-way quality that appealed to her. Far from placing her on a pedestal, she felt the term allowed her to reveal her clay feet. That was important, for she was put off when students idolized her. They needed to see her survive errors so they could learn to do the same. As long as they were hooked on their failures they would have difficulty seeing their successes.
>
> [The professor] had a special fondness for Jean. Like herself, Jean seemed to be honoring an inner voice that said it was time to care for herself. And Jean's curiosity, eagerness, enthusiasm, "inner sparkle," appealed to her. [The professor] was aware of her student's insecurity, her fear of the journey she was undertaking, so it was Jean's courage that [she] admired most of all—her "determination to get on with her life plan despite horrendous family problems" [pp. 107–108].

The professor held great hopes for Jean. She saw her student as standing at a threshold, ready to take on new challenges and do a lot of independent thinking. Jean also liked and respected her mentor.

As the year unfolded, Jean had mixed success in her coursework, became confused and discouraged, and almost dropped out. The barriers she faced were primarily at home. Her husband was recovering from a disabling accident, and her nineteen-year-old daughter had moved into the house with a baby. Daloz (1986, p. 109) says, "Her frustration is all the greater as she feels the impact of her education, both *what* she is studying and *that* she is studying. She enjoys being with other students, feels as though she is 'into the world' and 'participating in something.' And although she is not sure she is 'on the track I was when I started,' this does not worry her. There seems to be something more to it now than just learning how to be a secretary and more to her life than being 'only a mother.'"

Jean had minimal contact with her mentor during this difficult period, even though the invitation to drop by was always there. Yet she reports feeling her mentor's interest, concern, and warmth, and knew that she could talk to her about anything, "not just the school." Jean said, "'I see her supporting my goal, and I see her challenging, because she's where I want to be some day — not, say, this given job but her emotional attitudes toward her job and everything. I see her being where someday I want to be'" (p. 110). Daloz (1986, p. 109) describes the impact of this support on the growth of competence and autonomy:

> Knowing that she will be heard has allowed Jean to gain a greater sense of her voice during the past year. She is no longer as afraid as before to speak up in class; she feels freer to ask questions. If someone calls her on the phone, she feels "more authoritative," more self-confident than she used to. And although she is ambivalent about it, she sees her goal as somewhat closer now, feeling that even though her family may not know (or care), "inside myself, I'm growing."

Gaining a greater sense of voice is directly related to the growth of autonomy. Jean was gaining the courage to speak her mind, the confidence to act from her own center, and the growing sense of her self as a competent individual who could succeed. Her faculty mentor provided the support and challenge needed to foster this growing sense of competence. Daloz describes her the way the student saw her: the mentor seemed "to know everything, was very patient, committed to her work, and loved reading." She "had it all together," but that didn't mean she was perfect. Jean felt that she could disagree with her mentor, who was "super easy to talk to." She provided a climate "where students could talk freely without embarrassment, think aloud without being put down, and experiment with sometimes frightening ideas" (p. 107). The mentor challenged her by modeling her *own* independence and by helping Jean set goals and keep on track. She understood Jean's role as student as part of her larger role as an adult with very different responsibilities from those of residential students. She remained available to Jean without fostering dependence, and by doing so, let the student know that she was valuable enough to be cared about—a significant boon to one with a shaky identity.

Mentors can play key roles in helping students clarify purposes, values, aspirations, and career and educational goals. A young man at New College, Hofstra, spoke warmly of his mentor, Professor Anderson, who taught him to think. "He didn't answer questions; he said, 'What are the alternatives?' But he helped you along—'Now let me say this alternative won't do. Why not?' And he got you to work on every possibility, one after another" (Raushenbush, 1964, p. 86). The same young man went to Dr. Anderson three and a half months after he had begun work with him and said, "What I have to know now is whether you think I have what it takes to go into medicine. I have to make up my mind now, because this is my last chance to get into the Golden Gloves Competition." Raushenbush reports that the student gave up boxing that afternoon as a commitment to his academic work and by the end of the year had decided to become a theoretical chemist, saying, "'I don't want to do the experiments in the lab. It was the lab that first made me see what chemistry is—that and Dr. Anderson's talk—and how one *can* think about it—it was there I began to work out the alternatives—but I don't need that now'" (p. 87).

We turn now to the implications of mentoring for development.

Competence and Sense of Competence

Modeling the way we use our minds as teachers and as human beings has an impact on students' aspirations and sense of competence: "The extent of social interaction between students and faculty is significantly and positively related to educational aspirations at either the end of the freshman year, end of the sophomore year, or end of the senior year . . . . [The] degree of student-faculty social contact has a significant positive association with bachelor's degree completion and educational attainment through the doctoral degree" (Pascarella and Terenzini, 1991, p. 395). In national surveys (Baird, 1976; Baird, Clark, and Hartnett, 1973), graduate students reported on factors concerning senior-year decisions to attend graduate or professional school. Sixty-five percent in arts and humanities, 62 percent in the biological or physical sciences, and 56 percent in the social sciences said that personal encouragement from faculty was an important or very important factor.

Those relationships can be especially important for female students and black students. Astin and Kent (1983) report that "academic self-evaluations" were enhanced among women when faculty members had a research orientation and socialized with students. Komarovsky (1985) also found that student-faculty interaction positively affected women students' intellectual self-images. Gurin and Epps (1975) report similar results for the black students' self-images.

Purpose

Faculty members have an effect not only on students' competence and sense of competence but also, obviously, on the clarification of purpose. Wallace's (1966) report, which describes the relation between faculty members' expressed admiration, and students' grade-point average and graduate school aspirations, indicates their interaction. Grigg (1962) asked seniors whether any member of the college teaching faculty had made contact with them (as opposed to their approaching the faculty) during their college career to offer encouragement or suggestions about going to graduate or professional school. Students who had received such encouragement several times planned to go on for further study much more often than did students who reported little contact of this kind. Greeley (1962), who questioned students of both high and low achievement, found that those planning further education, regardless of their achievement level, had been influenced to do so by faculty members.

In summarizing the research, Feldman and Newcomb (1969, p. 253) say, "Evidence is accumulating that faculty are particularly important in influencing occupational decisions and educational aspirations. In over a dozen studies, in which students were asked to name the important sources of influence on their vocational planning and decisions, faculty along with parents ranked as extremely important. In fact, with only two or three exceptions in these studies, students perceived faculty to be either as influential as their parents or more so." Along the same lines, Pascarella and Terenzini (1991, p. 308) note that "with few exceptions, the findings indicate significant interactions between student-faculty contact and changes in students' occupational values. . . . Regardless of institutional type or size, most students tend to shift their occupational values away from the extrinsic rewards and (to a lesser degree) toward intrinsic rewards."

Frequent student-faculty contact has particular significance for women, students of color, and students entering with high SAT scores. The *quality* of student-faculty relations is most important for entering students who, relative to others, do not place great emphasis on graduating. Komarovsky (1985) found that as seniors career-oriented women who as freshmen had not been interested in careers had significantly more interaction with faculty than seniors who remained uninterested in a career. Thus, interaction with faculty in these cases did not simply accentuate a career orientation, but changed initial orientations. And Karman (1973) found that women's discussion with faculty of academic issues and problems had a direct effect on the choice of gender-atypical careers. Gurin and his colleagues (Gurin and Katz, 1966; Gurin and Epps, 1975) found that informal, out of class contact with faculty during the freshman year positively influenced the prestige of career choice by the end of that year. These findings show that high-quality, early, informal, out of class contact with faculty can have significant consequences for students' career aspirations and clarification of purpose.

Probably the principal way faculty members assist the development of purpose is by recognizing that effective teaching will raise questions of purpose or will add new dimensions to the questions already there. Faculty members help as students try to articulate the fit between their own developing purposes and an idea encountered in reading, discussion, or lecture, by responding to such questions in open and thoughtful manner—indeed, by granting that after all, a student may be working for something more than a grade. Fundamental questions reside in all areas of study—humanities, arts, natural sciences, and social sciences—and for more perceptive and thoughtful students, they reside in technical and professional training as well. Explicit recognition of this fact and willingness to deal with the issues that arise, either individually or in class, contributes substantially to development of purpose. Counselors and advisers can support the development of purpose more directly by exploring educational and career options, values, and lifestyle issues.

As Winter, McClelland and Stewart (1981, p. 126) put it, "Scholarly contact with the faculty, . . . together with the enthusiasm and interest they developed toward their courses, has strongly affected their choice of career." Raushenbush (1964, p. 135) captures this dynamic as follows:

> The ways in which teachers affect seriously the education of their students are many; but however the teachers function in the classroom, whatever their style, their subject, their way of talking to the students or with them, what students remember, what reached the heart of their learning, what they cherished more than any other one thing, is the sense of shared experience with a teacher. They know the teacher is going through something when the students are; the students speak of this when it is happening, and often afterward, for the sense of communion lasts. Such teachers care about what becomes of their students, but their concern for their students is not limited by a wish to do something for them. There is important experience to be discovered, work to be done, a world to function in; and the education of the students, . . . the personal

enlargement education should bring, has a better
chance of accomplishment if the teacher can forward the experience, reveal the work to do, help
them to find in study ways to function.

Research studies of living-learning centers, honors programs, and special programs involving flexible class meeting
schedules found significant effects on cultural sophistication and
on gains in cultural, aesthetic, and intellectual attitudes and
values (Endo and Harpel, 1982; Stakenas, 1972; Ory and Braskamp, 1988). But the critical influences were more a result of
students' interactions with program faculty members than of the
programs themselves.

Faculty members and administrators, secretaries, jani-
tors, and cooks — in short, any older person — can also contribute in another way: through appropriate self-disclosure. By letting students know our own occupational history, and by sharing
our feelings about it and the reasons for our moves, we permit
students to vicariously test their own occupational plans and
aspirations. By letting students know our home and family, the
way we spend our time, the organizing needs and satisfactions
for our particular life-style, we provide a wider base for clarification of their future existence. Not that they will follow our
example. Our difficulties and problems may be the most instructive things we offer, our blind spots and points of tension most
revealing. But with several such experiences, distortions carried from their own family settings can be tempered; and as
the range of encounters increases, so do opportunities for partial identification and emulation, for critical modeling. Disagreement, in the context of a warm relationship, can lead to positions contrary to our own, but positive for the student. Not all
faculty members can be so open, and not all can find satisfaction
in such relationships. But when they can, it makes a difference.

Autonomy

Such relationships of inspiration, informality, openness, and
warmth have particular implications for the development of autonomy. Achieving emotional independence is the first step

toward autonomy, and it begins with redefining relationships
with parents, sometimes through active rebellion and rejection
and other times more quietly, without overtones of anger and
disillusionment. But in either case, the support of peers and nonparental adults is helpful. Therefore, adults who are accessible
and sensitive can have substantial impact. With them, the habitual actions and reactions learned during childhood can be
reexamined and new behaviors can be tested. New modes of
relationship with authority figures can be formed. A student can
then move from dependence or defiant independence toward
relationships of mutual respect and regard where various kinds
of interdependence are recognized and from which an autonomous existence can be built.

Katz (1962, pp. 387–388), using a generic "he" typical
in earlier decades, puts it this way: "The college teacher is a
special transference object for his students. He is an 'in between'
object, in between parents and the adult relations the student
will establish in and after college. . . . Teachers thus may become 'associates' in the student's mind in his rebellion against
his parents. . . . This is a role to which teachers often lend themselves readily, being frequently permanent rebels themselves.
The intensity of the transference will of course vary much with
the school and with the individual students." Sanford (1966, p.
296) describes one form this dynamic takes for young women:

> One may sometimes observe quite clear-cut mother-
> transferences to older women teachers. A student
> involved in such a relationship will exhibit many
> signs of immaturity — often including a kind of com-
> pulsive devotion to duty that results in consistently
> good grades. Further observation, . . . however,
> will often show that the relationship is serving a use-
> ful means for gaining freedom from a rather over-
> whelming actual mother; powerful maternal influ-
> ence, supported by a host of response readiness
> brought over from childhood, could hardly be op-
> posed without a strong ally. Since the teacher usually
> represents more liberal values and a more flexible

and enlightened conscience than does the historical mother-image, there is a good chance for educational gain from the relationship.

A peer group or a close friendship with one or two others the same age provides the principal support during this period of redefinition. Frequently the new supports themselves can be binding. They may exact a high price for the support provided. A close relationship with an older person can temper total reliance on friends and can provide perspective on those relationships. With such help, it is often possible for the young person to leave one group and join another, where participation is less costly and where the values and behaviors better suit the developmental directions most desired. Alternatively, a student can move among several groups to acquire the diversity of experiences through which greater autonomy and tolerance can be achieved. Sanford's "Penny" illustrates this point (1966, pp. 67–69):

> Many aspects of Penny's experience at Vassar played a part in her development — faculty members, courses of study, the student society and culture, her friendship group, the general climate of the college — but the crucial factor has undoubtedly been, as she herself states, the relationship with Mr. A. . . .
>
> Mr. A's crucial role was to make it possible for her to break away from her original peer group, and breaking away was necessary to her new freedom, because this group had become the major support of her restrictive conscience and her authoritarian position. Only an adult — not a peer or group of peers — and an admired one who represented intellectual values and enlightened conscience could have played this role. No other agency could have stood in effective opposition to the values represented by the early peer group and fully espoused by Penny herself. She needed a figure that was in some part a representative of her conscience but

could at the same time nourish her developing confidence in her own intellectual powers. . . .

After the relationship with Mr. A became fully established Penny could make friends with an entirely different group of [women], who now became very important as supporters of her new value system and her new self-conception. She could also establish relationships with other faculty members, who served her in the same way . . . .

Be it noted, finally, that there is nothing in the material to suggest that Penny ever sexualized her relationship with Mr. A, or that he, for all his boyishness, ever indicated to the [women] that he valued them for anything other than their intellectual and human qualities. Any departure from these restraints by either one would, of course, have spoiled the whole drama. Deep and personal though her problems were, Penny managed to work them out at the level of intellectual activity — thereby taking advantage of one of the unique opportunities offered by the college or university to those whom it would change.

Relationships which have such potential for student development also create opportunities for teachers to exploit students for their own needs. Awareness about the dangers of sexual harassment has increased dramatically during the past several years. Some colleges and universities are debating whether to adopt codes of conduct prohibiting faculty-student dating relationships. Connelly and Marshall (1989) summarize several studies of inappropriate faculty relationships with students at large state universities in the 1980s. For example, one survey of 1,111 female students found that 20 percent of the graduate women and 17 percent of the undergraduate women experienced unwanted sexual attention from their professors; at another, 28 percent of the graduate students and 19 percent of the undergraduates reported being sexually harassed one or more times.

These are serious problems. A clear institutional policy is needed to counteract suggestive behavior, unwelcome requests for dates, demands for physical intimacy, or any behavior which injects sexual undertones into the learning environment. The unequal power of faculty over their students makes consensual romantic relationships risky. Subtle exploitation can be practiced by faculty whose self-esteem requires the continued nourishment that idolization provides, whose hostility, frustration, and insecurity require safe objects for expression, or who must induce dependence to support their own weak egos. Other ethical and interpersonal problems can alienate students and set poor examples. Who is not likely to become cynical when faculty put more energy into consulting than into good teaching, or when they bring departmental politics or interpersonal rivalries into a classroom or advising session?

Integrity

At least some students, though they may feel powerless in confronting entrenched authority figures, can sharpen their ethics by seeing what *not* to do. Faculty members and administrators should be paragons. That, despite occasional disclaimers, has been implicit in most of our discussion. But we must not forget the force of "anti-models" (Adelson, 1962) — people whom students actively reject. We have all known some of these anti-models — the tyrant, the haranguer, the no-show, the crowd-pleasing performer, the theoretician working out abstruse ideas, the boring lecturer using the same old notes. Such persons also provoke development. Each of us, if we have a clear and solid position, will be rejected by some. Comforting pillows can contribute to needed rest and recovery. But students also need anvils on which to hammer out their own shape. A college faculty and administration must provide both.

Faculty-student interactions can foster integrity by embodying positive values and ethical behavior. The classroom provides an excellent forum for questions of value: in readings, lectures, and class discussions; in all acts and contemplated acts; and in college policies and cultural standards. When such questions are raised in class, in advising, in committee meetings, and in individual conversations, humanizing of values and development of congruence are fostered. The instructional goals set by faculty members, and the degree to which questions of value and attitudes are raised by particular subject matter or by teachers themselves, can make a difference. Probably the greatest impact is on the humanizing of values, for development of congruence requires more than verbal exchange and intellectual discussion.

Daloz (1986) points out that there are few college-level subjects in which there is no legitimate controversy. He encourages faculty who want to be intentional about fostering growth to present a range of different perspectives on their subjects, to provide a context or map for students to clarify the beliefs and assumptions underlying the content, to offer ample opportunity for discussion and debate, and to pay attention to the developmental tasks confronting students (pp. 123–124).

Jacob (1957) found that institutions having a potent effect on values were characterized by (1) a distinctive climate, (2) individual teachers who had strong value commitments of their own, and (3) value-laden personal experiences on the part of students which were integrated with their own educational development. Heath (1968, pp. 204–205) says of students at Haverford College (one of the "potent" colleges singled out by Jacob) that they:

> value those faculty . . . who are professionally competent but who do not let their intellectual competence shield them from "being very human persons." Those faculty whose own lives were highly integrative, who revealed a humanness, including their frailties, who put into action what they believed, and who had developed a perspective within which to locate their own intellectual interests, strongly and emotionally move many of the men who were looking for models by which to make a similar integration in their own lives.

We all would back words with action, would make behavior consistent with belief. But most of us compromise in varying degrees, charting a course somewhere between total integrity and total comfort. Our agile intellects spin off rationalizations to gloss over gaps between what we espouse and what we do. Young adults hope mightily to avoid that fate, to sustain ideals in the face of seduction or sacrifice. Older persons who come close say that it can be done. Their example gives courage to many and provides a model when students meet tough choices.

Pascarella and Terenzini (1991, pp. 312–313), in discussing college impacts on attitudes and values, say, "Consistent evidence . . . suggests a relationship between student-faculty contact and attitude and value change. . . . In each instance, faculty contact is positively associated with positive changes in altruism, political liberalism, or civil libertarianism."

Components of Positive Student-Faculty Relationships

What general conditions for relationships among students and faculty seem to foster competence, autonomy, purpose, and integrity? Four major components run through the empirical findings and personal experiences described in the literature on higher education: accessibility, authenticity, knowledge, and an ability to communicate with students.

Accessibility

Accessibility means more than simply saying to students, "Feel free to come and see me." It requires an institutional climate where talking with faculty members is legitimized, where students feel free to "take up the professors' valuable time," and where such contacts are viewed as an important and necessary part of teaching and learning. In many studies, simple frequency of contact is associated with variables related to the general kinds of development with which we are concerned. When frequent contacts are characterized by informality and warmth, student development is augmented. This does not mean that professors should be available twenty-four hours a day or seven days a week. Different students need different amounts of contact with faculty members, and individual students vary at different times.

In some cases, delay or no assistance is appropriate. But where the climate legitimizes such contact and where people can respond flexibly according to their judgments about the significance and timing of particular requests, substantial contributions can be made.

Authenticity

Authenticity holds sway when the people that students encounter have a firm and well-integrated system of values and behaviors of their own. Students do not want to be told what they should be or what they should become, nor does such telling make much difference. They *do* want to know what others believe and the basis on which those beliefs rest. Empirical evidence is not the only valid or acceptable basis. When values rest on faith, on a religious or cultural tradition, or on basic assumptions that are part of an ethical humanism, candid admission of the fact is better than intellectual gymnastics that attempt to support a position through use of dubious evidence or rationalizations.

Knowledge

Knowledge about students and their development can be a great help. We assume that faculty members should be competent in their own disciplines. Faculty should also become familiar with the social, cultural, and spiritual backgrounds from which the students come, and the attitudes, ideals, and developmental problems they bring with them. College teachers should try to remember how *they* felt when facing college or graduate school. They should be attentive to learning theory, student characteristics, current issues affecting students, and strategies for making education meaningful to diverse adults with different learning styles and abilities.

Daloz (1986, pp. 232–233) offers students some maps in the form of readings in developmental literature and assigned reports on particular theorists who can address key issues for each student: "Levinson [*The Season's of a Man's Life*] for a young man in transition, Fowler [*Stages of Faith: The Psychology of Human*

Development and the Quest for Meaning] and *Christian Faith* for a woman of deep religious commitment, Gilligan [*In a Different Voice: Psychological Theory and Women's Development*] for a mother entangled in the demands of work and family. Because each knew I had selected that work for him or her, they each took special interest in that particular map and drew unique value from it."

You do not have to be a trained psychologist or human development specialist to understand some of the basic conceptual frameworks concerning human development and learning. Loevinger's *Ego Development: Conceptions and Theories* (1976), Perry's *Forms of Ethical and Intellectual Development in the College Years: A Scheme* (1970), Kegan's *The Evolving Self: Problem and Process in Human Development* (1982), Belenky, Clinchy, Goldberger, and Tarule's *Women's Ways of Knowing: The Development of Self, Mind, and Voice* (1986)—all these provide insights that help us "listen with a third ear" and hear better some of the fundamental developmental dynamics that underlie the cognition and affect our ability to come through in our encounters. They help us understand some of the diverse reactions we get from different students when our own reactions and behaviors remain constant. So increasing our own knowledge of the literature on human development can be very useful. Sharing it selectively with our students can help them put their own development into a larger perspective; it can give them conceptual tools to think about where they are and where they want to go, what they are and what they want to be.

Ability to Communicate with Students

Finally, we can learn better how to listen and how to talk with our students. Kuh, Schuh, Whitt, and Associates (1991, p. 178) have described the positive effects when faculty are experienced as real human beings. Not only do faculty at "involving colleges" discuss academic issues after class with students; many of them "take time to help a student who faces debilitating personal experiences, such as parental (or their own) divorce, illness of a child or parent, a roommate with a serious illness, or financial difficulties."

Sometimes a passing comment or question presents an opportunity for dialogue. "I can't study." "I can't stand the thought of going home to my parents." "I used to enjoy my church group, but now I am questioning everything." "I'm having a really hard time with my history teacher." "I don't know what to do when I graduate." "I don't see how I can live with my roommate for eight more weeks." "Something awful happened to me last night." Most faculty want to be helpful, and many feel a professional responsibility to respond. Yet few are trained in interviewing or counseling techniques, nor do they want to play the role of amateur psychotherapist.

An in-depth exploration of helpful listening skills is beyond the scope of this chapter. However, a short review of the qualities associated with skilled helping may remind us of what can be helpful. Trust and respect are key ingredients, as are empathy, warmth, concreteness, immediacy, and a nonjudgmental attitude. Ivey (1988) summarizes the basic components. The most basic is the ability to enter into the student's frame of reference, to attempt to truly understand the student's experiences, thoughts, feelings, and beliefs. Positive regard involves paying attention to the positive aspects of the student's experiences (even if the student cannot see them), and focusing on assets or strengths that the student can build on. This needs to be done sensitively, not discounting negative feelings or simply trying to make the student feel better superficially. Ivey describes other important dimensions of caring, such as genuine warmth, an emphasis on specifics rather than vague generalities, a focus on the here-and-now rather than the past or future, and a willingness to carefully offer feedback and suggestions that will help students move toward their goals.

Respect is also necessary, recognizing each student's basic worth and uniqueness, refraining from patronizing advice or quick solutions. By helping students clarify the situation, the problem, and the context, and discover what actions are possible, we empower them to take charge of their own adaptation and maturation. We may grow impatient with their bumbling experimentation, but better the bumbling be theirs than ours. Our respect for their thinking and solutions strengthens their autonomy and integrity.

Respecting students' thinking precludes certain rewards. We do not receive the satisfaction that comes from giving sage advice or from the lucid exposition of our own point of view. Dogmatic teachers usually alienate students. Those who pontificate will be tuned out. Neither can we have the satisfaction of pursuing our own curiosity. Any voyeuristic interest in the details of the students' sexual experiences, drug or alcohol use, or conflicts with parents or supervisors is unethical and intrusive. We can forgo this satisfaction passively, by not pursuing details that are superfluous, and we can forgo it actively by summarizing the core message, focusing the students' attention on goals and plans rather than on thrilling or titillating tangents. This helps students realize that we are not together for mutual amusement but for constructive purposes.

Above all, respect means that we seek only information or clarification that benefits the students; we do not seek gratification or prestige at their expense. We do not engage in behavior that threatens harm, injury, or loss or fails to respect the students' privacy, dignity, and individual rights. We may socialize with students, but we are careful about forming connections that may interfere with our objectivity, or may appear to other students like favoritism. We do not bring our personal issues or needs into the dialogues. We make referrals to more competent professionals — that is what the campus counseling center is for — and we consult with colleagues when we feel unsure of how to handle something.

Active listening involves using our eyes, voice, gestures, and body language to convey our interest, and being fully present to the speaker. This kind of attention demands restraint. It means no doodling, no thinking about tomorrow's class, this evening's dinner, or that interesting and upsetting luncheon discussion. It means deliberately tuning out the "static," such as our own counterarguments and opinions, and concentrating so intently on what the student is communicating that we can paraphrase it accurately.

We need to listen not only for facts and feelings but for students' interpretations of what they mean. Does the low grade received on a test mean "total failure"? Does it mean that he did not understand the assignment or needs more work on study skills? Does it mean that she could not concentrate because of personal problems? By helping students see their assumptions and interpretations, we probe cognitive constructs that underlie their thoughts, feelings, and actions. Alternative frames of reference can then be explored.

Listening to and talking with students effectively can be exhausting, frustrating, and difficult, especially with students diverse in age and national or ethnic backgrounds. But it is in one-to-one exchanges that we can be models, mentors, and friends. The four general conditions conducive to productive relationships among students and faculty—accessibility, authenticity, knowledge, and the ability to communicate with students—are not complicated to arrange. But on many campuses, such arrangements will require modification of priorities, funds, and energies. While many students do not miss an individual connection with faculty, others yearn to know us better. Institutions which do not have built-in traditions and rewards for informal student-faculty relationships may continue to leave most students nameless and faceless. They contribute little to the development of competence, autonomy, purpose, and integrity.

TWELVE

Curriculum

The word *curriculum* comes from the Latin verb, *currere,* which means to run a course. Thus, a *curriculum vitae* gives the course of one's life. In that sense, curriculum ought to be thought of as including all the diverse activities and investments that a student's experience of college comprises: classes, sports, student activities, residential life, co-op programs, love affairs, hassles with the registrar, dozing in the library. The dictionary collapses the original meaning to encompass simply "the courses of study offered by an educational institution." We use that restricted definition in this chapter. But we also recognize that in a more fundamental way the activities and experiences addressed in other chapters are critical elements that, for some students, may have more impact than their "courses of study."

Colleges have always served both liberal education and professional or vocational education. Six centuries ago, the first students who came to meet with tutors in Cambridge, England, were poor, slept where they could, and often went hungry. Like many students since then, they endured those hardships because education could lead to jobs in teaching, the church, the courts, and the royal administration. The first college in this country,

Harvard, was established principally to prepare men for teaching, medicine, law, and the ministry. Since those early beginnings, each college, student, and parent has assumed that a college education would lead to a better job and a better life. So the traditional assumption of colleges and universities has been that liberal education and preparation for work should and can go hand in hand.

But we need to make a critical distinction between preparation for work and preparation for a job. While one person understands career as a succession of jobs, another sees the succession of jobs held as contributing to the accomplishment of some work, as part of a purposeful calling. Green (1977) wonders whether it is possible for people to find work through the limited number of roles validated by today's employment structure. Alienation results when people do not see possibilities for paid employment linked to meaningful purposes. Green (1977, pp. 42–43) puts it this way:

> If we are to understand the relation between education and work we need to mark a *sharp distinction between work and job.* There is an enormous difference between the person who understands his career as a succession of jobs and a person who understands the succession of jobs he has held . . . as all contributing to the accomplishment of some work. . . . What is often referred to as *alienation from work* is seldom that. It is rather, alienation from the job structure of modern society. . . . Work is basically the way that people seek to redeem their lives from futility. It therefore requires the kind of world in which hope is possible, which is to say, the kind of world that yields to human effort. A world in which these conditions are unsatisfied is a world filled with labor, but without work — a world perhaps with "free time" but without leisure.

With this perspective on the distinction between work and a job, we can address some of the key relationships between (1) liberal education and the developmental vectors and (2) the skills, abilities, and characteristics required for effective work.

Liberal Education and the Developmental Vectors

If there is one thing the literature of higher education does not need, it is another definition of liberal education. Let us, therefore, share one of the first, and in our judgment, one of the best. The following passage is from Cardinal Newman's *The Idea of a University* ([1852] 1973, pp. 177–178). While its masculine pronouns remind us of the earlier exclusionary nature of higher education, its eloquently stated ideas provide an alternative to our more impoverished educational and psychological jargon:

> University training . . . aims at raising the intellectual tone of society, at cultivating the public mind, at purifying the national taste, at supplying true principles to popular enthusiasm and fixed aims to popular aspiration . . . at facilitating the exercise of political power, and refining the intercourse of private life. It gives a man a clear conscious view of his own opinions and judgments, a truth in developing them, an eloquence in expressing them, and a force in urging them. It teaches him to see things as they are, to go right to the point, to disentangle a skein of thought, to detect what is sophisticated, and to discard what is irrelevant. It prepares him to fill any post with credit, and to master any subject with facility. It shows him how to accommodate himself to others, how to throw himself into their state of mind, how to bring before them his own, how to influence them, how to come to an understanding with them, how to bear with them. He is at home in any society, he has common ground with every class; he knows when to speak and when to be silent; he is able to converse, he is able to listen; he can ask a question pertinently and gain a lesson seasonably, when he has nothing

to impart himself; . . . he is a pleasant companion
and a comrade you can depend upon; he knows
when to be serious and when to trifle with grace-
fulness and to be serious with effect. He has the repose of a mind which lives in itself, while it lives
in the world, and which has resources for its happiness at home when it cannot go abroad.

This paragraph can be translated into key objectives of
liberal education and components of the seven vectors. In the
phrase "a clear conscious view of his own opinions and judgments, a truth in developing them, an eloquence in expressing
them, and a force in urging them," we have integrity and interpersonal competence. In "to see things as they are, to go right
to the point, to disentangle a skein of thought, to detect what
is sophisticated, and to discard what is irrelevant," we have
intellectual competence — analysis, synthesis, and evaluation. "To
fill any post with credit and to master any subject with facility"
speaks to vocational purpose and lifelong self-directed learning.
"He is at home in any society, he has a common ground with
every class" calls for intercultural tolerance. "How to accommodate himself to others, throw himself into their state of mind,
bring before them his own, come to an understanding, bear with
them" gives us the empathy, understanding, and respect for
others that is essential for mature interpersonal relationships.
"A pleasant companion and a comrade you can depend on" proposes a loyalty and capacity for intimacy that goes beyond mere
understanding and tolerance. And, finally, "a repose of mind
which lives in itself, while it lives in the world" refers to our
basic sense of self in a social and historical context — part of establishing identity.

Skills, Abilities, and Characteristics
Required for Effective Work

How do these liberal education or developmental goals relate
to the skills, abilities, and characteristics required for successful work? Substantial research has addressed this area. Klemp

and his associates (1977) have made major contributions. Their approach involves three steps: (1) identifying successful individuals in a variety of occupations and professional roles, (b) finding out what they are doing that makes them successful, and (c) examining how and why they are doing what they do. They have studied diverse career areas: human services, military services, alcohol abuse counseling, small businesses, police work, sales, process consulting, civil service, the State Department, and industry management. Their research relies on observation, interviews, and direct assessment. What did they find?

> Our most consistent — though unexpected — finding is that the amount of knowledge one acquires of a content area is generally unrelated to superior performance in an occupation and is often unrelated even to marginally acceptable performance. Certainly many occupations require a minimum level of knowledge on the part of the individual for the satisfactory discharge of work-related duties, but even more occupations require only that the individual be willing and able to learn new things. . . .
> In fact, it is neither acquisition of knowledge nor the use of knowledge that distinguishes the outstanding performer, but rather the *cognitive skills* that are developed and exercised in the process of acquiring and using knowledge. These cognitive skills constitute the first factor of occupational success [p. 103].

Which cognitive skills are most important to success at work? Klemp (p. 103) lists four:

1. Information processing skills related to learning, recall, and forgetting.
2. Conceptualizing skills that involve both ability to analyze and ability to synthesize information from a prior analysis. This skill enables individuals to bring order to the informational chaos that constantly surrounds them.

3. The ability to understand many sides of a con-
    troversial issue. This skill enables people to
    resolve informational conflicts better than those
    who cannot conceptualize in this way. People
    without such skills typically resolve conflicts by
    denying the validity of other points of view and
    are not well qualified to mediate disputes or
    to understand what their positions have in com-
    mon with the positions of others.
4. The ability to learn from experience. This in-
    volves the ability to translate observations from
    work experience into a theory that can be used
    to generate behavioral alternatives.

In addition to these cognitive skills, success in the world
of work involves *interpersonal* skills. Klemp (p. 107–108) identifies
two inclusive ones:

1. Communication skills, including both fluency
    and precision in speaking and writing, and skill
    at nonverbal communication, both in sending
    and receiving information.
2. Accurate empathy, which includes both the di-
    agnosis of a human concern (based on what
    a person says of how he or she behaves) and
    an appropriate response to the needs of the per-
    son. Use of this ability helps clients and co-
    workers understand what is being said or done
    in a way that makes them feel they are them-
    selves understood. Three aspects to this skill
    are positive regard for others, giving another
    person assistance, either solicited or unsoli-
    cited, that enables the other person to be effec-
    tive, and the ability to control impulsive feel-
    ings of hostility or anger that, when unleashed
    on another person, make that other person feel
    powerless and ineffective.

But these cognitive and interpersonal skills do not by themselves guarantee effectiveness. The third critical factor found was *motivation*. Klemp (1977, pp. 107–108) describes this factor as a prerequisite for effective action:

> For a variety of reasons people are often unable to translate their dispositions into effective action. Recent research strongly suggests that *cognitive initiative* — the way one defines oneself as an actor in the motive-action sequence — is an important variable. This variable describes a person who habitually thinks in terms of causes and outcomes as opposed to one who sees [him- or her-]self as an ineffective victim of events that have an unknown cause. It has been empirically demonstrated, for instance, that women who think of themselves in terms of cause-action-effect sequences are more successful in careers ten years after college than women who do not think of themselves as the link in the cause-effect chain (Stewart and Winter, 1974, pp. 238–259). Our own analysis of complex managerial jobs and the people in them has shown that a person who takes a proactive stance, who initiates action and works to dissolve blocks to progress, will with few exceptions, have the advantage over a person who is reactive, who does not seek new opportunities, but sees the world as a series of insurmountable obstacles.

To sum up, then, effective performance in the world of work involves a set of clearly identifiable cognitive skills, interpersonal skills, and motivational characteristics. Stated in terms of our theory, intellectual and interpersonal competence must be accompanied by emotional and instrumental autonomy. The basic areas of competence and personal characteristics that characterize liberal education and success at work have major implications for curriculum and teaching. They have implications

for course content, for distribution requirements and core curricula, and for some of the fundamental ways we think about
the place of liberal education in our two- and four-year colleges
and universities and in our technical and professional programs
and institutions.

The basic point is that learning and personal development
in virtually all these areas can be fostered through a very wide
range of "content" areas. The kinds of cognitive skills, interpersonal competence, and motivational characteristics described
by Klemp and his colleagues can be encouraged through the
full range of our courses in humanities, natural sciences, and
social sciences that characterize typical arts and science curricula. They also can be fostered through a wide range of courses
devoted to professional preparation in business administration,
engineering, health sciences, social services, and law. In addition, they can be addressed in many complex areas for technical training. Unfortunately, however, we seem locked into the
notion that the objectives of liberal education should be relegated
to a relatively small number of courses within the arts and science
curriculum, usually offered at the introductory level, in a com-
partmentalized fashion set apart from the rest of the educational
enterprise. But the basic kinds of competence can be powerfully augmented through most other academic activities as well.
What this means in practice is that there needs to be much more
concern about educational processes and teaching practices than
is typically the case.

Process Issues

It is not that content is irrelevant. But if we start thinking about
content as a vehicle for encouraging such learning and personal
development, our selection of readings and writing assignments,
performances, laboratory experiences, and other learning activities will be enriched. We need not give up our objectives
concerning particular areas of knowledge and content. In fact,
these will probably be more effectively built into students' working knowledge; retention of the critical facts, competence, and
inquiry skills will almost certainly be substantially enhanced.

Palmer (1987, p. 22) addresses the "content versus process" issue in a fundamental way. He states

> My thesis is a very simple one: I do not believe that epistemology is a bloodless abstraction; the *way* we know has powerful implications for the *way* we live. I argue that every epistemology tends to become an ethic, and that every way of knowing tends to become a way of living. I argue that the relation established between the student and the subject tends to become the relation of the living person to the world itself. I argue that every mode of knowing contains its own moral trajectory, its own ethical direction and outcomes.

Palmer then characterizes the mode of knowing most prevalent in higher education — objectivism — as having three traits. First, it is objective. It holds the topic at arm's length, distances knowledge from personal life, and protects it from contamination by subjective biases. Second, it is analytic. It assumes that an object can be discussed in order to understand it. Third, it is experimental. Once we cut up an object into pieces, we can move them around and reshape them to fit our purposes.

Palmer contends that this seemingly abstract way of knowing then becomes an ethic of competitive individualism which works against community — a capacity for relatedness not only to people but to events in history, to nature, to the world of ideas, and to things of the spirit. He goes on to discuss new epistemologies which are illustrated by feminist thought and Native American studies. Then he says:

> I want to make it clear that these new epistemologies do not aim at the overthrow of objectivity, analysis, and experimentation. Indeed, the feminist thinkers that I know use those very tools in their writing. But they want to put those tools within a context of affirming the communal nature of reality itself, the relational nature of reality. So in these

studies, objectivist modes are used in creative tension with their related counterparts. For example,
the mode of objectivity is held in creative tension
with another way of knowing, the way of intimacy,
the way of personally implicating yourself with the
subject. Virtually every great scholar finds this way
of appropriating knowledge, of living it and breath-
ing it and bringing it so close to your heart that
you and it are almost one. Objectivity and intimacy
can go hand in hand; that's what the new epistemologies are calling for [p. 24].

These radical ideas — radical in the sense of going to the
root of the issue — have fundamental implications for our orientation toward the curriculum and toward the teaching practices,
student-faculty relationships, and peer relationships that characterize the ways of knowing through which learning and personal
development take place.

From a different, though complementary perspective,
Snyder (1970) reminds us that there are really two curricula,
the "formal curriculum" and the "hidden curriculum." His small
but insightful book begins with this quote from a student who
turned down membership in the National Honor Society: "I have
a few reasons for this action. . . . I see [the National Honor So-
ciety], in general, as merely an indication that an individual
has succeeded in a system that I feel wastes human potential,
blunts and distorts natural curiosities, and de-emphasizes creativity, individualism, and responsibility, in order to render him
more malleable. Furthermore, the Honor Society, along with
current grading procedures, can be seen as a goal that redirects
students into an "answer-oriented" versus a "problem-oriented"
outlook on education where answers become more important
than the process of learning" (p. 3).

This bright student recognizes the difference between the
espoused formal goals of the curriculum and the teachers, and
the quite different, contradictory behaviors required to obtain
high grades and other types of academic recognition. Snyder
differentiates between the formal curriculum, with its explicit

assignments ("Do problems 1 through 8 on page 67," "Read Chapter Three and be prepared to discuss the period 1792–94 in French politics") and the hidden curriculum of covert, implied tasks, and the means to their mastery, rooted in the professors' assumptions and values, the students' expectations, and the social context in which both the teacher and the taught find themselves.

> Each student figures out what is actually expected as opposed to what is formally required. A professor may explain at the beginning of the term that he requires knowledge and competence and creativity and originality. In many cases, the professor may mean it; or he may believe what he has said but then sets the tasks in such a way that rote memory rather than knowledge is rewarded. It takes the class a little time to sort out these messages, to locate the disparity, to interpret the mixed signals created by the presence of both a formal and a hidden curriculum. What is crucial is not the presence of formal rules and informal responses but rather the kinds of dissonance that are created by the distance between the two [p. 9].

The fundamental issues Palmer and Snyder address are like the air we breathe, like the water in which fish are immersed. They are so much a part of our daily rounds, our ongoing existence, that we do not recognize their pervasive significance. Like low levels of air pollution, acid rain, or toxic waste, their malevolent consequences go unrecognized because they do not drastically impair each person's ability to function. But they show up more generally in the gradual degradation of the environment and in reduced efficiency and energy. They show up in student cynicism and apathy, and in increased recourse to expedient, shortterm solutions. They are reflected in increased symptomatology in both physical and mental health. Most important, they show up in learning that evaporates quickly rather than lasting a lifetime.

In his powerful research report, *Literacy in the Open Access College,* Richardson (1983) gives us some sharp illustrative data. He identifies two highly contrasting categories of written language. The first is "texting" — the use of reading and writing to comprehend or compose connected language without the assistance of specific cues. "Examples are reading a textbook chapter to gain an overview of the important events of the 1920s and writing an essay that argues for or against capital punishment. Texting represents a traditional (liberal arts) view of the type of written language use that colleges should promote and should expect their students to demonstrate. Consistent with this traditional view, the students we interviewed described themselves as 'really reading' and 'really writing' only when they were dealing independently with connected language" (p. 65).

The second kind of operation was called "bitting"— the use of reading or writing to understand or produce fragmented language when presented with specific external cues. "Students were bitting when they read and copied from the blackboard a list of names that the instructor pointed to and identified as important and when they later were engaged in a somewhat more independent form of bitting when they skimmed a textbook to find answers to study-guide questions in preparation for a multiple-choice text. Bitting might involve either connected discourse (a textbook) or disconnected discourse (a list of names or definitions). In both instances, however, an information source was used to obtain fragments of meaning, and strong external cues were present" (pp. 65–66).

Richardson and his associates observed that bitting had become the norm for classroom written language in one of the institutions studied. Information in written materials remained bits of isolated facts that were not integrated or analyzed to achieve more holistic meaning. Students did not read textbooks to grasp both major themes and supportive detail, nor did they listen actively and critically to lectures and record comprehensive notes. They were not required to synthesize, analyze, or evaluate information from texts and lectures.

> Instead, they learned discrete pieces of information
> in order to recognize or reproduce them intact on

objective exams. In addition, student reading and writing were highly dependent activities, shaped by the general nature of students' roles in the classroom. The most typical form of social interaction involved students serving as attentive audience, and in this situation students used reading and writing as part of passive, receptive activity. Concurrently, in the basic language skills courses, reading and writing became little more than procedures that students performed under the direction of watchful instructors. Only in the less numerous vocational lab courses did the use of written language acquire any degree of independence, although it was quite minimal and was integrated into the "job" activities of the "worker" students [p. 71].

When these "hidden curriculum" dynamics work through time they drive similarly dysfunctional attitudes and behaviors on the part of faculty. Richardson found that faculty members at this institution came to view their students as having limited academic preparation. They adapted by preserving disciplinary content at the expense of literacy demands, by extensive cuing, by covering text material in class, and by constructing objective exams primarily testing knowledge-level objectives in the cognitive domain. They reduced or eliminated the need for students to compose or read connected discourse. The classroom environment became actively hostile to students who wanted to learn actively and use information. Instead, the environment reinforced students' use of instrumental bitting and other time-saving strategies to preserve as much time as possible for non-school-related facets of their lives.

To summarize, we must attend to the fundamental issues underlying our assumptions and the implementation of our curricula. If we and our students are living out lives in an environment polluted by unremitting objectivism and by contradictory hidden curricula, then the espoused values and significant aims of our formal curricula are unlikely to be achieved, no matter what our content priorities.

Content Issues

Our emphasis on process does not mean that selecting content is a frivolous task. The choice of appropriate content is one of the most difficult challenges we face. Unfortunately, faculty conversations about curriculum and recommendations for curricular change focus almost entirely on "what every educated person should know" or what "essential body of knowledge" should be covered in a major. Framing the issues this way usually assumes that economic or cultural conditions, the backgrounds of the students, and the rapid growth and changing nature of knowledge are irrelevant. Furthermore, as long as the issue is defined as finding the one menu that will nourish all students, discussion quickly becomes anchored in turf battles to preserve departmental and course enrollments, usually disguised with erudite justifications of the importance of one area over others. Most of us have heard the arguments about why "no one can live in today's world without a knowledge of history," why "philosophy is an absolutely critical foundation for everything else," why "no one can understand cultural context without thorough introduction to classical literature and the arts," and why "mathematics and the natural sciences are critical to understanding our technological revolution."

Rejecting this "essentialism" — this one-diet-for-all approach — does not mean that anything goes. Instead, it means doing some hard thinking about helping particular students with particular backgrounds, using content appropriate to their purposes in ways that lead to the more general outcomes important for effective living and success at work. Thinking about content this way does not at all treat it lightly. In fact, we must take its potential contributions to more general outcomes much more seriously. We must think hard about the curricular elements we create and how we help students make sound judgments about the course they run.

As Gamson and her associates (1984, pp. 114–115) say:

Once and for all, let us dispense with the notion
that there is one content that all students in this

country ought to study. Let us say finally, even regretfully, that not all may need to read Shakespeare or Plato. For a liberating education, a faculty must select subjects that will help students achieve a broad critical awareness with the commitment and skills to apply that awareness. Within this broad conception, many different subjects and texts can be taught — including Shakespeare and Plato. In some schools, for example, the study of women is seen as a legitimate part of a liberating education because it extends the understanding of the human condition by bringing attention to people whose experience has been inaccessible, even to themselves. . . . Black studies and studies of other groups that have been denigrated or ignored in the standard curriculum (workers, for example) offer some schools the opportunity to stretch their students' awareness in other ways. . . . Non-Western cultures, international studies, environmental studies, humanities, and technology have all been suggested as suitable content at one school or another. Choosing appropriate content is a complex matter for a teacher or an institution interested in a liberating education, for attention must be paid not only to the intrinsic characteristics of texts and assignments but also to their potential for stimulating the changes in students they believe should occur. This presumes that enough is known about students to make such a judgment. Yet most faculty are unaccustomed to deliberately selecting what they teach on the basis of an assessment of who their students are, however much they would like to stimulate changes in them.

The alternative to the standardized approach just described is distribution requirements. These range from general area requirements to lists of specific courses. Here is an example from George Mason University (Kearney, 1991, p. 53) which illustrates the general end of the continuum:

Core Requirements

Each undergraduate degree program requires a substantial core from the arts and sciences (24 semester hours). Six semester hours must be in English composition. . . . Of the remaining 18 hours, 6 must be in each of the following three areas:

Area A:
> Art
> Communication
> English
> Foreign Languages
> Literature
> Performing Arts
> Philosophy
> Religion
> Speech

Area B
> Astronomy
> Biology
> Chemistry
> Computer Science
> Engineering
> Geology
> Mathematics
> Physics

Area C
> Anthropology
> Economics
> Geography
> Government
> History
> Linguistics
> Psychology
> Sociology

Here's another approach from George Washington University (1993, pp. 23–24):

Students are obliged to demonstrate, either by course work or through examination, that they have attained an acceptable level of cultural literacy and intellectual competence and that they have acquired familiarity with the breadth and diversity of liberal learning.

Students must satisfy these requirements in eight distinct areas . . .

1. *Literacy* — 6 hours: Engl 9 or 10 or EFL 50, and Engl 11 or 13. Unless waived, the first semester of English Composition must be taken in the freshman year. The second semester (Engl 11 or 13) must be taken no later than the second semester of the sophomore year.

2. *Quantitative and/or Logical Reasoning* — 6 hours chosen from one of the following combinations: Phil 45 and 121; Stat 51 or 53 or 91, and 105 or 129; Stat 111–12 or 129–30; Math 9 and 10, 12 and 13, 30 and 31, 30 and 41, or 51–52; Phil 45 and Math 120 or Stat 51 or 52 or 91; Honr 23–24.

3. *Conceptual Foundations and Development of Natural Science* — 9 hours chosen from the courses listed below, distributed so that 3 or 6 hours come from Group A and 3 or 6 hours come from Group B (the 6-hour group must be a paired sequence): Group A: BiSc 3–4 or 11–12; Geol 1–2; Geol 5 and either 2 or 105; Honr 36. Group B: Chem 3–4 or 11–12 or 17–18; Honr 33–34; Phys 1–2 with 5–6; Phys 1–2 with 5–6; Phys 9–10; Phys 21–22 with 5–6.

The list goes on. Any first year student ought to get three credits just for creating a meaningful plan of study from this list of possibilities.

The problem with distribution requirements is that they seldom add up to any coherent collection of educational experiences governed by a larger organizing principle. Pick ten recent undergraduates at random and look at their final transcripts. In most cases, it will be difficult to discern any logic for the courses chosen to meet the general education requirements, except that they are scattered across the required terrain. Instead, some key considerations were probably teachers' reputation as interesting or easy; interest in the topic; time of day; and whether or not a friend was enrolling. In the absence of any larger rationale or thoughtful advising process, it is not surprising that these considerations drive the actual—as opposed to the espoused—general education curriculum.

The other common solution is to define a "core curriculum" through which each person meets general education requirements. Sometimes the "core" is a collection of courses organized under several categories; on other occasions, there is a prescribed set of broad courses required for all. Harvard's core curriculum, which was adopted in 1979, received a great deal of publicity. Its guiding philosophy is stated in its 1991–92 *Courses of Instruction* (Standing Committee on the Core Curriculum, 1991, p. 1):

> The philosophy of the Core Curriculum rests on the conviction that every Harvard graduate should be broadly educated, as well as trained in a particular academic specialty or concentration. It assumes that students need some guidance in achieving this goal, and that the faculty has an obligation to direct them toward the knowledge, intellectual skills, and habits of thought that are the hallmarks of educated men and women.
>
> But the Core differs from other programs of general education. It does not define intellectual breadth as the mastery of a set of Great Books, or the digestion of a specific quantum of information, or the surveying of current knowledge in certain fields. Rather, the Core seeks to introduce students to the major *approaches to knowledge* in areas that the faculty considers indispensable to undergraduate education. It aims to show what kinds of knowledge and what forms of inquiry exist in these areas,

how different means of analysis are acquired, how they are used, and what their value is. The courses within each area or subdivision of the program are equivalent in the sense that, while their subject matter may vary, their emphasis on a particular way of thinking is the same.

The six areas that make up the core are Foreign Cultures (27), Historical Study (29), Literature and Arts (48), Moral Reasoning (12), Science (27), and Social Analysis (11). The numbers in parentheses indicate how many courses are listed under each of these areas. The basic orientation of each area is given, followed by course titles and descriptions. Here, for example, are the orientations given for Foreign Cultures, Moral Reasoning, and Social Analysis (Standing Committee on the Core Curriculum, 1991):

Foreign Cultures
The common aim of courses in Foreign Cultures is to expand the range of one's cultural experience and to provide fresh perspectives on one's own cultural assumptions and traditions. Whatever the particular focus, each course seeks to identify the distinctive pattern of thought and action that account for the configuration or ethos of the foreign culture(s) studied. Consideration of the historical background and the contemporary significance of the culture(s) is normally included [p. 2].

Moral Reasoning
The common aim of courses in Moral Reasoning is to discuss significant and recurrent questions of choice and value that arise in human experience. They seek to acquaint students with the important traditions of thought that have informed such choices in the past and to enlarge the student's awareness of how people have understood the nature of the virtuous life. The courses are intended to show that it is possible to reflect reasonably about such matters as justice, obligation, citizenship, loyalty, courage, and personal responsibility [p. 10].

Social Analysis
The common aim of courses in Social Analysis is to
acquaint students with some of the central concepts
and methods of the social sciences and to show how
these approaches can enhance our understanding of
contemporary human behavior. Social Analysis
courses are not intended to provide a survey of a particular discipline, but rather to show how, by the use
of formal theories that are systematically related to
empirical data, one can better understand the application of analytical methods to important problems involving the behavior of people and institutions [p. 19].

This approach helps the student move one step closer to a rationale for choice and provides at least a modicum of information
about the various areas within which the menus are offered. It
certainly is more enlightening than a simple list of courses that
satisfy distribution requirements. Recognizing the limitations of
distribution requirements, George Mason University proposed
a required core.

A General Education Task Force found that faculty agreed
on four things (Bergoffen, 1988):

1.   Students cannot write.
2.   Students cannot compute or adequately interpret quantita-
     tive or statistical data.
3.   Students cannot read or think critically.
4.   Students lack basic information about their heritage and
     the world in which they live.

Many faculty members saw problems with the current
cafeteria system — classes are too large; there are insufficient sections of courses offered; too many part-timers are teaching general education courses. The Task Force therefore proposed that
the university replace the cafeteria approach with a core general
education program:

The current system of having students take a variety of introductory courses in several different dis-

ciplines conveys the idea that general education is a series of different elementary courses. It suggests that general education is a somewhat random affair and that the serious business of learning begins with the choosing of a major.

We think this misses the essence of general education. It is not an introductory, elementary phenomenon. It is not a preliminary affair. It is the core of a student's undergraduate university experience — the key to their intellectual development. It is central to our stated mission of providing students with an education which will enable them to exercise their role as citizens of a democracy in responsible and honorable ways.

General education needs to be as carefully thought through and structured as our major and professional programs. In focusing on students' thinking skills and enlarging their stock of information general education needs to help students develop an overall mind set which is sensitive to the complexities and ambiguities of the human situation. It needs to promote students' intellectual curiosity, and it needs to instill in them a confidence in their ability to understand and make choices about issues in areas outside of their area of concentration.

Having articulated these broad goals, the Task Force proposed a multidisciplinary four-year core that will assure that graduates from GMU will have:

1. Become familiar with the diverse ideas and values of the Western tradition
2. Developed an awareness of the global context within which this tradition has evolved and continues to live
3. Become aware of and sensitive to issues of race, class, and gender
4. Achieved university-level competencies in writing, speaking, reading, listening, analytic reasoning and library research
5. Explored the moral dimensions and ethical implications of their chosen area of specialization

This approach does represent a kind of enlarged "essentialism." But the breadth of material and topics studied and its distribution through all four years of the undergraduate curriculum help the goals to become an integral part of the ongoing educational experience. Furthermore, in a large university with a high proportion of commuting students, the approach has the virtue of creating a sense of shared educational experiences that can provide a basis for out-of-class dialogues and discussion. It also provides an intellectual framework to which varied student activities, cultural events, artistic performances, and community forums can be tied. Finally, it provides a curricular organizer for creating a community of faculty members who are truly interested in undergraduate students and liberal education. Neither the typical distribution requirements nor the Harvard core, expressed as clusters of courses under defined rubrics, has those added values.

In light of these varied approaches, how should we think about selecting content? What are some sound grounds for choice, some criteria that we might apply as we contend with this tough issue? We propose four axioms that can help us encourage growth along our developmental vectors and help students develop the capacities for living and working in the twenty-first century.

1. *Make content relevant to students' backgrounds and prior experiences.* Baxter Magolda (1992, p. 378) emphasizes that "situating learning in the students' own experience legitimizes their knowledge as a foundation for constructing new knowledge." Philosopher and educator Dewey (1938) addresses this point powerfully:

> It is a cardinal precept of the newer school of education that the beginning of instruction shall be made with the experience learners already have . . . [p.74].
>
> It is a mistake to suppose that the principle of the leading on of experience to something different is adequately satisfied simply by giving pupils some new experiences. It is also essential that the new objects and events be related intellectually to

those of earlier experiences . . . . [The educator] must constantly regard what is already won not as a fixed possession but as an agency and instrumentality for opening new fields . . . [p. 75].

The problem of selection and organization of subject matter is fundamental . . . [p. 78]. The basic material of study cannot be picked up in a cursory manner. . . . Occasions which are not and cannot be foreseen are bound to arise wherever there is intellectual freedom.

Unless a given experience leads out into a field previously unfamiliar, no problems arise, while problems are the stimulus to thinking. . . . Growth depends upon the presence of difficulty to be overcome by the exercise of intelligence. . . . The new facts and new ideas thus obtained become the ground for further experiences in which new problems are presented. The process is a continuous spiral [p. 79].

Note the critical role that Dewey assigns to the "selection and organization of subject matter" so that new ideas, issues, and events are related to prior experiences. We know from neurological research that the brain functions as a complex web of interconnected networks of neural pathways. When new information, insights, or experiences are connected to, and integrated with, those pre-existing networks, they enlarge our working knowledge and remain with us. When those connections are not made and content is left as isolated, disconnected, free-floating fragments, the ideas and events fade from memory.

Palmer's comments concerning the problems associated with traditional academic objectivism, mentioned earlier in this chapter, are pertinent here. Baxter Magolda (1992, p. xv) puts the issue well: "The dominance of objectivism has fostered separation in educational practice: between teacher and student and between knowledge and experience. . . . This separation hinders students' ability to construct their own perspectives. The objectivist view of knowledge also separates curricular from cocurricular knowledge, thereby distancing the process of knowing from the arena in which students feel most comfortable. Transforming educational practice requires eliminating separation in favor of connection. Constructing one's own perspective requires encouragement, which often comes from interactions between teacher and student, between knowledge and experience, between curricular and cocurricular life."

Our second axiom is required if the first is to be sensitively exercised.

2. *Recognize significant dimensions of individual difference between students.* The impact of any particular content will depend on the characteristics of the person who encounters it. When individuals differ, a single experience (with a person, program, object, or event) can have diverse developmental outcomes — and different experiences can have similar outcomes. Small dosages of arsenic are a stimulant for most persons; large ones are usually fatal. But individual tolerances can vary widely. As murder mystery buffs know, tolerance for lethal dosages can be developed. So the consequences of eating the same chicken pie may be different for the cook or the diner. Fitness centers recognize that individuals must enter the sequence according to their own strengths and weaknesses, must proceed at their own pace, and will reach different limits. Similarly, the impact of curriculum content will vary with the backgrounds, ability levels, and personality characteristics of the students.

But higher education has given little attention to this obvious principle. Instead, students have been treated as though they were billiard balls, all alike in shape, size, and density, all stationary until struck. The administration wields the stick, sending cue balls at students on the assumption that if the proper angle can be found, if students are struck in just the right spot, they all will behave in proper fashion and be impelled in the ordained direction. The trouble, of course, is that only a few students are smooth and well-rounded. Others are square or egg-shaped, knobby or dented, flat or curvy. Some are Ping-Pong balls, some bowling balls. Some look symmetrical, but inside, weight is concentrated at particular points so they roll along in irregular and unpredictable fashion. Further, some cues are badly twisted. So the game is frustrating and full of surprises.

We know some of the significant dimensions of difference between students that need to be explicitly recognized, but we are still struggling with how to take them into account. Differences in ability level and prior preparation pose problems for most curricula at most institutions. One option has been to "dumb down" the content so it is easy enough for all students — hardly a constructive response, as the outcries concerning basic skill deficiencies in college graduates attest. "Maintaining standards" by forcing complex materials on all students and living with high failure and drop-out rates is another option available to institutions with strong enrollment pools. But the human damage and institutional waste which results and the amplification of a two-tier society make that alternative even worse. We need to become much more sophisticated about selecting content alternatives across difficulty levels than we have been to date.

The complexities do not stop there. We are increasingly recognizing the importance of age, gender, and ethnicity as dimensions of individual difference that have serious consequences for the way students experience particular content. Baxter Magolda's detailed study of gender-related patterns of knowing and reasoning in college (1992), and more specifically her epistemological reflection model, make clear the significance of these differences for student development. The consequences of the differences are not subtle. They range from low-level disaffection and passivity to outright protests and active resistance. To remedy the problem, we need to select content throughout varied curricula — not only for general education but for majors as well — that is responsive to such differences, depending on the mix of students that characterizes a particular institution or program.

3. *Create encounters with diverse perspectives that challenge pre-existing information, assumptions, and values.* Some time ago, Festinger (1957) gave us his theory of cognitive dissonance. Since then, his basic propositions have been well documented. If people know things that are not consistent with one another, they will try in various ways to make them more consistent. The strategies can vary: change the opinion, change behavior and thereby change the kind of information and feedback received, or dis-

tort perceptions and screen out discordant input. Our task is to choose content that generates the dissonance and then help students resolve that dissonance by reaching more complex levels of understanding and action.

This is not an easy task. Most of us stand firmly on our own two feet. We have a pretty solid position, which allows us to bend with, or lean against, the pressures we encounter. When the pressure goes away, we usually snap back to our stance. Sometimes, however, we can be enticed to take a step. Other times we are pushed hard enough to be knocked off balance and have to move our feet to recover. Occasionally the rug is pulled out and when we pick ourselves up we find ourselves in a different spot. Significant education and significant development often involve some disruption and disequilibrium. Heath (1968, p. 18) puts it this way:

> To be educable means to be in a potential state of disorganization, to allow oneself to plunge into contradictory theories and points of view sharply contrasting with one's own, to entertain the prejudices and biases of others, to even permit oneself, in the search for new ideas, to slip into the dream world of hunch, reveries, narrowed awareness where the form of life's images is blurred, where strange and frightening and monstrous combinations of the familiar and unfamiliar romp and play, and where no words are either powerful nor subtle enough to capture emerging feelings, intuitions, and vivid sensory impressions. While maturity is no guarantee against some disorganization, it is a guarantee that disorganization can be used for adaptive and playful purposes.

Significant learning, therefore, often means taking risks. And in a college where powerful forces for student development are at work, turmoil will also be found; temporary dislocation and disorientation is part of the process.

Our fourth axiom is closely related to the second.

4. *Provide activities that help students integrate diverse perspectives, assumptions, value orientations.* Education is essentially the amplification of two basic developmental processes: differentiation and integration. Increased differentiation occurs when one comes to see the interacting parts of something formerly seen as unitary, when one distinguishes between concepts formerly seen as similar, when actions are more finely responsive to purposes or to outside conditions, and when interests become more varied, tastes more diverse, reactions more subtle. In short, differentiation occurs as we become more complex human beings. To foster the process of differentiation, liberal arts programs try to free students from the limited outlook they bring from their own locale, family, social class, and national heritage — a freeing that opens awareness to all the possibilities and impossibilities of the world, a freeing that can lead to heightened sensitivity. It also can open the path to coldness and insensitivity as the monstrous inconsistencies in the ways of the world are more clearly seen and more sharply experienced.

But increasing differentiation must be accompanied by increasing integration. This is the other major task of education. Relationships among parts must be perceived or constructed so that more complex wholes result. Concepts from different disciplines must be connected in ways appropriate to varied tasks and problems. Consistencies between word and word, word and deed, and deed and deed must be achieved. Impulse and emotion must pull together with conscience and reason. Short-run hedonism must coordinate with long-run purposes.

Thus, differentiation and integration are what education is about, and such education makes people different — different from what they were before and different from each other. It is, therefore, contrary to training. Training serves to make people more alike. It aims to develop a shared language, shared skills, shared information, shared objectives, and with time, shared values. Thus, while training starts with the task and conforms the learner to it, education starts with the learners and uses tasks in the service of their increased differentiation and integration. As Sanford (1962, p. 257) says, "A high level of development in personality is characterized chiefly by complexity and wholeness. It is expressed in a high degree of differentiation, that is, a large number of different parts having different and specialized functions, and a high degree of integration, that is, a state of affairs in which communication among parts is great enough so that the different parts may, without losing their essential identity, become organized into larger wholes."

In offering these axioms as guides to content selection, we do not pretend that they encompass all the complexities for such decisions. But we seldom act with even these simple grounds for judgment. When we use these principles for content selection — relevance to student backgrounds, individual differences, encounters with diverse populations, differentiation, and integration — we will also be strengthening some of the key areas of competence required for a fulfilling life, effective citizenship, and useful work. Content selected on these grounds will foster intellectual competence and cognitive skills, our "ability to understand many sides of a controversial issue." It will contribute to the development of identity, our basic sense of self in a social and historical context. It will help strengthen interpersonal relationships by encouraging empathy — our capacity to accommodate ourselves to others, to throw ourselves into their state of mind, to come to an understanding and bear with them. And it will strengthen the development of integrity — a conscious view of our own opinions and judgments and truth in developing them.

THIRTEEN

Teaching

We recognize that much significant "teaching" occurs in admissions and orientation processes, club and cultural activities, sports, career planning seminars and conferences, late-night bull sessions in residence halls, and the like. We know that all programs and services can contribute to educational goals. But we restrict the term *teaching* to activities that are directly related to the academic program and that are carried out by faculty members or other professionals.

Four propositions underlie this chapter:

1. Most teaching, as currently practiced, falls short of its potential to contribute to human development. This condition is reinforced by the unbalanced reward systems that characterize most institutions.
2. Principles of good teaching are well-known. Effective practices have been documented in numerous research and evaluation projects.
3. Good teaching can be learned. It is a craft where initial talents can be strengthened through reflection and practice.
4. The quality of teaching is critical to student development in college. Good teaching can powerfully encourage the

development of intellectual and interpersonal competence, identity, mature interpersonal relationships, purpose, and integrity. Poor teaching can actually hinder development in one or more of these areas.

Most Teaching Falls Short

At the heart of the problem with current practice is that few of us think of ourselves primarily as professional *teachers*. Especially in four-year institutions, we think of ourselves as professionals in our disciplinary or occupational specialty but not in our teaching role. Therefore, we spend little energy reflecting on teaching strategies, actively working to improve our teaching, or discussing practices with colleagues. We can spend many hours in most faculty lounges and not hear much conversation about teaching. We share lots of other experiences. We discuss our latest research and writing, grant proposals, consultation activities, institutional politics, and the like. But seldom do we share how things are going with particular students or courses, how this or that teaching strategy seems to be working, or what new approaches someone may have heard of that might be helpful.

A second problem is that we still tend to use lecturing as a preferred method of teaching. Cohen and Brawer (1989) report that even in community colleges, where teaching has been the top priority, "traditional methods of instruction still flourish. Visitors to a campus might be shown the mathematics laboratories, the media production facilities, and the computer-assisted instructional programs. But on the way to those installations, they will pass dozens of classrooms with instructors lecturing and conducting discussions just as they and their predecessors have been doing for decades" (pp. 156–157).

Relying on the lecture method as the predominant teaching strategy has serious limitations, as Cross (1986, pp. 3–4) points out:

> Lecturing to students has long been decried, yet it
> is the overwhelming method of choice for college
> teachers. It is estimated that teachers in the average

classroom spend about 80 percent of their time lecturing to students, who are attending to what is being said only about half of the time. . . . Added to the evidence of rather poor attention in the first place is the finding that the curve for forgetting course content is fairly steep. A generous estimate is that students forget 50 percent of the content within a few months (Brethower, 1977); a more devastating finding comes from a study that concluded that even under the most favorable conditions, "students carry away in their heads and in their notebooks not more than 42 percent of the lecture content" (Macleish, 1968, p. 9). Those were the results when students were told that they would be tested immediately following the lecture; they were permitted to use their notes; and they were given a prepared summary of the lecture. The test for immediate understanding was bad enough, but when students were tested a week later, without the use of their notes, they could recall only 17 percent of the lecture material.

When we look later in this chapter at what we know about educationally powerful teaching, we will see why lectures, which leave students the passive recipients of predigested information, create little impetus for student development. Lectures dominate teaching for many reasons: reward systems that give high priority to research, academic habits, students' prior experiences, lack of adequate assessment and feedback, and in some cases more or less explicit complicity between students and faculty. Richardson (1983) documents this latter phenomenon. As noted earlier, he describes "bitting"—the process whereby teachers provide isolated bits of information and give machine-scored multiple-choice exams that students can pass using rote memory and simple recall. Students like the approach because they know clearly what is needed to get by, and faculty like multiple-choice tests that minimize their workload. It takes a great deal of time to read papers, conduct pre- and post-tests, or evaluate student presentations.

Palmer (1990) contends that a fundamental reason for the pervasiveness of lecturing is the objectivist idea of knowing. The knower, in this mode, is supposed to observe from a distance. "This image of knowing is both reflected in and conveyed by our dominant mode of teaching, which, as Dewey said, turns education into a spectator sport. Students are kept in the grandstand so they can watch the pros play the knowledge game but not interfere with its 'objectivity'" (p. 12). He criticizes this pedagogy for making learning passive and joyless and turning too many educated people into spectators of life itself. A powerful learning experience requires active engagement and exchange, personal investment, sustained attention, and effort. Good teachers help make that happen.

Good Teaching

Tim Pitkin, former president of Goddard College, defined teaching as "creating the conditions for learning." One implication of that definition is that if learning is not going on, then neither is teaching. The proper conditions have not been created. Another implication is that the environment created and the processes employed need thoughtful attention. Sophisticated control of content is necessary, but good teaching calls for much more than that.

Pascarella and Terenzini (1991, p. 94) note substantial evidence that certain teaching behaviors systematically improve intellectual competence — especially the acquisition of subject matter knowledge. After reviewing the factor-analytic studies of the dimensions of student evaluations of teaching, they state that while various studies use different names for the dimensions, those offered by Cohen (1981) are clear and concise:

1. *Skill:* the instructor's overall pedagogical adroitness, including good command of subject matter and ability to give clear explanations.
2. *Rapport:* the instructor's empathy, accessibility and friendliness.
3. *Structure:* the instructor's ability to plan and organize the course and make good use of class time.

4. *Difficulty:* the amount and difficulty of work expected in the course.
5. *Interaction:* the extent to which the instructor facilitates student involvement and discussion.
6. *Feedback:* the extent to which the instructor provides feedback on the quality and progress of a student's work.

Moving to a level beyond pedagogy, with help from a task force of recognized scholars of higher education, A. W. Chickering and Z. F. Gamson identified *Seven Principles for Good Practice in Undergraduate Education.* These principles apply directly to teaching and assert that good practice "(1) encourages student-faculty contact, (2) encourages cooperation among students, (3) encourages active learning, (4) gives prompt feedback, (5) emphasizes time on task, (6) communicates high expectations, (7) respects diverse talents and ways of learning" (1987, p. 1). The Johnson Foundation supported the work of the task force in refining the principles and published them in the June 1987 issue of the *Wingspread Journal.* In the next eighteen months, more than 150,000 copies were ordered from the foundation by colleges and universities throughout the United States, as well as Canada, the United Kingdom, and several other countries. They were copied or reprinted in numerous other publications. Because they were not copyrighted, unknown numbers were reproduced by teaching improvement centers and others for institutional use.

The enthusiastic reception of the principles led Chickering and Gamson, with help from Louis Barsi (then a graduate student at George Mason University), to create a Faculty Inventory and an Institutional Inventory. These inventories aim to help teachers, departments, and colleges and universities examine individual behaviors and institutional policies and practices to see whether they conform to the seven principles. The response to the inventories was remarkable. They were published in fall of 1989, and by the spring of 1991, 500,000 copies had been requested. We share the principles (Chickering and Gamson, 1987, p. 1) and sample items from the "Principles for Good Practice in Undergraduate Education: Faculty Inventory" (1989, pp. 4–10) because they clarify what an outstanding faculty member would consistently do:

1.   *Good Practice Encourages Student-Faculty Contact.*
     Frequent student-faculty contact in and out of
     classes is the most important factor in student
     motivation and involvement. Faculty concern
     helps students get through rough times and
     keep on working. Knowing a few faculty mem-
     bers well enhances students' intellectual com-
     mitment and encourages them to think about
     their own values and future plans.
     • Students drop by my office just to visit.
     • I share my past experiences, attitudes, and
       values with students.
     • I know my students by name by the end
       of the first two weeks of the term.
     • I serve as a mentor or informal adviser to
       students.

2.   *Good Practice Encourages Cooperation Among Stu-
     dents.* Learning is enhanced when it is more like
     a team effort than like a solo race. Good learn-
     ing, like good work, is collaborative and so-
     cial, not competitive and isolated. Working
     with others often increases involvement in learn-
     ing. Sharing one's own ideas and responding
     to others' reactions sharpens thinking and deep-
     ens understanding. Even in large classes, stu-
     dents can learn from one another.
     • I ask students to tell each other about their
       interests and backgrounds.
     • I encourage my students to prepare together
       for classes or exams.
     • I ask my students to evaluate each other's
       work.
     • I ask my students to discuss key concepts
       with other students whose backgrounds and
       viewpoints are different from their own.
     • I create "learning communities," study
       groups, or project teams within my courses.

3.   *Good Practice Encourages Active Learning.* Learn-
     ing is not a spectator sport. Students do not

learn much just by sitting in classes listening to teachers, memorizing pre-packaged assignments, and spitting out answers. They must talk about what they are learning, write about it, relate it to past experiences, apply it to their daily lives. They must make what they learn part of themselves.

Active learning is encouraged in classes that feature structured exercises, challenging discussions, team projects, and peer critiques. Active learning can also occur outside the classroom. There are thousands of internships, independent study opportunities, and cooperative job programs in all kinds of fields, for all kinds of students. Students also can help design and teach courses or parts of courses.

- I ask my students to summarize similarities and differences among different theorists, research findings, or artistic works.
- I ask my students to relate outside events or activities to the subjects covered in my courses.
- I encourage students to challenge my ideas, the ideas of other students, or those presented in readings or other course materials.
- I give my students concrete, real-life situations to analyze.
- My students and I arrange field trips, volunteer activities, or internships related to the course.

4. *Good Practice Gives Prompt Feedback.* Knowing what you know and don't know focuses learning. Students need appropriate feedback on performance to benefit from courses. In getting started, students need help in assessing existing knowledge and competence. In classes, students need frequent opportunities to perform and receive suggestions for improvement. At various points during college, and at the

end, students need chances to reflect on what
they have learned, what they still need to know,
and how to assess themselves.

- I prepare classroom exercises and problems
  which give students immediate feedback on
  how well they do.
- I give students detailed evaluations of their
  work early in the term.
- I ask my students to schedule conferences
  with me to discuss their progress.
- I give my students written comments on
  their strengths and weaknesses on exams
  and papers.
- I ask students to keep logs or records of
  their progress.

5. *Good Practice Emphasizes Time on Task.* Time plus
   energy equals learning. There is no substitute
   for time on task. Learning to use one's time well
   is critical for students and professionals alike.
   Students need help in learning effective time
   management. Allocating realistic amounts of
   time means effective learning for students and
   effective teaching for faculty. How an institution
   defines time expectations for students, faculty,
   administrators, and other professional staff can
   establish the basis for high performance for all.

- I expect my students to complete their assignments promptly.
- I clearly communicate to my students the
  minimum amount of time they should spend
  preparing for classes.
- I make clear to my students the amount of
  time that is required to understand complex material.
- I underscore the importance of regular
  work, steady application, sound self-pac-
  ing, and scheduling.
- I meet with students who fall behind to dis-

cuss their study habits, schedules, and other commitments.

6. *Good Practice Communicates High Expectations.* Expect more and you will get it. High expectations are important for everyone — for the poorly prepared, for those unwilling to exert themselves, and for the bright and well motivated. Expecting students to perform well becomes a self-fulfilling prophecy when teachers and institutions hold high expectations of themselves and make extra efforts.

- I make clear my expectations orally and in writing at the beginning of each course.
- I help students set challenging goals for their own learning.
- I suggest extra reading or writing tasks.
- I publicly call attention to excellent performance by my students.
- I periodically discuss how well we are doing during the course of the semester.

7. *Good Practice Respects Diverse Talents and Ways of Learning.* There are many roads to learning. People bring different talents and styles of learning to college. Brilliant students in the seminar room may be all thumbs in the lab or art studio. Students rich in hands-on experience may not do so well with theory. Students need the opportunity to show their talents and learn in ways that work for them. Then they can be pushed to learning in new ways that do not come so easily.

- I discourage snide remarks, sarcasm, kidding, and other class behaviors that may embarrass students.
- I use diverse teaching activities to address a broad spectrum of students.
- I select readings and design activities related to the background of my students.

- I integrate new knowledge about women and other under-represented populations into my courses.
- I try to find out about my students' learning styles, interests, or backgrounds at the beginning of each course.

According to Chickering and Gamson (1987, p. 1), these principles rest on "50 years of research on the way teachers teach and the way students learn." Together with the Faculty Inventory, they provide useful guides for faculty members, student services staff members, and administrators, all of whom often are in teaching relationships with students.

In addition to applying these teaching principles, good teachers think systematically about arranging conditions for learning. Pascarella and Terenzini (1991, p. 141) report an effective general approach—the use of learning cycles. They say:

> A considerable body of inquiry has focused on the effectiveness of instructional interventions designed to increase students' formal reasoning. In our synthesis of this evidence, we found one particular approach, termed *inquiry* or *learning cycle* . . . to have the most consistently positive effects. The purpose of the learning cycle–inquiry approach is to move students from concrete to formal reasoning. It does this essentially by making the learning process highly inductive or concrete in nature. Concepts are taught in three stages: (1) exploration—students participate in an activity or laboratory with concrete materials (for example, collect data or conduct an experiment); (2) invention—students draw together ideas and/or concepts out of the concrete activities; and (3) discovery—students generalize or apply the concept.

D. A. Kolb's (1984) "experiential learning theory" is similar to this general approach. Its four elements provide an exellent way to think about diverse teaching and learning activities and how they might best be sequenced. (See Figure 13.1.)

Figure 13.1. The Experiential Learning Model.

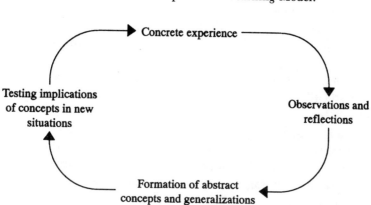

Source: Kolb (1981, p. 235). Reprinted by permission.

According to Kolb and Fry (1975, p. 1), experiential learning occurs through a four-stage cycle: "Immediate concrete experience is the basis for observation and reflection. These observations are assimilated into a 'theory' from which new implications for action can be deduced. These implications or hypotheses then serve as guides interacting to create new experiences." Effective learning therefore has four ingredients that themselves call for four different abilities. Learners must be able to enter into new experiences openly and fully, without bias; they must be able to stand back from the experiences, observe them with some detachment, and reflect on their significance; they must be able to develop a logic, a theory, a conceptual framework that gives some order to the observations; and they must be able to use those concepts to make decisions, to solve problems, to take action.

Application of the experiential learning cycle can increase teaching effectiveness. For example, Malcolm Knowles (personal communication, Feb. 1979) reported on an experiment in learning for medical students. Half the students in the entering class were sent out to hospitals and assigned to simply observe physicians and nurses at work. They were to record words they did not understand, to ask questions about what was going on, and to observe everything they could about the workings of the hospital over several weeks. The other half of the students remained in the classroom setting. Students in the field then returned to the campus for an accelerated introduction to terminology and clinical theory. On objective tests at the end of the term, students who had had what Kolb would call "concrete experience" and "reflective observation" outperformed their classmates who had not been in the field.

The learning cycle involves two quite different types of direct experience: active experimentation and hypothesis testing that systematically apply general theories or propositions, and more open engagement in which such prior judgments or assumptions are suspended or held in the background. The learning cycle also involves two quite different cognitive processes: (1) straightforward recording of reflections and observations related as closely as possible to the direct experiences themselves, unfettered by preexisting conceptual frameworks that might screen out or distort incongruous perceptions; and (2) analyses of the interrelationships among these, followed by syntheses that suggest larger meanings and implications.

Note some critical consequences of this approach when it is carried out well. First, experiential learning attaches major importance to ideas. When ideas are used as hypotheses and tested in action, their significance and the attention given to them is greater than when they are simply memorized or left as unexamined abstractions. An idea taken as a fixed truth gives no cause for further thought. An idea as a working hypothesis must undergo continual scrutiny and modification. That, in turn, creates pressures for accurate and precise formulation of the idea itself. Second, when an idea is tested for its consequences, results must be acutely observed and carefully analyzed. Activity not checked by observation and analysis may be enjoyable, but intellectually it usually leads nowhere, neither to greater clarification nor to new ideas and experiences. Third, reflective review requires both discrimination and synthesis to create a record of the significant elements of the experience. It involves looking back on experience to find meanings that provide new contexts for future learning.

Murrell and Claxton (1992) list teaching strategies that can be associated with each of Kolb's four elements. Under *Concrete Experience,* they list activities that involve the learner in the experience, either physically or emotionally (these may also involve vicarious experience), for example, field experience; interviews; role play; simulations, case studies, and games; debates; and slide presentations. Under *Reflective Observation* they list activities that require the student to step back and look at experience, get others' perspectives, or make connections with other experiences, such as structured small-group discussions, class discussion, and Socratic dialogue. Under *Abstract Conceptualization* fall information sources that use symbols. Students must use research and methods of the discipline to develop hypotheses and principles when relying on print, programmed or computer-assisted instruction, lectures, films, and videotapes. Under *Active Experimentation,* Murrell and Claxton list opportunities for the learners to apply principles or theories in problem-solving such as role play, individual or group projects, videotaping of practice session, "what if" situations, and action planning.

The particular emphasis and sequence will vary depending on the background of the students and the desired learning outcomes, but judicious combinations of these activities can create powerful conditions for learning. Some students come experience-rich and theory-poor. For such students, beginning with an exercise that helps bring to the surface or recreate experiences and then moving on to reflection and pertinent abstract concepts often works best. For students who bring little or no relevant experience, beginning with some of the more concrete activities will probably be most useful. For advanced students, who already have been "around the cycle" several times — so to speak — it may work best to introduce new, more complex and challenging concepts first and then turn to application.

Awareness of what skills and strategies are needed for excellent teaching is a vital step. Reviewing principles of good teaching and assessing one's strengths and weaknesses can lead to a plan for professional development and experimentation with new approaches.

Learning the Craft of Good Teaching

As the preceding comments make clear, applying Kolb's ideas or any other systematic approach to creating the conditions for learning is a complex task. But these things can be learned. Eble (1988, p. 5) explains why teaching can be thought of as a craft:

> Teaching can be taught. This is why I choose to think of teaching as a craft, even though my ego would have it recognized as an art and myself an artist. I had good reasons, though I was not aware of all of them at the time, for calling [my] book *The Craft of Teaching*. But I did not anticipate how many readers would be curious about that choice of title and how that would open up discussions about teaching. Craft has many shades of meaning and application. In thinking of a teacher as "crafty as a fox," of fashioning some useful object that works, of a craft not taking on some of the pretensions associated with art, of an honest craft—in all these and other ways I was endorsing a belief that in anything we do well we are both born and made. More made, generally, I think than we allow.

One way to learn the craft is to apply Kolb's theory to ourselves. We can take our concrete experiences as teachers, reflect on what seems to work and what does not, identify some pertinent generalizations, and try again. In *The Reflective Practitioner* (1983), Schön makes a powerful case for the importance of this kind of behavior as the route to increased professional competence. When he describes how the process works, we see close similarities with Kolb's experiential learning cycle.

> I have tried . . . to show how practitioners in very different sorts of professions reveal an underlying similarity in the art of their practice, and especially in the artful inquiry by which they sometimes deal with situations of uncertainty, instability, and uniqueness. This is the pattern of reflection-in-

action which I have called "reflective conversation with the situation." In all of these examples, inquiry begins with an effort to solve a problem as initially set. In some cases, the initial problem is framed as a problem of making something (a semiconductor amplifier, a higher-absorbency paper product); in some cases, it is framed as a problem of understanding something (why a traditional industrial process works, the sources of malnourishment) [p. 268].

Schön then describes how the inquirer may reframe the problem based on the discovery of phenomena incongruent with the initial problem setting. In order to do this, the inquirer must "remain open to the situation's back-talk" and must draw on some element of past experience, which then becomes generative metaphor for the new phenomenon. Furthermore, as the inquirer reflects on the similarities that have been perceived, new hypotheses are formulated and tested by experimental actions that also function "as moves for shaping the situation and as probes for exploring it" (pp. 268, 269).

Schön (1983, pp. 298–299) highlights the contrasts between a "reflective contract" and a "traditional contract." With the traditional contract, instructors are expected to play the role of the expert, keep their expertise private and mysterious, and enjoy freedom to practice without challenge to their competence. The reflective contract invites them to reveal their uncertainties, reflect publicly on their knowledge-in-practice, and be open to confrontation. Instead of the gratifications of deference and the comforts of relative invulnerability, they find new satisfactions: discoveries about knowledge-in-practice, recognition of ways to be more effective, and renewal that comes from the work itself.

Classroom research can be a very useful vehicle for becoming more systematic about the process just described. Cross (1986, p. 10) says:

Schön's work gives me the basis for the proposal for action that I am about to make. I believe that research on teaching and learning should be done in thousands of classrooms across this nation by classroom teachers themselves. What is needed if higher education is to move toward our goal of maximum student learning is a new breed of college teacher that I shall call a Classroom Researcher. A Classroom Researcher is one who uses the classroom as a laboratory, collecting data and using a variety of research methodologies appropriate to the study of teaching and learning in his or her particular discipline.

This idea has slowly been making inroads in higher education, though so far it has been more widespread at community colleges than at universities. While some faculty members *are* putting up resistance, others see the potential for new directions. A task force on improving teaching at the Graduate School of Education, George Mason University (George Mason University, 1989, p. 7), for example, found that:

> Faculty classroom research is emerging as a key vehicle for improving college and university teaching. . . . The primary purpose here is not to add to general knowledge about teaching and learning but to find out what specific students are learning as a result of particular practices undertaken with reference to specific content or desired outcomes, or to determine the workability of various new alternatives.
>
> This powerful strategy for professional development can be built into the faculty planning and evaluation system recommended above. The activities undertaken might be viewed as legitimate research and scholarship and included under that category or they might be included under the professional development category, depending upon the goals, conclusions and dissemination of the results.

Implementing the approach will require significant up-front investment in helping interested faculty learn about various approaches that can be useful. Then continued investments will be needed in order to help faculty members design and carry out their own data collection, data analyses, reflection, and attempts at modification. Public endorsements by deans, provosts, and presidents are needed to ensure that faculty members who invest significant time and energy in such activities will not find themselves punished when decisions are made concerning promotion and tenure.

Some colleges have made institutional commitments to vigorous new approaches to outcomes assessment. Miami Dade Community College has taken the bold step of building classroom research into professional load descriptions and reward systems. Beginning in 1990–91, every community college in Washington State received $60,000 per year, channeled through the State Board for Community College Education, to support institutional improvement through assessment activities. Shoreline Community College in Seattle is using a substantial portion of its allocation for research by professors. Steps like these, backed by a modicum of resources and support services, are critical if we are to become reflective practitioners in our role as teachers. When that happens, we should see real progress in learning the craft of teaching.

Impacts of Teaching on Student Development

The potential consequences for student development, if all of us in higher education *did* become effective teachers, would be enormous. Even the limited interventions we currently make have significant impact. Pascarella and Terenzini's summary of research concerning the impact of academic experiences (1991, pp. 616, 619) reveals how much could be gained if top-notch teaching pervaded our colleges and universities:

> Simply put, the greater the student's involvement or engagement in academic work or in the academic · experience of college, the greater his or her level of knowledge acquisition and general cognitive development. Though less extensive, evidence also suggests that academic involvement enhances de-

clines in authoritarianism and dogmatism and increases in autonomy and independence, intellectual orientation, and the use of principled moral reasoning. . . . A substantial amount of evidence indicates that there are instructional and programmatic interventions that not only increase a student's active engagement in learning and academic work but also enhance knowledge acquisition and some dimensions of both cognitive and psychosocial change. Instructional strategies such as note taking, peer teaching, and various individualized learning approaches (for example, personalized system of instruction, audio-tutorial instruction, computer-based instruction) are based to a large extent on increasing students' active engagement in learning. Each has been shown to enhance knowledge acquisition under experimental conditions. . . . [p. 616].

The learning-cycle or inquiry approach, which stresses inductive learning based on concrete activities, shows evidence of enhancing the development of abstract reasoning and perhaps cognitive complexity. Similarly, there is at least modest evidence to suggest that critical thinking and the use of principled moral reasoning may be enhanced by instruction that stresses active student discussion at a relatively high cognitive level and instruction that engages students in problem solving.

A second general conclusion is that change in a wide variety of areas is stimulated by academic experiences that purposefully provide for challenge and/or integration. For example, cognitive-developmental instruction, which presents the student with cognitive conflict and forces the altering of previously held values and constructs for reasoning, shows evidence of uniquely stimulating growth in postformal reasoning abilities. Similarly, a curricular experience in which students are required to integrate learning from separate courses around a central theme appears to elicit greater growth in critical thinking than does the same curricular experience without the integrative requirement.

A third conclusion is that student learning is unambiguously linked to effective teaching, and we know much about what effective teachers do and how they behave in the classroom. Although a number of teacher behaviors are positively associated with student learning (rapport with students, interpersonal accessibility to students, feedback to students, and the like), two . . . [are] particularly salient. These are instructor skill (particularly clarity of presentation) and structuring of the course (for example, class time is structured and organized efficiently). What is perhaps most important is that many of the elements of both dimensions of effective teaching can themselves be learned [p. 619].

How long can we get by with neglecting this critical craft? How long can we ignore the fact that teaching, and teaching well, is the primary justification for our existence, for our support from public and private sources, the tax-exempt status of our institutions? The signals are becoming clearer and stronger every year. Assessment mandates from statewide coordination boards and legislatures — some emphasizing improvement, others explicitly interested in accountability — have spread nationwide. Mandatory testing at some levels has been adopted in several states. Movements are growing to increase consumer choice between institutions so that the market can be driven by quality considerations. If we do not take initiatives ourselves, others will move to undermine the kind of institutional culture we require for serious, self-motivated professional improvement.

Gamson and her associates (1984, pp. 167–168) write passionately about the impact of higher education on the development of the whole person:

We have seen that education of the highest quality is possible not only for those who are typically thought to be college material but also for people considered incapable of it in times past: those in the midst of the full responsibilities of adulthood, members of minority groups, people with few financial means, those whose preparation for academic work has been minimal. To them, a liberating education offers a vision of life. In many ways, this vision stands in opposition to the world of Orwell's 1984 — and aspects of the world today. Against loneliness, liberating education offers community. Against fragmentation, it brings a sense of wholeness. Against helplessness, it offers understanding and a certain power. Most of all, a liberating education means vitality. Instead of the many stupefactions of modern life, it brings awakening.

Social fragmentation, apathetic citizenship, and economic malaise seem to be growing throughout the United States. Unless we take teaching seriously, we are unlikely to sustain the capacity to make democracy work in our increasingly pluralistic nation. As Gamson and her associates emphasize:

> Schools, and higher education even more, must recognize that they should be engaged in a mammoth reclamation project: the teaching of the arts and skills of democracy and community. How do people learn these things? By participating in communities that require them to cooperate with others and make decisions that matter. The key to the social implications of a liberating education lies in what [have been called] small republics of the intellect, what we have been calling learning communities. In them, students and faculty members experience the meaning of community, often for the first time in their lives. They learn what it means to take into account people who are not close friends or members of their families. In practicing the arts

of discourse and the application of the mind in everyday life, they come to understand these people and cooperate with them in the common tasks of learning.

Without communities and structures to support the learning of democracy, liberating education or any other scheme for reviving the civic tradition (Boyer and Hechinger, 1981) or bringing morality back into the curriculum (Hesburgh, 1981) will be empty. For arrayed against such schemes are powerful forces, some of them within higher education itself. In a society in which a national commission on excellence in education must invoke the fear of foreign powers to get attention, it is not surprising that universities and even some colleges might have become preoccupied with big-time research and politics — and have forgotten about education [pp. 168–169].

Higher education's critical contributions to society will not be realized until our teaching is the best we can make it. We do not get much mileage on cognitive skills if students are simply reading a single text, listening to lectures, and completing multiple-choice exams. What we need instead are educational resources, teaching practices, and homework assignments that ask students themselves to analyze and draw inferences from readings, films, and other sources of insight and understanding and that ask students to synthesize materials from diverse sources, to evaluate the validity and reliability of different kinds of evidence and argument. We do not get much leverage on interpersonal competence and developing relationships if students are working in isolation, in competition with each other, without any opportunity or need to work with others or to obtain information and broaden their understanding by using human as well as print resources.

What we need instead are collaborative projects requiring students to work together on challenging problems or to create a joint product or performance. We need methods for evaluation and grading that do not pit one student against another, that recognize the value of cooperation and respect for diverse points of view and varied talents. We do not make much contribution to intellectual or interpersonal competence, tolerance, or autonomy when our academic studies make no connection with real-life situations, when students have no opportunity to apply theoretical principles or abstract concepts to concrete realities.

We need a much heavier dose of "experiential learning" throughout our curriculum so that the links between theory and practice and the social and professional relevance of our academic studies become much more apparent. Most significant performance in the world of work requires those personal qualities, yet there is little in our typical teaching practices that encourage them. Active learning needs to be encouraged in classes that use structured exercises, challenging discussions, team projects, and peer critiques. Active learning can also occur outside the classroom. There are thousands of internships, independent study opportunities, and cooperative job programs in all kinds of colleges and universities across the country, in all kinds of fields, for all kinds of students. Students also can help design and teach courses or parts of courses.

Learning can be individualized in recognition of differences. Individualized degree programs allow for both independent study and specialized seminars. Personalized systems of instruction and mastery learning let students work at their own pace. Contract learning helps students define their own objectives, determine their learning activities, and define the criteria and methods of evaluation. These options provide vehicles for developing autonomy, identity, and purpose. In many colleges and universities, students with poor past records or test scores do extraordinary work, supported by learning centers, developmental studies programs, and other special services. When students and faculty hold high expectations for themselves and for each other, day-to-day and week-in and week-out, high achievement leads to increasing sense of competence and self-esteem.

These principles of good teaching are well-known and can be learned. We owe ourselves the satisfactions that come from working as competent professional educators who are learning and growing along with our students. We owe future generations the legacy of enriched human development that will come when we remember that creating the conditions for powerful learning is our primary responsibility.

FOURTEEN

Friendships
and Student
Communities

A student's most important teacher is often another student. Bonds formed in college with classmates, hallmates, teammates, or blind dates may last one semester or a lifetime. Friends and reference groups filter and modulate the messages from the larger student culture. They amplify, dampen, or distort the force of curriculum, instruction, codes of conduct, and institutional norms. They can trump the best teacher's ace and stalemate the most thoughtful dean.

Relationships are labs for learning to communicate, empathize, argue, and reflect. Encounters with others who have diverse backgrounds and strongly held opinions create the context for increased tolerance and integrity. Feelings and judgments may be traded, along with outlines and anecdotes. In the process, the biases, histories, and idiosyncrasies of each person are revealed. Growth can be tangible when bonds are formed with those of different backgrounds, lifestyles, and values. So can upheaval, when relationships turn up unfinished business, unconscious needs, and unexamined projections. Friendships grounded in honesty and empathy can bring lasting gifts of acceptance, enjoyment, and loyalty.

Dialogue clarifies values and purposes. Many words are spent on mutual interests, plans, dreams, and existential questions. What my family is like, what they would have me be, and what I want to do—such questions are passed around, turned over, argued about, and applauded. In groups, we learn to care and to compromise, to play for the first time those roles we will refine throughout life. Thus, relationships with close friends and participation in student communities can be primary forces influencing student development in college; and all seven vectors for change are affected.

Pascarella and Terenzini (1991, p. 190) emphasize the importance of "socializing agents"—the people with whom students come into contact—as playing a critical role in identity and ego development during college. Citing a number of studies, they suggest that "it is the diversity of individuals (particularly other students) that developmentally challenges students' conceptions of themselves and that requires adaptation and commitment to certain attitudes, values, beliefs, and actions" (p. 190).

Whether living on campus, joining a sorority or fraternity, or commuting, students will form new relationships at college. They may find one new friend or a small circle of acquaintances. They may immerse themselves in new subcultures within a living unit, a student organization, or an off-campus social network. Daily behavior then becomes planned and patterned with closest friends in mind. The deeper the friendships, the more pronounced the impact. Unassigned books read are those friends recommend. Films, concerts, lectures, or art exhibits are often those enjoyed with close friends. Music for listening, topics for reflection, brands of beverage, styles of dress, figures of speech—all are influenced by students' close relationships. Furthermore, the influence of friends is amplified and enriched by the values, standards, and interests of the groups to which they belong.

A residence hall or Greek house has the most impact when it becomes an effective—and affective—subculture or reference group for its members. Like a new floor plan, the values and behavioral norms of an adopted group become the background for the individual's personal actions and attitudes. When students themselves form the community, shared standards and rules for conduct are not as likely to be seen as arbitrary or coercive. It is ironic that the group may demand more obedience than parents would, or more conformity than administrators would. It may even reinforce self-defeating behavior, but since we tend to defend what we identify with, those subcultural tyrannies may not be questioned.

Of course, decisions are not made in perfect harmony with group standards. Individuals test alternatives and find their own opinions through continuing interaction. Responses from others in the group powerfully influence the development of integrity. Gaps between expressed beliefs and behavior will not go unchallenged, nor will perceived breaches of ethics. When a person is known and observed over a year or more, discrepancies become apparent. All may be fooled for a while and some may be fooled forever — but most, before long, see us clearly for who we are. Given sufficient concern and a supportive atmosphere, they will not keep their knowledge from us.

Once a student identifies with a particular group, it becomes both an anchor and a reference point. The extent to which new groups influence behavior and thinking depends first on how much the older ties to family and friends have loosened and second on how much the group supports the individual's goals, emerging interests, or preferences. Students usually sever ties with groups whose purposes seem antithetical to their own, but the desire to belong may make them stay, silently resentful or outwardly ambivalent. When the subculture becomes important, individuals try to fit into it. If the hall leaders favor late-night discussions and intramural sports, new members may find themselves sleeping less and competing more. If a pledge must prove endurance or grace under pressure, poise and discipline begin to emerge. If the group values great parties, social skills bloom, but grades may suffer.

In addition to exerting influence on individual students' thinking and behavior, subcultures can define norms for relating to the entire campus community. The student culture interprets to the newcomers the range of tolerated deviations and the consequences of stepping out of bounds. The culture may carry values of its own, distinct from those of the institution; or it may go beyond the faculty and administration in endorsing and acting on institutional priorities. For example, student governments teach newly elected representatives by modeling formal procedures, informal discussions, or disorganized conflicts. They can directly or indirectly convey respect or distrust of the administration. The student newspaper staff can inculcate in cub reporters the value of sniffing out scandals, working all night, or striving for national recognition. Some students may find that sit-ins, banners, and interminable consensus-based meetings are acceptable responses to perceived injustices. At other institutions, no public protest has been seen since the Vietnam War, and reaching political consensus is the last thing on anyone's mind. What is politically or socially "correct" becomes a norm, and when it clashes with individual preference, students must think about where they stand.

It is the student culture that principally defines the appropriate responses to institutional authority and accepted ways of interacting with faculty. Faculty-student relationships are encouraged or blocked by word-of-mouth information about who is a good adviser, a dynamic teacher, or a hard grader. Whether the group supports or limits individual autonomy, whether it reinforces academic achievement or undermines it, whether its rumor mill is accurate or off-base, the subculture's norms may not be questioned, since they are both unwritten and subconsciously adopted.

The norms of the student subcultures both affect and are affected by the institutional culture. Catalysts are necessary for individual and institutional growth. But when students disdain involvement, steal equipment, or vandalize furniture, then authorities can become more rigid, and constructive challenges to the status quo do not occur. When the community tacitly supports intransigence, so that listening, reflection, or compromise are blocked, then both students and the institution remain at an antidevelopmental impasse.

Student culture can affect the development of identity and purpose by encouraging wide-ranging exploration or curtailing it. The sense of self is strengthened when students encounter different kinds of people and situations, observe their reactions, try out different roles with varying degrees of investment, and receive feedback uncontaminated by others' prejudices. But when the community affords status to only a limited set of roles, such as that of athlete or intellectual, activist or socialite, liberal or conservative, then the development of identity suffers.

When friendships and the intimate exchanges that accompany them are valued and promoted, identity and purpose become clearer. When the culture inhibits personal or cross-cultural connections, or assigns second-class citizenship to certain types of students or relationships, then avenues for dialogue and exploration may be closed. This is a challenge for campuses where students from different cultures are present but tend to stay in their own groups, or where insensitivity or intolerance exist beneath superficial niceness. Successful recruitment of diverse populations is not enough. They must seriously encounter each other. If the student culture is open to varying life-styles, belief systems, and backgrounds, and if the institution actively promotes deeper levels of multicultural understanding, then students move toward more mature relationships.

The campus ethos may be more powerful than any one department or subculture in affecting development along certain vectors. For example, Knox, Lindsay, and Kolb (1988) analyzed data from 7,500 participants over a fourteen-year period. They looked at students' independence from parents or peers and found that it was positively and significantly correlated with "institutional cohesion," a characteristic based on a number of variables, such as the proportion of freshmen on campus, the "full-timeness" of the student body, the proportion of out-of-state freshmen, and institutional selectivity, and others. Graffam (1967) found that increases in independence were due more to general institutional factors than to specific degree programs. The culture of a college may be based on these kinds of quantifiable factors. It is certainly based on its shared values, assumptions, and beliefs, which may be set forth in its mission statements (although not always adhered to), or implied by how staff members react to issues or determine their priorities. Kuh and his associates (1991) describe two striking examples of how well-defined missions affect the development of community. At Earlham College in Richmond, Indiana, Quaker traditions support relationships and integrity.

> First, it is assumed that the "light of truth" can be found in each individual, and so value is placed on consensual ways of learning and knowing. People are expected to participate in discussions without a firmly held position and to be prepared to hear the words and insights spoken by all members of the community. . . . Typically, a period of silence is used to initiate and to conclude campus meetings; silence insulates the experience from the outside world and encourages active listening on the part of participants. . . . The second assumption expressed by Earlham's mission is contained in the phrase, "Let your lives speak"; knowledge is not only to be appreciated but, more important, it is also to be lived. Quakers traditionally have been skeptical of learning for its own sake; knowledge must be applied to be of value. Students not only read about the causes of illiteracy, for example, but are also urged to identify ways to eliminate this problem [pp. 44–45].

Campus buildings at Earlham have been positioned around "the heart," which is an oval area of grass, trees, and shrubs surrounded by a sidewalk. Vigils are held in silence at this site in demonstration of support for various causes. A vigil is considered successful if enough people participate so that by holding hands they can encompass the "heart." Hierarchical relationships among all members of the community are discouraged. First names are used for everyone, including the president, and faculty members with the same first names are identified by their department ("Sue in economics" or "Sue in English").

Berea College in Berea, Kentucky, promotes the development of both physical and intellectual competence by adhering to its Seven Great Commitments, which were adopted during the Civil War era. One of them is "to provide an educational opportunity primarily for students from Appalachia who have high ability but limited economic resources" (Kuh, Schuh, Whitt, and Associates, 1991, p. 46). Another is to demonstrate the dignity of labor, both mental and physical. Since no one pays tuition, and money is scarce, everyone works. Each student is assigned to one of 130 different types of labor, from custodial services to skilled crafts.

Kuh and his associates also examine seven types of cultural "artifacts," which are more visible than values and assumptions. These include history, traditions, language, heroes and heroines, sagas, the physical setting, and symbols and symbolic action (p. 71), and they influence identity, purpose, and other vectors. For example, the graduating seniors at Mount Holyoke College carry a laurel chain that stretches symbolically back to the founding of the college, when founder Mary Lyon vowed to help women stretch beyond their assumed limits. It has traditions like Mountain Day, when classes are canceled for outdoor activities, and Founder's Day, when students eat ice cream at 6:00 A.M. at Mary Lyon's gravesite. While the ice cream on a November morning may be a reward or a trial, students carry away memories and messages from these traditions, which in effect say that "learning occurs off campus, in the world of nature," "balance work, exercise, and fun," and "you, too, can be a heroine."

Development is fostered when students feel part of a community. For optimum development, the community, whether it takes the form of residence hall unit, sorority or fraternity house, student organization, or informal circle of friends, should have the following characteristics:

1. It encourages regular interactions among students, and provides a foundation for ongoing relationships.
2. It offers opportunities for collaboration and shared interests, for engaging in meaningful activities and facing common problems together.
3. It is small enough so that no one feels superfluous.
4. It includes people from diverse backgrounds.

5. It serves as a reference group, where there are boundaries that indicate who is "in" and who is "out." It has norms that inform those with different roles, behaviors, and status that they are "good" members or that what they are doing is unacceptable.

To foster student development, institutional leaders need to assess how communities function within their institution. What subcultures exist? What norms do they reinforce? How do they reinforce or diminish institutional influences? Do they encourage friendships to develop? Do they foster intercultural communication? Do they support or block student development?

Where communities do not exist, colleges need to create them. Institutions with living units, such as residence halls or student apartment complexes, can wield the greatest influence. Greek houses also provide communities that can be governed by campus regulations and national sorority and fraternity administratrors. Where most students live off campus or commute, institutions face the greatest challenges in fostering student friendships and communities. Whether they operate residence halls or not, institutions can support relationship-building activities both inside and outside the classroom. We will now discuss a few of the ways that development can be affected by residential living arrangements, programs for commuters, and learning communities.

Residential Living

Powerful learning occurs in situations where people come to know each other as friends. Effective and affective exchange requires going beyond the persona to the person, behind the contrived image to the real self. Most of us know from experiences with out-of-town workshops, retreats, or excursions that staying together in a communal setting fosters a unique kind of bonding. College-operated residence halls provide ready-made communities that can have major impact on students. Research indicates that most changes in residents' attitudes, values, future plans, and intellectual interests occur during the first two years, as students form new relationships and find new reference groups.

Because the college can control student placement within residence halls, train and supervise live-in staff, and organize governance and judicial systems, it has leverage for fostering development. Residence hall arrangements can affect development of competence, purpose, integrity, and mature interpersonal relationships, depending on the diversity of backgrounds and attitudes among the residents, the opportunities for significant interchange, the existence of shared intellectual interests, and the degree to which the unit becomes a meaningful culture for its members.

Yet overly protective or homogeneous environments may screen out the intellectual and social challenges needed for development. Winter, McClelland, and Stewart (1981), for example, found that student involvement in hall-sponsored activities at a selective liberal arts college was negatively associated with gains in critical thinking, as measured by the Test of Thematic Analysis. Moos and his colleagues examined the ways that specific residential environments differed in their impact on students. They found that much of the variability depended on the students occupying the space and what their priorities were (Moos, DeYoung, and Van Dort, 1976). The hall can be insulating or stimulating and can promote academic achievement or rowdy escapism, depending on who the residents are and whether they partake of the growth opportunities around them (Moos, Van Dort, Smail, and DeYoung, 1975; Moos, 1978).

Developmental benefits appear to be greater for students living on campus, in residence halls or Greek societies, than for students living off campus. After analyzing data from 14,600 students at sixty-two colleges from 1979 to 1982, Pace (1984) found that the largest differences in self-reported gains in personal and social development were between on-campus and off-campus subjects. Chickering (1974a) found that campus residents rated themselves higher than commuters on six of eight skills, including academic, writing, artistic, public speaking, and leadership skills — all except artistic at statistically significant levels. Living at home during the freshman year was negatively related to measures of social confidence and popularity, with initial differences growing during the year. In fact, these patterns were found to continue through the senior year; gains in self-confidence and popularity were greatest among resident students and lowest among commuter students. Astin (1973, 1977) found similar results, even after extensive controls for students' precollege characteristics.

Furthermore, living on campus increases opportunities for intellectual, academic, and social involvement, which have been found to enhance principled moral judgment. Rest and Deemer (1986) found that living on campus (versus commuting to college) was positively related to higher scores on the Defining Issues Test (DIT) over a ten-year period. Living in a residence hall is consistently and positively associated with increases in altruism, support for civil liberties, racial integration, and political liberalism (Pascarella and Terenzini, 1991, pp. 310–311). Students have also reported the importance of interactions with upperclassmen in residential facilities and the value of new responsibilities, such as becoming hall officers or resident assistants, in supporting ethical development (Pascarella and Terenzini, 1991, p. 365). This is consistent with Kohlberg's identification (1969) of the types of experiences that foster moral development: exposure to more advanced stages of moral reasoning, social role-taking, exposure to divergent perspectives, and cognitive moral conflict.

Having reviewed the research on the effects of living in residence halls versus living in off-campus quarters and commuting, Pascarella and Terenzini (1991, p. 262) found that "living on campus tends to promote somewhat greater increases in personal autonomy and independence, intellectual disposition, and the development of more mature interpersonal relationships." Studying the effects of residence arrangements, they found recurring evidence that students' interpersonal relations with peers and faculty strongly affected psychosocial development. Faculty have greater influence in intellectual areas and peers have greater influence in noncognitive areas. As with student-faculty interaction, there is evidence that the frequency of interaction with peers is less important than the nature and

quality of it. Living on campus increases opportunities for social, cultural, and cocurricular involvement, and "it is this involvement that largely accounts for residential living's impact
on student change" (p. 611). Those who live off campus and
commute to college have a disadvantage — they miss the social-
psychological context created by on-campus living, which Pascarella and Terenzini find to be "perhaps the single most consistent within-college determinant of impact" (p. 611).

It is in residence hall units that the all-important propinquity factor can operate. Newcomb (1962) found that even
within a small, two-floor house accommodating only seventeen
students, significantly more close relationships existed among
the eight men on one floor and among the nine men on the other
than between the men on different floors. Newcomb points out
that while there are many potential relationships all around us,
those we actually develop are made possible by opportunities
for contact and reciprocal exploration, which in turn are affected
by physical propinquity. And other things being equal, we are
likeliest to maintain close relationships already established instead of launching a search for new ones (p. 76).

Two major variables affect development in residence hall
settings: the nature of close friendships and reference groups, and
the general attitudes and values carried by the living unit as a cultural entity. Staff members can work with these variables to foster
movement along several vectors by (1) incorporating learning
activities into living units; (2) adapting existing halls to allow a
balance of interaction and privacy and to permit a more personalized environment; (3) enhancing community by building new
units that are small enough to allow maximum participation but
large enough to allow more experienced students to induct newer
ones into the culture; (4) improving both the "fit" and the diversity by placing students carefully; (5) using regulations, policies,
and hall management strategies as tools for fostering autonomy,
interdependence, and integrity.

Incorporating Learning Activities

Students who live together learn together — when studies and activities overlap sufficiently to permit it. Residence halls heighten

their impact by becoming "living and learning centers," putting books, classes, and instructors' offices in the halls and building academic and cultural programs into the residential community. Experimental units at Michigan State University, the University of Michigan, and the University of California, Berkeley were established to foster continued discussion of issues raised in class and to promote cooperative study. When 197 freshmen who entered the University of Michigan's Residential College in 1967 were compared with 410 freshmen in three different control groups on the family independence scale of the College Student Questionnaire (Educational Testing Service), gains among the Residential College students were most substantial, although all groups showed increased scores. On the peer independence scale, scores for all groups decreased, indicating the growing importance of fellow students over family (Newcomb and others, 1971). Pascarella and Terenzini (1981) found further evidence of the impact of residence in a living-learning center compared to a conventional residence hall. With fifteen preenrollment characteristics held constant, they found that residing in a living-learning center at a large Northeastern university had positive effects on freshman students' year-end reports of progress in gaining a better understanding of self, developing interpersonal skills, and developing self-reliance and self-discipline. Increases in autonomy and intellectual orientation and decreases in dogmatism and authoritarianism were also found. Thus, curricular coordination and allocation of students to residences can foster development along several vectors. And without such efforts, a large university offers little chance for classmates in Freshman English, Western Civilization, or Advanced Calculus to encounter each other outside class.

Intramural teams formed from unit halls may entice nonvarsity athletes to emerge and develop physical abilities. Jogging and walking groups, stress management and nutrition workshops, dances and aerobic workouts, indoor recreation programs, and stop-smoking classes can help students improve physical health and self-esteem. Group efforts to build homecoming floats or ice sculptures, design sets and costumes for musical satires, or transform hall lounges and lobbies with holiday decorations can foster artistic and manual competence while enhancing frindships.

Leafgren (1981) proposes that student development experts present theoretical models to residence hall staff. They can then discuss these with residents, help them assess current levels of development, clarify developmental goals and activities, identify or design programs to bring about desired behavioral changes, and evaluate results (p. 28). For example, if a student's goal is to make new friends, the resident advisers can invite specific commitments to initiate conversation, sit at a different table in the dining commons, or ask a neighbor to have coffee. Staff members could also design programs that use films, discussions, or structured workshops to explore the basis of best friendships, desires for independence and dependence in relationships, the basis of traditional roles and the implications of those roles in relationships, and expectations in relationships with the opposite sex (p. 30). Residence hall staff may not wish to be this structured, but certainly a knowledge of student development theories can inform both one-to-one dialogues and plans for group activities.

Creating a More Personalized Environment

What goes on inside university housing can also be influenced by the housing itself. Beginning in the 1960s, colleges and universities built more residence halls. The era of expansion now seems to be over. An array of clean, attractive, low-cost accommodations now exists, including high-rise or low-rise buildings, small cell-like rooms and suites with movable furniture, and long linoleum corridors and carpeted pathways around courtyards. Research on the effects of architectural decisions is instructive.

Smaller living units foster peer involvement, emotional support, and innovation (Moos, 1978). Baum, Aiello, and Colesnick (1978) found that students who live on long corridors spent less time studying and socializing in their residence hall, experienced more housing-related problems, described their buildings as more crowded, and had more difficulty controlling interaction than short-corridor residents did. Students in low-rise structures expressed more satisfaction and established more friendships in the halls than those living in high-rise buildings, according to Valine and Baum (1973). Gerst and Sweetwood (1973) found that students living in suites reported more interaction with peers, more spontaneity, and more contentment than those in corridor bedroom arrangements. Suite arrangements provide more privacy for sleeping and studying, as well as a separate living room space for socializing and relaxing. Students living in rooms with built-in furniture reported spending less time in their rooms and using their rooms less often for interpersonal recreation than students living in rooms with movable furniture (High and Sundstrom, 1977).

Where possible, adaptations should be made in existing units to allow for more personalizing of space. Schroeder (1981) proposes that students need a balance between their needs for privacy, control, and social interaction. A relatively good fit is required between the environment and the preferred activities, such as sleeping, studying, relaxing, or interacting. Faced with too much forced interaction and larger groups, students may isolate themselves in their rooms or stay away from the halls. When private rooms cannot be rearranged or redecorated in order to regulate the amount of stimulation, privacy, freedom, and order, stress increases. Drab walls and uniform furniture are depersonalizing, as are lounge spaces removed from foot traffic and maintained as an extension of the institution's territory, not the students'.

Other benefits may be gained by allowing students to create a more agreeable decor. Schroeder (1976) found that retention increased by 40 percent, damages decreased by 82 percent, and both occupancy and academic achievement increased substantially following a three-year room and hallway personalization program. Georgia Southwestern College reported a reduction in damage costs of over 300 percent during the first year that rooms were personalized (Schroeder, 1979). Auburn furnished $1,200 worth of paint for women residents in one medium-sized residence hall. They used it to paint their rooms and hallways, costing the university a great deal less than the physical plant's estimate of $67,000 (Schroeder, 1981).

Residence hall managers can foster development by encouraging students to add color, texture, and individual decoration, within bounds that preserve the safety and a certain amount of decorum. Let them build partitions or lofts, or rearrange desks and bookcases to divide up the room to make it more comfortable or more functional. Give students greater control and ownership of hallways and lounges. Paint, graphics, plants, murals, drapes, or symbols can serve as territorial markers which distinguish "our" space from another's. Make student lounges accessible and inviting. If lounges for entertaining or socializing are separate from areas central to the daily life of students, consider converting centrally located student rooms into group rooms, so that corridors lead right into them. Provide areas where students can take a break from studying and do something other than sit in small lounges and talk. Consider new uses for old lounges. They might become health clubs with exercise equipment or recreation areas for pinball machines, video games, board games, or music, thereby providing ways to relax and socialize.

Building New Units That Allow
Maximum Participation and Interaction

Small size, both in absolute numbers and the ratio of persons to opportunities and pressures for active participation, is important. Three to five hundred students are enough to support a wide range of activities and programs. Competition then exists for only a few of the most attractive programs, and the rest welcome additional participants. In a residential complex of that size, there are few strangers. Ten or twelve hundred students seems to be about the maximum. By then, the rate of increase for activities and programs starts to level off, so further gains in enrollment simply increase the load and the competition, with consequent reduction of opportunities for those who enter less qualified. Individuals become lost, their presence neither noted nor missed.

Institutions planning new residence halls have an opportunity to create smaller-scale communities, thereby reducing the potential for redundancy. New complexes can be designed to be small enough to encourage maximum participation and familiarity. They can provide flexibility with suites, double rooms with movable furniture, and distinctive designs that reduce uniformity and impersonality.

Size is important also because the rate of flow through the community is high. In most colleges, each year's freshman class comprises more than 30 percent of the total enrollment. Developing and sustaining a strong sense of community in the face of such continual turnover requires frequent, intense interaction, beginning at entrance and continuing throughout. New members need to be inducted and assimilated through interactions with more experienced students and staff; otherwise, they will form their own subgroups, bypassing the benefits of older friends.

More than a few small colleges tripled their enrollment in the 1960s. Many of these were small, tight ships, sailing a clear course. All hands pulled together, and despite some grumbling about who managed the tiller, neither the general direction nor the operating procedures were sharply questioned. But the increased enrollment and increased faculty size outstripped the capacity for induction and assimilation. The course began to be questioned. Debates concerning roles and responsibilities arose. The institutions were soon plagued by discontent, disaffection, and disillusionment. Not that questioning is inappropriate or redirection uncalled for, but as subcultures become polarized, questioning and redirection become masks for power struggles and outlets for hostility. Exit reason and temperate solutions. Many small colleges caught in this dynamic have not yet fully recovered. The trend in the early 1990s seems to be toward downsizing, which can be as traumatic as unbridled expansion. Either way, conflicts that lead to emotional rigidity, suppression of differences, elimination of dissidents, and arbitrary decisions can poison the environment.

Assuming that there *is* agreement about the mission and values of the system, students need to be initiated into the ways of the new culture. Hopefully they will form relationships with faculty members and advisers who will help define norms and explain procedures. Students who have survived the first year can also be valuable sources of information. If they are placed in proximity to new residents—in adjoining rooms or floors or as resident assistants—interaction that can help the sense of community is virtually guaranteed.

Placing Students Carefully

A good interpersonal and environmental fit can foster development by reducing stress, conflict, and feelings of powerlessness. More energy can thus be spent on increasing competence and building friendships. For example, roommates at Auburn University were matched by commonalities, on the basis of the Myers-Briggs Type Indicator (MBTI). Requests for roommate changes declined by over 65 percent during the first year. In addition, twenty-four pairs of the self-selected roommates were randomly picked and their MBTI scores compared. Twenty-one of the twenty-four pairs had matched themselves in the same manner as that employed by the housing staff (Schroeder, 1976, 1981). At Ohio State University, students were placed in suites on the basis of compatible MBTI scores. They reported a higher degree of emotional support and involvement than students assigned in the traditional way (Kalsbeek, 1980).

While matching roommates for compatibility within the room, diversity within the hall must also be considered. Each unit should comprise students with varying backgrounds, interests, and values, as far as possible, given the range in characteristics of students enrolled. The number of students per unit should be small enough so that each student can know the others and so the impact of an individual's behavior on the whole community is visible. Allow students to live in the same unit as long as they choose. Let them change to a different unit if they want to, and if space is available, let the students' wish to remain take precedence over new students' requests. Let the members of each unit allocate to themselves the spaces within the unit, arranging their preferences according to whatever schedule of priority or hierarchy they prefer. A staff member can then fill the empty spaces with new students or older students who request transfer.

Using Regulations, Policies, and
Hall Management to Foster Development

Residence hall managers can influence development through the ways they organize programming and implement governance procedures. As we have already mentioned, they can involve residents and student staff members in planning events and incorporating learning activities into the residence hall experience whenever possible. They can introduce residents and student staff members to student development models. In addition, housing rules and judicial procedures can have an impact. For example, regulations should permit spontaneous, heated, and extended discussions, held without the imposition of arbitrary cutoff times and free from adult interruption, intrusion, or surveillance. Standards of behavior should be explicit, both to heighten their visibility and to provide a clear point of view for students to contest. The values of the administration and faculty need to be clearly communicated, and each residence unit needs to provide its own public statement of rules, rights, and judicial procedures.

Administrators should involve residents in conducting hearings, determining sanctions, and responding to peers who disrupt the community or violate codes of ethics or conduct. They should provide training for hall officers and modeling of assertive communication which holds residents accountable for illegal drug or alcohol use, property damage, loud music, or insensitive behavior. Managers could foster autonomy and integrity by giving each house some funds to work with and requiring an accounting at the end of each term. Perhaps each hall could take some responsibility for its own interior decoration and its own maintenance. Each unit could be billed for breakage or deterioration, and members could deal with the individuals responsible. Funds could also be used to plan activities or entertainment. By allowing members of each unit to make meaningful decisions that require significant discussion, the diversity of orientation may be revealed, examined, and tested.

Off-Campus Housing

Similar principles can be applied in managing off-campus housing or in advising sororities and fraternities. Workshops on
parenting or couples communication can be organized in married student housing units. Workshops on alcohol abuse and
date rape are needed both on and off campus. While students
in off-campus apartments may be forced to develop autonomy
and purpose, Greeks may have less impetus for developing independence and integrity if the subculture promotes conformity.
For example, a study of Bucknell University students by Wilder
and his associates examined seven cohorts of entering freshmen
from 1965 to 1981. In each cohort, Greeks were significantly
lower than non-Greeks on the family independence scale of the
College Student Questionnaire at entrance, and their gains during college were significantly smaller than those of non-Greeks.
Furthermore, students who had joined but then withdrew from
a Greek organization showed significantly greater increases in
peer independence than either Greeks or non-Greeks, and significantly greater gains than Greeks on the family independence
scale (Wilder and others, 1978, 1986).

Other researchers have gotten mixed results. Winston and
Saunders (1987) find little evidence that Greek society membership promotes autonomy but also find that it did not block
the growth of independence. Marlowe and Auvenshine (1982)
compared fraternity-affiliated freshmen with nonfraternity freshmen on the Defining Issues Test. No statistically significant
differences in moral reasoning were found over a nine-month
period. Researchers have found smaller increases in liberalism
among Greeks than among independents (Astin, 1977; Longino
and Kart, 1973). Krasnow and Longino (1973) found that the
Greek influence was a moderating one: conservative for students
initially more liberal than the fraternity norm and liberalizing
for new members who were more conservative than the norm.

More research needs to be done on the impact of sororities and fraternities on student development. While operating
much more independently of college authorities than residence
halls, they still provide a crucial community experience for their

members. Greek advisers and Panhellenic councils can institute programs and practices that enhance independent thinking and ethical behavior. Residents in off-campus housing may
lose touch with each other and become more like commuter students unless the college is proactive in creating programs for
them.

Commuter Students

The advantages of living on campus have already been mentioned. Pascarella and Terenzini (1991) reiterate that commuter
schools are less likely to provide their students with the kinds
of interpersonal and academic experiences associated with increases in cultural and aesthetic attitudes and values, in social,
political, and religious tolerance, in self-awareness and independence, and in persistence and degree attainment. Without the
natural meeting place that residence halls provide, fewer students can "encounter, confront, question, examine, analyze,
challenge, criticize, reflect, differentiate, and evaluate. The significance of this inequality becomes all the more striking and
urgent when one considers that more than half of America's college students commute, and even more are likely to do so in
the future. Given economic pressures and, for many, limited
or nonexistent space for new buildings, current commuter institutions are unlikely to open residential facilities in the fore-
seeable future" (pp. 639–640).

Chickering (1974a) found major differences in commuters
versus residents. Data in a large national sample were consistent with earlier research findings that commuters had lower
high school grades, defined their primary purpose in college as
vocational preparation, reported more financial and interpersonal problems with peers and family, and showed less interest
in national and world affairs. Commuters tend to have grown
up in moderate-sized towns or cities and had parents who were
more frequently skilled, semiskilled, or unskilled workers. Residents tended to come from suburbs and had parents who were
more advantaged in education, occupation, and income. Substantially more commuters than residents had applied only to

the college they were attending (61 percent versus 38 percent). Thus, they might not have been seeking out the college with the best academic or social fit but simply choosing what was close to home.

Resident students may have different priorities. For example, residents more frequently judge several items "essential" or "very important" to their future lives compared with commuters. In order of magnitude, they are as follows: to "keep up with political affairs," "become a community leader," "develop a philosophy of life," "have friends different from me," and "influence social values." Proportionally, three times as many commuters as residents plan to stop with an associate degree, whereas substantially more residents plan to obtain at least a master's degree.

Commuting students in private universities, compared with their resident counterparts, combine high academic aspirations with limited resources and limited past achievements. Despite the fact that their parents' backgrounds and high school achievements may often exceed those of their commuting peers who have chosen other institutions, the gap between where they start and where they hope to finish is great. It is as though the private four-year institutions set up a race on a mile track, but commuters start a quarter of a mile behind. The point of education, obviously, is to accelerate learning and development. Most important, therefore, is how far people travel during the experience, not whether they reach some arbitrary defined finish line within a set time.

Commuting students increasingly go to the nearest community college. Faced with tight job markets and higher tuition at four-year institutions, they compete with rising numbers of freshmen and transfer students for limited seats. Classes fill more quickly. Desperate students sign up for anything that is open or take electives until seats appear in more popular vocational programs. Like crowds in a giant funnel, they create pressure for larger classes, more adjunct instructors, and more delays in buying books and seeing advisers. Crowding and frustration add to the barriers that may already exist—work and family responsibilities, transportation, housing, and financial problems.

As a result, commuters may rush in and out, without even sampling the food service, the cultural events, or the student organizations. They may select vocational courses regardless of their goals or aptitudes. They may intend to complete a liberal arts degree and transfer to a four-year college, but a large percentage cannot manage it within two years.

Given these challenges, colleges must be especially creative in bringing commuters together and encouraging friendships to form. Student organizations and events must be planned to appeal to adult learners, single parents, and ethnic groups eager for programs that celebrate their heritage. Parents can be invited or required to participate in cooperative child-care centers that augment the daycare with parenting workshops and support groups. First-time college students may be drawn to a single course on self-esteem, life skills, or career exploration. A special lounge for returning adults, with peer advisers and relevant programs, may provide a sense of community. Busy adults may not come to meetings every week but might participate in a short-term volunteer project, such as donating for the food bank or cleaning up the neighborhood. Others may be drawn to group meetings or outreach efforts aimed at specific groups (for example, veterans, disabled students, public assistance recipients, single parents, and so on).

Commuters may find it easier to spend more time on campus if appealing spaces are available in which to congregate. Many colleges overlook corridors, stairwells, foyers, and grassy areas as potential gathering spots that can be made more inviting with well-placed benches, sofas, snack bars, espresso carts, or sidewalk cafés. It may take more than printed brochures, posters, or calendars to lure commuters. Electronic bulletin boards or newsprint banners taped to the sides of buildings may be needed. An enthusiastic statement or course requirement from an instructor may do more than the best-designed promotional pieces in getting students to a film series, guest lecture, candidate forum, Earth Day, or symphony concert.

Teams traveling to tournaments, bands riding to halftime shows, and debate squads carpooling to contests know the potential for relationships that can deepen during trips. Short-term residential experiences can be offered in a variety of forms. Overnight retreats, vans to professional meetings, field trips to drama festivals, mountaineering expeditions — all can be organized to combine learning with informal activities. Community colleges can arrange for intersession or summer session visits to selected four-year institutions for potential transfers, with overnight or weeklong visits included. Continuing education can augment credit-bearing courses with educational tours of historic places, walks around ethnic neighborhoods or architectural wonders, ecology awareness trips, or adventures abroad. For students tracing Darwin's steps in the Galapagos, reading James Joyce in Dublin, or admiring Giotto's paintings in Assisi, the arts, humanities, and sciences come to life.

Honors programs have provided interactive communities and accelerated intellectual development. King (1973) found greater increases in internal locus of control and self-esteem among honors program participants than among students enrolled in regular curricula. Community colleges can establish honors programs which offer mentoring, interdisciplinary courses, transfer information, encouragement to become leaders, and motivation to do community service. The success of such programs can boost the image of the college in the surrounding high schools and make it a more appealing alternative for talented students on a budget.

Learning Communities

Perhaps the closest facsimile to residence hall communities for commuters is involvement in a learning community. This innovative restructuring of curriculum involves linking courses around a common theme and enrolling students as a cohort group of twenty-five to one hundred in a self-contained learning group. In addition to receiving credit for two or more general education requirements, they are asked to build explicit connections between ideas and disciplines, since the courses are team designed and frequently team taught. Under the impetus of the Washington Center for Improving the Quality of Undergraduate Education at The Evergreen State College, learning communities were organized in different forms during the late 1980s. Whether they are called coordinated studies as at many Washington community colleges; Freshman Interest Groups as at the University of Washington; federated learning communities as at the State University of New York, Stony Brook; learning communities as at LaGuardia Community College in New York City and Daytona Beach Community College in Orlando, Florida; or the honors cluster as at Western Michigan University, all embody the principles of student involvement and active learning.

They create a sense of group identity, cohesion, purpose, and specialness, help students see the relationships between different disciplines, apply concepts from one area to another, and balance academic life with the demands of family and work (Matthews, 1986). They can also lift faculty morale. As Matthews says, "Participation in communities provides too-often beleaguered community college faculty with the opportunity to work in close cooperation with colleagues and take a new look at ossified courses and stale methodologies. When small groups of faculty from different disciplines work together to define and deliver a common learning experience for a group of students, they revitalize each other and discover in old acquaintances new talents, interests and friendships. The actual teaching experience contributes to increased involvement with students" (p. 47).

Coordinated studies programs often have engaging themes, like The American Spirit in Literature, Humanities, and History, Conscience and Cowardice, or The Problem of Prejudice. Rather than disciplines confining content, interesting topics form bridges between departments: Close Encounters: Gender and Relationships (taught by instructors from speech, psychology, English, and the library), Political Arabesques: Disentangling the Middle East (taught by instructors from anthropology, economics, and English), Seeing Beyond the Surface (combining photography, and chemistry), The Zoo Is You (combining biology, English, and speech communication), and Dancing Bears, Raging Bulls: Tracking Down the Rhythm of Money, Markets, and the Economy (combining economics and mathematics) ("What's Happening: Learning Community and Faculty Exchanges at Participating Institutions," 1991, pp. 31–34).

Other models of learning communities link college study skills courses, writing modules, or speech labs with regular general education classes, emphasizing small group problem solving, minilectures, and collaborative preparation for weekly tests. Biology teachers at Yakima Valley Community College compared the retention and performance of 650 students in new, collaborative biology classes to results in their "old" biology classes. Retention increased from 80 to 92 percent; students who persisted but earned a failing grade decreased from 9.2 to 2.4 percent; 30.4 percent of the students in the collaborative learning classes earned A's and 26.4 percent earned B's, compared to 17.3 percent A's and 19.9 percent B's in the lecture format class (MacGregor, 1991, p. 5).

The University of Washington offers triads of courses, known as Freshman Interest Groups, or "FIGs." For example, a prelaw FIG might link American Government, Fundamentals of Public Speaking, and Introduction to Philosophy: Ethics. Each FIG has a more advanced student who serves as a peer adviser. This student convenes the students every week to form study groups, learn about campus resources, and plan social gatherings. A study of 1988 and 1989 FIGs at the University of Washington found that more students stayed in courses if they were in a FIG and that the overall grade point averages were significantly better for FIG students, even after adjustment for academic potential. FIG students at Eastern Washington University also had significantly higher retention levels than other, comparable freshmen, from quarter to quarter and from year to year, into the sophomore year (MacGregor, 1991, pp. 5-6).

Most learning communities demand levels of student participation and responsibility not typically found in general education offerings. Several studies in Washington and elsewhere have used the Perry scheme to examine student intellectual development in learning community programs (MacGregor, 1987). Using the Measure of Intellectual Development (MID), which assesses student-written essays along Perry's positions, most studies indicated that students enter learning communities as late "Dualists," with mean scores falling in a range of 2.6 to 2.0 on a scale of 2.0 to 5.0. MacGregor (1991, p. 7) found that "students generally made a significant and unusual leap in intellectual development during their learning community experience. [They] exited as early 'Multiplists' (3.1 to 3.5), significantly more advanced developmentally than their counterparts in control groups. This indicates that the meanings these learning community students are making of their academic environment are more typical of college juniors and seniors."

Such programs apparently generate major payoffs for students. For example, ten faculty members at Seattle Central Community College analyzed student self-evaluations written at the end of coordinated studies programs, in order to see what students reported as the most important things they had learned. The outcomes that students described most frequently were developing self-esteem and motivation, developing sensitivity and respect for others, building community, making interdisciplinary connections, becoming lifelong learners, and building fundamental communication and writing skills (MacGregor, 1991, p. 9).

Encouraging students to work together and to discover their own excitement about content enhances development by helping students to care not only about their own work and each other but also about what they are learning. For many students, the fear of being wrong or looking inept keeps them from truly acknowledging the value of their own questions and interpretations. The norm in academia, as we have already discussed, is to separate self from subject and to favor objective, impersonal, analytical, data-based ways of knowing. Palmer (1987, p. 25) asserts that regardless of how many small-group experiences are built into the curriculum, if the dominant epistemology is objectivism, and the prevailing ethic is competition, we will continue to breed "silent, sub rosa, private combat for personal reward."

Learning communities, in addition to bringing students into relationships with each other, can also help them actively connect with content and with their own feelings and values. Objectivism, or separate knowing, as Belenky, Clinchy, Goldberger, and Tarule (1986, p. 104) have called it, emphasizes critical thinking, caution, and being "right."

> Separate knowers are tough-minded. They are like
> doormen at exclusive clubs. They don't want to let
> anything in unless they are pretty sure it is good. . . .
> Presented with a proposition, separate knowers im-
> mediately look for something wrong — a loophole,
> a factual error, a logical contradiction, the omission
> of contrary evidence. Separate knowing is in a sense
> the opposite of subjectivism. While subjectivists as-
> sume that everyone is right, separate knowers as-
> sume that everyone — including themselves — may
> be wrong. If something feels right to subjectivists,
> they assume it to *be* right. Separate knowers, on the
> other hand, are especially suspicious of ideas that
> feel right; they feel a special obligation to examine
> such ideas critically, whether the ideas originate in
> their own heads or come from someone else.

Too much emphasis on separate knowing can teach technical skills at the expense of compassion. For example, Simpson's study (1967) of students entering a nursing program found that all the entering students were inspired by a desire to help suffering peo-ple. After the first semester, academic coursework and the prac-tice of routines and procedures were top priorities. They prac-ticed twenty-one consecutive steps in making a bed, without considering the welfare of the patient occupying it. "After two semesters, a shift in values began to emerge. Their humanistic concerns gave way to concerns about mastery of technical skills. This trend continued so that by the end of their professional train-ing, the student nurses had internalized the values of professional proficiency. They no longer evaluated hospital personnel in terms of their sympathy for patients, but in terms of their technical virtuosity" (Bartsch, Girrell, and Yost, 1976, p. 111).

To analyze objectively means to exclude personal concerns and to speak dispassionately, to choose the well-reasoned argu-ment even if it contradicts a strongly held but poorly articulated belief. It also means to exclude feelings, including those of the adversary, and to examine issues from a pragmatic, strategic point of view. In contrast, connected knowing honors feelings, experience, and understanding. It does not emphasize defending positions, proving points, or converting dissenters. Ideas can be shared as works in progress, since connected knowers assume that others will contribute greater clarity rather than being critical and competitive. Such a process requires trust, support, and a nonjudgmental attitude in listeners, who, like midwives, help emerging insights struggle into being. In order to have this collaborative approach, classmates need to know each other relatively well, to accept life experience as a necessary ingredient rather than an irrelevant diversion, and to take into account individual personalities, just as a family would accommodate its various members, with their sometimes irritating habits. When classrooms become learning communities, subjective knowing can be balanced with objective inquiry.

Palmer (1987, p. 20) says, "Community is that place where the person you least want to live with always lives." To truly make a safe environment for development, students need to tolerate the presence of people, ideas, and facts that they do not particularly like. Using interpersonal skills, they can commune with classmates. Using objective analysis, they can ask "What is it?" and "What caused it?" and "How does it work?" They can also engage subjectively with objects of study by asking "What are my reactions?" and "Why am I reacting this way?" and "What more do I want to know?" Learning through relationship, with others and with the material, fosters a lasting ability to think beyond the boundaries of self and to link content with experience.

When students relate to works of art and bodies of knowledge, they become players, not spectators. When they focus only on the product rather than the people who created it and the context of their individual lives, they miss the human element, the foundation for empathy. Viewing what we are studying from a position of superiority and detachment can take the enjoyment out of the learning process. A former student recalls voicing her frustration in a poetry class:

> I remember having such a strong reaction to one
> of the assigned poems. I think it was one by Yeats,
> or maybe Gerard Manley Hopkins. I didn't even
> know how to put words to my reaction, but I was

tremendously interested in what the class discussion would yield. As usual, the instructor began to dissect it and critique it. He discussed the metaphors, examined the wording, analyzed the meter, ranked it in terms of other poems, and reported that some critics didn't think it was one of his best. I surprised myself by raising my hand and saying, "I can see that you put a lot of work into this analysis, but it has taken all the enjoyment out of the poem for me. For once, could we spend some time just talking about why we appreciated it?" His young face went completely blank, and he said, "I don't think I know how to do that."

This instructor, with his facile analysis and scholarly rigor, illustrates how objectivism without the capacity for relatedness turns the world into what Palmer calls a "bloodless abstraction." Yet his willingness to be a little vulnerable dispelled the distance.

Good class discussions and ongoing conversation about what happened in class can counteract the tendency to learn in isolation. Our cultural context of individualism perpetuates a myth that learning is best done alone—studying or writing or listening to an expert. Since it is a race for the highest grades, the best schools, and later the best jobs, why help others succeed? Students with this mentality get nervous about group projects. What if the others do not carry their weight and my own grade suffers as a result? Instructors also may balk at collaborative approaches. What if the students resist it and give lower evaluations? What if the students learn so well that they all earn A's? Grade inflation looks bad. Palmer (1987, p. 25) says:

> The root fallacy in the pedagogy of most of our institutions is that the individual is the agent of knowing and therefore the focus of teaching and learning. We all know that if you draw the lines of instruction in most classrooms, they run singularly from the teacher to each individual student . . . there simply for the convenience of the instructor. . . . But

to say the obvious, knowing and learning are *communal acts*. They require many eyes and ears, many observations and experiences. They require continual cycle of discussion, disagreement and consensus over what has been seen and what it all means. This is the essence of the community of scholars and it should be the essence of the classroom as well.

The impersonal structure of the academic community has a similar effect on faculty. Status goes to rigorous graders, prolific publishers, and good grant writers. Yet minimal supervision and accountability may allow low performers to continue undisturbed, year after year. Glaring discrepancies in rank, salary, and workload can heighten separation between adjuncts and full professors, between the hard workers and those who rarely hold office hours. Few faculty have the time or inclination to relate to each other, let alone to their students. Yet faculty might be more effective if their own sense of community were strong and positive. Respect, caring, humor, equity, and high standards are needed; so is the courage to disagree and the will to support each other. Palmer (1987) sees conflict, not competition, as essential to a communal way of teaching and learning. Most of us do not like confrontation in the meeting room or the classroom.

> What prevents conflict in our classrooms is a very simple emotion called fear. And it's fear that's in the hearts of teachers as well as students. It's fear of exposure, of appearing ignorant, or being ridiculed. And the only antidote to that fear is a hospitable environment created, for example, by a teacher who knows how to use every remark, no matter how mistaken or how seemingly stupid, to upbuild both the individual and the group. When people in the classroom begin to learn that every attempt at truth, no matter how off the mark, is a contribution to the larger search for corporate and consensual truth,

they are soon emboldened and empowered to say what they need to say to expose their ignorance, to do all those things without which learning cannot happen. Community is not opposed to conflict. On the contrary, community is precisely that place where an arena for creative conflict is protected by the compassionate fabric of human caring itself [p. 25].

Restoring a sense of community in academia may help graduates reverse the erosion of community in America. In *Habits of the Heart: Individualism and Commitment in American Life* (1985, pp. 284–285), Robert Bellah and his associates describe how individual judgments, personal preferences, and short-sighted interests have blocked our understanding of the "social ecology" of shared traditions and collective decision making:

For several centuries, we have embarked on a great effort to increase our freedom, wealth, and power. For over a hundred years, a large part of the American people, the middle class, has imagined that the virtual meaning of life lies in the acquisition of ever-increasing status, income, and authority, from which genuine freedom is supposed to come. Our achievements have been enormous. They permit us the aspiration to become a genuinely humane society in a genuinely decent world, and provide many of the means to attain that aspiration. Yet we seem to be hovering on the very brink of disaster, not only from international conflict but from the internal incoherence of our own society. What has gone wrong? How can we reverse the slide toward the abyss? . . . What has failed at every level — from the society of nations to the national society to the local community to the family — is integration: we have failed to remember "our community as members of the same body," as John Winthrop put it. We have committed what to the republican founders of our nation was the cardinal

> sin: we have put our own good, as individuals, as
> groups, as a nation, ahead of the common good.

The assumption that we are free individuals, that the good life
for each consists of pursuing personal satisfaction, and that we
are morally and rationally self-directing agents has become what
Bowers (1987) calls a "loose canon." "Few students," he says,
"have the maturity or conceptual basis for questioning a cultural myth that, at the same time, enhances the sense of self"
(p. 151). Unless faculty and staff can model community values,
this obsession with self-interest will continue.

The Carnegie Foundation, observing a decline in the commitment to teaching and learning, a breakdown of civility, and
an upsurge of campus crime, racial tensions, and substance
abuse, calls for a "more integrative vision of community in higher
education" (Carnegie Foundation for the Advancement of Teaching, 1990, p. 7). It describes the ideal institution as

- A purposeful community, where faculty and students share
  intellectual goals and values
- An open community, where freedom of expression is protected but which has a civility that respects the dignity of all
- A just community with a commitment to heterogeneity and
  diverse opportunities in the curriculum and social activities,
  and an honoring of the individual person
- A disciplined community, in which individuals are guided
  by standards of conduct for academic and social behavior
  and governance procedures that work for the benefit of all
- A caring community that supports individual well-being
  through positive relationships, sensitivity, and service to
  others
- A celebrative community, which unites the campus through
  rituals that affirm both tradition and change and instill a
  sense of belonging

Peavey (1986, p. 1) finds an analogy for our fundamental, though often invisible, connectedness. She writes that human beings are a lot like crabgrass. "Each blade of crabgrass

sticks up into the air, appearing to be a plant all by itself. But when you try to pull it up, you discover that all the blades of crabgrass in a particular piece of lawn share the same roots and the same nourishment system. . . . Human beings may appear to be separate, but our connections are deep and we are inseparable." In learning to care about each other as friends, to learn with each other in groups, and to realize the connections between content and process, theory and application, disagreement and compromise, students move through autonomy toward interdependence. When learning experiences make room for feelings as well as ideas and beliefs and facts, integration and integrity flourish. With the skills to analyze objectively and appreciate subjectively, to respect the self and others, and to align individual goals with those of the larger community, students are well prepared for purposeful responsibility.

FIFTEEN

Student Development Programs and Services

In drafting this chapter, we have debated about what to call professionals who have previously been referred to as student personnel administrators or student services or student affairs professionals. A survey of forty-seven graduate preparation programs found that some combination of the words *college, student, personnel,* and *services* was used by twenty-nine programs in 1987. *Development* was part of the program description at only three institutions (Keim, 1991, pp. 233–234). We would like to see the term used more often. The old vocabulary conveys an image of managers moving "personnel" through the system or staff members dispensing services to consumers. Schlossberg, Lynch, and Chickering (1989, p. 12) make the following recommendation:

> We suggest shifting the emphasis to a point where we see ourselves as educators who make fundamentally useful educational contributions pertinent to the educational objectives of our institutions. Such a shift calls for a very different way of thinking about our professional roles, the criteria for program evaluation, the kinds of professional prepara-

tion and ongoing professional development required, and the nature of our interactions with students, faculty, and administration. It also means that we must actively work to shift the way our faculty and administrative colleagues see us. But the change must begin at home, with us. The language, self-perceptions, and behaviors of "service" point us in the wrong direction. As an expression of this shift, we recommend a change in terminology, replacing *student personnel services* with *student educational services* and replacing *student personnel professionals* with *student development professionals*.

Student development professionals are once again at a crossroads in their interesting history. Having evolved from their early role as wardens enforcing proper behavior and clerks preparing rosters and recording grades, they defined a profession grounded in concern for all aspects of the students' college experience. Despite the trend toward specialized administrative functions, they embraced a holistic philosophy and a growing body of theory and research on student development. This philosophy was reinforced when they met in conference, shared ideas, and studied in graduate schools. Well into the 1970s, they proactively defined themselves as equal partners with faculty in educating students. Yet often their actual status and mission did not match these aspirations.

During the 1980s and 1990s, changing demographics and reductions in state, federal, and local funding forced many institutions to reduce or reorganize student development functions. More resources were shifted toward basic support services for students who were increasingly diverse in age, ethnicity, ability, and attitude. While invoking student development as the lasting outcome of what they did, many practitioners had less time to reflect, experiment, and communicate with colleagues, less money to support in-house workshops or travel to conferences, and fewer staff members to move students and information to the next destination. More time was devoted to crisis management. Facing recurring budget cuts, increasing com-

plaints, and growing demands for compliance and accountability by outside agencies, few staff members had energy left
to focus on the applications of student development theory.

Yet it is important for student development staff not to
lose sight of their responsibility as advocates for the education
of "the whole student." They must periodically step back from
the fray, update their knowledge, and redefine their identity and
purpose within the changing realities of higher education. They
must redefine their relationship with faculty and revitalize their
ways of working with students, incorporating student development principles into systems that fit today's environment, or they
risk becoming expendable cogs in a costly machine. They must
articulate their role and relevance, or they risk being viewed
as hand-holders or technicians ancillary to the "real" educators —
the tenured faculty. If teaching faculty are the bricks, student
development staff members are the mortar. Both must be in good
condition or the building will crumble.

Many student development professionals do not have a
clear sense of their professional heritage, which was evolved
along with changes in the role of colleges and universities. Though
many faculty feel that students' physical, interpersonal, emotional, and ethical development is none of their concern, many
historians report that until relatively recently, the primary mission of higher education and the most important function for
faculty has been the shaping of character. Only in the last
hundred years has the emphasis shifted, as faculty focused more
on scholarship and teaching and less on developing their students as individuals. Student development professionals picked
up the fallen gauntlet, although they did so by a circuitous route.

A Historical Overview

The fascinating history of higher education reveals the roots of
the student development profession and sheds light on its evolution. For more than eight hundred years, master educators
have brought their knowledge to younger scholars, most of whom
were literally bachelors. Through its first six centuries, the college experience occurred in small groups, in pastoral, semi-

monastic settings, and in close quarters with authorities deeply concerned about their students' moral character. American colleges trace their ancestry to medieval Europe, to a time when books were rarities and clerics pored over ancient manuscripts preserved and duplicated by the only institution older than the college — the church. It is hard to picture colleges the size of a parsonage, a financial aid office with iron-bound chests full of daggers, silver cups, furs, or whatever students pledged as collateral for loans, and libraries with a single shelf of books.

Such were the first colleges at Oxford, founded in the thirteenth century as self-governing religious foundations. The prototype, Merton College, had sixteen names on its admissions rolls in 1285 and twelve books, including Aquinas, Aristotle, Augustine, the Book of Job, and "Half the psalter, glossed" (Morris, 1987, p. 23). No wonder that lecturing was the preferred mode of instruction, since the texts could probably not be borrowed or purchased. Original documents describing these colleges reveal the founders' rarefied vision of college life. Scholars "devoted to the study of letters, or Arts or Philosophy, the Canons, or Theology" were to obey the Warden — "a man of circumspection in spiritual and temporal affairs." They were to "dress as nearly alike as possible" and dine in silence at their common table while listening to a reader. When in their chambers, they were to speak in Latin and "live meekly in fellowship, without burdening each other, but sharing all things fairly" (pp. 20–22).

We can only imagine what the townspeople thought of these scholars in their fur-trimmed gowns, immersed in disputations about whether more than one angel could occupy the same place, multiplying in Roman numerals, and studying to be priests but probably acting like adolescents. Lofty ideals and actual behavior probably did not match, to the consternation of the wardens and the local citizens. One legend is that the mortarboard cap originated when students stuffed their writing slates into their knit caps, freeing their hands to defend themselves from hostile townspeople. We can imagine why they were hostile when we read an account of a visitor to Magdalen College in 1507 reporting on early student conduct problems:

The college was found to be in a terrible state, its functions in disorder and its Fellows spitefully at odds. Among the complaints made to the inquiry were these:

Stokes was unchaste with the wife of a tailor.

Stokysley baptized a cat and practiced witchcraft.

Gregory climbed the great gate by the tower, and brought a Stranger into College.

Kendall wears a gown not sewn together in front.

Pots and cups are very seldom washed, but are kept in such a dirty state that one sometimes shudders to drink out of them.

Gunne has had cooked eggs at the Taberd in the middle of the night.

Kyftyll played cards with the butler at Christmas time for money.

Smyth keeps a ferret in College, Lenard a sparrow-hawk, Parkyns a weasel, while Morcott, Heycock and Smyth stole and killed a calf in the garden of one master Court [p. 39].

In 1636, the same year that Harvard was founded, William Laud, Archbishop of Canterbury and chancellor of Oxford University, organized "the jumbled mass of rules and statutes by which Oxford confusedly governed itself" into Laud's Code (Morris, 1987, p. 78). Among other things, it barred students from "idling about," from going anywhere where wine or the "Nicotian herb" was sold, from visiting houses where harlots were kept, or from "every sort of sport or exercise, whence danger, wrong or inconvenience may arise to others." All stage players, rope dancers, or fencers were to be incarcerated. Under no condition was football to be played. Students were not to carry bows and arrows, hunt wild animals with hounds, walk publicly in boots, or encourage the growth of curls. The vice-chancellor and heads of colleges were to publish their opinions about any new and unusual fashion in dress, in the event that anyone was in doubt about appropriate decorum. The lecturers were to follow the opinion of those who dissented least from prevailing religious or philosophical canons (pp. 78-80).

The Statutes of Harvard were patterned after those of Cambridge (Hofstadter and Smith, 1961, pp. 8-10). They directed the students to read the scriptures twice a day, to publicly repeat sermons whenever called on, to honor their parents, elders, and tutors by being silent in their presence, and to "studiously redeem their time" by diligently praying and studying. Students were to "eschew not only oaths, lies, and uncertain rumors, but likewise all idle, foolish scoffing, frothy wanton words and offensive gestures." College personnel must have expended a great deal of energy on enforcement efforts.

The codes of conduct suited Puritan settlers. Schools were established to produce literate church members who could read the Bible for themselves, and pious young men who would train as ministers at Harvard (Monroe, 1972). William and Mary College, founded in 1693, offered not only classes for promising colonials, but also continuing education for the Indians, who were instructed in Christianity (Hofstadter and Smith, 1961, pp. 39-49). Yale, founded in 1701, drafted statutes instructing students to "live Religious, Godly and Blameless Lives according to the Rules of God's Word, diligently Reading the holy Scriptures, the Fountain of Light and Truth" (Hofstadter and Smith, 1961, pp. 49-61). The long list of rules of conduct specified punishments for violators, mostly fines collected by vigilant tutors who lived on the collections. One shilling was charged for picking locks, going to a tavern, using cudgels, or jumping out of windows; two shillings for loud, indecent noises, "turbulent words," or wearing women's apparel.

In these colleges, the president, trustees, faculty, and tutors literally stood in for parents, imposing a heavily moralistic discipline and a biblical perspective on the world. They lived with the students, taught class, conducted chapel services, and punished and prayed over backsliders. In their own way, they were united in their commitment to developing their students into respectable citizens. Fenske (1989b, pp. 8-9) states:

Surely the religiously oriented college that dominated the American higher education scene for two-thirds of its history provided a setting in which student services, although not yet differentiated and professionalized, were at their zenith in the functional sense — in the sense that they involved all participants and were inseparable from the academic program. Contemplation of these early models tempts one to speculate that only in a setting in which an absolute unifying principle (such as a specific orthodox religion) permeates the life and aims of a college can the field of student services, with its concern for the whole person, become a full partner in the academic enterprise. But that source of unity is gone from all but a small minority of present-day colleges, a minority that constitutes only a tiny fraction of total U.S. enrollment.

As American society grew more pluralistic, secular, and technological, single-minded approaches to student behavior and course content were challenged. Thomas Jefferson attempted a more secular approach, proposing that higher education was a public trust and establishing the University of Virginia in 1825 as a state-supported, nondenominational enterprise; it even gave students the right to choose which curriculum to follow. Yet the private colleges clung to their classical curriculum, following the Harvard model. Instead of seeing the writing on the wall, they wrote the Yale Report of 1828, denouncing the upstart Jefferson and defending their narrow curriculum and sectarian control. After all, how could something as precious as a college be entrusted to the whims of state legislators?

This set the development of secular higher education back for several decades, and along with it, the relaxation of the *in loco parentis* relationship colleges had with students. Yet an increasingly literate population in a growing agricultural and industrial society needed colleges responsive to their needs. Other developments reinforced pressure for change. The opening of the frontiers democratized the West. Capitalists wanted educated citizens as better workers and more affluent consumers. Free elementary schools proliferated, as did special interest colleges, and "normal schools" needed to train teachers. Finally the landmark Morrill Land Grant Act of 1862 created a federal funding base for large state universities. Thousands of students began to look beyond high school for places at the fledgling land-grant institutions. Many faculty winced at the inevitable lowering of standards. The University of Wisconsin grudgingly accepted poorly educated farm boys to fill out its enrollment, and the first remedial courses were born (Fenske, 1989b, p. 12).

The trend toward egalitarianism in admissions paralleled a shift in faculty orientation — away from students and toward their own departments and scholarly interests. Allied with neither the trustees and presidents nor with the students, they became their own constituency group. American instructors doing graduate work at prestigious German research universities returned with their hosts' laissez-faire attitude about what students did outside the classroom. Faculty priorities shifted away from surrogate parenting. The trend was toward less constraint and more freedom of choice as the classical curriculum fragmented into proliferating disciplines. The brightest students were taught how to do scholarly research, not how to become good citizens or well-integrated human beings. Yet someone had to be responsible for enrolling students, handling discipline problems, and "supervising such daring activities as unmarried young men and women dining together in a campus dining hall" (Fenske, 1989a, p. 30). The deans of women and men charged with warding off the dangers of coeducation joined the first deans of students as members of the nineteenth-century college student development profession.

Other managers were appointed as registrars, deans of men or women, or admissions directors. They became part of "the administration" — a group distinct from the academics. As the twentieth century approached, students began to look to each other for social and intellectual stimulation, forming literary societies, athletic squads, debating teams, and sororities and fraternities. Accordingly, universities hired student activities advisers.

Some leading educators noticed the growing rift between the purely academic faculty concerns and the other aspects of student life. A. L. Lowell became president of Harvard in 1909 and warned "that the recent emphasis upon graduate education and research scholarship was sabotaging the unique function of the American college. Undergraduates must be helped to develop as well-rounded individuals as well as scholars" (Brubaker and Rudy, 1976, p. 335). Woodrow Wilson agreed and as president of Princeton, developed a Quadrangle Plan to recreate the collegial atmosphere at Oxford and Cambridge (Fenske, 1989a, p. 32). Nevertheless, faculty continued to institutionalize the German model, and looked primarily to ever-more-specialized scholarly work as their primary purpose.

Concern for the students' overall development was kept alive by "student personnel movement" after World War I. Mental testing and counseling techniques used extensively by the Army were applied on the campuses. Student health services, intercollegiate and intramural athletics, and placement services joined the field, which was differentiating and specializing as the curriculum diversified. The pragmatic ideas of John Dewey and other humanists reinforced the notion of the "whole student," who learned best when there was a balance of thought with action. In 1937, the Committee on College Personnel of the American Council on Education published a philosophical statement and a list of twenty-three specific student services that should be adapted to the environment of each college and university. It called on educational institutions to consider the student as a whole, taking into account intellectual capacity and achievement, emotional make-up, physical condition, social relationships, vocational aptitudes and skills, moral and religious values, economic resources, and aesthetic appreciations (American Council on Education, 1937, p. 1). In 1949, another committee reaffirmed the basic philosophy, and added new commitments to strengthening democracy in every phase of living, expanding international programs, and applying creativity in solving social problems (American Council on Education, 1949).

These statements guided the profession through the expansive 1950s and 1960s. Social scientists interested in studying college student behavior added new findings. Bolstered by the work of Erikson, Chickering, Perry, Kohlberg, and Sanford, the Council of Student Personnel Associations in Higher Education (COSPA) reaffirmed the developmental orientation of student personnel work in 1975. Self-directedness was the primary goal, and collaboration with faculty and administration was the recommended mode (Council of Student Personnel Associations in Higher Education, 1975, pp. 1–2). The commission report introduced the term "student development specialist" to identify student services staff, saying that "in general, faculty tend to emphasize content, and student development specialists tend to emphasize process" (p. 3).

The Unrealized Potential

Despite the grounding of the profession in holistic and developmental principles, a gap between the rhetoric and the reality has existed. Knefelkamp (1974) identified one reason that the potential of student services had not been realized: administrators and faculty members continued to view student services as secondary to the real work of the institution. After analyzing theorists and critics since 1950, Knefelkamp (1974, p. 31) concluded that the profession itself stopped short of practicing what it preached. It "recognized the interrelationship between the intellectual and the affective but consistently failed to enter both areas of the student's life." Some did not view the classroom as a legitimate setting for student development strategies, advocating educational efforts outside the classroom in response to students' needs and difficulties, rather than a cooperative model of student development professionals using their knowledge to collaborate with faculty in designing more effective teaching and advising methods (Mueller, 1961).

By continuing down this road, Korn (1966, p. 138) says "we have abandoned our responsibility; student development is left to chance or to those with little zest for it." Despite advocacy about taking individual differences into account and recognizing the interrelationship of intellectual and emotional maturity, developmental perspectives fell on deaf ears. Parker

(1970) called for a "permeable membrane" between in-class and out-of-class activities that allows faculty, students, and student services staff to move into each sphere. But in most colleges, there is a wall rather than a membrane, and the result is second-class citizenship for student development professionals. As long as the transmission and advancement of knowledge are valued over the development of the whole student, this pattern will continue.

Despite the lines of demarcation, the theme of collaboration recurs whenever leaders convene to draft statements of purpose. One of the most recent is the 1984 Traverse City Statement, *Toward the Future Vitality of Student Development Services* (American College Testing Program, 1985). Drafted by student development leaders for two-year colleges at a colloquium sponsored by the National Council on Student Development and the American College Testing Program, it affirmed "integrating student development into the educational experience" as one of seven major goals:

> This challenge emphasizes collaboration with faculty and other campus educators to incorporate student development concepts into the college mission, academic program competencies, co-curricular programs, and, ultimately, course objectives. . . . At the local level, student development professionals should:
>
> a. Assume leadership roles in integrating student development concepts into college missions and expected student outcomes.
> b. Assess student needs in terms of development.
> c. Provide for student development through co-curricular programs.
> d. Collaborate with instructional leaders in integrating student development competencies into academic programs and courses.
> e. Enhance their own knowledge and competencies in student development [p. 5].

In 1989, some of the participants in the 1984 colloquium returned to Traverse City, along with thirty-five other leaders, to review progress and make further revisions. They added one to the above list: "Collaborate with institutional leaders in integrating student development philosophies into all components of the institution" (Keys, 1990, p. 32), perhaps reflecting the realization that without support from the highest levels in the institution, change is difficult. They reviewed results of a survey of two-year college chief student services officers across the country, inquiring about their use of the 1984 Traverse City Statement. The survey found fairly high levels of support for the value of the student development objectives listed above, as well as a considerable degree of personal involvement in achieving them on the part of the respondents. Institutional accomplishment of the objectives, however, tended to receive lower ratings. There were generally positive reports on how student development was being integrated into the education experience—for example, "College mission statements have been reviewed and revised to include student development concepts"; "Institutions are requiring student assessment programs prior to enrolling so that students' needs can be identified and addressed when they enter the institution"; "Student life programs are adding leadership programs for all students. Orientation and College Life programs are now being offered as credit courses" (Keys, 1990, p. 22).

Colloquia such as these help institutional leaders reflect on their mission and recommit to the goals of the profession. But how many staff members attend such meetings or read their proceedings? How many have initiated collaborative efforts with faculty? How many have challenged their institutions to measure the actual impact of college mission statements or encouraged their staff to update their knowledge of theory, research, and innovative models? Like students struggling with identity by making hard choices, student development professionals must constantly choose between a demanding array of priorities. Some may feel that studying theory is low on the priority list, and applying it may be feasible in residential colleges with large counseling centers but is less possible on a bare-bones budget. Many student development staff members remain invisible to faculty, unless they serve with them on campus wide committees. If they are only regarded as helpers or bureaucrats who get students registered, advised, insured, informed, controlled, and graduated, the staff may also see these tasks as their only *raison d'être*.

When a college commits to a student development framework as a guide for practice in and out of the classroom, it is newsworthy. One rare example is Ursuline College, a small Roman Catholic women's college near Cleveland, Ohio. After trying to refine their educational mission, the faculty found *Women's Ways of Knowing: The Development of Self, Mind, and Voice* (Belenky, Clinchy, Goldberger, and Tarule, 1986). "We latched onto it; we said, 'This is written about our students,' explained Sister Rosemarie Carfagna, who is director of Ursuline Studies, the core curriculum required of all students, which has now been reorganized on the basis of the book's developmental model (Chira, 1992, p. B7). The first-year seminar encourages students to find their own voice through writing introspective essays and to express their own opinions, not what they think the teacher wants. The second-year seminar is an interdisciplinary humanities course focusing on cities in different historical eras and incorporating material on the lives of women who lived there. Students read classic works like Machiavelli's *The Prince* but also feminist critiques of the texts. They also read about the lives of feminist critics. In the third year, students are asked to integrate both the personal and the academic approaches so that ethical and personal commitments drive their academic and career choices. Asked what Ursuline graduates will have that they did not have before, Sister Rosemarie replied, "Moxie."

We would like to believe that more faculty members will discover ways to apply student development theories to their teaching. But in the meantime, student development professionals must do what they can to use theory as a guide for practice and a foundation for program evaluation. Applying developmental principles does not require increased staff, residence halls, large counseling staffs, or endless one-to-one dialogues with students. It involves looking through developmental lenses, listening for readiness, tuning our ears to turning points. It can occur in short interactions—in questions that foster independent thinking, in careful phrasing that stimulates informed choices rather than acquiescence, in challenging students to learn from consequences and consider the larger community. As one chief student affairs officer said, "If we did not allow students to wrestle with a task, and we dealt with it for them, as a parent would for a child, they wouldn't develop or learn to be fully functioning, effective, independent adults, which is our desired outcome. We challenge them to take on as much responsibility for self-management as appropriate and at the same time provide the support that they need" ("Student Development: A Combination of Challenge and Support," 1991, p. 2). Ten minutes of respectful listening can boost self-esteem and provide a reason for a return visit. One decision that makes the institution more supportive and responsive can make a difference. These are the minimums, but with a review of developmental models and support from deans and department heads, staff can create ways to work smarter, not harder, to let go of what has been done out of habit, and to be intentional about new priorities that lead to measurable student development outcomes.

Fostering Development Through Three Service Clusters

Schlossberg, Lynch, and Chickering (1989) proposed viewing student development programs and services from a student's point of view, as clusters of necessary functions in sequence. One cluster involves *entering services*—preadmissions, recruitment, admissions, financial aid, employment, orientation, educational planning, academic skills assessment, prior learning assessment, and registration. *Supporting services* assist students in moving through the institution and enrich their in-class experiences with developmental cocurricular activities; they include academic support services, career development, life and personal counseling, educational programming, recreational, athletic, and cultural activities, health services and wellness programs, student government and organizations, residential life, child care, support groups, and developmental mentoring. *Culminating services* assist students in the transition to work or further education; they include practica and internships, academic review and graduation assessment, job search, résumé-writing, interviewing, placement services, and development transcript review. Overlap exists among the clusters. For example, orientation may extend into the supporting services cluster when it becomes an introductory course. And educational planning needs to be done periodically throughout the college career. Using this format, we will describe some examples of how student development programs and services can have developmental impact.

Entering Services

The transition to college begins with admissions information and continues throughout the student's first term. Admissions officers may not see the applications they design or the interviews they conduct as tools for student development; yet they may provide the first stimulus for students to reflect on what competencies they have developed, what vocational goals they wish to achieve, and what strengths and experiences have contributed to their identity. Careful admissions counseling sets the stage for students of all ages to begin the rite of passage to a new sense of self.

Recruiters and orientation coordinators can make a clear connection between daily practice and the fostering of autonomy, relationships, and purpose. Western Washington University created a developmental approach to freshman orientation based on these three vectors (Copeland and Cress, 1988). The process involves three transitional time periods: (1) exploration and assessment, (2) formalizing commitment, and (3) initial assimilation. The sequential steps are aimed at supporting gradual disconnection from parents and increasing self-reliance, first involving students and parents in their own communities, then bringing them both to the campus to engage in separate activities, and finally bringing students to disengage from their parents by moving onto the campus or beginning classes. This sequential approach also addresses students' limited readiness to take in all the orientation information in one sitting. Because it is a model program, we will describe it in some detail.

Western Information Nights begin in the fall, often at community colleges. During the winter break, current students, accompanied by admissions and financial aid counselors, visit their alma maters to talk about campus life with high school seniors. High school seniors are also invited to visit the university, spend the night in a residence hall, and attend classes for a day, escorted by student advisers. In the spring, students and parents are invited to Western Preview Day on campus, where they can tour the campus, attend departmental presentations, and ask questions of representatives from various university offices. Next, a summer orientation/advising/registration program called SUMMERSTART is given in early August. Parents and students spend a full day on campus in separate programs, meeting for only an hour at lunch and late in the afternoon for a closing reception. In the fall, there are workshops on study skills, choosing a major, time management, and test anxiety, and an information fair where clubs and activities are represented. Parents are encouraged to visit their students' new home in a Fall Parents' Open House. In mid-November, students attend a mandatory Freshman Advising Night. Meeting in the same small groups formed at SUMMERSTART, they assess their fall quarter performance, receive assistance in planning a winter quarter schedule of classes, and ask about any university policies that may be unclear.

An important aspect of the program is providing the same information to both students and parents, which helps reduce the dissonance that can be caused when one party or the other gains too much or too little information. It also reduces anxiety about the impending separation from home. The importance of student responsibility is explained to parents, who are encouraged to redefine themselves as extensions of the university's referral network instead of as agents acting on behalf of their offspring. Peer advisers lead new students through a separate session aimed at answering immediate questions, such as where to eat, when to buy books, whether to schedule all one's classes before noon, and so on. In facilitating interaction with each other while learning the system, advisers foster both instrumental autonomy and the development of relationships. Such interactions complement the icebreakers in residence halls, the assignment of roommates based on personal assessment questionnaires, and an extensive intramural program.

The designers of the orientation process understood the relationship between growing self-confidence and increasing clarity about the physical environment, the services available, and the way things are done. Peer advisers model knowledgeability and faculty-student teamwork as they work with faculty partners. Advisers help students feel less anonymous by eliciting shared personal information (Where are you from? Where are you going to live? What major are you thinking about and why? What are you looking forward to? What are you anxious about?) They engage the group in accomplishing a common task that has immediate relevance (learning how to read the schedule of classes and fill out their fall registration form). They also introduce the students to general education requirements by leading them through a specially designed minicatalogue of introductory courses, which describes not only the content, but also the size of the class and the basis for grading. They highlight courses in disciplines that might seem exotic (environmental studies, liberal studies, or American cultural studies). The orientation process reinforces exploration of diverse intellectual possibilities and gives permission to students to sample broadly before committing to a major. It also introduces the liberal arts requirements as tools for developing purpose.

Juniata College in Pennsylvania takes a similar approach. Orientation is designed as an interactive program for both parents and students. New students have the opportunity to interact with other freshmen and upperclass orientation leaders. The program addresses personal, social, and developmental concerns for parents and students. An administrator explains that "orientation is a time when we begin to educate students and parents to this idea of student development theory. We stress that there's an underlying rationale for why we do what we do. We want students to go through a developmental process" ("Student Development: A Combination of Challenge and Support," 1991, p. 2). For example, occasionally parents cannot understand why freshman student-athletes are not permitted to live together. The staff explains that they are deliberately trying to enlarge the circle of interactions beyond the familiar teammates and that residence hall assignments integrate new students with upper-level ones in order to encourage interaction.

A different orientation process may be needed for adult learners. They may be especially heartened by a panel of returnees talking about what helped and how they succeeded. But like younger freshmen, they are part of a larger familial and social system, and movement toward competence, autonomy, interdependence, and freedom from anxiety may be fostered when partners, spouses, and children feel oriented and when relevant concerns are addressed.

Other offices can help the transition to college and the broadening of perspectives. Admissions officers can work with graphic artists to create materials designed not only to sell the college but also to present it accurately so that students begin to establish a realistic connection. Registrars can design class schedules to highlight alternative ways to gain credit—through contracts, telecourses, self-study labs, assessment of life and work experience, and so on. Institutional researchers can integrate their questions into the design of the admissions application, and computerized data-management systems can be tailored for advising purposes. Automation of the more mundane advising tasks, such as reviewing transcripts, checking prerequisites, and monitoring progress, frees up academic advisers to spend more time building mentoring relationships.

Assessment of incoming students has focused on reading, writing, and mathematical skills and on placement at appropriate course levels. Fewer institutions have created "upstream intervention" systems for students on the basis of specific predictor variables. Variables might include economic, physical, or academic disadvantages; low high school grades; a lapse of many years since the last school experience; low scores on measures of career decidedness, study habits, and attitudes; or barriers identified during an intake interview. On the basis of "early warning" signals, students would then be required to take developmental or orientation courses designed to prepare them psychologically for college level work. This may be especially critical for community college students. Rouche (1990, pp. 4–5) proposes that community college orientation programs should be required for all entering first-time degree-seekers, and that the major goal should be to socialize them and transmit the values and expectations of the college.

> More important, these students need some quality time with faculty and/or counseling mentors. The objective of mentor relationships as part of orientation is to leave the student with the feeling that a faculty member or counselor honestly cares about the student, is available, friendly, open, communicative, and exhibits keen listening skills as well. . . . I would also recommend that entry-level orientation be followed by a freshman year course, titled "college success" or "college survival," which provides much needed reinforcement and assistance to students throughout the first year. These courses have also been researched and found to pay tremendous dividends in college-wide retention efforts.

Just as employees need different styles of supervision based on their ability and motivation, so college students need different levels of structure and support. A reactive approach informs students about counseling services or special programs and hopes they will seek them out. A more proactive, individualized approach would monitor progress, offer support as needed, and record outcomes. On the basis of thorough assessment at entrance, students who might benefit from extra support (those typically called "high risk") would be identified and invited or required to meet regularly with an adviser, who would maintain contact, assess problems, suggest interventions, and check on results. This person would coordinate with all the other faculty and staff who are interacting with the advisee during the first term, and if appropriate, the adviser would request progress reports and encourage attendance at study tables, skills workshops, or tutoring programs. At the end of the term, another assessment would determine if the student is making progress. If so, structured support could be reduced.

Whether staff members adopt a case-management approach or a required orientation course, or whether they offer voluntary information sessions or well-designed student guides, the system should be evaluated to see if it helps the critical transition during the students' first term. Those who master the logistics, bond with other students, discover mentors, and find the institution congenial will more likely persist and reap the longer-range developmental benefits.

Supporting Services

Support services and programs assist students to move successfully through the college or university. We have used the term "cocurricular" to highlight the value of college experiences that are not only "extra" or outside the curriculum but complementary to it and equally important. The term can also refer to new additions to traditional course offerings, such as seminars on becoming a successful student, coping or communication skills, career exploration, or wellness. The medieval curriculum was circumscribed. Enrollment was limited to courses in the Seven Liberal Arts—Grammar, Logic, Rhetoric, Music, Arithmetic, Geometry, and Astronomy (such as it was in the days before Copernicus), the Three Philosophies—Moral, Metaphysical, and Natural, and the Two Tongues—Greek and Hebrew (Morris, 1987). The categories now are slightly different, but students pursuing academic programs must typically choose from a menu of English and other humanities courses, social science classes, and mathematics and science courses, all more or less interchangeable within their categories. To many faculty members, the configuration is as sacred as the classical curriculum was to the leaders of the English and colonial colleges. And students are not inclined to stray from the more familiar textbook-bound introductory courses. Proposals for adding new disciplines, let alone developmental or "nonacademic" course options have often expired under the weight of committee debates, scorn from faculty, and resistance from students.

But there have been some worthy experiments. For example, researchers at the University of Maryland saw the importance of certain nonacademic factors that affected student success. They reviewed the literature on retention and found some key factors associated with student success: good interpersonal relationships, student involvement, faculty-student interaction, commitment to personal values and goals, a successful leadership experience, a positive self-concept, and the availability of a support person (McIntire and others, 1992). They looked for new ways to help students (1) improve time management and study skills, (2) discuss academic concerns and receive weekly guidance about course progress, (3) identify career choices and skills, (4) improve interactions with faculty, (5) improve interpersonal skills, and (6) facilitate involvement in college activities. They explain why they addressed these goals through a course:

> Programs with these goals are not unusual on college campuses. Volunteer workshops are often available on study skills, campus adjustment, or career development. But in our pilot projects, such volunteer workshops compared unfavorably with a required course for college credit. Workshops did not make strong demands for students' time and their impact on retention rates was narrow and short-lived. A single extracurricular program cannot address the variety of factors related to retention. But a regular college course can provide the time and motivation for students to address many problems. Enrollment in a course ensures a minimum level of attendance, attention, and motivation, in a format where faculty are comfortable making demands of students and providing rewards for their efforts [p. 301].

A three-credit course (General Education 100) was designed to provide weekly practice in academic and social skills as well as teach time management, test-taking and writing skills. In addition, it provided for exploration of majors and careers. An extensive workbook helped students record their progress in these areas and in a concurrent course chosen by the student for special effort and evaluation. "At-risk" students (based on high school grade-point average and standardized test scores) were required to take General Education 100. Others chose it on the advice of academic counselors. The behavioral emphasis required students to apply techniques learned in the class. "All students, for example, recorded the amount of time they spent studying, devised a personalized plan for reinforcing their study behavior, and submitted a report on their success in a baseline and treatment design" (p. 303). The authors compared the performance of 407 students who completed the course over a two-year period (fall 1988 through spring 1990) with a matched sample of freshmen. Those who completed the course had a semester grade-point average one point higher than their counterparts in the control group; retention rates were also consistently higher. The outcome probably signifies greater movement along the developing competence vector and reflects enhanced self-esteem.

Many decision makers hesitate to screen students or mandate a structured approach to retention, even if it is in the students' best interest. It smacks of the old *in loco parentis* approach. Others balk at the time and energy needed to sell the idea, organize materials, recruit and train instructors, and manage the process. Yet poor performance during the initial semesters can leave students in debt, ineligible for financial aid, and out in the job market with few skills. This is especially true for community college students who have no other higher education option. K. P. Cross (1971) warned that the open door could become the revolving door unless colleges adapted their teaching methods to the "new students"—those least prepared for college work. Rouche (1990) advocates an intrusive approach—a kind of "tough love" translated into mandatory placement policies, coordinated by student development staff who keep communication "up front and personal" and who bring faculty and administrators together to clarify their expectations for students and the conditions for remaining at the institution.

A parallel issue involves behavior problems, which seem to be increasing on campus. Dannells and Stuber (1992) report that the numbers of the emotionally disturbed may be increasing at a higher rate among college students than in the rest of the population. They propose two possible reasons: "First, many recently released psychiatric patients are encouraged to enroll in colleges and universities as a means of assisting with recovery and personal development. Second, nontraditional re-entry students, who constitute the fastest-growing segment of the student population, appear to be at a greater risk for mental and emotional problems" (p. 163). Other contributing factors may include the escalation of economic hardships, family problems, poor impulse control or learning problems, or resentment, in cases where students cannot afford their first-choice four-year institution and end up in a local college.

While many of these students can benefit from the college experience, however difficult, others are simply not ready or able to adjust and can disrupt the learning environment for others. Faculty need to feel supported by student development staff in confronting problem behavior. Some are skilled at taking students aside when they see signs of trouble and clarifying the terms for remaining in class. Others allow disruptive behavior to continue until they run out of patience and insist that the student be removed. Student development staff must then step in, navigating the course between confronting the behavior, respecting the student, ensuring due process, and enforcing faculty rights. Dealing with grievances takes up many stress-filled hours.

The alternative may be a consultative relationship between faculty members and the student development staff. Through workshops with academic departments, in-depth orientation for new faculty members, or proactive networking between counselors and instructors, more effective early interventions can be designed. Are students missing classes or tests? If so, are faculty encouraged to contact them and find out what the problem is? Is there a referral mechanism in place that triggers staff contact with the student? Do faculty have clear syllabi that spell out not only the objectives of the course and the reading assignments but also the consequences if students come late, miss deadlines, intimidate others, or engage in academic dishonesty? Can they initiate respectful but direct communication when inappropriate behavior occurs? Student development professionals can provide assistance in strategizing with faculty members and in focusing on ways to develop student responsibility, while assuring consistency and due process.

Students having difficulty in class may also need work on managing emotions and shifting from self-interest to interdependence. Involvement in campus activities helps the sense of belonging and respect for the rights of others. Students may learn about community values and ethical principles when they either violate the conduct code or serve in judicial systems. The latter case represents an opportunity to develop integrity. In hearing cases, reviewing disciplinary procedures, and determining sanctions, students consider moral dilemmas in a concrete way. Is the accused guilty of the alleged rule violation? What is the evidence? What was the intent? What kind of punishment fits the transgression? Are we here to punish students or to help them learn? What do we consider "inappropriate" behavior? Shall we state it as a positive expectation or as a list of prohibitions? What rights and responsibilities should students have? By serving on hearing committees, students also benefit from watching faculty members, administrators, and staff members grapple with the arguments. The need for rules has not disappeared, although paternalism declined when the German university model came into vogue and curfews and dress codes vanished in the 1960s. The challenge now is engaging students to take more responsibility for maintaining a safe and positive learning environment, becoming aware of the institution's code of conduct, and respecting the processes for enforcing and amending regulations.

Cocurricular and academic success build on each other. Programs organized by student leaders and student activities staff have traditionally provided stimulation for development as well as enjoyment. Speakers who present different perspectives, films that provide vicarious learning, exhibits that expand awareness, and discussions that clarify personal values all foster student development. Campus ministries can help students explore beliefs and strengthen commitments. Participation in student government, athletics, and organizations sharpens interpersonal skills.

Staff members can speed the process by explaining not only the procedures but also the developmental opportunities, as one administrator states: "Particularly with student organizations, we try to inform the students of our developmental approach. Many times students get caught up in the functional aspect of the organization and see the functional side as the sole purpose. We see these organizations as an opportunity for increased student development. They serve as laboratories for interpersonal and leadership skills" ("Student Development," 1991, p. 4).

Some colleges have created cocurricular transcripts, knowing that evidence of leadership ability, volunteer work, and team spirit are of value to potential employers. For example, Juniata College's Co-Curricular Transcript (CCT) lists the student's activities, describes leadership and related skill development, and records verification and evaluations by others. With the transcript in mind, advisers help students plan their cocurricular involvement:

> At the outset of each academic year, special programs highlighting learning opportunities available through co-curricular activities and explaining the CCT concept are presented to groups of students in residence hall meetings and in volunteer leadership seminars. Thereafter, the CCT Program is highly individualized. Students identify personal goals and plan their participation in appropriate student activities and organization with advisors. "For example, . . . wanted to improve her public speaking skills. As a prospective teacher, this was very important to her. We targeted the opportunities she had for public speaking during her term as student government president." . . . The completed Co-Curricular Transcript becomes a permanent part of the student's placement credentials ["The CCT," 1991, p. 11].

Student activities coordinators and residence hall staff can work creatively with students to organize special events based on student interests. Other activities may emerge spontaneously, as an administrator at the Savannah College of Art and Design in Georgia (SCAD) reports:

> In the fall quarter of 1989, SCAD's residence life staff offered 31 educational and social programs and filed 212 incident reports. Last fall, the staff offered 65 educational and social programs and filed only 52 incident reports. . . . "Resident assistants are trained," Roberson says, "to report everything they see — whether students are breaking school rules or endangering themselves or others." So he doesn't attribute the decrease in reported incidents to his RAs. Instead, he says, it's the result of a grass-roots effort to get more students involved in the educational and social aspects of residence life. "If someone is going to the museum, for instance, we encourage them to put up a flier or something and take a group of people," he says. "That's a program. You've developed something for 10 or 15 people who wouldn't have gone otherwise" ["More Programs, Less Conflict," 1992, p. 2].

The strong potential for residence halls programs to foster student development has already been discussed in Chapter Fourteen. Student development staff can also look for ways to link student activities to academic departments. Commuters are much less likely than residents to stay on campus beyond their class times to attend lectures, films, debates, concerts, exhibits, or club meetings. It may help to set aside a "common hour" at midday when classes are not scheduled. Instructors can motivate engagement by encouraging study groups, requiring attendance at relevant programs, organizing projects and field trips, inviting student development staff into their classrooms to do mini-workshops, encouraging students to carry out group projects, plan potlucks, or organize study groups or carpools. Student development staff need to plant ideas for increasing student involvement whenever possible. Pascarella and Terenzini (1991, p. 193) cite a small (but growing) and consistent body of research showing that "the most powerful forces acting on academic and social self-images may flow from students' involvement in the formal and informal academic and social systems of their institutions." Formal systems consist of classes, grades, cocurricular activities, and regulations, while informal systems involve the interactions students have with other students and faculty members.

Programs and services that support student development are consistently provided by counseling and career planning centers and offices for such special populations as returning adults, disabled students, international students, senior citizens, athletes, students of color, and so on. State-funded, grant-funded, and student government-sponsored programs add to the richness of the developmental environment, providing legal information, emergency housing or food, health information, men's centers, women's centers, multicultural centers, veterans' offices, child care, parent education, and myriad other support services. One of the most important services as regards purpose and identity is assistance with life, career, and educational planning. Ideally, such assistance involves reflection on past experience, exploration of career options and majors, clarification of values and personal goals, and tentative commitments.

Rockland Community College has incorporated all the components, plus a review of various adult development theories, learning styles, and decision-making skills, into a series of Life Skills courses. Instructors are required to take a thirty-three hour workshop before teaching the course. Since the program began with five students in 1981, more than five thousand have taken Life Skills seminars, more than ninety instructors have been trained, and a workbook has been published (Liberace and others, 1990). In 1986, an extensive evaluation was done using mail and telephone surveys (Kirschner and others, 1986). Over 75 percent of the respondents acknowledged the usefulness of all three dimensions (self-awareness, career exploration, and goal setting), but they were most enthusiastic about the self-understanding components. More than 82 percent indicated that they had been somewhat or highly successful in reaching the goals that they had set for themselves during the semester. Whether they are first-generation college students, disadvantaged, or highly able college students, the institution can add essential doses of self-confidence when it offers this kind of support. Neumann and Riesman (1980) found this to be true even for the "community college elite"—those who transfer to highly selective private colleges and universities in the northeast. The students unanimously agreed that their community college experience was the key to their success. The primary advantage they derived from the community college experience was self-confidence (p. 70).

Fewer students in two-year or four-year colleges are completing their degrees within those time limits, if they complete them at all. The National Collegiate Athletic Association surveyed 297 institutions and found that only 53 percent of the full-time freshmen who entered college in 1984 had graduated within six years (Cage, 1992). A critical factor consistently identified by retention researchers is commitment to an educational goal. For example, at the University of Massachusetts, relatively few students who select a major leave the university. "Eighty percent of the class of 1991 history majors have graduated. . . . Students with declared majors get special attention. Engineering students in danger of probation, for example, are required to meet monthly with the associate dean of the engineering school, who helps them set grade point average goals and keeps track of their progress" (Shea, 1992, p. A30). Students who find their sense of direction may need help in sticking it out through the years of closed classes and endless prerequisites. Advocates for returning adults can help by lobbying the institution to make degree requirement courses available on evenings and weekends and to make services accessible when students need them.

Culminating Services

Whether students are completing their degrees, transferring to another institution, dropping out, or stopping out, placement offices, exit interviewers, or transfer planning services can assist with a smooth departure. With a developmental perspective, these services can do more than assist with job interviewing and résumé writing, or providing information about transfer requirements and graduate schools. They can probe into how decisions are being made, how plans are being revised, and how the college has affected them. Just as the entry point should be a data-gathering opportunity—for developmental purposes as well as record keeping—the exit point is a chance to evaluate program effectiveness and provide further guidance.

Culminating ceremonies acknowledge accomplishment, celebrate relationships, and recognize a change in status, from undergraduate to alumnus, from bachelor's degree recipient to master's or doctoral degree holder, and, less obviously, from dependent, anxious newcomer to autonomous, purposeful achiever. Induction ceremonies for honors societies, awards programs, receptions, and departmental events can serve as memorable reminders that transformation has occurred and that together, a group of peers, supported by faculty, staff, and administrators, has achieved significant goals. Commencement ceremonies reconnect all members of the campus community with the traditions of academia—the clerical hoods displaying the alma mater's colors, the fur or velvet trim marking the discipline, the maces, medals, and banners heralding history and authority. Gold cords, honor society stoles, pins, certificates, and processionals through a congratulatory gauntlet of staff members can have real meaning for students and their families.

Marching together, faculty, administrators, and student development professionals look identical in academic regalia. The divisions are temporarily forgotten. Such solidarity should persist during the rest of the school year, for the good of students. As Miller and Prince (1976, p. 155) emphasize: "The institution's commitment to student development is directly proportional to the number of collaborative links between student affairs staff and faculty." If all members of the college community can refocus on the individual student, who is more precious than any publication, more complex than any curriculum, and more worthy of our attention than any committee work, we can restore the balance of personal growth and academic achievement, and can reestablish the links between the life of the mind and the life of the person.

SIXTEEN

Creating
Educationally
Powerful
Environments

To say that higher education faces critical challenges as we approach the future is to state the obvious—like telling people with measles they itch. Some say we are at a crossroads, but that metaphor is too simple. It is more like being at the center of a web, an interconnected system with numerous options. The web image is apt in another sense. An institution tries to move. The web jiggles. System forces rush forth, wrap it in bureaucratic tape, constrain its freedom, hold it in place. But higher education must move. Since the 1980s, there have been calls for reform, in keynote addresses, panel discussions, books, and reports like *Involvement in Learning: Realizing the Potential of American Higher Education* (National Institute of Education, 1984). An assessment movement, largely initiated by state legislators concerned about educational quality, has swept the country. Many students must work part-time to pay escalating tuition and fees. Serious budget reductions have forced many institutions to reorganize and reevaluate their priorities. Thus, both internal and external forces signal a need for change.

The most critical task of higher education for the twenty-first century is to create and maintain educationally powerful environments. Given our orientation, that means environments that promote human development along the seven vectors described in Part One. We know a good bit about the key ingredients of such environments. The most important elements are addressed in the preceding chapters of Part Two. But we are only beginning to understand how to create and sustain a mix of interdependent parts.

Conceptual Frameworks

Perhaps the place to begin is to decide how we want to conceptualize the major elements and their interactions. Models proposed by Pascarella (1985b) and by Weidman (1989) supply a good starting point. (See Figures 16.1 and 16.2.) Pascarella's model proposes that five sets of variables act directly and indirectly to influence student learning and cognitive development. Student background and precollege characteristics, together with the structural and organizational characteristics of the institution, determine the institutional environment. All three sets of variables influence the nature and frequency of interactions with faculty, peers, and other socializing agents. The socializing agents, the institutional environment, and student background characteristics combine to influence the quality of student effort. Finally, learning and cognitive development are directly affected by quality of effort, socializing agents, and student backgrounds.

Weidman's model is more complex. It recognizes both psychological and social structural influences on student development. Furthermore, it adds a critical distinction between the formal and informal aspects of the college experience and between normative contexts and socialization processes. It also gives explicit attention to noncognitive changes: career choices, life-style preferences, attitudes, and values. Like Pascarella, Weidman notes the importance of student background characteristics. But he also assigns an important role to normative pressures from parents and noncollege reference groups. These pressures are especially significant for adult learners, for whom the forces — positive and negative — exerted by family, peers, employers, and community relationships and activities typically play an

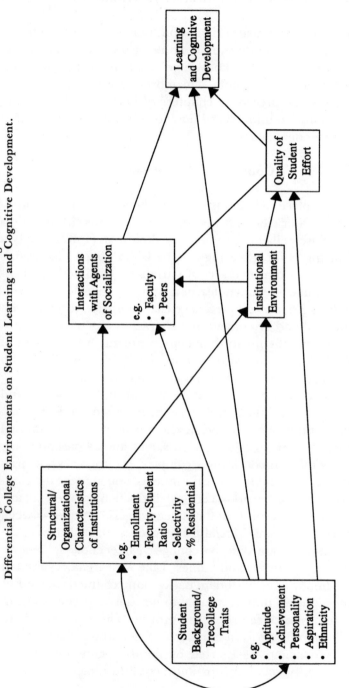

Figure 16.1. A General Causal Model for Assessing the Effects of
Differential College Environments on Student Learning and Cognitive Development.

Source: Reprinted from Pascarella, E. "College Environmental Influences on Learning and Cognitive Development: A Critical Review and Synthesis." In J. Smart (ed.), *Higher Education: Handbook of Theory and Research,* Vol. 1, 1985. By permission of Agathon Press, New York.

Figure 16.2. A Conceptual Model of Undergraduate Socialization.

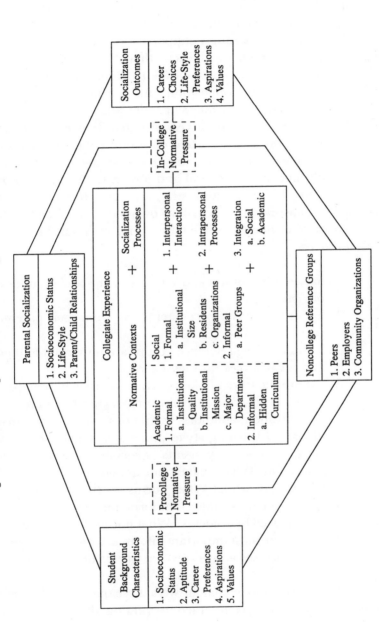

Source: Reprinted from Weidman, J. "Undergraduate Socialization: A Conceptual Approach." In J. Smart (ed.), *Higher Education Handbook of Theory and Research,* Vol. 2, 1989. By permission of Agathon Press, New York.

important role. The three sets of variables exert powerful forces that operate both before entrance and during the college experience. They can be strongly supportive or strongly constraining. Or they can conflict with each other. Employers and peers may strongly support college aspirations, family or spouses may offer active or passive opposition, and earlier experiences of failure or low self-esteem may engender ambivalence or anxiety. If all the factors are positively oriented, they can be major sources of support as the student encounters the challenges of college. If they are negative, they increase the challenge.

Both models are general and abstract. But they can be useful starting points for an institution trying to create a conceptual framework that captures its own particular characteristics. Answers to questions like these could flesh out the appropriate boxes:

What are the cultural and socioeconomic backgrounds of our students?

What are the basic forces stemming from their parental socialization?

What noncollege reference groups are important to them and what forces do they exert?

What are the students' key characteristics with regard to prior learning and academic preparation? With respect to motivation, aptitudes, aspirations, values, and career plans? In learning styles and ways of knowing?

Who are the primary agents of socialization within our institution? What are the contexts and processes through which they work? What norms do they express?

What are the most important formal normative contexts experienced by students? What norms do they express?

What are the most important informal normative contexts and processes at work? What norms do they express?

Elaborate a model that answers those questions. Describe the direct and indirect interactions among them. Then you will have created a map that identifies the aspects which most reinforce progress toward your institutional objectives and those which conflict. Use the map to identify specific arenas for action to create and sustain a more educationally powerful environment.

Challenging Traditional Assumptions

We need an approach like this to get through the smoke screen of our conventional wisdom and self-serving shibboleths. John F. Kennedy said, "The great enemy of truth is very often not the lie—deliberate, contrived, dishonest—but the myth, persistent, persuasive, and unrealistic. Too often we hold fast to the clichés of our forebears. We subject all facts to a prefabricated set of interpretations. We enjoy the comfort of opinion without the discomfort of thought" (Schlesinger, 1965, p. 238). In more stable and less complex times, when change was measured by generations, not years, the opinions of forebears reformulated in the light of personal experience could serve. But that way no longer works. Pascarella and Terenzini (1991, p. 260) repeatedly make the point that "conventional descriptors of institutional characteristics appear not to be useful predictors of impacts on student development." For example, they say that traditional definitions of quality focus more on resource wealth than on the aspects of student life and experience that strongly affect learning, such as curricular flexibility, informal interaction with faculty and peers, and a general education emphasis in the curriculum (p. 592).

> We need to focus less on a college's resources and more on such factors as curricular experiences and course work patterns, the quality of teaching, the frequency and focus of student-faculty nonclassroom interactions, the nature of peer group and extracurricular activities, and the extent to which institutional structures and policies facilitate student academic and social involvement. It is likely that colleges of equal selectivity, prestige, and financial resources may differ substantially in the more proximal influences on student development [p. 596].

If resources such as library holdings, endowment, and faculty degrees do not guarantee a high-quality education, what does? Standard answers no longer serve. Pascarella and Terenzini (1991, p. 637) criticize the assumption that selectivity, reputation, curricular emphasis, or "simpleminded outcomes (such as the quality of an institution's graduates unadjusted for their precollege characteristics)" are valid foundations for the current pecking order.

> Such conceptions imply institutional advantages and greater personal benefits that may be more mythical than real. When such notions of quality, singly or in the aggregate, receive public and presumably authoritative expression in the form of institutional rankings reported in the news media, they may be not only misleading but pernicious. Such contrasts do a disservice to non "elite" institutions, to the students and faculty members of those schools, and to the high school students and parents who rely on such rankings when choosing a college. The evidence also clearly points out the need for more useful taxonomies, for better measures of college effectiveness and quality, and for more circumspection in our beliefs and claims about the benefits of attendance at different kinds of institutions, and for moderation and candor in our recruiting literature. The quality of undergraduate education may be much more a function of what colleges do programmatically than it is of the human, financial, and educational resources at their disposal [p. 637].

These findings imply that all of us — community colleges, struggling small private institutions, underfunded public institutions — can create and sustain educationally powerful environments. We do not have to wait for a large endowment. We do not have to recruit and find the wherewithal to employ a highly credentialed, well-published faculty from "the best" graduate schools. We do not need a massive public relations campaign that gives us widespread name recognition. We do not need to raise our selection criteria whenever we get enrollment pressure. We can create a top-quality institution through rigorous planning and creative action. The knowledge base is clear and solid. Diverse institutional examples are available to us to mix, match, and adapt to our own special mission, resources and constituencies.

Principles for Good Practice — Institutional Inventory

The Principles for Good Practice in Undergraduate Education, given in Chapter Thirteen — encouraging student-faculty contact, cooperation among students, active learning, prompt feedback, time on task, high expectations, and respect for diverse talents and ways of knowing — are anchored in the research summarized above. As part of the same project, an Institutional Inventory identified six areas that can be assessed to see how well they support those "good practices": (1) Climate, (2) Academic Practices, (3) Curriculum, (4) Faculty, (5) Academic and Student Support Services, and (6) Facilities. Items from the inventory suggest the wide range of policies, practices, norms, and expectations involved ("Principles for Good Practice in Undergraduate Education: Institutional Inventory," 1989).

1. *Climate.* Pascarella and Terenzini report, "There is evidence in several areas that institutional context — a college or university's educational and interpersonal climate (and subclimates) — may more powerfully differentiate among institutions in the extent of their influence on student change than do the typical descriptors" (1991, p. 589). For example, women's colleges and historically black institutions can apparently offer the kind of climate that encourages success. "The evidence suggests that women's colleges, in particular, have tended to enhance the educational attainment of undergraduate women. . . . The evidence tends to support those who claim that a women's college provides a uniquely supportive climate for women to experience themselves and other members of their gender (both students and faculty) in a wide range of intellectual and social leadership roles" (1991, p. 383). About historically black colleges,

they say, "Much evidence . . . suggests that black students who attend predominantly white colleges and universities experience significantly greater levels of social isolation, alienation, personal dissatisfaction, and overt racism than their counterparts at historically black institutions. . . . Given this evidence, one might hypothesize that attendance at historically black colleges enhances the persistence and educational attainment of black students, and indeed most evidence supports this hypothesis. . . . Black students were significantly less likely to drop out of college if they were enrolled in a predominantly black institution" (1991, p. 380). It is also worth noting that departmental environment, particularly homogeneity of values and consensus, may have a more important influence than the discipline itself on students' attitudes (1991, p. 614).

The following items suggest some of the characteristics of a climate that would support good practices:

- Students and faculty can get together at informal campus functions.
- Students are represented on major faculty and administrative committees.
- Students are publicly recognized for superior academic performance.
- The institution successfully recruits and retains minority faculty, staff, and students.
- Senior administrators explicitly recognize faculty and student contributions to institutional policies and practices.
- Institutional publications reflect the diversity of the student body, faculty, and staff.
- The administration encourages faculty to hold high expectations for student performance.
- The president and other senior administrators are accessible to faculty members and students.
- Faculty members and administrators go out of their way to create a hospitable climate on campus.
- Senior administrators, deans, and department heads set examples of collaborative relationships.
- Students know that people work hard on this campus.

2. *Academic Practices.* Academic practices, both those which are explicitly stated and those which characterize the "hidden curriculum," have pervasive consequences for supporting or undermining educationally powerful environments. Baxter Magolda (1992) describes the impact of curricular and cocurricular experiences on intellectual development:

> Until students feel that what they think has some validity, it is impossible for them to view themselves as capable of constructing knowledge. As most participants made meaning of their experiences from absolute or transitional perspectives when the study began, they needed recognition of the value of their ideas to move forward the development of voice. Their curricular life, characterized by lack of encounter with knowledge discrepancies and by large classes with minimal interaction, initially offered no such recognition. Their cocurricular life — with its opportunities for student responsibility and for exposure to diversity via peer interactions — did foster confirmation. As they increased their responsibilities in their cocurricular lives, involvement in curricular settings, and interactions with authorities, students began to entertain the notion that teachers were human like themselves. When authority figures expressed respect for students, asked their opinions, and directly encouraged self-reliance, this confirmation helped build the student voice. Speaking in their own voice through class involvement, evaluation techniques, leadership opportunities, and peer interactions helped students come to see themselves as sources of knowledge [p. 376].

The practices necessary to support the kind of environment suggested by Baxter Magolda cut across all the Principles for Good Practice in Undergraduate Education. The inventory signals only a few elements.

- Students may test out of requirements they have already met or subjects they know.
- The institution speaks to the relationship between the course load students assume and other responsibilities, such as work, family, and community activities.
- The institution compares salary levels for male and female staff.
- The institution keeps track of how its graduates are doing.
- Students are given opportunities to evaluate academic programs and suggest changes.
- The institution imposes limitations on the number of incompletes students can carry.
- Faculty members articulate clear criteria for evaluating students' work.
- The institution sends reports to students on their progress in meeting requirements.
- Part-time faculty play other important roles besides teaching their courses.
- The institution assesses changes in student knowledge and competence during their attendance.
- Athletes are held to the same academic expectations as other students.

3. *Curriculum.* In Chapter Twelve, we examined fundamental issues underlying our assumptions about the content and process of the curriculum. Astin's research findings concerning "What Really Matters in General Education" (1991) provide another way to evaluate curriculum. They are highly consistent with the Principles for Good Practice in Undergraduate Education and with behaviors that characterize educationally powerful institutions. Astin found that contrary to conventional wisdom, the form and content of general education programs—issues on which faculty spend inordinate time, energy, and emotion—were not significant factors in explaining differences in student outcomes. Instead, the key variables were (1) student-student interaction, (2) student-faculty interaction, (3) a student-oriented faculty, (4) discussions of racial and ethnic issues with other students, (5) the number of hours devoted to studying, (6) tutoring of other students, (7) socializ-

ing with students of different race/ethnicity, (8) a student body with high socioeconomic status, (9) an institutional emphasis on diversity, (10) a faculty positive about general education, and (11) students who valued altruism and social activism. All these variables, except the one concerning socioeconomic status, are directly pertinent to the Principles for Good Practice in Undergraduate Education and the institutional characteristics suggested by the Institutional Inventory. Reflecting on these, Astin suggests that since the way we implement our general education curriculum is much more important than its form or content, we need to radically rethink our traditional institutional approaches.

Gaff's findings (1991) concerning the directions of general education reform also are consistent with our views in Chapter Twelve and in this chapter. He found increasing recognition that emphasis on liberal arts and sciences is fundamental to good undergraduate education for all students. Innovative pedagogy, higher standards, more purposeful curricular structures, with more explicit emphasis on the freshman and senior years were key areas for change. Greater attention to global studies, cultural pluralism, and interdisciplinary approaches, and increased emphasis on moral reflection and reexamining values, were also part of the mix.

The items from the Institutional Inventory suggest policies and practices consistent with Astin's and Gaff's research and with the principles. Institutions that adhere to the practices are likelier to foster the development of competence, autonomy, mature interpersonal relationships, identity, and purpose.

- Courses incorporate field experiences or hands-on applications.
- Faculty revise and monitor the general education requirements.
- Faculty revise and monitor requirements in the major.
- Students engage in independent study, contract learning, or mastery learning.
- Freshmen enroll in special programs.
- Students participate in a cooperative work program or an internship program.

- Faculty and students are aware of the knowledge, skills, and attitudes that the institution expects its students to develop by the time they graduate.
- Students pursue their own individually designed majors.
- Students enroll in interdisciplinary majors.
- Students participate in programs that help them appreciate cultural diversity.
- Students enroll in learning communities, cluster courses, or special seminars designed to help them see relationships among the subjects they study.

4. *Faculty.* In Chapter Eleven, we discussed the importance of student-faculty relationships. Research on educationally powerful departments illustrates the importance of policies, practices, and norms that encourage high-quality relationships between students and faculty. Pascarella and Terenzini (1991) recommend conscious and systematic efforts by academic departments to create environments that engage students in both intellectual and interpersonal learning and that support meaningful faculty-student interaction.

> This is not a simplistic recommendation for hand-holding or for new or specially designed programs to bring students and faculty into greater contact. Rather, it is a suggestion for shaping departmental, as well as institutional, climates in ways that will promote desirable educational outcomes. It suggests elevation of the mentor's role. Much will depend, of course, on the presence of faculty members who are genuinely interested in students and willing to make the necessary personal efforts to engage them intellectually and personally in and out of class. The need here is for faculty members who neither intimidate nor are intimidated by students and their questions but who enjoy engaging with students in the learning process. . . . Where climates not conducive to student learning are identified, they can be altered through a variety of mech-

anisms, including resource allocation processes, faculty recruitment and hiring criteria and standards, and faculty recognition, promotion, tenure, and compensation policies [p. 653].

The following items address ways to improve the quality of teaching, advising, mentoring, and collaborating to contribute to students' increasing competence, identity, and purpose:

- Faculty members are on campus and available to students during the week.
- Explicit criteria are used for evaluating teaching performance.
- Faculty members receive release time and other support to develop new ways of teaching or to keep up with their fields.
- Faculty members receive feedback concerning their performance as teachers and advisers.
- Limits on outside consulting and other private ventures are discussed with faculty members.
- Faculty take academic advising seriously.
- Annual merit increases are directly tied to faculty performance in teaching.
- Faculty members work with student services staff members.
- The institution recognizes advising as a legitimate part of the faculty's work load.
- Faculty participate in key institutional decisions, such as those concerning long-range planning, budget, and personnel.
- Faculty evaluate administrators' contributions to the educational climate of the institution.

5. *Academic and Student Support Services.* In Chapters Fourteen and Fifteen, we explored the power of student friendships and communities to influence development, and the ways that student development programs and services can be organized to support movement along all seven vectors. Pascarella and Terenzini (1991, p. 604) say that "the environmental factors that maximize persistence and educational attainment include a peer culture in which students develop close on-campus friendships, participate frequently in college-sponsored activities, and perceive

their college to be highly concerned about the individual student, as well as a college emphasis on supportive services (including advising, orientation, and individualized general education courses that develop academic survival skills)."

Resource allocations are the most tangible indicators of institutional priorities. When budget cuts are anticipated, it is often the student development programs and services that are put on the block. Yet these support services may have a direct bearing on retention and degree completion. Hedlund and Jones (1970), for example, studied the relationship between the level of student services and graduation rates at twenty-one two-year colleges in New York State. They found that all of the colleges with a ratio of one student development professional to 150 students or fewer graduated 50 percent or more of their students in two years. In contrast, only 20 percent of the colleges with a ratio of more than 1:150 graduated 50 percent in two years.

Baxter Magolda (1992, pp. 296–297) confirmed the significant impact of the "cocurriculum."

> Students' stories about their most significant experiences were often in the cocurricular realm. . . . Life beyond the classroom intensely involved students. They were consumed, sometimes positively and sometimes negatively, with roommates and other relationships. The success of these relationships often affected the students' perceptions of themselves and the quality of their academic work. Involvement in organizations helped students build confidence, learn skills, make career decisions, build friendships, develop leadership qualities, and feel comfortable. The tasks of everyday living and working yielded insights about individual functioning, responsibility to others, and values. Relationships with others in all of these contexts broadened students' perspectives about human diversity and their own place in the larger community.

The following items from the Institutional Inventory suggest some of the ingredients worth recognizing, and can be related to competence, managing of emotions, mature relation-ships, and identity.

- Counseling services address a wide range of student con-cerns.
- Students go to a writing laboratory for help with papers and writing problems.
- Time-management seminars are offered to students.
- Students with poor academic preparation receive help in im-proving their academic skills.
- Student Affairs, Academic Affairs, and the student govern-ment jointly carry out the orientation program.
- Students serve as tutors, advisers, or resource persons for other students.
- Students receive professional assistance in preparing their financial aid forms.
- Educational objectives are specified for student activities.
- Students work with the same adviser during the entire period of their enrollment.
- The institution trains faculty, staff, and students to deal with student diversity.
- Financial aid checks are available for distribution on the first day of classes for those who apply by the deadline.

6. *Facilities.* Like the fresh or polluted air we breathe, our facilities exert constant and pervasive effects on our behavior. They send clear signals about the kinds of behaviors that are expected and valued. The facilities restrict some activities and encourage others. Any teacher stuck with a theater-style class-room with fixed seats who wants to promote active exchange among students — subgroup discussions, role-plays, fish bowls, simulations, group problem solving, and the like — experiences keenly the force of facilities. Barker's (1968) work on behavior settings vividly documents how the characteristics of setting in-fluence behavior. Kitchen, bedroom, and living room behaviors are much more consistent across social classes and cultures than within the settings themselves. So are behaviors for churches, schools, bars, playgrounds, and the like. Architects know how to design spaces both inside and between buildings to promote

interaction and exchange or to insulate people from one another. Thus, attending to facilities can send strong signals and make an important difference. The inventory items suggest some areas that are worthy of attention.

- Classrooms have movable furniture.
- Comfortable places where students can meet with faculty are available.
- Study spaces conducive to quiet concentration are available.
- Recreational and athletic facilities are open evenings and weekends.
- A cafeteria, snack bar, or other eating facility is open during the day and evening.
- Students use video, laboratory, and artistic equipment on campus.
- Students use computers provided by the university.
- Parking facilities are adequate to serve the needs of students, faculty, and staff.
- Public transportation to and from the campus is available to students during the day and evening.
- Over the course of the semester, the library is open late evenings and weekends.
- Administrative and student services offices are open for students who take courses at night.

Our point here is that creating and maintaining educationally powerful environments requires thoughtful attention to these six areas: climate, academic practices, curriculum, faculty, academic and student support services, and facilities. In most of our institutions, certain policies, practices, norms, expectations, and structural characteristics work against the educational outcomes we value for students. Creating an institutional map along the lines suggested by the Pascarella or Weidman models and using some information collection strategy like that suggested by the seven principles and the Institutional Inventory can help us identify the particular aspects that it is most important to tackle first. We do not need to address everything at once. The most important thing is to identify a clear, feasible agenda for institutional development and get started. Over time, we can change the environmental characteristics that are most counterproductive and strengthen those which provide positive impetus for student development. As we do that and experience positive consequences, a truly top-quality institution develops.

Three Admonitions

As we pursue changes, we need to keep three critical admonitions in the forefront of our institutional thinking. Each of them has assumed increasing force in the last twenty years and will continue to matter in the next twenty:

1. Integrate work and learning.
2. Recognize and respect individual differences.
3. Remember that significant learning and development move in cycles of challenge and response, differentiation and integration, disequilibrium and regained equilibrium.

Integrate Work and Learning

Integrating work and learning not only adds educational power for adult learners, it also is critical for typical college-age students. The myth that "full time" students — even those in residence — spend all their time on academic study and college activities is severely outdated. Residential students at George Mason University, for example, are typical middle and upper-middle class eighteen- to twenty-five-year-olds. When surveyed in 1990, 60 percent of the full-time residential students worked more than twenty hours a week. A 1991 survey indicated that 48 percent of all students had full-time jobs. It used to be that those who pursued higher education went to college and then went to work. Partnership, marriage, and family came after college and usually after the graduate had gotten a job. Now most students pursue work and learning simultaneously and sustain a significant relationship as well. Our knowledge society requires lifelong learning. We behave accordingly. More and more of us will do so in the future. Corporate expenditures for educa-

tion and training—human resource development, human capital
formation—exceed the total expenditures for higher education.

A significant report from the National Center on Education and the Economy, *America's Choice: High Skills or Low Wages!*
(1990, pp. 42, 91), emphasizes the importance of high-quality
education for global economic competitiveness.

> Work organization changes drive the demand for
> high skills. But without a skilled workforce, more
> companies will settle into low wage organizations.
>
> As we shall now see, we are not providing the
> education and skills to a majority of our students
> and workers which will be required to support a move
> to new high performance work organizations. . . .
>
> America is headed toward an economic cliff.
> We will no longer be able to put a higher propor-
> tion of our people to work to generate economic
> growth. If basic changes are not made, real wages
> will continue to fall, especially for the majority who
> do not graduate from four-year colleges. The gap
> between the economic "haves" and "have nots" will
> widen still further and social tensions will deepen.

Improved integration of work and learning responds to the
new realities. In Chapter Thirteen, we shared Kolb's experiential learning theory. That conceptual framework is one way to
think through effective integration of concrete experiences, reflective observations, abstract concepts, active experimentation, and
application. We need collaborative relationships not only with
the world of business, but with community organizations and
volunteer programs. Such integration will help students develop
knowledge, competence, and personal characteristics that will
persist for a lifetime. It will also strengthen our direct institutional contributions to local, regional, and national needs.

Recognize and Respect Individual Differences

In Chapter Twelve, we noted the importance of recognizing and
respecting individual differences. We return to that critical point

here because that orientation needs to pervade our institutional climate, academic practices, faculty attitudes and behaviors, academic and student support services, and even thinking about facilities. In the last twenty years, we have moved from a meritocratic to an egalitarian policy framework for higher education. We have also experienced dramatic increases in the diversity of students enrolled at most institutions. Coping with diversity in academic preparation, socioeconomic status, race, ethnicity, national origin, age, and gender has become our most significant challenge. Although the research base is still skimpy, it is sufficient to suggest significant interactions between individual differences and varied aspects of our institutional environment. From personal experience as well as from research findings, we know about some of the ways that individual differences such as prior academic preparation, gender, race, ethnicity, and motivation influence outcomes like academic achievement, persistence, and degree completion rates. We know about similar interactions for individual differences in learning styles, personality type, and stages of ego development, intellectual and ethical development, and cognitive-moral development. It is clear that diversity will only increase in the years ahead. It is also clear that if we are unable to deal with it, we are likely to face increasing social conflict, a two-tier society, and economic stagnation.

The impact of a given curriculum, course, teacher, residence hall, or fellow student will vary according to the characteristics of the student experiencing the situation or person. Thirty years of diverse studies testing and elaborating on Helson's (1964) *adaptation-level theory*—which maintains that judgments are relative to prevailing internal norms and adaptation levels—clearly document the pervasive interaction between frames of reference and functional considerations, and "stimulus" characteristics. You receive a weak shock and I a strong one. Then we both receive shocks of equal intensity. For me, the second shock is weaker and provokes less reaction than for you. Breakfast orange juice is sweet and tasty—but not after a bit of toast and jam. A six-inch ice cube is big; a six-foot room is small. Thus, our frames of reference make a difference. Functional considerations also modify meaning and impact. A comfortable apartment for newlyweds becomes impossible when two children arrive. The strong tether for the puppy will not hold the dog. Speaking about the implications of adaptation-level theory for motivation, Helson (1966, pp. 144, 147) says:

> We must distinguish between the *physical* stimulus and the *effective* stimulus. . . . The effective stimulus depends upon the state of the organism, upon preceding and accompanying stimuli, and, in some cases, upon possible future outcomes of stimulation. . . . Most of the difficulties of stimulus theories of motivation vanish if we take as the zero of intensity not the absolute threshold (the level at which a stimulus barely can be perceived) but the adaptation level. It then follows that stimuli below level as well as above level may possess motivating power because it is discrepancy from level in either direction that determines affective quality and its distinctiveness.

Similarly, for college students, the motivational force — the stimulus value — of a course, curriculum, or climate, depends on the students' past experiences and current purposes. Zero stimulation occurs when college turns out to be no different from high school. When there are high expectations concerning the anticipated challenges and stimulation, "more of the same" is not just neutral, but negative.

Typology theories describe distinct but relatively stable differences in perceiving the world or responding to it. They say that while we may travel in the same general direction, we own very different vehicles and we do not all drive the same way. We bring our roots with us — our culture, class, gender, and race. We have preferred styles of learning, thinking, processing information, and making decisions. For example, Jung saw patterns in human personality, which he called *psychological types*. In his theory, "all conscious mental activity can be classified into four mental processes. . . . What comes into consciousness, moment by moment, comes either through the senses or through intuition. To remain in consciousness, perceptions must be used—sorted, weighed, analyzed, evaluated—by the judgment processes, thinking and feeling" (cited in Lawrence, 1982, p. 6). In using the perception functions, a person may prefer "sensing" (using the five senses) or "intuition" (using insight and unconscious associations). In making judgments, a person may prefer either "thinking" (logic) or "feeling" (affective values) as a basis for choosing or deciding. An analogy would be preferring to use one's right or left hand. While a person may use all four functions at different times, each has a preference for using one or the other perception function and one or the other judgment function. The favored function is called "dominant," while the other polarity, which is least used and least trusted, is called "auxiliary." The Myers-Briggs Type Indicator (MBTI) is a popular paper-and-pencil instrument based on Jung's ideas.

The typology models remind us that students bring different frames of reference and different functional considerations to their work. They also differ in other ways. Some students are authoritarian, others rigidly antiauthoritarian, and still others are more flexible and rational (Stern, 1962); some are activists, some are alienated (Keniston, 1967), and some are apathetic. Reasons for going to college differ—to get a better job, to increase self-knowledge, to get a general education, to prepare for a specific profession. On intelligence test scores, differences among college freshmen span nearly four standard deviations (McConnell and Heist, 1962). Wide differences are found for measures of creativity (Hannah, 1967, 1968; Heist, 1968). But most of the diverse entrants encounter remarkably similar programs, similar patterns of teaching and expectations for study, and similar conditions for living and for faculty and peer relationships. High attrition rates and high transfer rates are not surprising when such diversity meets such similarity. More effective education requires taking clearer account of the differences among students and acting accordingly. Doing so does not mean catering to students, nor does it entail merely discovering what students want and providing it. On the contrary, the task of the college is to provide whatever is needed for learning and development to occur. And sound decisions about what is needed must derive from knowledge of where a student is, where he or she wants to go, and what equipment he or she brings for the trip. With such information at hand, intelligent planning can take place. But when significant differences are ignored, some students will be missed entirely and many barely touched.

Remember That Significant Learning and Development Involve Cycles

The basic point here is that, as noted, significant human development occurs through cycles of challenge and response, differentiation and integration, and disequilibrium and regained equilibrium.

Differentiation and integration refer to a familiar process. The notion has been with us for some time that learning and development occur as people encounter new conditions and experiences that are important to them, in which they invest themselves, and for which they must develop new courage, new competencies, and new attitudes. It is reflected in Dewey's "reconstruction of experience" (1938), Festinger's "cognitive dissonance" (1957), Heider's "balance theory" (1958), Newcomb's "strain for symmetry" (1961), Helson's "adaptation-level theory" (1964), and Rogers's "development of congruence" (1961).

Heider (1958, p. 176), for example, asked 101 high school students what would happen "nine times out of ten" in the following situation: "Bob thinks Jim very stupid and a first-class bore. One day, Bob reads some poetry he likes so well that he takes the trouble to track down the author in order to shake his hand. He finds that Jim wrote the poems." This story creates imbalance, conflict. Bob experiences new input that upsets his preexisting system. His view is challenged. How does he resolve it, according to the high school students? Heider found that 46 percent changed Bob's opinion of Jim — "He grudgingly changes his mind about Jim." Thus both Jim and his poetry become positive, and balance is regained. Twenty-nine percent changed Bob's opinion of the poetry — "He decides the poetry is lousy." Both become negative, and balance is achieved. Others sought balance in more complex ways: Bob questions Jim's authorship; he calls Jim smart in poetry but dumb in other ways; he tells

Jim, but "without much feeling," that he likes the poems. Heider, generalizing from diverse studies of this dynamic, says: "The concept of balanced state designates a situation in which the perceived units and the experienced sentiments coexist without stress; there is thus no pressure toward change, either in the cognitive organization or in the sentiment" (p. 176).

Heider's "balance" concept reminds us that significant change sometimes involves a period of disequilibrium, upset, disintegration, out of which a new equilibrium is established. Many conditions and experiences that offer strong potential for development also contain potential for damage. Venturing into a new job, a new culture, or a new relationship can be chancy. But if an individual wants to grow, and if an institution would have an impact, the risks must be taken. Sanford (1963, pp. 11–12) puts it this way:

> We could run an institution in the interest of positive mental health that would so protect individuals from challenging stimuli that they would not develop at all. They might remain quite healthy, in the sense that they managed such strains as were brought to bear, but they remain very simple, undeveloped people. Or . . . you could say that if we are going to have a democratic society in which we expect each individual to be independent, we automatically run very serious risks of mental ill health, because people are not always prepared for the kind of freedom that we expect them to have in our society. But if it comes to that, in general we would rather have freedom than the absence of any risks with respect to mental ill health.

Sanford goes on to say that health and development are by no means the same thing. A simple, undifferentiated person may be healthy but not well developed. Problems may not be in evidence, since the person is not aware of the things that would arouse problems in other people. Similarly, a highly developed person may be complex, tortured, and full of conflicts, but may also be a unique and fascinating individual. "We have to find challenges that are sufficient to require that the individual make a really new kind of adaptation, but not so intense or disturbing as to force the student to fall back on earlier primitive modes of adaptation which will serve him badly in the long run" (p. 13).

Satir's five-stage transition model is a nice elaboration of Sanford's ideas (Figure 16.3). The "status quo"—our smooth-running, predictable patterns of living, thinking, and behaving— gets disrupted by some "foreign element." This event or discovery disrupts the status quo. It can be an external event—injury, job change, family crisis, death of a friend or loved one—or it can be an internal shift in frame of reference or a conscious decision to make a change. The immediate consequence is often "chaos." Confusion, disorder, hopelessness, a feeling of being stuck, anxiety, and fear are some of the emotional counterparts. The path out of chaos requires support and practice. Support can come from other people and from internal resources, from self-care and self-coaching. Opportunities to learn and practice new behaviors, roles, coping strategies, cognitive skills, attitudes, and interpretations are required. In time, the combination of support and practice leads to a new level of integration, a higher level of development, which then becomes the new status quo.

Satir's model suggests a way to think about the contribution of higher education to human development. We need to

Figure 16.3. Satir's Model of Transition.

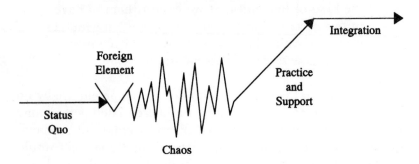

Source: Adapted from Wahbe, 1990.

introduce "foreign elements": new information, new ideas, new insights, new experiences, new skills and higher levels of competence, more complex self-understanding, and new perspectives on other individuals and on society. We need to recognize the chaos and disequilibrium that may result and let them happen, accepting them as a normal and necessary part of significant learning and personal development. Signs of discomfort and upset are not necessarily negative. On the contrary, they often signal that developmentally fruitful encounters are occurring, that stimuli for learning are at work. We need to control our impulse to cover them up, ignore them, or wish them away. At the same time, we need to provide appropriate supports and opportunities for learning and practicing the new orientations and behaviors required to achieve more complex, mature integration.

Differentiation and integration, challenge and response, then, are one basic principle to keep in mind when observing student reactions to varied programs and practices and when planning for change. This principle is important, because the past is piled up around us. We must work through it to obtain knowledge, understand ourselves and others, become what we can. We have gulped it down, but it must be chewed, tasted, and swallowed again if development is to be nourished.

The three admonitions concerning work and learning, individual differences, and challenge and response need to pervade our institutional consciousness and mind-set and provide the conceptual underpinnings for institutional change. The same admonitions need to drive professional development opportunities for administrators, faculty members, student development professionals, and support staff.

Leadership and Organizational Culture

Creating and maintaining educationally powerful environments requires effective leadership and an appropriate organizational culture. We identify eight characteristics of high-quality institutions. An institution becomes a "learning organization" when it does the following:

1. *Clearly defines core values, mission, and vision.* A strong sense of shared values and purposes is the foundation for institutional coherence and integrity. These values and purposes provoke and sustain human allegiance and energy. They provide the touchstone against which policies and practices can be tested. They establish the parameters and directions for innovation and improvement.

2. *Emphasizes an ethic of quality.* High-quality education, research, and service are achieved through hundreds of individual transactions, moment by moment, day by day, and only when responsibility for high-quality transactions is broadly based and personally assumed. Responsibility is shared, not categorized and pigeonholed. People hold high expectations for themselves and for each other. They expect the best and help others achieve it. Risk taking to improve performance is rewarded. Failure and shortfalls suggest lessons to be learned.

3. *Makes people the prime resource.* The root source of quality and productivity rests with rank-and-file administrators, faculty members, professional staff, and support personnel. Respect for these persons — for their individual needs and differences — pervades administrative and collegial relationships. Policies and practices reflect continual concern about the quality of their work life and day-to-day environments.

4. *Learns from the people it serves.* An educationally powerful institution has leaders who track societal trends, whether international, national, regional, or local, and who are sensitive to the potential symmetry in the relation between the institution and its many constituencies. Such an institution is oriented toward service in the broadest sense, which includes both teaching and research. It is immersed in the turbulent environment and honors multiple faculty roles inside and outside the institution. It is close to its students, responsive to their changing needs, interests, backgrounds, and future plans and aspirations. Systematic data about students' avocational, vocational, and intellectual interests, learning styles, and level of cognitive development inform decisions concerning curriculum and teaching.

5. *Emphasizes autonomy and entrepreneurship.* It is important to encourage leadership and innovation throughout the institu-

tion. Mistakes will sometimes be made. Experimentation shakes things up. Ad hoc pilot projects, centers, and institutes that cut through disciplines and professional categories are a good way to begin. Effective, self-terminating task forces and teams get things done, and their members recombine to tackle other tasks. Project teams can be given authority to act as well as to make recommendations about policies and practices. Autonomy can be pushed as far down the organization as possible, while clear values, purposes, and mission provide glue for diverse ventures.

6. *Orients toward sustained action.* Do it, fix it, try it again. Action is always taken on the basis of partial information, despite the usefulness of pertinent research and the experiences of others. Rapid change and significant situational differences make flexible initiatives taken with close monitoring and tenuous tenacity better than comprehensive studies, long-range plans, and grand designs. And we need to hang in there, to stick with it. Three years seems to be a minimum to move from initial ideas through pilot testing to initial institutionalization. Changes that involve several key elements or a new institutional culture require several years.

7. *Analyzes strengths and weaknesses.* Regularized assessment provides data for continual self-reflection and program development. Internal improvement, not external accountability, is emphasized. Formative evaluation accompanies experimentation and change.

8. *Invests in professional development.* High expectations and regular assessment create continual challenges for program improvement and individual performance. The quality of human resources determines institutional performance. Institutional reward systems support and encourage reflective practitioners throughout the organization. Dollars invested in professional development reduce costs stemming from rapid turnover, low morale, and litigation.

Such is the leadership and organizational culture we need to create and sustain educationally powerful environments consistent with research findings concerning college influences on student development. With that leadership, we need to articulate our conceptual framework to describe the major elements, norms, and socialization processes at work inside and outside our institutions. We need to challenge the persistent, pervasive and unrealistic myths about the characteristics of our "best" institutions. We need to use the Principles for Good Practice in Undergraduate Education and the associated inventories, or some similar resources, as a framework for self-diagnosis for improvement. And we need to keep our three key admonitions clearly in mind as we address those aspects of our climate, academic practices, curriculum, faculty, academic and student support services, and facilities to maximize their support of and consistency with top-quality education.

Systematic improvement in these areas over a reasonable time period does not require massive infusions of additional dollars or new hotshot administrators, faculty members, or student development professionals. It requires hard thinking and smart working, sustained to yield slow and steady progress. If we can do that, we will build an institution in which all students develop increased competence, manage emotions more effectively, learn to function effectively in an interdependent world, develop mature relationships, clarify identity, and develop strong purposes that they pursue with integrity.

Social Imperatives

Throughout the world—here in the United States and abroad, the poor are getting poorer, the hungry, hungrier, the homeless more numerous and destitute. The AIDS epidemic continues relentlessly. Health care reform is still on the horizon. Although the superpower confrontation has cooled, the number of countries with known nuclear capability continues to increase. Nationalism and highly localized autonomy run rampant. Tribal, ethnic, religious, and regional animosities, unleashed after seventy years of constraint by communism and the cold war, are causing bloodshed on all the major continents except Australia and Antarctica. Nonrenewable resources are running out. Geographical and economic distribution patterns for food, oil, lumber, precious woods, and key minerals create economic imbalances, starvation, shifting labor markets, and human migrations that require unprecedented global cooperation. For the first time in human history, the level of cooperation and the time perspective required of the "haves" will go far beyond token contributions. We will need to undertake levels of sharing and sacrifice that affect the living standards of all of us in the "developed" world. We have already been experiencing the impact on the economies of the United States and the "West."

We do not have to think globally to recognize our critical need for full competence, for the ability to manage our emotions, for interpersonal competence, and for integrity, purpose, and a sense of interdependence. Consider simply the relationships among population density and diversity, technological complexity, and human interaction here at home. In Colonial America, population density averaged one person per square mile: 314 people within a circle twenty-mile radius — a good day's walk. The chance of human contact was 313 to 1. People encountered in the woods or on the plains, if not Native Americans, would probably be from Western Europe, and most likely white, Anglo-Saxon Protestants striving to improve their status, free from the restrictions of hereditary privilege. Today Chicago has more than ten thousand people per square mile. Los Angeles and other parts of California have "minority majorities." Across the United States, our colors span the rainbow. But we do not share that natural symmetry and unity of a rainbow. More often we split off, jockey for position, or fight for advantage. Each day television and radio highlight our differences and relative standing, the policy implications that favor one group at the expense of another, and the difficult trade-offs necessary if all are to survive.

We confront problems so complex that few of us have confidence in rational responses. We resort to gut feelings anchored in anachronistic assumptions and long-gone cultures. But we are painfully aware of the gap between the positions we take and the quality of information, evidence, and logic behind them. We see our social institutions — education, law, medicine, government, finance — driven by self-centered short-run decisions, designed to maximize the benefits of those institutions and persons at the expense of the common good. Cynicism and apathy run rampant.

These changes and social conditions have enormous implications for higher education. We know that we cannot depend on a select few to lead us. We have experienced the consequences of leadership by "the best and the brightest." To respond to these conditions, we need a citizenry and a work force with sufficient breadth and personal characteristics to participate actively in social self-determination. As Bailey (1977, pp. 257–258) said:

> This nation is in woefully short supply of people equipped to look at problems as a whole, at life as a whole, at the earth as a whole. Without a sense of the whole we have no way of evaluating the parts, no way of appraising the importance of the expert, no way of seeing that the fragmentation and violence we lament in the world around us are but the mirror image of our own cluttered and frenetic psyches. Liberal learning at its best is not designed to relieve life of its pain and uncertainty. It is designed to help people have creative engagements with adversity, to discover and draw upon the well springs of existential joy, to recognize our common plight and need for one another.

We in the United States are neither better nor worse than most other peoples in the world. But our size, our resources, our economic power, our armed might, our wealth, our domination of the media, and our attractiveness to other struggling political and economic systems give us unequaled capacity for influence and leadership throughout the world. Thus, the values and behaviors we exemplify, the ability we demonstrate to rise above factionalism and fragmentation, to make our political, economic, and social systems work for all, can be forces for good far beyond our borders. Our colleges and universities remain our most significant resource for creating a polity with a "sense of the whole" and with the ability to act for the greater good.

But they can contribute to this future only if they effectively transform the lives of the students who pass through them.

To do so, they must not settle for unexamined practices or surrender to political paralysis. College and university administrators must emphasize top-quality teaching. Faculty members must expand their repertoire of teaching strategies to accommodate differences and to help students actualize their highest potential. Student development professionals must continue to articulate their educational role and to collaborate with faculty colleagues to bring about movement along the seven vectors. All members of the learning community then become allies in the development of the individual, the society, and the world.

References

Adams, G., and Fitch, S. "Ego Stage and Identity Status Development: A Cross-Sequential Analysis." *Journal of Personality and Social Psychology,* 1982, *42,* 547–583.

Adams, J. M. "For Many Gay Teenagers, Torment Leads to Suicide." *Boston Globe,* Jan. 3, 1989, pp. 1–8.

Adelson, J. "The Teacher as a Model." In N. Sanford (ed.), *The American College.* New York: Wiley, 1962.

Alcoff, L. "Cultural Feminism vs. Post-Structuralism: The Identity Crisis in Feminist Theory." *Signs,* 1988, *13*(3), 405–436.

Allport, G. W. *Pattern and Growth in Personality.* Troy, Mo.: Holt, Rinehart & Winston, 1961.

Alumni Office, Princeton University. *Twenty-Five Years Out.* Princeton, N.J.: Alumni Office, Princeton University, 1967.

Alverno College Faculty. *Assessment at Alverno College.* (Rev. ed.) Milwaukee, Wis.: Alverno Productions, 1985.

Alverno College Faculty. *Liberal Learning at Alverno College.* (Rev. ed.) Milwaukee, Wis.: Alverno Productions, 1992.

American College Testing Program. *Toward the Future Vitality of Student Development Services.* National Council on Student Development, 1985.

American Council on Education. *The Student Personnel Point of View.* American Council on Education Studies, ser. 1, vol. 1, no. 3. Washington, D.C.: American Council on Education, 1937.

American Council on Education. *The Student Personnel Point of View.* (Rev. ed.) American Council on Education Studies, ser. 6, vol. 1, no. 3. Washington, D.C.: American Council on Education, 1949.

Annis, L. F. "Improving Study Skills and Reducing Test Anxiety in Regular and Low-Achieving College Students: The Effects of a Model Course." *Techniques,* 1986, *2*(2), 115–125.

Archer, J., and Lamnin, A. "An Investigation of Personal and Academic Stressors on College Campuses." *Journal of College Student Personnel,* 1985, *26,* 210–215.

Argyris, C., and Schön, D. A. *Theory in Practice: Increasing Professional Effectiveness.* San Francisco: Jossey-Bass, 1974.

Aslanian, C. B., and Brickell, H. M. *Americans in Transition: Life Changes as Reasons for Adult Learning.* New York: College Entrance Examination Board, 1980.

Association of American Colleges. *Integrity in the College Curriculum: A Report to the Academic Community.* Washington, D.C.: Association of American Colleges, 1985.

Astin, A. W. "Differential College Effects on the Motivation of Talented Students to Obtain the Ph.D." *Journal of Educational Psychology,* 1963, *54*(1), 63–71.

Astin, A. W. "Personal and Environmental Factors Associated with College Dropouts Among High Aptitude Students." *Journal of Educational Psychology,* 1964, *55,* 219–277.

Astin, A. W. "The Impact of Dormitory Living on Students." *Educational Record,* 1973, *54,* 204–210.

Astin, A. W. *Four Critical Years: Effects of College on Beliefs, Attitudes, and Knowledge.* San Francisco: Jossey-Bass, 1977.

Astin, A. W. *Achieving Educational Excellence: A Critical Assessment of Priorities and Practices in Higher Education.* San Francisco: Jossey-Bass, 1985.

Astin, A. W. "What Really Matters in General Education: Provocative Findings from a National Study of Student Outcomes." Keynote address, Conference of the Association of General and Liberal Studies, 1991.

Astin, H., and Kent, L. "Gender Roles in Transition: Research and Policy Implications for Higher Education." *Journal of Higher Education,* 1983, *54,* 309–324.

Atkinson, D. R., Morten, G., and Sue, D. W. *Counseling American Minorities: A Cross-Cultural Perspective.* (2nd ed.) Dubuque, Iowa: Brown, 1983.

Bailey, S. K. "Needed Changes in Liberal Education." *Educational Record,* 1977, *58*(3) 250–258.

Baird, L. "Who Goes to Graduate School and How They Get There." In J. Katz and R. Hartnett (eds.), *Scholars in the Making: The Development of Graduate and Professional Students.* New York: Ballinger, 1976.

Baird, L. "The College Environment Revisited: A Review of Research and Theory." In J. Smart (ed.), *Higher Education: A Handbook of Theory and Research,* Vol. 4. New York: Agathon, 1988.

Baird, L., Clark, M., and Hartnett, R. *The Graduates: A Report on the Characteristics and Plans of College Seniors.* Princeton, N.J.: Educational Testing Service, 1973.

Banning, J. "Creating a Climate for Successful Student Development: The Campus Ecology Manager Role." In U. Delworth, G. R. Hanson and Associates, *Student Services: A Handbook for the Profession.* (2nd ed.) San Francisco: Jossey-Bass, 1989.

Banning, J., and Kaiser, L. "An Ecological Perspective and Model for Campus Design." *Personnel and Guidance Journal,* 1974, *52,* 370–375.

Barker, R. G. *Ecological Psychology: Concepts and Methods for Studying the Environment of Human Behavior.* Stanford, Calif.: Stanford University Press, 1968.

Barker, R. G., and Gump, P. V. *Big School, Small School.* Stanford, Calif.: Stanford University Press, 1964.

Barker, V. L. "The Minister in Higher Education: Theologian, Mentor, and Educator." Paper presented at the Southwestern Campus Ministers' Conference, Texas Christian University, June 1989.

Barnard, J. D. "The Lecture-Demonstration Versus the Problem-Solving Methods of Teaching a College Science Course." *Science Education,* 1942, *26,* 121–132.

Barron, F. *Creativity and Psychological Health*. New York: Van Nostrand Reinhold, 1963.

Bartsch, K., Girrell, K. W., and Yost, E. B. *Effective Personal and Career Decision Making*. New York: Westinghouse Learning Corporation, 1976.

Bassis, M. "The Campus as a Frog Pond: A Theoretical and Empirical Reassessment." *American Journal of Sociology*, 1977, *82*, 1318–1326.

Bateson, M. C. *Composing a Life*. New York: Penguin Books, 1989.

Baum, A., Aiello, J., and Colesnick, L. "Crowding and Personal Control: Social Density and the Development of Learned Helplessness." *Journal of Personality and Social Psychology*, 1978, *36*, 1000–1011.

Baumrind, D. "Sex Differences in Moral Reasoning: Response to Walker's (1984) Conclusion That There Are None." *Child Development*, 1986, *5*(21), 511–521.

Baxter Magolda, M. B. *Knowing and Reasoning in College: Gender-Related Patterns in Students' Intellectual Development*. San Francisco: Jossey-Bass, 1992.

Bayer, A. "Faculty Composition, Institutional Structure, and Students' College Environment." *Journal of Higher Education*, 1975, *46*(5), 549–555.

Bayer, A., and others. *The First Year of College: A Follow-Up Normative Report*. American Council on Education Research Report No. 5. Washington, D.C.: American Council on Education, 1970.

Beal, P. E., and Noel, L. *What Works in Student Retention*. Iowa City, Iowa: American College Testing Program, 1980.

Beck, A. T. *Depression*. New York: HarperCollins, 1967.

Beecher, G., Chickering, A., Hamlin, W. G., and Pitkin, R. S. *An Experiment in College Curriculum Organization*. Plainfield, Vt.: Goddard College, 1966.

Belenky, M. F., Clinchy, B. M., Goldberger, N. R., and Tarule, J. M. *Women's Ways of Knowing: The Development of Self, Mind, and Voice*. New York: Basic Books, 1986.

Bellah, R. N., and others. *Habits of the Heart: Individualism and Commitment in American Life*. New York: HarperCollins, 1985.

Bender, S. *Plain and Simple: A Woman's Journey to the Amish.* San Francisco: HarperCollins, 1989.

Bennett, M. J. "A Developmental Approach to Training Intercultural Sensitivity." *International Journal of Intercultural Relations,* 1986, 10(2), 179–196.

Bennett, S., and Hunter, J. "A Measure of Success: The WILL Program Four Years Later." *Journal of the National Association of Women Deans, Administrators, and Counselors,* 1985, *48,* 3–11.

Bergoffen, D. "Presentation to the College of Arts and Sciences Faculty on Core Course Proposal," George Mason University, Sept. 26, 1988.

Berne, E. *Transactional Analysis in Psychotherapy.* New York: Ballantine, 1961.

Bisconti, A., and Kessler, J. *College and Other Stepping Stones: A Study of Learning Experiences That Contribute to Effective Performance in Early and Long-Run Jobs.* Bethlehem, Pa.: CPC Foundation, 1980.

Bisconti, A., and Solomon, L. *College Education on the Job–The Graduates' Viewpoint.* Bethlehem, Pa.: CPC Foundation, 1976.

Bloom, B. S. "Thought Processes in Lectures and Discussion." *Journal of General Education,* 1953, *7,* 160–169.

Blos, P. "The Second Individuation Process of Adolescence." *Psychoanalytic Study of the Child,* 1967, *22,* 162–186.

Blunt, M., and Blizard, P. "Recall and Retrieval of Anatomical Knowledge." *British Journal of Medical Education,* 1975, *9,* 255–263.

Bootzin, R. R., and Acocella, J. R. *Abnormal Psychology: Current Perspectives* (5th ed.). New York: Random House, 1988.

Bourne, E. "The State of Research on Ego Identity: A Review and Appraisal, Part I." *Journal of Youth and Adolescence,* 1978a, *7,* 223–252.

Bourne, E. "The State of Research on Ego Identity: A Review and Appraisal, Part II." *Journal of Youth and Adolescence,* 1978b, *7,* 371–392.

Bower, E. M. "Personality and Individual Social Maladjustment." In W. W. Wattenberg (ed.), *Social Deviancy Among Youth.* National Society for the Study of Education. Chicago: University of Chicago Press, 1966.

Bower, P. A. "The Relation of Physical, Mental, and Personality Factors to Popularity in Adolescent Boys." Unpublished doctoral dissertation, University of California, Berkeley, 1940.

Bowers, C. A. *Elements of a Post Liberal Theory of Education.* New York: Teachers College Press, 1987.

Boydell, T. *Experiential Learning.* Manchester Monographs No. 5. Manchester, England: Department of Adult and Higher Education, University of Manchester, 1976.

Boyer, E. L. *College: The Undergraduate Experience in America.* Princeton, N.J.: Carnegie Foundation for the Advancement of Teaching, 1987.

Boyer, E. L. and Hechinger, F. M. 1981. *Higher Learning in the Nation's Service.* Washington, D.C.: The Carnegie Foundation for the Advancement of Teaching, 1981.

Brabeck, M. "Moral Judgment: Theory and Research on the Differences Between Males and Females." *Developmental Review,* 1982, *3,* 274–291.

Branch-Simpson, G. "A Study of the Patterns in the Development of Black Students at The Ohio State University." Unpublished doctoral dissertation, Ohio State University, Columbus, 1984.

Brawer, F. *New Perspectives on Personality Development in College Students.* San Francisco: Jossey-Bass, 1973.

Breen, P., Donlon, T. F., and Whitaker, U. *Learning and Assessing Interpersonal Competence — A CAEL Student Guide.* Princeton, N.J.: CAEL, Educational Testing Service, 1977.

Breen, P., and Whitaker, U. *Bridging the Gap: A Learner's Guide to Transferable Skills.* San Francisco: Learning Center, 1983.

Brethower, D. "Research in Learning Behavior: Some Implications for College Teaching." In S. Scholl and S. Inglis (eds.), *Teaching in Higher Education.* Columbus: Ohio Board of Regents, 1977.

Brubaker, J. S., and Rudy, W. *Higher Education in Transition.* New York: HarperCollins, 1976.

Brundage, D. H., and MacKeracher, D. *Adult Learning Principles and Their Application to Program Planning.* Toronto, Ontario: Ministry of Education, 1980.

Bucklin, R., and Bucklin, W. *The Psychological Characteristics of the College Persister and Leaver: A Review.* Washington, D.C.: U.S. Department of Health, Education, and Welfare, 1970. (ED 049 709)

Cage, M. C. "Fewer Students Get Bachelor's Degrees in Four Years, Study Finds." *Chronicle of Higher Education,* July 15, 1992, pp. A29–A31.

Campbell, J. *The Power of Myth.* New York: Doubleday, 1988.

Cannon, D. "Generation X: The Way They Do the Things They Do." *Journal of Career Planning and Employment,* 1991, *51*(2), 34–38.

Carnegie Foundation for the Advancement of Teaching. *Campus Life: In Search of Community.* Lawrenceville, N.J.: Princeton University Press, 1990.

Carroll, L. *Alice in Wonderland.* New York: Collier Books, (1865) 1962.

Cass, V. C. "Homosexual Identity Formation: A Theoretical Model." *Journal of Homosexuality,* 1979, *4,* 219–235.

"The CCT: Structuring and Documenting Co-Curricular Learning." Juniata College Bulletin, 1991, *90*(2), 11.

Center for the Study of Higher Education. *Omnibus Personality Inventory Research Manual.* Berkeley: University of California, 1964.

Center for the Study of Higher Education. *Omnibus Personality Inventory Form Fx — Brief Scale Descriptions.* Berkeley: University of California, 1965, (mimeographed).

Cerio, J. "The Use of Hypnotic Elements and Audio Recordings with the Fantasy Relaxation Technique." *Personnel and Guidance Journal,* 1983, *3*(2), 17–18.

Chickering, A. W. "Dimensions of Independence." *Journal of Higher Education,* 1964, *35,* 38–41.

Chickering, A. W. "Institutional Objectives and Student Development in College." *Journal of Behavioral Science,* 1967, *3,* 287–304.

Chickering, A. W. *Education and Identity.* San Francisco: Jossey-Bass, 1969.

Chickering, A. W. "The Best Colleges Have the Least Effect." *Saturday Review,* Jan. 16, 1971, pp. 48–50, 54.

Chickering, A. W. *Commuting Versus Resident Students: Overcoming Educational Inequities of Living Off Campus.* San Francisco: Jossey-Bass, 1974a.

Chickering, A. W. "The Impact of Various College Environments on Personality Development." *Journal of the American College Health Association,* 1974b, *23,* 82–93.

Chickering, A. W. *Experience and Learning. An Introduction to Experiential Learning.* Washington, D.C.: Change Magazine Press, 1977.

Chickering, A. W., and Associates. *The Modern American College: Responding to the New Realities of Diverse Students and a Changing Society.* San Francisco: Jossey-Bass, 1981.

Chickering, A. W., and Gamson, Z. F. "Seven Principles for Good Practice in Undergraduate Education." *American Association of Higher Education Bulletin,* 1987, *39*(7), 3–7.

Chickering, A. W., and Havighurst, R. "The Life Cycle." In A. W. Chickering and Associates, *The Modern American College: Responding to the New Realities of Diverse Students and a Changing Society.* San Francisco: Jossey-Bass, 1981.

Chickering, A. W., and Kuper, E. "Educational Outcomes for Commuters and Residents." *Educational Record,* 1971, *52,* 255–261.

Chickering, A. W., and McCormick, J. "Personality Development and the College Experience." *Research in Higher Education,* 1973, *1,* 43–70.

Chickering, A. W., McDowell, J., and Campagna, D. "Institutional Differences and Student Development." *Journal of Educational Psychology,* 1969, *60,* 315–326.

Chira, S. "An Ohio College Says Women Learn Differently, So It Teaches That Way." *New York Times,* May 13, 1992, p. B7.

Chodorow, N. "Family Structure and Feminine Personality." In M. Z. Rosaldo and L. Lamphere (eds.), *Woman, Culture and Society.* Stanford: Stanford University Press, 1974.

Clark, B., and others. *Students and Colleges: Interaction and Change.* Berkeley: Center for Research and Development in Higher Education, University of California, 1972.

Cohen, A. M., and Brawer, F. B. *The American Community College.* (2nd ed.) San Francisco: Jossey-Bass, 1989.

Cohen, P. "Student Ratings of Instruction and Student Achievement: A Meta-Analysis of Multisection Validity Studies." *Review of Educational Research,* 1981, *51,* 281–309.

Coleman, E. "Developmental Stages of the Coming Out Process." *Journal of Homosexuality,* 1981–1982, *7*(2/3), 31–43.

Collier, G., Wilson, J., and Tomlinson, P. *Values and Moral Development in Higher Education.* New York: Wiley, 1978.

Collins, P. H. *Black Feminist Thought: Knowledge, Consciousness, and the Politics of Empowerment.* Boston: Unwin Hyman, 1990.

Connelly, W. B., and Marshall, A. B. "Sexual Harassment of University or College Students by Faculty Members." *Journal of College and University Law,* 1989, *4,* 381–403.

Constantinople, A. "An Eriksonian Measure of Personality Development in College Students." *Developmental Psychology,* 1969, *1,* 357–372.

Coopersmith, S. *The Antecedents of Self-Esteem.* New York: Freeman, 1967.

Copeland, C. L., and Cress, C. M. "A Developmental Approach to Freshman Orientation and Advising." In L. Reisser and L. A. Zurfluh (eds.), *Student-Centered Learning: Selected Papers from the National Conference on Student-Centered Learning,* May 25–27, 1988. Bellingham: Western Washington University, 1988.

Corey, G. *Theory and Practice of Counseling and Psychotherapy.* (4th ed.) Pacific Grove, Calif.: Brooks/Cole, 1991.

Council of Student Personnel Associations in Higher Education. "Student Development Services in Post Secondary Education." *Journal of College Student Personnel,* 1975, *16,* 524–528.

Cray, D., Curry, T., and McWhirter, W. "Proceeding with Caution." *Time,* July 16, 1990, pp. 56–62.

Creamer, D. G., and Associates. *College Student Development: Theory and Practice for the 1990s.* Alexandria, Va.: American College Personnel Association, 1990.

Cross, K. P. *Beyond the Open Door: New Students to Higher Education.* San Francisco: Jossey-Bass, 1971.

Cross, K. P. *Adults as Learners: Increasing Participation and Facilitating Learning.* San Francisco: Jossey-Bass, 1981.

Cross, K. P. "Taking Teaching Seriously." Paper presented at the annual meeting of the American Association for Higher Education, Washington, D.C., Mar. 1986.

Cross, W. "Discovering the Black Referent: The Psychology of Black Liberation." In J. Dixon and B. Foster (eds.), *Beyond Black or White.* Boston: Little, Brown, 1971.

Crouse, R. H., Deffenbacher, J. L., and Frost, G. A. "Desensitization for Students with Different Sources and Experiences of Test Anxiety." *Journal of College Student Personnel,* 1985, *26,* 315–318.

Daloz, L. A. *Effective Teaching and Mentoring: Realizing the Transformational Power of Adult Learning Experiences.* San Francisco: Jossey-Bass, 1986.

Dank, B. M. "Coming Out in the Gay World." *Psychiatry,* 1971, *34,* 180–197.

Dannells, M., and Stuber, D. "Mandatory Psychiatric Withdrawal of Severely Disturbed Students: A Study and Policy Recommendations." *National Association of Student Personnel Administration Journal,* 1992, *29*(3), 163–168.

Davidson, W. G., House, W. J., and Boyd, T. L. "A Test-Retest Policy for Introductory Psychology Courses." *Teaching of Psychology,* 1984, *11*(3), 182–184.

Davis, J. *Great Aspirations: The Graduate School Plans of America's College Seniors.* Chicago: Aldine, 1964.

Dearden, D. F. "Autonomy and Education." In D. F. Dearden, P. F. Hirst, and R. S. Peters (eds.), *Education and the Development of Reason.* London: Routledge, 1972.

DeMan, A. F. "Autonomy-Control Variation in Child-Rearing and Anomie in Young Adults." *Psychological Reports,* 1982, *51,* 7–10.

Demiutroff, J. "Student Persistence." *College and University,* 1974, *49,* 553–565.

Denney, R. "American Youth Today: A Bigger Cast, A Wider Screen." In E. H. Erikson (ed.), *The Challenge of Youth.* New York: Doubleday, 1965.

Denny, N. "Socio-Moral Development Variability: Comparisons of Kohlberg's Moral Reasoning Stages for Jung's Thinking-Feeling Student Process, Educational Level, and Gender." Unpublished doctoral dissertation, Ohio State University, Columbus, 1988.

Dewey, J. *Education and Experience.* New York: Collier Books, 1938.

Dickinson, E. "The Props Assist the House." In T. H. Johnson (ed.), *The Poems of Emily Dickinson.* Cambridge, Mass.: Belknap Press, 1983. (Originally published 1890.)

Dodge, S. "Poorer Preparation for College Found in 25-Year Study of Freshmen." *Chronicle of Higher Education,* Nov. 21, 1991, pp. A38–A39.

Douvan, E. "Capacity for Intimacy." In A. W. Chickering and Associates, *The Modern American College: Responding to the New Realities of Diverse Students and a Changing Society.* San Francisco: Jossey-Bass, 1981.

Douvan, E., and Adelson, J. *The Adolescent Experience.* New York: Wiley, 1966.

Dressel, P. L. "On Critical Thinking." In P. L. Dressel (ed.), *Evaluation in the Basic College at Michigan State University.* New York: HarperCollins, 1958.

Dumont, R., and Troelstrup, R. "Measures and Predictors of Educational Growth with Four Years of College." *Research in Higher Education,* 1981, *14,* 31–47.

Eble, K. E. *The Craft of Teaching: A Guide to Mastering the Professor's Art.* (2nd ed.) San Francisco: Jossey-Bass, 1988.

Eddy, E. G., Jr. "The College Influence on Student Character." Washington, D.C.: American Council on Education, 1959.

Edelmann, R. J., and Harwick, S. "Test Anxiety, Past Performance, and Coping Strategies." *Personality and Individual Differences,* 1986, *7*(2), 255–257.

Endo, J., and Harpel, R. "The Effect of Student-Faculty Interaction on Students' Educational Outcomes." *Research in Higher Education,* 1982, *16,* 115–138.

Erikson, E. "Growth and Crisis of the Healthy Personality." In M.J.E. Senn (ed.), *Symposium on the Healthy Personality.* Supplement II. New York: Josiah Macy, Jr., Foundation, 1950, pp. 91–146.

Erikson, E. "Identity and the Life Cycle." *Psychological Issues Monograph,* 1959, *1*(1), 1–171.

Erikson, E. *Childhood and Society.* New York: Norton, 1963.

Erikson, E. *Insight and Responsibility.* New York: Norton, 1964.

Erikson, E. *Identity: Youth and Crisis.* New York: Norton, 1968.

Eron, L. D. "The Development of Aggressive Behavior from the Perspective of a Developing Behaviorism." *American Psychologist,* 1987, *42*(5), 435–442.

Eron, L. D., and Huesmann, L. R. "The Relation of Prosocial

Behavior to the Development of Aggression and Psychopathology." *Aggressive Behavior,* 1984, *4,* 399–413.

Evans, N., and Levine, H. "Perspectives on Sexual Orientation." In L. V. Moore (ed.), *Evolving Theoretical Perspectives on Students.* New Directions for Student Services, no. 51. San Francisco: Jossey-Bass, 1990.

Faculty of Arts and Sciences, Harvard University. Harvard University Courses of Instruction, 1991–1992. Allston, Mass.: Office of the University Publisher, 1991.

Feldman, K., and Newcomb, T. *The Impact of College on Students.* San Francisco: Jossey-Bass, 1969.

Fenske, R. H. "Evolution of the Student Services Profession." In U. Delworth, G. R. Hanson, and Associates, *Student Services: A Handbook for the Profession.* (2nd ed.) San Francisco: Jossey-Bass, 1989a.

Fenske, R. H. "Historical Foundations of Student Services." In U. Delworth, G. R. Hanson, and Associates, *Student Services: A Handbook for the Profession.* (2nd ed.) San Francisco: Jossey-Bass, 1989b.

Feshback, N., and Feshback, S. "Empathy Training and the Regulation of Aggression: Potentialities and Limitations." *Academic Psychology Bulletin,* 1984, *4,* 399–413.

Feshback, S., and Price, J. "Cognitive Competencies and Aggressive Behavior." *Aggressive Behavior,* 1984, *10,* 185–200.

Festinger, L. *A Theory of Cognitive Dissonance.* New York: HarperCollins, 1957.

Finkelstein, M. J., and Gaier, E. L. "The Impact of Prolonged Student Status on Late Adolescent Development." *Adolescence,* 1983, *18,* 115–128.

Fleming, J. *Blacks in College: A Comparative Study of Students' Success in Black and in White Institutions.* San Francisco: Jossey-Bass, 1984.

Flesch, R. (ed.). *The Book of Unusual Quotations.* New York: HarperCollins, 1957.

Fowler, J. W. *Stages of Faith: The Psychology of Human Development and the Quest for Meaning.* San Francisco: HarperCollins, 1981.

Frankl, V. *Man's Search for Meaning.* New York: Washington Square Press, 1963.

Freedman, M. B. "Studies of College Alumni." In N. Sanford (ed.), *The American College*. New York: Wiley, 1962.

Freud, S. *Civilization and Its Discontents*. New York: Norton, 1961. (Originally published 1930.)

Gaff, J. "The Rhetoric and Reality of General Education Reform: An Overview." Keynote address, conference of the Association of General and Liberal Studies, 1991.

Gallant, J. A., and Prothero, J. W. "Weight-Watching at the University: The Consequences of Growth." *Science*, 1972, *175*, 381–388.

Gamson, Z. F., and Associates. *Liberating Education*. San Francisco: Jossey-Bass, 1984.

Gaudry, E., and Spielberger, C. *Anxiety and Educational Achievement*. New York: Wiley, 1971.

George Mason University. *Improving Teaching at George Mason University*. Task force report. Fairfax, Va.: George Mason University, 1989.

George Mason University Board of Visitors. "George Mason University Mission Statement." Fairfax, Va.: President's Office, George Mason University, 1991.

George Washington University. *Undergraduate and Graduate Programs*. Washington, D.C.: George Washington University, 1982.

Gerst, M., and Sweetwood, H. "Correlates of Dormitory Social Climate." *Environmental Behavior*, 1973, *5*, 440–463.

Gibbs, B. "Autonomy and Authority in Education." *Journal of Philosophy of Education*, 1979, *13*, 119–132.

Gibbs, J. C., Arnold, K. D., and Burkhart, J. E. "Sex Differences in the Expression of Moral Judgment." *Child Development*, 1984, *55*, 1040–1043.

Gilligan, C. "In a Different Voice: Women's Conception of Self and of Morality." *Harvard Educational Review*, 1977, *47*, 481–517.

Gilligan, C. *In a Different Voice: Psychological Theory and Women's Development*. Cambridge, Mass.: Harvard University Press, 1982.

Gilligan, C. "Remapping Development: The Power of Divergent Data." In L. Cirillo and S. Wapner (eds.), *Value Presuppositions in Theories of Human Development*. Hillsdale, N.J.: Erlbaum, 1986a.

Gilligan, C. "Reply by Carol Gilligan." *Signs,* 1986b, *2,* 304–333.

Ginsberg, E. "The Pluralistic Economy of the U.S." *Scientific American,* 1976, *2,* 25–29.

Gold, M. S. *The Good News About Depression.* New York: Bantam Books, 1987.

Goldberger, N. "Ways of Knowing: Women's Constructions of Truth, Authority and Self." In B. De Chant (ed.), *Women and Group Psychotherapy.* New York: Guilford Press, forthcoming.

Goldscheider, F. K., and Davanzo, J. "Semiautonomy and Leaving Home in Early Adulthood." *Social Forces,* 1986, *65,* 187–201.

Gould, R. "The Phases of Adult Life." *American Journal of Psychiatry,* 1972, *5,* 521–531.

Graffam, D. "Dickinson College Changes Personality." *Dickinson Alumnus,* 1967, *44,* 2–7.

Greeley, A. M. *The Influence of Religion on the Career Plans and Occupational Values of June, 1961, College Graduates.* Unpublished doctoral dissertation, University of Chicago, 1962.

Greeley, A., and Tinsley, H. "Autonomy and Intimacy Development in College Students: Sex Differences and Predictors." *Journal of College Student Development,* 1988, *29,* 512–520.

Green, T. F. "Ironies and Paradoxes." In D. W. Vermilye (ed.), *Relating Work and Education: Current Issues in Higher Education 1977.* San Francisco: Jossey-Bass, 1977.

Grigg, C. M. "Recruitment to Graduate Study: College Seniors' Plans for Postgraduate Study and Their Implementation the Year After Commencement." *SREB Research Monograph,* no. 10. Atlanta, Ga.: Southern Regional Education Board, 1962.

Gurin, P., and Epps, E. *Black Consciousness, Identity, and Achievement: A Study of Students in Historically Black Colleges.* New York: Wiley, 1975.

Gurin, P., and Katz, D. *Motivation and Aspiration in the Negro College.* Office of Education, U.S. Department of Health, Education, and Welfare, Project No. 5-0787. Ann Arbor: Survey Research Center, Institute of Social Research, University of Michigan, 1966.

Gustav, A. "Retention of Course Material Over Varying Intervals of Time." *Psychological Reports,* 1969, *25,* 727–730.

Haan, N. "With Regard to Walker (1984) on Sex 'Differences'

in Moral Reasoning." Mimeographed paper. Berkeley: Berkeley Institute of Human Development, University of California, 1985.

Hannah, W. "Differences Between Drop-Outs and Stay-Ins at Entrance — 1965 Freshmen." Paper presented at the 1967 Workshop of the Project on Student Development in Small Colleges, Racine, Wis., Aug. 1967.

Harrison, R. "How to Design and Conduct Self-Directed Learning Experiences." *Group and Organizational Studies,* 1978, *3*(2), 149–167.

Haswell, R. H. "Student Self-Evaluations and Developmental Change." In J. MacGregor (ed.), *Student Self-Evaluation: Fostering Reflective Learning.* New Directions in Teaching and Learning, no. 56. San Francisco: Jossey-Bass, forthcoming.

Hatch, D. "Differential Impact of College on Males and Females." In *Women on Campus, 1970: A Symposium.* Ann Arbor: Center for Continuing Education for Women, University of Michigan, 1970.

Healy, C., Mitchell, J., and Mourton, D. "Age and Grade Differences in Career Development Among Community College Students." *Review of Higher Education,* 1987, *10,* 247–258.

Heath, D. *Growing Up in College: Liberal Health Education and Maturity.* San Francisco: Jossey-Bass, 1968.

Heath, D. "A Model of Becoming a Liberally Educated and Mature Student." In C. Parker (ed.), *Encouraging Development in College Students.* Minneapolis: University of Minnesota Press, 1978.

Heath, D. "A College's Ethos: A Neglected Key to Effectiveness and Survival." *Liberal Education,* 1981, *67,* 89–111.

Heath, R. G. "Pleasure Response of Human Subjects to Direct Stimulation of the Brain: Physiologic and Psychodynamic Considerations." In R. G. Heath (ed.), *The Role of Pleasure in Behavior — A Symposium by Twenty-Two Authors.* New York: HarperCollins, 1964.

Hedlund, D., and Jones, J. "Effect of Student Personnel Services on Completion Rates in Two-Year Colleges." *Journal of College Student Personnel,* 1970, *11,* 196–199.

Heider, F. *The Psychology of Interpersonal Relations.* New York: Wiley, 1958.

Heist, P. (ed.). *The Creative College Student: An Unmet Challenge.* San Francisco: Jossey-Bass, 1968.

Heist, P., and Yonge, G. *Omnibus Personality Inventory Manual (Form F)*. New York: Psychological Corporation, 1968.

Heller, S. "Race, Gender, Class, and Culture: Freshman Seminar Ignites Controversy." *Chronicle of Higher Education,* Jan. 19, 1992, p. A33.

Helms, J. "An Overview of Black Racial Identity Theory." In J. Helms (ed.), *Black and White Racial Identity: Theory, Research, and Practice*. New York: Greenwood Press, 1990.

Helson, H. *Adaptation-Level Theory*. New York: HarperCollins, 1964.

Helson, H. "Some Problems in Motivation from the Point of View of the Theory of Adaptation Level." In D. Levin (ed.), *Nebraska Symposium on Motivation*. Lincoln: University of Nebraska Press, 1966.

Hesburgh, T.M. 1981. "The Future of Liberal Education." *Change*, April, 1981, 36–40.

High, T., and Sundstrom, E. "Room Flexibility and Space Use in a Dormitory." *Environmental Behavior,* 1977, *9,* 81–90.

Ho, M. *Family Therapy with Ethnic Minorities*. Newbury Park, Calif.: Sage, 1987.

Hofstadter, R., and Smith, W. *American Higher Education: A Documentary History*. Vol. 1. Chicago: University of Chicago Press, 1961.

Holland, J. L. *The Psychology of Vocational Choice: A Theory of Personality Types and Model Environments*. Waltham, Mass.: Blaisdell, 1966.

Holland, J. L. *Making Vocational Choices: A Theory of Vocational Personalities and Work Environments*. Englewood Cliffs, N.J.: Prentice Hall, 1985.

Holland, J. L. *Self-Directed Search*. Assessment Booklet and College Majors Finder, Form R. Odessa, Fla.: Psychological Assessment Resources, Inc., 1990.

Hood, A. B., and Jackson, L. M. "The Iowa Managing Emotions Inventory." In A. B. Hood (ed.), *The Iowa Student Development Inventories*. Iowa City, Iowa: Hitech Press, 1986.

Huesmann, L. R., and Eron, L. D. "Cognitive Processes and the Persistence of Aggressive Behavior." *Aggressive Behavior,* 1984, *10,* 243–251.

Hyde, J. S. *Understanding Human Sexuality.* (3rd ed.) New York: McGraw-Hill, 1986.

Hyman, H., Wright, C., and Reed, J. *The Enduring Effects of Education.* Chicago: University of Chicago Press, 1975.

Ivey, A. E. *Intentional Interviewing and Counseling.* (2nd ed.) Pacific Grove, Calif.: Brooks/Cole, 1988.

Jacob, P. E. *Changing Values in College.* New York: HarperCollins, 1957.

Johnson, G. *State of the University Address.* George Mason University, Fairfax, Va., 1986.

Johnson, M., and Lashley, K. "Influence of Native-Americans' Cultural Commitment on Preferences for Counselor Ethnicity." *Journal of Multicultural Counseling and Development,* 1988, *17,* 115–122.

Johnston, D. K. "Two Moral Orientations—Two Problem-Solving Strategies: Adolescents' Solutions to Dilemmas in Fables." Unpublished doctoral dissertation, School of Education, Harvard University, 1985.

Josselson, R. "Psychodynamic Aspects of Identity Formation in College Women." *Journal of Youth and Adolescence,* 1973, *2,* 3–52.

Josselson, R. *Finding Herself: Pathways to Identity Development in Women.* San Francisco: Jossey-Bass, 1987.

Kalsbeek, D. "Balancing the Support-Challenge Ratio in Residence Hall Environments: A Study of the Effects of Roommate Matching by Personality Type Compared to Standard Procedures on Student Perceptions of Social Climate." Unpublished master's thesis, Department of Education, Ohio State University, 1980.

Kapp, G. J. "College Extracurricular Activities: Who Participates and What Are the Benefits?" Unpublished doctoral dissertation, University of California, Los Angeles, 1979. (University Microfilms No. 80-01, 378)

Karman, F. "Women: Personal and Environmental Factors in Career Choice." Paper presented at the meeting of the American Educational Research Association, New Orleans, La., 1973.

Katz, J. "Personality and Interpersonal Relations in the College Classroom." In N. Sanford (ed.), *The American College.* New York: Wiley, 1962.

Kearney, C. (ed.). *George Mason University Undergraduate Catalog, 1991–92.* Fairfax, Va.: University Publications, 1991.

Kegan, D. L. "The Quality of Student Life and Financial Costs: The Cost of Social Isolation." *Journal of College Student Personnel,* 1978, *19,* 55–58.

Kegan, R. *The Evolving Self: Problem and Process in Human Development.* Cambridge, Mass.: Harvard University Press, 1982.

Keim, M. C. "Student Personnel Preparation Programs: A Longitudinal Study." *National Association of Student Personnel Administration Journal,* 1991, *28*(3), 231–242.

Keirsey, D., and Bates, M. *Please Understand Me: Character and Temperament Types.* (3rd ed.) Del Mar, Calif.: Prometheus Nemesis, 1978.

Keniston, K. *The Sources of Student Dissent.* In E. E. Samson (ed.), "Stirrings Out of Apathy: Student Activism and the Decade of Protest." *Journal of Social Issues,* 1967, *23*(3), 108–137.

Keys, R. C. (ed.). *Toward the Future Vitality of Student Development Services: Traverse City Five Years Later.* Iowa City, Iowa: American College Testing Program, 1990.

Keyser, J. S. *Toward the Future Vitality of Student Development Services.* Iowa City, Iowa: American College Testing Program, 1985.

King, P. M. "Assessing Development from a Cognitive-Developmental Perspective." In D. G. Creamer and Associates, *College Student Development: Theory and Practice for the 1990's.* Alexandria, Va.: American College Personnel Association, 1990.

King, S. "The Clinical Assessment of Change." In J. Whiteley and H. Sprandel (eds.), *The Growth and Development of College Students.* Washington, D.C.: American Personnel and Guidance Association, 1970.

King, S. *Five Lives at Harvard: Personality Change During College.* Cambridge, Mass.: Harvard University Press, 1973.

Kinsey, A. C., Pomeroy, W. B., and Martin, C. E. *Sexual Behavior in the Human Male.* (2nd ed.) Philadelphia: Saunders, 1953.

Kirschner, J., and others. *Life Skills Five Year Follow Up Report.* Suffern, N.Y.: Rockland Community College, 1986.

Kitchener, K., and King, P. "Reflective Judgment: Concepts of Justification and Their Relationship to Age and Education." *Journal of Applied Developmental Psychology,* 1981, *2,* 89–116.

Kitchener, K., and King, P. "The Reflective Judgment Model: Ten Years of Research." In M. Commons and others (eds.), *Adult Development: Models and Methods in the Study of Adolescent and Adult Thought.* New York: Praeger, 1990a.

Kitchener, K. S., and King, P. M. "The Reflective Judgment Model: Transforming Assumptions About Knowing." In J. Mezirow and Associates, *Fostering Critical Reflection in Adulthood: A Guide to Transformative and Emancipatory Learning.* San Francisco: Jossey-Bass, 1990b.

Kitchener, K. S., King, P. M., Wood, P. K., and Davison, M. L. "Consistency and Sequentiality in the Development of Reflective Judgment: A Six-Year Longitudinal Study." *Journal of Applied Developmental Psychology,* 1989, *10,* 73–95.

Kitto, H.D.F. *The Greeks.* Baltimore, Md.: Penguin Books, 1963.

Klemp, G. O. "Three Factors of Success." In D. Vermilye (ed.), *Relating Work and Education: Relating Current Issues in Higher Education 1977.* San Francisco: Jossey-Bass, 1977.

Knefelkamp, L. "Developmental Instruction: Fostering Intellectual and Personal Growth of College Students." Unpublished doctoral dissertation, Department of Education, University of Minnesota, 1974.

Knefelkamp, L., Widick, C., and Parker, C. (eds.). *Applying New Developmental Findings.* New Directions for Student Services, no. 4. San Francisco: Jossey-Bass, 1978.

Knowles, M. *The Adult Learner: A Neglected Species.* (2nd ed.) Houston, Tex.: Gulf, 1979.

Knox, A. B. *Adult Development and Learning: A Handbook on Individual Growth and Competence in the Adult Years.* San Francisco: Jossey-Bass, 1977.

Knox, W., Lindsay, P., and Kolb, M. "Higher Education Institutions and Young Adult Development." Unpublished Manuscript, University of North Carolina, Greensboro, 1988.

Koapp, S., and Mierzwa, J. A. "Effects of Systematic Desensitization and Self-Control Treatments in Test-Anxiety Reduction Programs." *Journal of College Student Personnel,* 1984, *25*(3), 229–233.

Koestler, A. *The Act of Creation.* New York: Dell, 1967.

Kohlberg, L. "Stage and Sequence: The Cognitive-Developmental Approach to Socialization." In D. Goslin (ed.), *Handbook of Socialization Theory and Research.* Skokie, Ill.: Rand McNally, 1969.

Kohlberg, L. "Stages of Moral Development." In C. M. Beck, B. S. Crittenden, and E. V. Sullivan (eds.), *Moral Education.* Toronto: University of Toronto Press, 1971.

Kohlberg, L. "A Cognitive-Developmental Approach to Moral Education." *Humanist,* 1972, *6,* 13–16.

Kohlberg, L. *Essays on Moral Development, Vol. 2: The Psychology of Moral Development: The Nature and Validity of Moral Stages.* New York: HarperCollins, 1984.

Kohlberg, L., Levine, C., and Hewer, A. *Moral Stages: A Current Formulation and Response to Critics.* Contributions to Human Development Series, no. 10. New York: Karger, 1983.

Kolb, D. A. *Learning Styles Inventory Technical Manual.* Boston: McBer, 1976.

Kolb, D. A. "Learning Styles and Disciplinary Differences." In A. W. Chickering and Associates, *The Modern American College: Responding to the New Realities of Diverse Students and a Changing Society.* San Francisco: Jossey-Bass, 1981.

Kolb, D. A. *Experiential Learning.* Englewood Cliffs, N.J.: Prentice Hall, 1984.

Kolb, D. A., and Fry, R. "Toward an Applied Theory of Experiential Learning." In C. Cooper (ed.), *Theories of Group Processes.* New York: Wiley, 1975.

Komarovsky, M. *Women in College: Shaping New Feminine Identities.* New York: Basic Books, 1985.

Korn, H. A. "Counseling and Teaching: An Integrated View." *Journal of College Student Personnel,* 1966, *7,* 137–140.

Krasnow, R., and Longino, C. "Reference and Membership Group Influence of Fraternities on Student Political Orientation Change." *Journal of Social Psychology,* 1973, *91,* 163–164.

Kuh, G. "Persistence of the Impact of College on Attitudes and Values." *Journal of College Student Personnel,* 1976, *17,* 116–122.

Kuh, G., Schuh, J. H., Whitt, E. J., and Associates. *Involving Colleges: Successful Approaches to Fostering Student Learning and Development Outside the Classroom.* San Francisco: Jossey-Bass, 1991.

Kuhlman, T. "Symptom Relief Through Insight During Systematic Desensitization: A Case Study." *Psychotherapy Theory, Research, and Practice,* 1982, *19,* 88–94.

Kurfiss, J. "Sequentiality and Structure in a Cognitive Model of College Student Development." *Developmental Psychology,* 1975, *13*(6), 565–571.

Langdale, S. "Moral Orientations and Moral Development: The Analysis of Care and Justice Reasoning Across Different Dilemmas in Females and Males from Childhood to Adulthood." Unpublished doctoral dissertation, School of Education, Harvard University, 1983.

Lange, C. G., and James, W. *The Emotions.* New York: Hafner, 1967.

Lannholm, G. V., and Pitcher, B. *Achievement in Three Broad Areas of Study During the First Two Years of College.* Princeton, N.J.: Educational Testing Service, 1956a.

Lannholm, G. V., and Pitcher, B. *Achievement in Three Broad Areas of Study During the Second Two Years of College.* Princeton, N.J.: Educational Testing Service, 1956b.

Lannholm, G. V., and Pitcher, B. *Mean Score Changes on the Graduate Record Examinations Area Tests for College Students Tested Three Times in a Four-Year Period.* Princeton, N.J.: Educational Testing Service, 1959.

Lawrence, G. *People Types and Tiger Stripes.* Gainesville, Fla.: Center for Applications of Psychological Type, 1982.

Leafgren, F. "Educational Programming." In G. S. Blimling and J. H. Schuh (eds.), *Increasing the Educational Role of Residence Halls.* New Directions for Student Services, no. 13. San Francisco: Jossey-Bass, 1981.

Lerner, H. G. *The Dance of Anger.* New York: HarperCollins, 1985.

Levinson, D. J. *The Seasons of a Man's Life.* New York: Ballantine Books, 1978.

Levitt, E. *The Psychology of Anxiety.* Hillsdale, N.J.: Erlbaum, 1980.

Lewin, K. "Group Decision and Social Change." In G. E. Swanson, T. M. Newcomb, and E. L. Hartley (eds.), *Readings in Social Psychology.* (2nd ed.) New York: Holt, Rinehart & Winston, 1952.

Lewinsohn, P. M., Muñoz, R. F., Youngren, M. A., and Zeiss, A. M. *Control Your Depression.* Englewood Cliffs, N.J.: Prentice Hall, 1986.

Lewis, H. G. *The Role of Shame in Symptoms Formation.* Hillside, N.J.: Erlbaum, 1987.

Liberace, M., and others. *Life, Career, and Educational Planning.* Needham Heights, Mass.: Ginn Press, 1990.

Loacker, G., Cromwell, L., and O'Brien, K. "Assessment in Higher Education: To Serve the Learner." In C. Adelman (ed.), Assessment in Higher Education: Issues and Contexts. Report no. or86-301. Washington, D.C.: U.S. Department of Education, 1986.

Loevinger, J. *Ego Development: Conceptions and Theories.* San Francisco: Jossey-Bass, 1976.

Loevinger, J., Wessler, R., and Redmore, C. *Measuring Ego Development.* 2 vols. San Francisco: Jossey-Bass, 1970.

Longino, C., and Kart, C. "The College Fraternity: An Assessment of Theory and Research." *Journal of College Student Personnel, 1973, 14,* 118–125.

Lopez, F. G. "Family Structure and Depression: Implications for the Counseling of Depressed College Students." *Journal of Counseling and Development,* 1986, *64,* 508–511.

Luttrell, W. "Working-Class Women's Ways of Knowing: Effects of Gender, Race, and Class." *Sociology of Education,* 1989, *62,* 33–46.

Lyons, N. P. "Two Perspectives: On Self, Relationships, and Morality." *Harvard Educational Review,* 1983, *53,* 125–145.

Mabry, M. and Rogers, P. "Bias Begins at Home." *Newsweek,* Aug. 5, 1991, p. 33.

McConnell, T. R., and Heist, P. "The Diverse College Student Population." In N. Sanford (ed.), *The American College.* New York: Wiley, 1962.

McGeoch, J. A., and Irion, A. L. *The Psychology of Human Learning.* White Plains, N.Y.: Longman, 1952.

MacGregor, J. "Intellectual Development of Students in Learning Community Programs, 1986–1987." *Washington Center Occasional Paper No. 1.* Olympia, Wash.: Washington Center for Improving the Quality of Undergraduate Education, Evergreen State College, 1987.

MacGregor, J. "What Differences Do Learning Communities Make?" *Washington Center News,* 1991, *6*(1), 5–9.

McIntire, R. W., and others. "Improving Retention Through Intensive Practice in College Survival Skills." *National Association of Student Personnel Administration Journal,* 1992, *29*(4), 229–306.

McKeachie, W. J. "Procedures and Techniques of Teaching: A Survey of Experimental Studies." In N. Sanford (ed.), *The American College.* New Work: Wiley, 1962.

McLaughlin, G., and Smart, J. "Baccalaureate Recipients: Developmental Patterns in Personal Values." *Journal of College Student Personnel,* 1987, *28,* 162–168.

Macleish, J. "The Lecture Method." *Cambridge Monograph on Teaching Methods No. 1.* Cambridge, England: Cambridge Institution of Education, 1968.

Makepeace, J. M. "Courtship Violence Among College Students." *Family Relations,* 1981, *30,* 97–102.

Makepeace, J. M. "Life Events Stress and Courtship Violence." *Family Relations,* 1983, *32,* 101–109.

Malamuth, N. M. "Predictors of Naturalistic Sexual Aggression." *Journal of Personality and Social Psychology,* 1986, *50,* 953–960.

Malamuth, N. M., and Briere, J. "Sexual Violence in the Media: Indirect Effects on Aggression Against Women." *Journal of Social Issues,* 1986, *42*(3), 75–92.

Marcia, J. "Determination and Construct Validity of Ego-Identity Status." Unpublished doctoral dissertation, (*Dissertation Abstracts International,* 1965, *25,* 6763A).

Marcia, J. "Development and Validation of Ego-Identity Status." *Journal of Personality and Social Psychology,* 1966, *3,* 551–559.

Marcia, J. "Studies in Ego-Identity." Unpublished manuscript, Simon Frazier University, 1976.

Marlowe, A., and Auvenshine, C. "Greek Membership: Its Impact on the Moral Development of College Freshmen." *Journal of College Student Personnel,* 1982, *23,* 53–57.

Marmor, J. "Overview: The Multiple Roots of Homosexual Behavior." In J. Marmor (ed.), *Homosexual Behavior: A Modern Reappraisal.* New York: Basic Books, 1980.

Martinez, C., Jr. "Mexican Americans." In L. Comas-Diaz and E. Griffith (eds.), *Clinical Guidelines in Cross-Cultural Mental Health.* New York: Wiley, 1988.

Matthews, R. "Learning Communities in the Community College." *Community, Technical, and Junior College Journal,* 1986, *57*(2) 44–47.

Mayo, L., and Norton, G. R. "The Use of Problem Solving to Reduce Examination and Interpersonal Anxiety." *Journal of Behavior Therapy and Experimental Psychiatry,* 1980, *11*(4), 287–289.

Mentkowski, M. and Doherty, A. *Careering After College: Establishing the Validity of Abilities Learned in College for Later Careering and Professional Performance.* (Rev. ed.) Milwaukee, Wis.: Alverno Productions, 1983.

Meyer, G. "An Experimental Study of the Old and New Types of Examinations. II: Method of Study." *Journal of Educational Psychology,* 1936, *26,* 30–40.

Mezirow, J. *Transformative Dimensions of Adult Learning.* San Francisco: Jossey-Bass, 1991.

Mezirow, J., and Associates. *Fostering Critical Reflection in Adulthood: A Guide to Transformative and Emancipatory Learning.* San Francisco: Jossey-Bass, 1990.

Michael, R. "Education and Consumption." In F. Juster (ed.), *Education, Income, and Human Behavior.* New York: McGraw-Hill, 1975.

Middleton-Moz, J. *Shame and Guilt: The Masters of Disguise.* Deerfield Beach, Fla.: Health Communications, Inc., 1990.

Miller, G. A., Galanter, E., and Pribram, K. H. *Plans and the Structure of Behavior.* Troy, Mo.: Holt, Rinehart & Winston, 1960.

Miller, J. B., *Toward a New Psychology of Women.* Boston: Beacon Press, 1976.

Miller, T. K., and Prince, J. S. *The Future of Student Affairs: A Guide to Student Development for Tomorrow's Higher Education.* San Francisco: Jossey-Bass, 1976.

Minton, H. L., and McDonald, G. J. "Homosexual Identity Formation as a Developmental Process." *Journal of Homosexuality,* 1983–1984, *9*(2/3), 91–104.

Monroe, C. *Profile of the Community College: A Handbook.* San Francisco: Jossey-Bass, 1972.

Mooney, C. J. "Professors Feel Conflict Between Roles in Teaching and Research, Say Students Are Badly Prepared." *Chronicle of Higher Education,* May 8, 1991, pp. A15–17.

Moore, D., and Hotch, D. F. "The Importance of Different Home-Leaving Strategies to Late Adolescents." *Adolescence,* 1983, *18,* 413–416.

Moore, L. V. (ed.). *Evolving Theoretical Perspectives on Students.* New Directions for Student Services, no. 51. San Francisco: Jossey-Bass, 1990.

Moos, R. *The Human Context: Environmental Determinants of Behavior.* New York: Wiley, 1976.

Moos, R. "Social Environments of University Student Living Groups: Architectural and Organizational Correlates." *Environment and Behavior,* 1978, *10,* 109–126.

Moos, R. *Evaluating Educational Environments: Procedures, Measures, Findings, and Policy Implications.* San Francisco: Jossey-Bass, 1979.

Moos, R., DeYoung, A., and Van Dort, B. "Differential Impact of University Student Living Groups." *Research in Higher Education,* 1976, *5,* 67–82.

Moos, R., Van Dort, B., Smail, P., and DeYoung, A. "A Typology of University Student Living Groups." *Journal of Educational Psychology,* 1975, *67,* 359–367.

"More Programs, Less Conflict?" *National On Campus Report* (Magna Publications, Madison, Wis.), 1992, *20*(6), 2.

Morris, J., ed. *The Oxford Book of Oxford.* Oxford, England: Oxford University Press, 1987.

Muelenhard, C. L., Friedman, D. E., and Thomas, C. M. "Is Date Rape Justifiable?" *Psychology of Women Quarterly,* 1985, *9*(3), 297–310.

Mueller, K. H. *Student Personnel Work in Higher Education.* Boston: Houghton Mifflin, 1961.

Murphy, G. *Human Potentialities.* New York: Basic Books, 1958.

Murrell, P. H., and Claxton, C. S. "Teaching Strategies for Kolb's Experiential Learning Cycle." Unpublished paper. Memphis, Tenn.: Center for the Study of Higher Education, Memphis State University, 1992.

Myers, I. *Gifts Differing.* Palo Alto, Calif.: Consulting Psychologists Press, 1980a.

Myers, I. *Introduction to Type.* Palo Alto, Calif.: Consulting Psychologists Press, 1980b.

Nagelberg, D. B., Pillsbury, E. C., and Balzer, D. M. "The Prevalence of Depression as a Function of Gender and Facility Usage in College Students." *Journal of College Student Personnel*, 1983, *24*, 525–529.

National Center on Education and the Economy. *America's Choice: High Skills or Low Wages!* Report of the Commission on the Skills of the American Workforce. Rochester, N.Y.: National Center on Education and the Economy, 1990.

National Institute of Education. *Involvement in Learning: Realizing the Potential of American Higher Education.* Washington, D.C.: U.S. Government Printing Office, 1984.

Nelson, E., and Johnson, N. "Attitude Changes on the College Student Questionnaires: A Study of Students Enrolled in Predominantly Black Colleges and Universities." Paper presented at the meeting of the American Educational Research Association, New York, 1971.

Nelson, E., and Uhl, N. "The Development of Attitudes and Social Characteristics of Students Attending Predominantly Black Colleges: A Longitudinal Study." *Research in Higher Education*, 1977, *7*, 299–314.

Neugarten, B. *Personality in Middle and Later Life.* New York: Atherton, 1964.

Neugarten, B. *Middle Age and Aging.* Chicago: University of Chicago Press, 1968.

Neugarten, B. "Adult Personality: Toward a Psychology of Life Cycle." In W. Sze (ed.), *The Human Life Cycle.* New York: Aronson, 1975.

Neumann, W., and Riesman, D. "The Community College Elite." In G. B. Vaughn (ed.), *Questioning the Community College Role.* New Directions for Community Colleges, no. 32. San Francisco: Jossey-Bass, 1980.

Newcomb, T. *Personality and Social Change.* New York: Dryden Press, 1943.

Newcomb, T. *The Acquaintance Process.* Troy, Mo.: Holt, Rinehart & Winston, 1961.

Newcomb, T. "Student Peer-Group Influence and Intellectual Outcomes of College Experience." In R. L. Sutherland, W. H. Holtzman, E. A. Koile, and B. K. Smith (eds.), *Personality Factors on the College Campus.* Austin, Tex.: Hogg Foundation for Mental Health, University of Texas, 1962.

Newcomb, T., Koenig, K., Flacks, R., and Warwick, D. P. *Persistence and Change: Bennington College and Its Students After Twenty-Five Years.* New York: Wiley, 1967.

Newcomb, T., and others. "Self-Selection and Change." In J. Gaff (ed.), *The Cluster College.* San Francisco: Jossey-Bass, 1970.

Newcomb, T. and others. "The University of Michigan's Residential College." In P. Dressel (ed.), *The New Colleges: Toward an Appraisal.* Iowa City, Iowa: American College Testing Program and American Association for Higher Education, 1971.

Newman, Cardinal J. H., *The Idea of a University.* Westminster, Md.: Christian Classics, 1973. (Originally published 1852.)

Newton, L., and Gaither, G. "Factors Contributing to Attrition: An Analysis of Program Impact on Persistence Patterns." *College and University,* 1980, *55,* 237–251.

Ory, J., and Braskamp, L. "Involvement and Growth of Students in Three Academic Programs." *Research in Higher Education,* 1988, *28,* 116–129.

Pace, C. R. *College and University Environment Scales.* Princeton, N.J.: Educational Testing Service, 1962.

Pace, C. R. *Demise of Diversity? A Comparative Profile of Eight Types of Institutions.* New York: McGraw-Hill, 1974.

Pace, C. R. *Measuring the Quality of College Student Experiences.* Los Angeles, Calif.: Higher Education Research Institute, University of California, 1984.

Painton, P. "The Shrinking Ten Percent." *Time,* Apr. 26, 1993, pp. 27–29.

Palmer, P. J. "Community, Conflict, and Ways of Knowing." *Change,* 1987, *19*(5), 20–25.

Palmer, P. J. "Good Teaching: A Matter of Living the Mystery." *Change,* 1990, *22*(1), 11–16.

Parker, C. A. "Ashes, Ashes. . . ." Paper presented at the American College Personnel Association Convention, St. Louis, Mo., Mar. 1970.

Pascarella, E. "Academic and Interpersonal Experience as Mediators of the Structural Effects of College." Unpublished manuscript, University of Illinois, Chicago, n.d.

Pascarella, E. "Student-Faculty Informal Contact and College Outcomes." *Review of Educational Research,* 1980, *50,* 545–595.

Pascarella, E. "The Influence of On-Campus Living Versus Commuting to College on Intellectual and Interpersonal Self-Concept." *Journal of College Student Personnel,* 1985a, *26,* 292–299.

Pascarella, E. "Students' Affective Development Within the College Environment." *Journal of Higher Education,* 1985b, *56,* 640–663.

Pascarella, E. "A Program for Research and Policy Development on Student Persistence at the Institutional Level." *Journal of College Student Personnel,* 1986, *27,* 100–107.

Pascarella, E., and Smart, J. "Impacts of Intercollegiate Athletic Participation for Black-American and White-American Men: Some Further Evidence." Unpublished manuscript, University of Illinois, Chicago, 1990.

Pascarella, E., and Terenzini, P. "Student-Faculty and Student-Peer Relationships as Mediators of the Structural Effects of Undergraduate Residence Arrangement." *Journal of Educational Research,* 1980, *73,* 344–353.

Pascarella, E., and Terenzini, P. "Residence Arrangement, Student/Faculty Relationships, and Freshman-Year Educational Outcomes." *Journal of College Student Personnel,* 1981, *22,* 147–156.

Pascarella, E. T., and Terenzini, P. T. *How College Affects Students: Findings and Insights from Twenty Years of Research.* San Francisco: Jossey-Bass, 1991.

Pearson, C. S. *The Hero Within.* San Francisco: HarperCollins, 1986.

Peavey, F. *Heart Politics.* Philadelphia: New Society Publishers, 1986.

Perls, F. S. *In and Out of the Garbage Pail.* Moab, Utah: Real People Press, 1969.

Perry, W. G. *Forms of Intellectual and Ethical Development in the College Years: A Scheme.* Troy, Mo.: Holt, Rinehart & Winston, 1970.

Pervin, L. "A Twenty-College Study of Student × College Interaction Using TAPE (Transactional Analysis of Personality and Environment): Rationale, Reliability, and Validity." *Journal of Educational Psychology,* 1967, *58,* 290–302.

Pervin, L. "The College as a Social System: Student Perceptions of Students, Faculty, and Administration." *Journal of Educational Research,* 1968a, *61,* 281–284.

Pervin, L. "Performance and Satisfaction as a Function of Individual-Environment Fit." *Psychological Bulletin,* 1968b, *69,* 56–68.

Peterson, C., Schwartz, S., and Seligman, M.E.P. "Self-Blame and Depressive Symptoms." *Journal of Personality and Social Psychology,* 1981, *42,* 23–28.

Peterson, S. A., and Franzese, B. "Correlates of College Men's Sexual Abuse of Women." *Journal of College Student Personnel,* 1987, *28,* 223–228.

Piaget, J. *The Moral Judgment of the Child.* Orlando, Fla.: Harcourt Brace Jovanovich, 1932.

Pike, D. K. "The Structure of the Individual." Audiotaped class no. 1. Scottsdale, Ariz.: Teleos Institute, 1985.

Plummer, K. *Sexual Stigma: An Interactionist Account.* London: Routledge, 1975.

Prager, K. "Identity Development, Age, and College Experience in Women." *Journal of Genetic Psychology,* 1986, *147,* 31–36.

"Principles for Good Practice in Undergraduate Education Faculty Inventory." Racine, Wis.: The Johnson Foundation, Inc., 1989.

"Principles for Good Practice in Undergraduate Education: Institutional Inventory." Racine, Wis.: The Johnson Foundation, Inc., 1989.

Raushenbush, E. *The Student and His Studies.* Middletown, Conn.: Wesleyan University Press, 1964.

Redmore, C. "Ego Development in the College Years: Two Longitudinal Studies." *Journal of Youth and Adolescence,* 1983, *12,* 301–306.

Rest, J. *Development in Judging Moral Issues.* Minneapolis: University of Minnesota Press, 1979.

Rest, J. *Moral Development.* New York: Praeger, 1986.

Rest, J., and Deemer, D. "Life Experiences and Developmental Pathways." In J. Rest (ed.), *Moral Development: Advances in Research and Theory.* New York: Praeger, 1986.

Richardson, R. C., Jr. *Literacy in the Open-Access College.* San Francisco: Jossey-Bass, 1983.

"Risky Business." *National On Campus Report.* (Magna Publications, Madison, Wis.), 1992, *20*(4), 4.

Rodgers, R. F. "Recent Theories and Research Underlying Student Development." In D. G. Creamer and Associates (1990), *College Student Development: Theory and Practice for the 1990s.* Alexandria, Va.: American College Personnel Association, 1990.

Rogers, C. *On Becoming a Person.* Boston: Houghton Mifflin, 1961.

Rosen, S. "Measuring the Obsolescence of Knowledge." In F. Juster (ed.), *Education, Income, and Human Behavior.* New York: McGraw-Hill, 1975.

Rosenbaum, E. E. *A Taste of My Own Medicine.* New York: Random House, 1988.

Rouche, J. "Student Development 2000 or Traverse City Revisited." In R. C. Keys (ed.), *Toward the Future Vitality of Student Development Services: Traverse City Five Years Later.* Iowa City, Iowa: American College Testing Program, 1990.

Rubin, T. I. *The Angry Book.* New York: Macmillan, 1969.

Ryan, F. "Further Observations on Competitive Ability in Athletics." In B. M. Wedge (ed.), *Psychosocial Problems of College Men.* New Haven, Conn.: Yale University Press, 1958a.

Ryan, F. "An Investigation of Personality Differences Associated with Competitive Ability." In B. M. Wedge (ed.), *Psychosocial Problems of College Men.* New Haven, Conn.: Yale University Press, 1958b.

Ryan, F. "Participation in Intercollegiate Athletics: Affective Outcomes." *Journal of College Student Development,* 1989, *30,* 122–128.

Saigh, P. A. "Unscheduled Assessment: Test Anxiety, Academic Achievement, and Social Validity." *Educational Research Quarterly,* 1985, *9*(4), 6–11.

Sale, K. *Human Scale.* New York: Perigee, 1980.

Sandberg, G., Jackson, T. L., and Petretic-Jackson, P. "College Students' Attitudes Regarding Sexual Coercion and Aggression: Developing Educational and Preventative Strategies." *Journal of College Student Personnel,* 1987, *28,* 302–310.

Sanford, N. *The American College.* New York: Wiley, 1962.

Sanford, N. "Factors Related to the Effectiveness of Student Interaction with the College Social System." In B. Barger and E. E. Hall (eds.), *Higher Education and Mental Health*. Proceedings of a conference, University of Florida, Gainesville, 1963, pp. 9–26.

Sanford, N. *Self and Society: Social Change and Individual Development*. New York: Atherton Press, 1966.

Schenkel, S., and Marcia, J. E. "Attitudes Toward Premarital Intercourse in Determining Ego Identity Status in College Women." *Journal of Personality*, 1972, *40*(1), 472–482.

Schlesinger, A. M., Jr. *A Thousand Days*. Boston: Houghton Mifflin, 1965.

Schlossberg, N. K., Lynch, A. Q., and Chickering, A. W. *Improving Higher Education Environments for Adults: Responsive Programs and Services from Entry to Departure*. San Francisco: Jossey-Bass, 1989.

Schmitz, J. A. (ed.). Alverno College Bulletin, 1992–94. Milwaukee, Wis.: Alverno Productions, 1992.

Schön, D. A. *The Reflective Practitioner*. New York: Basic Books, 1983.

Schroeder, C. "New Strategies for Structuring Residential Environments." *Journal of College Student Personnel*, 1976, *17*, 386–390.

Schroeder, C. "Territoriality: Conceptual and Methodological Issues for Residence Educators." *Journal of College and University Student Housing*, 1979, *8*, 9–15.

Schroeder, C. "Student Development Through Environmental Management." In G. S. Blimling and J. H. Schuh (eds.), *Increasing the Educational Role of Residence Halls*. New Directions for Student Services, no. 13. San Francisco: Jossey-Bass, 1981.

Schumacher, E. F. *Small Is Beautiful: Economics as if People Mattered*. New York City: HarperCollins, 1973.

Sedlacek, W. E. "Black Students on White Campuses: Twenty Years of Research." *Journal of College Student Personnel*, 1987, *28*, 484–495.

Shawn, W., and Gregory, A. *My Dinner with André*. New York: Grove Press, 1981.

Shea, C. "At U. of Massachusetts at Amherst, Students Graduate at a Rate Above the National Average." *Chronicle of Higher Education*, July 15, 1992, p. A30.

Sheehy, G. *Passages: Predictable Crises of Adult Life*. New York: Dutton, 1974.

Siegel, S. F. "Reduction of Test Anxiety Using Pavlovian Condition Principles: A Preliminary Note." *Psychological Reports,* 1986, *59*(1), 48–50.

Simpson, I. H. "Patterns of Socialization into Professions: The Case of Student Nurses." *Sociological Inquiry,* 1967, *37*(1), 47–54.

Smart, J., and Pascarella, E. "Socioeconomic Achievements of Former College Students." *Journal of Higher Education,* 1986, *57,* 529–549.

Smith, M. B. "Personal Values in the Study of Lives." In R. H. White (ed.), *The Study of Lives.* New York: Atherton Press, 1963.

Smith, V. B., and Bernstein, A. R. *The Impersonal Campus: Options for Reorganizing Colleges to Increase Student Involvement, Learning, and Development.* San Francisco: Jossey-Bass, 1977.

Snyder, Benson R. *The Hidden Curriculum.* New York: Knopf, 1970.

Spaeth, J., and Greeley, A. *Recent Alumni and Higher Education: A Survey of College Graduates.* New York: McGraw-Hill, 1970.

Spielberger, C. (ed.). *Anxiety: Current Trends in Theory and Research.* New York: Academic Press, 1972.

Spivak, L., and Shire, M. *Social Adjustment of Young Children: A Cognitive Approach to Solving Real-Life Problems.* San Francisco: Jossey-Bass, 1974.

Spohn, H. "Vocational Orientation and Growth." In L. B. Murphy and E. Raushenbush (eds.), *Achievement in the College Years.* New York: HarperCollins, 1960.

Spurr, J., and Stevens, V. "Increasing Study Time and Controlling Student Guilt: A Case Study in Self-Management." *Behavior Therapist,* 1980, *3*(2), 17–18.

Stakenas, R. "Student-Faculty Contact and Attitude Change: Results of an Experimental Program for College Freshmen." In K. Feldman (ed.), *College and Student: Selected Readings in the Social Psychology of Higher Education.* New York: Pergamon Press, 1972.

Standing Committee on the Core Curriculum. *1991–92 Courses of Instruction.* Faculty of Arts and Sciences. Cambridge, Mass.: Harvard University, 1991.

Stern, G. G. "Environments for Learning." In N. Sanford (ed.), *The American College.* New York: Wiley, 1962.

Stern, G. G. "Student Ecology and the College Environment." In *Research in Higher Education.* New York: College Entrance Examination Board, 1964.

Stern, G. *People in Context: Measuring Person-Environment Congruence in Education and Industry.* New York: Wiley, 1970.

Stewart, A. J., and Winter, D. G. "Self-Definition and Social Definitions in Women." *Journal of Personality,* 1974, *42,* 238–259.

Strange, C., and King, P. "The Professional Practice of Student Development." In D. G. Creamer and Associates, *College Student Development: Theory and Practice for the 1990s.* Alexandria, Va.: American College Personnel Association, 1990.

Straub, C. "Women's Development of Autonomy and Chickering's Theory." *Journal of College Student Personnel,* 1987, *28,* 198–204.

Straub, C., and Rodgers, R. "An Exploration of Chickering's Theory and Women's Development." *Journal of College Student Personnel,* 1986, *27,* 216–224.

"Student Development: A Combination of Challenge and Support." Juniata College Bulletin, 1991, *90,* (2), 2–9.

Sue, S., and Sue, D. "Chinese-American Personality and Mental Health." *Amerasia Journal,* 1971, *1,* 36–49.

Szasz, T. *The Myth of Mental Illness.* New York: Dell, (1961) 1967.

Taylor, H. Address given at the College of Education, Wayne State University, Apr. 23, 1964.

Terry, P. W. "How Students Review for Objective and Essay Tests." *Elementary School Journal,* 1933, *33,* 592–603.

Thistlethwaite, D. L. "College Press and Student Achievement." *Journal of Educational Psychology,* 1959, *50*(5), 183–194.

Thistlethwaite, D. L. "College Press and Changes in Study Plans of Talented Students." *Journal of Educational Psychology,* 1960, *51*(4), 222–233.

Thistlethwaite, D. L. "Rival Hypotheses for Explaining the Effects of Different Learning Environments." *Journal of Educational Psychology,* 1962, *53*(6), 310–331.

Thomas, D. "Light Breaks Where No Sun Shines." In D. Thomas, *Collected Poems.* New York: New Directions Books, 1939.

Thomas, R., and Chickering, A. W. "Institutional Size, Higher Education, and Student Development." In S. Goodlad (ed.),

Economies of Scale in Higher Education. Guildford, Surrey, England: Society for Research into Higher Education, 1983.

Torbert, W. R. "Interpersonal Competence." In A. W. Chickering and Associates, *The Modern American College: Responding to the New Realities of Diverse Students and a Changing Society.* San Francisco: Jossey-Bass, 1981.

Troiden, R. R. "Becoming Homosexual: A Model of Gay Identity Acquisition." *Psychiatry,* 1979, *42,* 362–373.

Vaillant, G. *Adaptation to Life.* Boston: Little, Brown, 1977.

Valine, S., and Baum, A. "Residential Group Size, Social Interaction, and Crowding." *Environmental Behavior,* 1973, *5,* 421–439.

Vandenberg, B. "Is Epistemology Enough? An Existential Consideration of Development." *American Psychologist,* 1991, *46*(12), 1278–1286.

Veysey, L. *The Emergence of the American University.* Chicago: University of Chicago Press, 1965.

Wahbe, M. "Current Issues in Human Services: The Satir Model: Theory and Practice." Workshop sponsored by Western Washington University and the Northwest Satir Institute, Bellingham, Wash., July 1990.

Walker, L. "Sex Differences in the Development of Moral Reasoning: A Critical Review." *Child Development,* 1984, *55,* 677–691.

Wallace, W. L. *Student Culture.* Hawthorne, N.Y.: Aldine, 1966.

Walters, A. S. "College Students' Knowledge About AIDS and Reported Changes in Sexual Behavior." *National Association of Student Personnel Administration Journal,* 1992, *29*(2), 91–99.

Waluconis, C. "Self-Evaluation: Settings and Uses." In J. MacGregor (ed.), *Student Self-Evaluation: Fostering Reflective Learning.* New Directions for Teaching and Learning, no. 56. San Francisco: Jossey-Bass, 1993.

Weathersby, R. P. "A Developmental Perspective on Adults' Uses of Formal Education." Unpublished doctoral dissertation, Graduate School of Education, Harvard University, 1977.

Weathersby, R. P. "Ego Development." In A. W. Chickering and Associates, *The Modern American College: Responding to the New Realities of Diverse Students and a Changing Society.* San Francisco: Jossey-Bass, 1981.

Webster, H., Freedman, M.B., and Heist, P. "Personality Changes in College Students." In N. Sanford (ed.), *The American College.* New York: Wiley, 1962.

Wegscheider, S. *Another Chance.* Palo Alto, Calif.: Science and Behavior Books, 1981.

Weidman, J. "The World of Higher Education: A Socialization-Theoretical Perspective." In K. Hurrelmann and U. Engel (eds.), *The Social World of Adolescents: International Perspectives.* Hawthorne, N.Y.: Aldine, 1989.

"What's Happening: Learning Community and Faculty Exchanges at Participating Institutions." *Washington Center News* (Washington Center for Improving the Quality of Undergraduate Education, The Evergreen State College), 1991, *6*(1), pp. 31–34.

White, D. B., and Hood, A. B. "An Assessment of the Validity of Chickering's Theory of Student Development." *Journal of College Student Development,* 1989, *30,* 354–361.

White, K. "Mid-Course Adjustments: Using Small-Group Instructional Diagnosis to Improve Teaching and Learning." *Washington Center News* (Washington Center for Improving the Quality of Undergraduate Education, The Evergreen State College), 1991, *6,* (1), 20–22.

White, R. W. *Lives in Progress.* New York: Dryden Press, 1958.

White, R. W. "Sense of Interpersonal Competence: Two Case Studies and Some Reflections on Origins." In R. W. White (ed.), *The Study of Lives.* New York: Atherton Press, 1963.

White, R. W. "Humanitarian Concern." In A. W. Chickering and Associates, *The Modern American College: Responding to the New Realities of Diverse Students and a Changing Society.* San Francisco: Jossey-Bass, 1981.

Wilder, C., Sherrier, J., and Berry, W. "Learning Activity Proposal for PDA 101 (Pluralism and Diversity in America)." Suffern, N.Y.: Office of Instructional and Community Services, Rockland Community College, 1991.

Wilder, D., and others. "The Impact of Fraternity or Sorority Membership on Values and Attitudes." *Journal of College Student Personnel,* 1978, *19,* 445–449.

Wilder, D., and others. "Greek Affiliation and Attitude Change in College Students." *Journal of College Student Personnel,* 1986, *27,* 510–519.

Wilson, E. K. "The Entering Student: Attributes and Agents of Change." In T. M. Newcomb and E. K. Wilson (eds.), *College Peer Groups.* Hawthorne, N.Y.: Aldine, 1966.

Winston, R. B., Miller, T. K., and Prince, J. S. "Student Development Task and Lifestyle Inventory." Athens, GA: Student Development Associates, 1987.

Winston, R. B., Jr., and Saunders, S. "The Greek Experience: Friend or Foe of Student Development?" In R. B. Winston, Jr., W. R. Nettles III, and J. H. Opper, Jr. (eds.), *Fraternities and Sororities on the Contemporary College Campus.* New Directions for Student Services, no. 40. San Francisco: Jossey-Bass, 1987.

Winter, D. G., McClelland, D. C., and Stewart, A. J. *A New Case for the Liberal Arts: Assessing Institutional Goals and Student Development.* San Francisco: Jossey-Bass, 1981.

Wylie, R. *The Self-Concept.* Vol. 2: *Theory and Research on Selected Topics.* (rev. ed.) Lincoln: University of Nebraska Press, 1979.

Yalom, I. D. *Existential Psychotherapy.* New York: Basic Books, 1980.

Yonge, G., and Regan, M. "A Longitudinal Study of Personality and Choice of Major." *Journal of Vocational Behavior,* 1975, *7,* 41–65.

Name Index

A

Acocella, J. R., 186
Adams, G., 178
Adams, J. M., 186
Adelson, J., 116, 270, 333
Adler, A., 21, 30, 158
Aiello, J., 404
Alcoff, L., 20
Allport, G. W., 158
Annis, L. F., 108
Aquinas, T., 428
Archer, J., 91
Argyris, C., 253–254
Aristotle, 428
Arnold, K. D., 20
Astin, A. W., 82, 214, 216, 271, 291, 308, 310, 311, 312, 314, 318, 321, 401, 410, 464–465
Astin, H., 326
Atkinson, D. R., 35, 193–194
Augustine, 428
Auvenshire, C., 410

B

Bailey, S. K., 484
Baird, L., 294, 326

Balzer, D. M., 94
Banning, J., 3, 5
Barker, R. G., 3, 268, 299, 300n, 301, 305, 314, 469
Barker, V. L., 113
Barnard, J. D., 272
Barron, F., 236
Barsi, L., 373
Bartsch, K., 418
Bates, M., 3
Bateson, M. C., 195
Baum, A., 404, 405
Baumrind, D., 19
Baxter Magolda, M. B., 2, 6, 15–17, 20, 56, 317–318, 362, 363–364, 365, 463, 468
Bayer, A., 309
Beal, P. E., 310
Beauvoir, S. de, 192
Beck, A. T., 94
Beecher, G., 119–121, 231
Belenky, M. F., 2, 6, 9, 12–15, 17, 56, 57, 99, 116, 337, 417, 437
Bellah, R. N., 422–423
Bender, S., 233–234
Bennett, M. J., 151–152
Bennett, S., 89

Bergoffen, D., 360
Bergson, H., 71
Berne, E., 21, 201
Bernstein, A. R., 311
Berry, W., 153–154
Bisconti, A., 55, 64
Blizard, P., 56
Bloom, B. S., 272
Blos, P., 115
Blunt, M., 56
Bootzin, R. R., 186
Bourne, E., 174
Bower, E. M., 61–62, 71
Bower, P. A., 65
Bowers, C. A., 423
Boyd, T. L., 108
Boyer, E. L., 283–284, 289–290, 318, 321, 389
Brabeck, M., 20
Branch-Simpson, G., 35, 190
Braskamp, L., 329
Brawer, F. B., 89, 148, 370
Breen, P., 75–76
Brethower, D., 56, 371
Briere, J., 104
Brubaker, J. S., 433
Brundage, D. H., 135
Buber, M., 261
Bucklin, R., 216
Bucklin, W., 216
Burkhart, J. E., 20

C

Cage, M. C., 452
Campagna, D., 89
Campbell, J., 144, 225
Cannon, D., 213
Carfagna, R., 437
Carroll, L., 264
Cass, V. C., 35, 187–188, 193
Cerio, J., 108
Chickering, A. W., 2, 6, 22–24, 66, 89, 119–121, 148, 200, 231, 296n, 307–308, 373–378, 400, 411–412, 425–426, 434, 438
Chira, S., 437
Chodorow, N., 28–29
Clark, B., 89
Clark, M., 326

Claxton, C. S., 381
Clinchy, B. M., 2, 6, 9, 12–15, 17, 56, 57, 99, 116, 337, 417, 437
Cohen, A. M., 370
Cohen, P., 372–373
Coleman, E., 35
Colesnick, L., 404
Collins, P. H., 17
Connelly, W. B., 332
Conrad, J., 191
Constantinople, A., 176
Coopersmith, S., 179
Copeland, C. L., 439
Copernicus, N., 444
Corey, G., 261–262, 264
Cray, D., 213, 214
Creamer, D. G., 190
Cress, C. M., 439
Cromwell, L., 291
Cronan, W., 223
Cross, K. P., 3, 322, 370–371, 383–384, 446
Cross, W., 2, 35, 192–193
Crouse, R. H., 91
Curry, T., 213, 214

D

Daloz, L. A., 318, 322–325, 334, 336–337
Dank, B. M., 35
Dannells, M., 446–447
Dante, 113–114
Darwin, C., 414
Davanzo, J., 133
Davidson, W. G., 108
Davis, J., 273, 309, 317
Davison, M. L., 59
Dearden, D. F., 117
Deemer, D., 401
Deffenbacher, J. L., 91
DeMan, A. F., 123–124
Demiutroff, J., 216
Denny, N., 20
Dewey, J., 58, 127, 362–363, 372, 433, 476
DeYoung, A., 400
Dickens, C., 191
Dickinson, E., 203
Dodge, S., 213

Doherty, A., 291
Donlon, T. F., 75-76
Dostoyevsky, F., 191, 261
Douvan, E., 116, 161-162, 169, 170
Dressel, P. L., 273
Dumont, R., 55

E

Eble, K. E., 382
Eddy, E. G., Jr., 307
Edelmann, R. J., 108
Einstein, A., 280
Eliot, T. S., 95
Ellis, A., 21
Endo, J., 329
Epps, E., 326, 327
Erikson, E., 1, 2, 6, 18, 21-23, 35,
    40, 115, 138, 149, 161, 173-176,
    181, 197, 202-203, 205, 207,
    253, 274, 434
Eron, L. D., 93
Evans, N., 186-187, 188

F

Feldman, K., 89, 215-216, 237, 327
Fenske, R. H., 430-431, 432, 433
Ferlinghetti, L., 95
Feshback, N., 93
Feshback, S., 93
Festinger, L., 365, 476
Finkelstein, M. J., 131
Fitch, S., 178
Flacks, R., 288
Flesch, R., 141
Fowler, J. W., 2, 240, 336-337
Frankl, V., 261, 262-264
Franzese, B., 104
Freedman, M. B., 89, 141
Freud, S., 21, 160, 201
Friedman, D. E., 104
Frost, G. A., 91
Frost, R., 229
Fry, R., 379

G

Gaff, J., 465
Gaier, E. L., 131

Gaither, G., 216
Galanter, E., 209-211
Gallant, J. A., 308
Gamson, Z. F., 354-355, 373-378,
    387-389
Gaudry, E., 91
Gerst, M., 405
Gibbs, B., 118
Gibbs, J. C., 20
Gilligan, C., 2, 6, 18-21, 29, 116,
    243-244, 251, 337
Giotto, 414
Girrell, K. W., 418
Gold, M. S., 94, 99
Goldberger, N. R., 2, 6, 9, 12-15,
    17, 56, 57, 99, 116, 337, 417,
    437
Goldscheider, F. K., 133
Gould, R., 2
Graffam, D., 396
Greeley, A., 55
Greeley, A. M., 24, 326-327
Green, T. F., 342
Gregory, A., 211
Grigg, C. M., 326
Gump, P. V., 268, 300n, 301, 305,
    314
Gurin, P., 326, 327
Gustav, A., 56

H

Haan, N., 19
Hamlin, W. G., 119-121, 231
Hannah, W., 475
Hannibal, 191
Hardy, T., 99
Harpel, R., 329
Harrison, R., 134-135
Hartnett, R., 326
Harwick, S., 108
Haswell, R. H., 57
Hatch, D., 119, 148
Havighurst, R., 2
Hawthorne, N., 99
Healy, C., 216
Heath, D., 2, 89, 119, 288-289,
    306-307, 308, 317, 334, 366
Hechinger, F., 389
Hedlund, D., 468

Heidegger, M., 261
Heider, F., 476-477
Heist, P., 89, 475
Heller, S., 151
Helms, J., 35
Helson, H., 473-474, 476
Hemingway, E., 256
Hesburgh, T. M., 389
Heston, C., 211
Hewer, A., 18
High, T., 405
Ho, M., 35
Hofstadter, R., 430
Holland, J. L., 3, 5
Hood, A. B., 88-89, 134
Hopson, 192
Hotch, D. F., 133
House, W. J., 108
Huesmann, L. R., 93
Hunter, J., 89
Hyde, J. S., 186
Hyman, H., 55, 56

I

Irion, A. L., 272
Ivey, A. E., 338

J

Jackson, L. M., 88-89
Jackson, T. L., 93
Jacob, P. E., 288, 307, 334
James, W., 86
Jefferson, T., 431
Job, 264, 428
Johnson, G., 285-286
Johnson, M., 35
Johnson, N., 119
Johnson-Powell, G., 192
Johnston, D. K., 19
Jones, J., 468
Josselson, R., 2, 13, 35, 116,
    117-118, 131, 139, 145, 149-150,
    163-164, 176-178, 181, 229-230
Joyce, J., 414
Jung, C. G., 21, 474-475

K

Kaiser, L., 3
Kalsbeek, D., 408

Kapp, G. J., 321
Karman, F., 327
Kart, C., 410
Katz, D., 327
Katz, J., 330
Kearney, C., 355-356
Kegan, D. L., 321
Kegan, R., 2, 6, 24-30, 62, 116,
    162, 164, 337
Keim, M. C., 425
Keirsey, D., 3
Keniston, K., 475
Kennedy, J. F., 280, 459
Kent, L., 326
Kessler, J., 64
Keys, R. C., 436
Keyser, E., 89
Kierkegaard, S., 261-262
King, P. M., 2, 17, 36, 57-59
King, S., 89, 414
Kinsey, A. C., 186
Kirschner, J., 451
Kitchener, K., 2, 17, 57-59
Kitto, H.D.F., 40-41
Klemp, G. O., 77, 344-348
Knefelkamp, L., 2, 5, 207, 278, 434
Knowles, M., 379-380
Knox, A. B., 2
Knox, W., 396
Koapp, S., 108
Koenig, K., 288
Koestler, A., 85-86, 87-88, 111-113
Kohlberg, L., 2, 6, 14, 17-18, 19,
    20, 21, 36, 37, 116, 250-251,
    252, 255-256, 260, 401, 434
Kolb, D. A., 3-4, 6, 378, 379, 380,
    381, 382, 472
Kolb, M., 396
Komarovsky, M., 326, 327
Korn, H. A., 434
Krasnow, R., 410
Kuh, G., 148, 318, 320, 321-322,
    337, 396-397, 398
Kuhlman, T., 180
Kurfiss, J., 37

L

Lamnin, A., 91
Langdale, S., 19
Lange, C. G., 86

Lannholm, G. V., 55
Lashley, K., 35
Laud, W., 429
Lawrence, G., 475
Leafgren, F., 404
Lerner, H. G., 108
Levine, C., 18
Levine, H., 186–187, 188
Levinson, D. J., 2, 336
Lewin, K., 272
Lewinsohn, P. M., 94
Lewis, H. G., 95
Lindsay, P., 396
Loacker, G., 291
Loevinger, J., 2, 6, 30–34, 35, 36,
    37, 58, 116, 143, 161, 175, 178,
    206, 337
Longino, C., 410
Lopez, F. G., 94, 104
Lovelace, L., 110
Lowell, A. L., 433
Luttrell, W., 17
Lynch, A. Q., 425–426, 438
Lyon, M., 398
Lyons, N. P., 19

M

Mabry, M., 192
McClelland, D. C., 64, 328, 400
McConnell, T. R., 475
McCormick, J., 89
McDonald, G. J., 35
McDowell, J., 89
McGeoch, J. A., 272
MacGregor, J., 416–417
Machiavelli, N., 437
McIntire, R. W., 445
McKeachie, W. J., 272
MacKeracher, D., 135
Macleish, J., 56, 371
McWhirter, W., 213, 214
Makepeace, J. M., 93
Malamuth, N. M., 104
Marcia, J. E., 2, 131, 174–175,
    176, 178, 187
Marlowe, A., 410
Marmor, J., 187
Marshall, A. B., 332
Martin, C. E., 186

Martinez, C., Jr., 35
Maslow, A., 34
Matthews, R., 415
Mature, V., 191
May, R., 261
Mayo, L., 108
Mentkowski, M., 291
Meyer, G., 273
Mezirow, J., 57, 249
Michael, R., 55
Middleton-Moz, J., 99
Mierzwa, J. A., 108
Milgram, S., 256
Miller, G. A., 209–211
Miller, H., 192
Miller, J. B., 21, 149
Miller, T. K., 148, 453
Minton, H. L., 35
Mitchell, J., 216
Monroe, C., 430
Mooney, C. J., 54
Moore, D., 133
Moore, L. V., 2
Moore, M. T., 104
Moos, R., 3, 400, 404
Morris, J., 428–430, 444
Morten, G., 35, 193–194
Mourton, D., 216
Mozart, W. A., 112
Muelenhard, C. L., 104
Mueller, K. H., 434
Muñoz, R. F., 94
Murphy, G., 48, 212
Murrell, P. H., 381
Myers, I., 3

N

Nagelberg, D. B., 94
Narcissus, 48
Nelson, E., 119
Neugarten, B., 2
Neumann, W., 452
Newcomb, T., 89, 119, 215–216,
    237, 287–288, 327, 402, 403,
    476
Newman, J. H., 343–344
Newton, L., 216
Nietzsche, F., 261, 262
Nin, A., 192
Nixon, R. M., 253

Noel, L., 310
Norton, G. R., 108

O

O'Brien, K., 291
Orwell, G., 388
Ory, J., 329

P

Pace, C. R., 55, 291, 318, 400
Painton, P., 186
Palmer, P. J., 270-271, 349-350,
    351, 363, 372, 417, 419, 420-422
Parker, C. A., 2, 5, 207, 434-435
Pascarella, E. T., 1-2, 37, 55, 56,
    64, 80-81, 82, 89, 118-119,
    147-148, 149, 158, 175, 178,
    179-180, 183, 185, 192, 193,
    216, 237, 251-252, 256, 259-260,
    294-295, 305-306, 308-309, 310,
    311, 316, 318, 320-321, 322,
    325-326, 327, 335, 372, 378,
    385-387, 393, 401-402, 403, 411,
    450-451, 455, 456n, 459-460,
    461-462, 466-468, 470
Pearson, C. S., 66-67, 121,
    128-129, 131, 159-160, 203
Peavey, F., 423-424
Perls, F. S., 21, 204
Perry, W. G., 2, 6, 7-11, 12, 14,
    15, 17, 36, 37, 56, 57, 58, 116,
    128, 238, 240, 246, 337, 416,
    434
Pervin, L., 3
Peterson, C., 95-96
Peterson, S. A., 104
Petretic-Jackson, P., 93
Piaget, J., 6, 14, 18, 36, 238, 260
Pike, D. K., 198, 203
Pillsbury, E. C., 94
Pirandello, L., 139
Pitcher, B., 55
Pitkin, R. S., 119-121, 231
Pitkin, T., 372
Plato, 40, 127, 355
Plummer, K., 35
Pomeroy, W. B., 186
Prager, K., 175

Pribram, K. H., 209-211
Price, J., 93
Prince, J. S., 148, 453
Prothero, J. W., 308

R

Raushenbush, E., 317, 325,
    328-329
Redmore, C., 178
Reed, J., 55, 56
Regan, M., 148
Reisser, L., 45
Rest, J., 20, 35, 36, 251, 401
Richardson, R. C., Jr., 352-353,
    371
Riesman, D., 452
Rodgers, R. F., 2, 6, 23, 162-163
Rogers, C., 21, 40, 253, 476
Rogers, P., 192
Rosen, S., 56
Rosenbaum, E. E., 25
Rouche, J., 442-443, 446
Rubin, T. I., 93
Rudy, W., 433
Ryan, F., 64

S

Saigh, P. A., 108
Sale, K., 298-299, 302, 305
Salinger, J. D., 95
Sandberg, G., 93
Sanford, N., 1, 51, 238, 274,
    330-332, 367-368, 434, 477-478
Sartre, J. P., 192, 261
Satir, V., 21, 478
Saunders, S., 410
Schenkel, S., 176
Schlesinger, A. M., Jr., 280, 459
Schlossberg, N. K., 425-426, 438
Schmitz, J. A., 291-294
Schön, D. A., 253-254, 382-383
Schroeder, C., 405, 408
Schuh, J. H., 318, 320, 321-322,
    337, 398
Schumacher, E. F., 297-298, 302,
    305
Schwartz, S., 95-96
Sedlacek, W. E., 192

Seligman, M.E.P., 95–96
Shakespeare, W., 95, 355
Shawn, W., 211
Shea, C., 452
Sheehy, G., 2
Sherrier, J., 153–154
Shure, M., 93
Siegel, S. F., 108
Simpson, I. H., 418
Skinner, B. F., 21
Smail, P., 400
Smart, J., 64
Smith, M. B., 246
Smith, V. B., 311
Smith, W., 430
Snyder, B. R., 350–351
Solomon, L., 55
Spaeth, J., 55
Spielberger, C., 91, 108
Spivak, L., 93
Spohn, H., 220
Spurr, J., 108
Stakenas, R., 329
Stern, G. G., 3, 291, 475
Stevens, V., 108
Stevens, W., 212
Stewart, A. J., 64, 328, 347, 400
Strange, C., 2
Straub, C., 23–24
Stuber, D., 446–447
Sue, D. W., 35, 193–194
Sue, S., 35
Sullivan, H. S., 21
Sundstrom, E., 405
Sweetwood, H., 405
Szasz, T., 155–156

T

Tarule, J. M., 2, 6, 9, 12–15, 17,
    56, 57, 99, 116, 337, 417, 437
Taylor, H., 315
Terenzini, P. T., 1–2, 37, 55, 56,
    80–81, 82, 89, 118–119, 147–148,
    149, 158, 175, 178, 179–180,
    183, 185, 192, 193, 216, 237,
    251–252, 256, 259–260, 294–295,
    305–306, 308–309, 310, 311, 316,
    318, 320–321, 322, 325–326, 327,
    335, 372, 378, 385–387, 393,
    401–402, 403, 411, 450–451,
    459–460, 461–462, 466–468
Teresa, Mother, 159
Terry, P. W., 273
Thistlethwaite, D. L., 273, 309–310,
    317
Thomas, C. M., 104
Thomas, D., 43
Thomas, M., 104
Thomas, R., 296n
Tinsley, H., 24
Torbert, W. R., 254
Troelstrup, R., 55
Troiden, R. R., 35
Twain, M., 141

U

Uhl, N., 119

V

Vaillant, G., 2
Valine, S., 405
Vandenberg, B., 260–261
Van Dort, B., 400
Vennum, T., 222
Virgil, 113

W

Wahbe, M., 478n
Walker, A., 99
Walker, L., 20
Wallace, W. L., 309, 326
Walters, A. S., 172
Waluconis, C., 59–61, 79
Warwick, D. P., 288
Weathersby, R. P., 161
Webster, H., 89
Wegscheider, S., 201–202
Weidman, J., 455, 457n, 470
Whitaker, U., 75–76
White, D. B., 134
White, K., 319
White, R. W., 7, 72, 74, 77–78,
    146, 157–159, 181, 238
Whitt, E. J., 318, 320, 321–322,
    337, 398
Widick, C., 2, 5, 207

Wilder, C., 153–154
Wilder, D., 410
Wilson, E. K., 321
Wilson, W., 433
Winston, R. B., Jr., 148, 410
Winter, D. G., 64, 328, 347, 400
Winthrop, J., 422
Wood, P. K., 59
Wright, C., 55, 56
Wylie, R., 179

Y

Yalom, I. D., 261, 264
Yonge, G., 89, 148
Yost, E. B., 418
Youngren, M. A., 94

Z

Zeiss, A. M., 94

Subject Index

A

Academic practices, for student development, 463–464

Accessibility, for student-faculty relationships, 335–336

Adaptation-level theory, 473–474, 476

Admissions, for student development, 439, 442

Adult students: and autonomy, 115, 131–132, 136–137, 140; and competence development, 59, 69, 79; emotional development of, 91–92, 96–97, 105–106, 107–108, 110–111; orientation for, 442; and purpose, 214–216

African-American students: and cognitive theories, 17; emotional development of, 91–92; identity formation for, 190–194; institutional climate for, 461–462. *See also* Minority students

Aggression. *See* Anger

AIDS, and interpersonal relationships, 146, 172

Altruism: and institutional size, 314; and tolerance, 158–159

Alverno College: interpersonal competence at, 76–77; objectives at, 291–294

American College Testing Program, 278–279, 435–436

American Council on Education, 82, 433

American Psychological Association, 186

Amish, and intentionality, 233–234

Anchoring, and identity, 177–178

Anger, managing, 92–93, 103, 104, 108–110

Anxiety: and autonomy, 142; managing, 91–92, 108

Appearance, and identity formation, 183–184, 204

Aretê, concept of, 40–41

Association of American Colleges, 54–55

Auburn University, residence halls at, 405, 408

Australia: identity formation in, 180; integrity in, 252

Authenticity, in student-faculty relationships, 336

Autonomous stage, in ego development, 31, 33, 34, 116

Autonomy toward interdependence: acceptance of, 140-144; aspects of moving through, 115-144; and cognitive theories, 21; and community, 275, 401, 403, 409, 410, 424; components of, 117; concept of, 118; and curriculum, 347; developmental direction for, 38; and emotional independence, 121-132; and family, 123-128, 131, 141; and feedback, 198; growth of, 118-121; and instrumental independence, 132-140; and integrity, 242; and intellectual competence, 60; and orientation, 440; and physical competence, 72; and psychosocial theories, 28, 29, 31, 34; and recovery programs, 129-130; rethinking, 40; and student-faculty relationships, 269, 324-325, 329-333; summarized, 47-48; and teaching, 272, 273-274, 390

B

Balance: stages of, 25-29; theory of, in learning cycle, 476-477

Baseball, settings and redundancy in, 302-304

Battelle Human Affairs Research Centers, 186

Bennington College: emotional development at, 89; objectives at, 287-288

Berea College, community at, 397-398

Body, and identity formation, 183-184, 204

Bucknell University, community at, 410

C

California at Berkeley, University of: course for tolerance at, 151; residence programs at, 403

California at Los Angeles, University of: Cooperative Institutional Research Program at, 82; Higher Education Research Institute at, 54, 213; identity formation at, 180; student athletes at, 66

Cambridge University: atmosphere of, 433; gowns at, 49; rules of, 430; vocational education at, 341

Canada: homosexuality in, 186; teaching in, 373

Caring: and integrity, 251; and moral development, 19-20, 29; and tolerance, 159-160

Carnegie Foundation for the Advancement of Teaching, 423

Center for the Study of Higher Education, 89

Ceremonies, culminating, 453

Challenges: current, 43-44, 454-455, 482-485; in development, 1, 22; and identity, 175; impact of, 386-387; and integrity, 240; in learning cycle, 477-478; by student development professionals, 438

Chicago, University of, surveys by, 186

China, and integrity, 241

Classroom research, for teaching, 383-385

Climate, for student development, 461-462

Cocurriculum: and autonomy, 142-144; impact of, 468; supporting services as, 444-452; transcripts for, 449

Cognitive development: and curriculum, 345-346; and intellectual competence, 56-57; and teaching, 389

Cognitive dissonance, and curriculum, 365-366

Cognitive theories: on autonomy, 116-117, 128; on integrity, 260-261; on student development, 2, 6-21

College Student Questionnaire, 403, 410

Commitment, and identity formation, 196

Commitment in relativism, elements in, 11
Communication: and emotional development, 103–104; in student-faculty relationships, 337–340
Communities, student: aspects of, 392–424; characteristics of, 277, 398–399; for commuter students, 411–414; creating, 399, 402, 404, 405–406, 407, 408, 409, 413–424; functions of, 392–399; hypothesis on, 275–277; for learning, 414–424; in off-campus housing, 410–411; in residence halls, 399–410; and size, 306–308
Commuter students: and cocurriculum, 450–451; communities for, 411–414; learning communities for, 414–424
Competence: aspects of developing, 53–82; background on, 53–54; and cognitive theories, 17; and community, 275, 400, 403; and curriculum, 270, 344, 347, 368; developmental direction for, 38; faculty as models of, 318–319, 320; intellectual, 54–63; interpersonal, 72–77; and interpersonal relationships, 160; and objectives, 289; physical and manual, 63–72; and self-concept, 80–82; sense of, 53, 65, 74, 77–82, 312; and size, 268, 311–312, 315; and student-faculty relationship, 269, 325–326; summarized, 45–46; and teaching, 272–273, 372–373, 389–390
Conformist stage: in ego development, 31, 32; and intimacy, 161
Congruence: concept of, 52; and institutional size, 315; and integrity, 253–264
Conscientious stage: and autonomy, 116; in ego development, 31, 32
Cooperation: in learning communities, 420–421; teaching for, 374, 389–390
Cooperative Institutional Research Program, 82
Council of Student Personnel Associations in Higher Education, 434

Counseling, for student development, 443–444
Crabgrass, humans as, 423–424
Creativity, and physical competence, 69–71
Crises, and identity, 174–175, 181
Critical thinking, and physical competence, 64
Culminating services, by student development professionals, 438–439, 452–453
Cultural and aesthetic development, and intellectual competence, 56
Curriculum: aspects of, 341–368; axioms for, 362–368; and cognitive dissonance, 365–366; concept of, 341; content issues of, 354–368; core, 358–362; differentiation and integration in, 367–368; distribution requirements in, 356–358; hidden, 270–271, 350–351, 353; hypothesis on, 270–271; and individual differences, 364–365; liberal and vocational, 341–348; process issues of, 348–353; relevance of, 362–364; for skills and abilities, 344–348; for student development, 464–466

D

Daytona Beach Community College, learning communities at, 415
Defining Issues Test, 251–252, 401, 410
Denmark, homosexuality in, 186
Depression, managing, 94–96, 97–98, 99, 104
Developing Autonomy Inventory, 134
Development. See Student development
Differentiation and integration: in curriculum, 367–368; in learning cycles, 476–477
Disaggregation, need for, 305–306
Dualism: elements of, 11; and learning communities, 416–417; and reflective judgment, 58

E

Earlham College, community at, 397

Eastern Washington University, learning communities at, 416

Educational Testing Service, 55, 403

Ego development: and autonomy, 116, 117–118; and identity, 174–178, 180, 205–206; and intimacy, 161; psychosocial theories of, 30–34

Emotional independence: and autonomy, 121–132; concept of, 47, 117; steps toward, 117, 129; and student-faculty relationships, 329–330

Emotions: accepting, 101–103; aspects of managing, 83–114; and autonomy, 118, 125–126, 142; awareness of, 88, 97–106; background on, 83–84; and behavior problems, 448; changes in, 88–90, 113; and cognitive theories, 21; and communities, 275; developmental direction for, 38; and family history, 97–99, 101–102, 104–105; identifying, 100–101; and identity formation, 204–205; integration of, 107–114; and intellectual competence, 61; and interpersonal relationships, 160; and physical competence, 65, 66–67; positive, 110–113; and psychosocial theories, 28; reactions to, 85–87, 112–113; rethinking, 39; self-transcending, 88, 111–113; summarized, 46–47; toxic, 90–97; validity of, 105–106

Empathy, and tolerance, 157–160

Entering services, by student development professionals, 438, 439–444

Environments: admonitions on, 471–479; aspects of creating, 454–485; conceptual frameworks for, 455–459; hypotheses on, 279–281; and identity formation, 207; interaction with, 3, 5–6, 7; leadership and organizational cul-

ture in, 479–482; personalized, in residence halls, 404–406; principles for, 280–281, 461–471; and social imperatives, 482–485; as system, 279–280; traditional assumptions on, 459–461

Epigenetic principle: and ego development, 22; and identity, 174, 196

Epistemology. *See* Knowledge

Ethics: cognitive theories on development of, 7–11; and integrity, 238; of quality, 480; in student-faculty relationships, 333

Ethnocentrism, and interpersonal relationships, 147–148, 151–152

Ethos, and institutional size, 306–308

Evergreen State College, Washington Center for Improving the Quality of Undergraduate Education at, 414–415

Evolutionary truces, helix of, 24–26

Existentialism, and integrity, 261–264

Expectations, high, in teaching, 377

F

Facilitating Anxiety Scale, 91

Facilities, for student development, 469–470

Faculty: and autonomy, 126–128, 134–136, 138; cultures of, 320; and emotional development, 99, 108, 114; feedback for, 319; and integrity, 248–249, 264; and learning communities, 415, 421; and objectives, 288; priorities of, 432; self-disclosure by, 329; for student development, 466–467; and tolerance, 150–151, 154–155. *See also* Student-faculty relationships

Faculty Inventory, 373–378

Fairhaven College: integrity at, 247–248; purpose at, 220–224, 226–227

Family: and autonomy, 123–128, 131, 141; and emotions, 97–99,

101–102, 104–105; and identity formation, 189–190, 203–204; and integrity, 238; and intimacy, 168–169; and purpose, 229–231

Fear. *See* Anxiety

Feedback: for faculty, 319; and identity formation, 197–199; in teaching, 375–376

Florida, University of, academic stressors at, 91

Foreclosure: and autonomy, 131; and identity, 13, 177; and interpersonal relationships, 149–150

Frame-changing. *See* Reframing

France: autonomy in, 138–139; homosexuality in, 186

Friendships. *See* Communities, student

G

Gallaudet University, emotional development at, 109

Gender, comfort with, and identity, 184–188

Gender differences: in autonomy, 116–117, 119; and cognitive theories, 9, 12–17, 18–21; and community, 410–411; in emotional development, 92, 93, 94; in identity formation, 176, 178, 187; in interpersonal relationships, 149, 169–170; in knowing, 365; and physical competence, 64, 65; and psychosocial theories, 23–24, 28–29

George Mason University: curriculum at, 355–356, 360–361; students at, 471; teaching at, 384

George Washington University, curriculum at, 356–357

Georgia Southwestern College, residence halls at, 405

Germany, university model from, 432, 433, 448

Goddard College: autonomy at, 119–121; identity formation at, 200–201; purpose at, 217–220, 231–233

Guilt, managing, 95, 105

H

Habitat for Humanity, 72

Handball, and feedback for identity formation, 198

Harvard University: curriculum at, 358–360, 362; history of, 429, 430, 431, 433; student interviews at, 7; vocational education at, 342

Haverford College: and objectives, 288–289; and values, 334

Health, and identity formation, 183

Heinz dilemma, 18, 19

Higher education: challenges for, 454–455, 482–485; history of, 427–434

Hofstra University, New College at, 325

Homosexuality. *See* Sexual orientation

Hong Kong, integrity in, 252

House, identity formation as, 203–207

Humanizing values: concept of, 51; in integrity, 237–245, 334

I

Iceland, integrity in, 252

Identity: adolescent formation of, 173–175; aspects of establishing, 173–208; and autonomy, 131; and cocurriculum, 451; and cognitive theories, 8, 13; and comfort with gender, 184–188; and community, 276, 395–396; concepts of, 181–182, 205; and curriculum, 270, 344, 368; developmental direction for, 38; and ego development, 174–178, 180, 205–206; and emotional development, 105–106; and feedback, 197–199; growth of, 175–183; and interpersonal relationships, 156–157; and physical competence, 70; and psychosocial theories, 22–23; rethinking, 40; and self-concept through roles and life-style, 194–197; and self-esteem, 80, 179–180, 199–200; and sense of self, 188–194, 197–199; and sexual orientation, 184–188; and size, 268, 312–313; and social context, 188–194; stability and integration in, 200–208; stages in forming, 187–188, 193–194; summarized, 48–50; and teaching, 272, 274

Identity Achievement: and autonomy, 131; and identity formation, 177–178

Identity Diffusion: and autonomy, 139; and identity formation, 178

Independence. See Autonomy toward interdependence

Individual differences: and curriculum, 364–365; respect for, 472–476; teaching for, 377–378, 390

Individualistic stage, in ego development, 31, 33

Institutional Inventory, 373, 461–471

Institutions: culture of, 479–482; ideal, 423; as learning organizations, 281, 479–481; objectives of, 283–295; and sense of competence, 82; size of, 268–269, 296–315

Instrumental independence: and autonomy, 132–140; concept of, 47, 117

Integrated stage, in ego development, 33, 34

Integration: and autonomy, 142; concept of, 107; differentiation and, 367–368, 476–477; of emotions, 107–114; in identity, 200–208; in learning, 136; of work and learning, 471–472

Integrity: aspects of developing, 235–264; and behavior problems, 448; and cognitive theories, 8, 20; and community, 394, 397, 400, 409, 410, 424; concepts of, 235–236, 253; and congruence, 253–264; and curriculum, 270, 344, 368; developmental direction for, 39; humanizing values in,

237–245, 334; and interpersonal relationships, 243, 256–260; and personalizing values, 52, 245–253; and physical competence, 72; and psychosocial theories, 34; and religious/spiritual issues, 239–242, 256–259, 261, 264; and size, 268, 314–315; stages in, 236–237; and student-faculty relationships, 269, 333–335; summarized, 51–52

Intellectual competence: areas of, 55–57; aspects of developing, 54–634; concept of, 45, 54–55; and physical competence, 66, 70; and reframing, 57–58; research needed on, 62–63; and symbolism, 61–62

Intellectual development: and autonomy, 134–135; cognitive theories on, 7–11; and integrity, 238

Intentionality, and purpose, 231–234

Interdependence: acceptance of, 140–144; concept of, 117. See also Autonomy toward interdependence

Interests, personal, and purpose, 217–220, 225–229

Interpersonal competence: aspects of developing, 72–77; concept of, 46, 72; subskills in, 75–77

Interpersonal relationships: aspects of developing mature, 145–172; and cognitive theories, 8; and community, 275–276, 400, 401–402; components of, 146; and curriculum, 344, 346, 368; developmental direction for, 38; growth in, 147–150; and integrity, 243, 256–260; and intimacy, 160–172; and orientation, 440; and psychosocial theories, 31; and purpose, 226, 229–231; rethinking, 39, 40; and size, 268, 313–314; summarized, 48; and teaching, 272, 274–275, 389–390; tolerance in, 150–160

Intimacy: aspects of developing capacity for, 160–172; concept of, 48, 147; and curriculum, 344;

and family, 168-169; and
homosexuality, 170-171; and insights, 165-167; mature,
161-162, 172; pitfalls of,
162-163; sexual, 171-172; steps
in, 167
Iowa Student Development Inventories, 88-89

J

Japan: and consensus, 154; and integrity, 245
Johnson Foundation, 373
Juniata College: cocurricular transcript at, 449; orientation at,
441-442
Justice: and integrity, 251; and
moral development, 19-20

K

Knowledge: connected and separate,
14, 276, 417-419; and curriculum, 345, 349-350, 365; in developmental models, 12-17; perspectives on, 12-15; in
student-faculty relationships,
336-337; subject matter, and intellectual competence, 55
Korea, integrity in, 252

L

LaGuardia Community College,
learning communities at, 415
Language, texting and bitting of,
352-353, 371
Leadership, in environment,
479-482
Learning: active, 374-375, 390;
communities for, 414-424; cycles
for, 378-380, 386, 476-479; experiential, 378-380, 390; organizations for, 281, 479-481; residence hall activities for, 402-404;
stages in autonomous, 135-136;
styles of, 3-4; work integrated
with, 471-472
Learning Style Inventory, 3

Lecture method: early use of, 428;
teaching by, 370-372
Liberal education, and developmen-
tal vectors, 343-344
Life-style, identity through, 194-197
Listening, skills of, 338-340
Logotherapy, and integrity, 263-264
Losing, and physical competence,
66-68

M

Manual competence, developing, 46,
63-72
Maryland, University of, retention
at, 444-446
Massachusetts, University of, reten-
tion at, 452
Measure of Intellectual Develop-
ment, 416-417
Men. *See* Gender differences
Mentors: for emotional develop-
ment, 113-114; in student-faculty
relationship, 322-325
Mexican-American student, identity
formation for, 189-190. *See also*
Minority students
Miami Dade Community College,
teaching at, 385
Miami University, student inter-
views at, 15
Michigan, University of, Residential
College at, 403
Michigan State University, residence
programs at, 403
Minority students: and cognitive
theories, 17, 35; identity forma-
tion for, 188-194. *See also*
African-American students
Mission statements, and objectives,
284-286, 290
Mobility, and autonomy, 138-140
Moral development: cognitive the-
ories of, 17-21; and community,
401; levels of, 250-251, 252,
255-256
Moral Judgment Interview, 252
Moratorium: and autonomy, 131;
and identity, 178; and purpose,
229-230

Morrill Land Grant Act of 1962,
    432
Motivation, and curriculum, 347
Mount Holyoke College, community
    at, 398
Multiplicity: and autonomy, 128;
    elements of, 11; and learning
    communities, 417
Myers-Briggs Type Indicator, 4, 20,
    148, 408, 475
Mystery-mastery strategy, 254

N

National Center on Education and
    the Economy, 472
National Collegiate Athletic Associa-
    tion, 452
National Council on Student Devel-
    opment, 435–436
National Honor Society, 350
National Institute of Education, 54,
    454
National Institute of Mental Health,
    186
New York, student services in,
    468
Norway, homosexuality in, 186

O

Objectives: aspects of clear and con-
    sistent, 283–295; hypothesis on,
    266–268; impact of, 287–295;
    and institutional size, 296; need
    for, 283–287; and self-selection,
    291
Off-campus housing, student com-
    munities in, 410–411
Ohio State University, residence
    halls at, 408
Omnibus Personality Inventory, 89,
    148
Orientation, for student develop-
    ment, 439–442
Orphan, and autonomy, 121,
    128–129, 130
Oxford University: atmosphere of,
    433; gowns at, 49; history of,
    428–430

P

Person-environment interaction
    theories, of student develop-
    ment, 3, 5–6. *See also* Envir-
    onment
Personalizing values: concept of,
    52; and integrity, 245–253
Philippines, integrity in, 252
Physical and manual competence:
    aspects of developing, 63–72;
    concept of, 46; and creativity,
    69–71; winning and losing and,
    66–68
Pitchfork, competence as, 53
Plans, and purpose, 210–211,
    212–225
Princeton University: Alumni Office
    of, 64; Quadrangle Plan at,
    433
Principled reasoning, and integrity,
    250–251, 256–260
Programs and services. *See* Student
    development professionals
Psychosocial theories: on autonomy,
    115; on intimacy, 161; on stu-
    dent development, 2, 21–34
Purpose: aspects of developing,
    209–234; and cocurriculum, 451;
    and community, 276, 395–396,
    400, 424; concept of, 209–210;
    and curriculum, 270, 344; de-
    velopmental direction for, 39,
    224–225; elements in, 212; and
    family, 229–231; and intellectual
    competence, 60; and intentional-
    ity, 231–234; and interpersonal
    relationships, 226, 229–231; and
    personal interests, 217–220,
    225–229; and plans, 210–211,
    212–225; and psychosocial the-
    ories, 34; and student-faculty
    relationship, 269, 325, 326–329;
    summarized, 50; and teaching,
    272; and vocational plans,
    212–225

Q

Quality, ethic of, 480

R

Recovery programs, and autonomy, 129–130

Recruitment, for student development, 439–440

Redundancy, and institutional size, 268–269, 301–305, 311–312, 315

Reflective judgment, and intellectual competence, 58–59

Reframing: and emotional development, 104–106, 107–108; and integrity, 250; and intellectual competence, 57–58; and tolerance, 156

Registrars, and student development, 442

Relationships. *See* Interpersonal relationships; Student-faculty relationships

Relativism, elements of, 11

Religious/spiritual development: and integrity, 239–242, 256–259, 261, 264; and purpose, 228

Residence halls: community in, 399–410; and emotional development, 100; functions of, 399–402; impact of, 275–276; learning activities in, 402–404; personalized environment in, 404–406; placement in, 408; policies and regulations of, 409; size of, 406–408; as subculture, 393–394

Respect, in student-faculty relationships, 338–339

Retention: factors in, 442–443, 445–446, 452; and size, 310

Rochester, University of, identity formation at, 176

Rockland Community College: course for tolerance at, 153–154; Life Skills courses at, 451–452

Roles, identity through, 194–197

S

Sarah Lawrence College, purpose at, 212, 220

Savannah College of Art and Design, cocurriculum at, 450

Seattle Central Community College, learning communities at, 417

Self: concepts of, 201–202; sense of, 188–194, 197–199

Self-concept: and competence, 80–82; roles and life-style for, 194–197

Self-esteem: concept of, 179; and identity, 80, 179–180, 199–200; and physical competence, 65

Self-sufficiency, development of, 132–138

Self-talk, and emotional development, 91, 102–103

Semiautonomy, concept of, 133

Settings, and size, 300–305

Sexual impulses: and emotional development, 93, 96–97, 98–99, 104; and intimacy, 171–172; and student-faculty relationships, 332–333

Sexual orientation: and identity, 184–188; and integrity, 258–259; and intimacy, 170–171

Shame, managing, 95–96, 105

Shoreline Community College, teaching at, 385

Silence, perspective of, 9, 12

Size, institutional: appropriate, 299–305; aspects of, 296–315; and context, 304–305; ethos and community and, 306–308; factors in increased, 296–298; and faculty concern for students, 309–310; and human scale, 298–299; hypothesis on, 268–269; impact of, 305–310; for residence halls, 406–408; and student development, 311–315; and student involvement and participation, 308–309; and student persistence and retention, 310

Social context, and identity formation, 188–194

Stability, in identity, 200–208

Stages, simple and complex, 35–37

State Board for Community College Education, 385

State University of New York at Stony Brook, learning communities at, 415

Student development: aspects of theories on, 1–41; background on, 1–2; cognitive theories of, 2, 6–21; cycles in, 476–479; environments for, 454–485; influences on, 265–485; as organizing purpose, 265–281; person-environment theories of, 3, 5–6; psychosocial theories of, 2, 21–34; and size, 311–315; typology theories of, 3–5; vectors of, 34–264

Student development professionals: aspects of, 425–453; culminating services by, 438–439, 452–453; early practitioners of, 432–434; entering services by, 438, 439–444; in higher education, 427–434; hypothesis on, 277–279; potential unrealized for, 434–438; professional development for, 481; roles of, 425–427; service clusters for, 438–453; supporting services by, 438, 444–452

Student Development Task and Lifestyle Inventory, 148

Student Development Task Inventory, 23–24

Student-faculty relationships: arrangements for, 340; aspects of, 316–340; and community, 395; components of, 335–340; hypothesis on, 269–270, 316–317; influential, 317–321; and institutional size, 309–310; interactions in, 321–335; mentoring in, 322–325; and teaching, 374

Students: autonomy to, 122–134, 136–139, 141–143; behavior problems of, 446–447; emotions to, 84–85, 95, 96–97, 98, 100–103, 104–106, 107–108, 109–111; identity to, 185, 189–190, 191–192, 199–200; and individual differences, 364–365, 377–378, 390, 472–476; and institutional size, 301, 306, 311–315; integrity to, 238–245, 247–250, 254–259; intellectual competence to, 59–61; interpersonal competence to, 73–75; interpersonal relationships to, 154–157, 164–171; involved, 308–309, 318, 385–386, 406–408, 415; and objectives, 289; physical competence to, 65, 68–70; predictor variables for, 442–443; purpose to, 214–224, 226–228, 230–231; retention of, 310, 442–443, 445–446, 452; sense of competence to, 78–80, 81; ways of knowing to, 419–420. *See also* Adult students; African-American students; Communities, student; Commuter students; Minority students

Suicide, and depression, 94

Support services: for student development, 467–469; by student development professionals, 438, 444–452

Symbolism, and intellectual competence, 61–62

Symphony, and identity formation, 208

Synthesis, and integrity, 244–245

T

Taps in bar, emotions as, 87–88, 90

Teaching: and accountability, 387; aspects of, 369–391; classroom research for, 383–385; good, 372–381; hypothesis on, 272–275; impact of, 385–391; learning craft of, 382–385; by lecture method, 370–372, 428; propositions on, 369–370

Test of Thematic Analysis, 64, 400

Time on task, in teaching, 376–377

Tolerance: aspects of developing, 150–160; concept of, 48, 146–147; and curriculum, 344; and empathy, 157–160; factors in, 157

Typology theories: and individual differences, 474–476; of student development, 3–5

U

United Kingdom: identity formation in, 180, 186, 191–192; teaching in, 373. *See also* Cambridge University; Oxford University
Urban development, humanizing values as, 238
Ursuline College, moxie at, 437

V

Values: applying, 236; changes in, 237–238; clarification of, 314; and community, 395; espoused, 253–254; humanizing of, 51, 237–245, 334; institutional, 480; and institutional size, 307–308, 314; personalizing of, 52, 245–253; and purpose, 234; and student-faculty relationships, 333–335
Vassar College: autonomy at, 141, 331–332; emotional development at, 89
Vectors of development: as conceptual lenses, 44; contexts for, 34–41; developmental directions for, 38–39; and liberal education, 343–344; original, 23–24; overview of, 43–52; summarized, 45–52. *See also* Autonomy toward interdependence; Competence; Emotions; Identity; Integrity; Interpersonal relationships; Purpose
Virginia, University of, history of, 431
Vocation, concept of, 50
Vocational plans: changing, 215–217, 219–220; and integra-tion of work and learning, 471–472; limits on, 213–214; and purpose, 212–225

W

Washington: intellectual competence in, 59–61; teaching improvement in, 385
Washington, University of: Center for Instructional Development at, 319; Freshman Interest Groups at, 415, 416; sense of competence at, 79
Web, higher education as, 454
Western Michigan University, honors clusters at, 415
Western Washington University: faculty-student teams at, 319–320; Fairhaven College at, 220–224, 226–227, 247–248; orientation at, 439–441
William and Mary College, history of, 430
Winning, and physical competence, 66–68
Wisconsin, University of, history of, 432
Women: institutional climate for, 461; and student-faculty relationships, 326, 327, 330–331, 332. *See also* Gender differences
Wooster, College of, course for tolerance at, 151

Y

Yakima Valley Community College, learning communities at, 416
Yale University, history of, 430, 431